This is a further volume ||||||||||||||||
philosophers. Each vol   MW01138375
essays by an international team of scholars together with a
substantial bibliography and will serve as a reference work for
students and non-specialists. One aim of the series is to dispel
the intimidation that such readers often feel when faced with
the work of a difficult and challenging thinker.

Aristotle is one of the very greatest thinkers in the Western tradition, but also one of the most difficult. The contributors to this volume do not attempt to disguise the nature of
that difficulty, but at the same time they offer a clear exposition of the central philosophical concerns in his work. Their
approaches and methods vary, and the volume editor has not
imposed any single interpretation, but has allowed legitimate differences of interpretation to stand. An introductory
chapter provides an account of Aristotle's life and works.
Subsequent chapters cover Aristotle's writings on logic,
metaphysics, science, psychology, ethics, politics, rhetoric,
and poetics. It is an assumption of the companion that its
readers will not know Greek.

New readers and non-specialists will find this the most
accessible and comprehensive guide to Aristotle currently
available.

THE CAMBRIDGE COMPANION TO
ARISTOTLE

The Cambridge Companion to
ARISTOTLE

Edited by Jonathan Barnes
University of Geneva

CAMBRIDGE
UNIVERSITY PRESS

Published by the Press Syndicate of the University of Cambridge
The Pitt Building, Trumpington Street, Cambridge CB2 1RP
40 West 20th Street, New York, NY 10011-4211, USA
10 Stamford Road, Oakleigh, Melbourne 3166, Australia

© Cambridge University Press 1995

First published 1995
Reprinted 1995 (twice), 1996 (twice)

Printed in the United States of America

Library of Congress Cataloging-in-Publication Data is available.

A catalogue record for this book is available from the British Library.

ISBN 0-521-41133-5 hardback
ISBN 0-521-42294-9 paperback

CONTENTS

vi   Contents

CONTRIBUTORS

JONATHAN BARNES is Professor of Ancient Philosophy in the University of Geneva. He was educated at Oxford, where he taught for twenty-five years. His numerous publications include *Aristotle* (1982) and the revised edition of the 'Oxford Translation' of Aristotle's works (1984).

STEPHEN EVERSON was educated at Corpus Christi College, Oxford, and currently teaches philosophy at Trinity College, Cambridge. His publications include *Aristotle: The Politics* (1988) and a sequence of *Companions to Ancient Thought* (1990–).

R.J. HANKINSON was educated at Balliol College, Oxford, and King's College, Cambridge, where he was also a Research Fellow. He has taught at McGill University, Montreal, and the University of Texas at Austin, where he is currently Professor of Philosophy. He has written numerous articles on Greek philosophy and science; his *Galen: On the Therapeutic Method* appeared in 1991.

D.S. HUTCHINSON studied at Queen's University, Kingston, and Balliol College, Oxford, and is now a Fellow of Trinity College, Toronto. He teaches ancient philosophy in the University of Toronto and is the author of *The Virtues of Aristotle* (1986).

ROBIN SMITH is Professor of philosophy at Kansas State University. His publications include translations with commentary of Aristotle's *Prior Analytics* (1989) and Books I and VIII of the *Topics* (1994).

vii

C.C.W. TAYLOR is a Fellow of Corpus Christi College, Oxford. He is the author of *Plato: Protagoras* (1976) and of many articles in ethics, philosophy of mind, and history of philosophy. He is co-author (with J. Gosling) of *The Greeks on Pleasure* (1982) and co-editor (with J. Dancy and J.Moravcsik) of *Human Agency: Festschrift for J. O. Urmson* (1985).

INTRODUCTION BY JONATHAN BARNES

The essays which make up this book are all new; but the book is not
yet another collection of New Essays on Aristotle. Rather, it is – it
has striven to be – what its title proclaims it to be: a companion to
Aristotle.

It is a philosophical companion. That is to say, first, it addresses
its topic in a philosophical manner: it is not primarily concerned to
divine the various influences on Aristotle's thought or to uncover
the historical origins of his ideas and to trace their development. Nor
is it primarily concerned to set Aristotle's philosophy in the larger
intellectual context of his age. Rather, it is primarily concerned to
offer a philosophical exposition – and sometimes a philosophical
criticism – of the theses and arguments which are set down in Aristotle's writings.

Secondly, the *Companion* is primarily concerned with the philosophical parts and aspects of Aristotle's thought – that is to say, with
those parts and aspects which we now should be inclined to judge
philosophical. The first chapter provides some general information
about the man and his works; but in the main body of the book there
is very little about Aristotle as an historian, and relatively little
about Aristotle as a man of science. It is Aristotle the philosopher to
whom the book is devoted. The *Companion* thus regards Aristotle's
works from our point of view and not from the point of view of their
author and of his contemporaries; and it divides up his work in ways
which he did not acknowledge and might not have welcomed. There
are evident dangers in such an enterprise – we may miss connections which were plain to Aristotle, and the modern idiom may
disguise his original mode of thought. But the dangers are not insur-
mountable, nor is the enterprise frivolously anachronistic: we have

a legitimate interest in what Aristotle represents for *us*, as philosophers, now.

(And it may be worth observing that the term "philosophy," so far as the *Companion* is concerned, refers to what is sometimes called the analytical tradition of philosophy. Philosophers working in other traditions have studied Aristotle – there are, for example, Thomist interpretations of Aristotle and "continental" interpretations of Aristotle. The *Companion*, for wholly unpolemical reasons, does not address itself to these things.)

In principle, a work of this sort might be expected to have comprehensive aspirations; that is to say, the *Companion* might be expected to cover the whole of Aristotle's philosophy – or at any rate, most and the most important of his ideas. In practice, such aspirations cannot be realized within the covers of a single volume: the subject is too large, and too difficult. Too large: some aspects of Aristotle's thought which some philosophers would deem to be important have not been mentioned at all; and many points which many philosophers would consider important have been only lightly touched upon. Too difficult: comprehensive surveys of tough texts degenerate into superficial and unsatisfying summaries, and the *Companion* is intended to be a philosophical guidebook rather than a flat epitome: the contributors have sometimes chosen to labour hard in this or that area rather than skim softly over their whole domain. Nonetheless, the *Companion* claims to give a reasonably serious treatment of many of the most important aspects of Aristotle's philosophy.

The treatment is elementary. The *Companion* is intended for philosophical readers who are new to Aristotle. It is not a book for scholars who are already practised Aristotelians (they are too old for companions); nor, on the other hand, is it written for that fabulous creature, the general reader. It is for students, undergraduate and graduate, who have acquired – or would like to acquire – an incipient philosophical interest in Aristotle. The students are not supposed to know Greek or to have any prior acquaintance with Greek philosophy; and although they are assumed to be philosophy students (in a generous sense of the phrase), they are not supposed to be advanced philosophers. What they are supposed to be is determined – and intelligent. For although the *Companion* purports to be introductory, it does not claim to be easy. Aristotle is a

difficult author and the subjects he addresses are difficult subjects –
if the *Companion* made no demands on its readers, it would be a
poor guide to Aristotle.

The contributors to the *Companion* were urged to be elementary; but they were not urged to be orthodox. Scholarly orthodoxies
are ephemeral things; and on many issues in the interpretation of
Aristotle's philosophy it is not plain where the orthodoxy lies. In
any event, it is tedious to read – and very tedious to write – a survey of current orthodoxies. On the other hand, the book has not
striven for novelty, and it is never surreptitiously zany: a *Companion* is not the place for airing old hobby-horses or for giving new
notions a preliminary canter. In short, the views which the *Companion* presents are, in principle and for the most part, views which
most modern scholars in the analytical tradition would probably
regard as initially reasonable, whether or not they would also find
them ultimately defensible.

This may read like a recipe for a bland dish. (And the dish certainly lacks the spice of scholarly controversy, for the contributors
were given no room for polemics.) Blandness is no doubt something
for readers to assess. But the editor can affirm that the ingredients of
the *Companion* have not been homogenized. The different contributors naturally adopted different approaches to their tasks, and they
preferred different methods and different styles; and from time to
time it becomes clear that they disagree with one another on issues
of interpretation. The editor has not attempted to efface these differences: he has regularized the abbreviations, but he has not otherwise
intervened. And this not merely from idleness: uniformity is a drab
virtue, if it is a virtue at all.

Blandness is the vice of authority. Whether or not the *Companion*
has avoided the vice, it certainly has no pretension to authority – it
does not claim to serve up a definitive account of the topics it
covers. Whether or not there ever will or ever could be a definitive
account of Aristotle's philosophy, the *Companion* has not the least
intention of producing such an item: it hopes to guide readers
to Aristotle's philosophy, not to instruct them in what Aristotle
thought. I write this not as a preemptive strike against hostile re-
viewers, but as an honest advertisement for friendly readers. Suppose that you read a chapter of the *Companion* in which it is suggested that Aristotle believed such-and-such or argued thus-and-so.

If you turn over the page and say to yourself, "Oh, so Aristotle believed such-and-such or argued thus-and-so," then the *Companion* will have failed, and failed wretchedly. For you are meant, as you put the book down, to converse with yourself in the following sort of way: "Oh, so Aristotle is supposed to have believed such-and-such or argued thus-and-so. What an interesting – or perplexing, or perverse – thing to have thought. Might it be true? How best can it be defended (or attacked)? Should it perhaps be modified or qualified or otherwise embellished? Come to that, *did* Aristotle really mean exactly that? Perhaps a subtler version of the interpretation is possible? Perhaps a different interpretation altogether? Let me now look more nearly at Aristotle's own words and see what he actually *says*."

Well, no *Companion* will evoke such thoughts in every reader all the time; but if you never find yourself thinking in this way, then either you are not made for Aristotle or else you should return the *Companion* to the publisher and claim your money back.

Aristotle has not always had a good press. At some periods and in some quarters it has been urged that his influence on philosophy was malign. (And I recently heard a Nobel laureate assert – it was an assertion based on the most perfect ignorance – that Aristotle had a malign influence on the development of science.) Nonetheless, he has always been judged an important philosopher, and he has always been judged a difficult philosopher. And these twin judgments make it un-astonishing that Aristotle's writings have been subjected, ever since antiquity, to profound and continuous critical attention. Learned articles and learned books, scholarly commentaries and popular accounts, philological inquiries and philosophical investigations, the products of solitary reflection and the proceedings of conferences and colloquia and symposia – scribble, scribble, scribble, for two thousand years, and never faster than in recent decades. No waste paper basket can keep up with the stuff.

Much of this secondary literature is without intellectual merit – indeed, it is produced for reasons that have little to do with the intellect. Yet the excellent material, though small in proportion, is comfortable enough in girth: a bibliography on Aristotle which included only eminent items would run to several hundred pages.

This luxuriant growth has had its pedagogical effect. At any rate, students in many British and North American universities often seem to adopt – and are tacitly encouraged to adopt – a peculiar approach to Aristotle. First, you choose – or are assigned – an established "Aristotelian topic": Aristotle's Doctrine of the Mean, let us say. Then you are given a "reading list" which catalogues a few articles and books on the topic (all in English, of course, and the more recent the better). You read some of these items, in which scholar X takes issue with scholar W, and scholar Y with scholar X. Glancing quickly at a passage or two in Aristotle, you try to decide whether X refuted W and whether Y finally got the matter straightened out (of course he didn't); and you write your paper or essay. If you do this well enough, you will later publish it under the title "Y on Aristotle's Doctrine of the Mean"; you will become Z; and future students will try to decide whether Z finally got the matter straightened out . . .

This is no doubt a calumny – and perhaps it is a caricature. But I am persuaded that it is not far from the truth. I have no desire to ban articles on Y's criticisms of X's account of W's interpretation of Aristotle. To be sure, such things have their disadvantages. (They are both a cause and a symptom of the extraordinary conservatism of modern scholarly interest in Aristotle.) But they also have their place in the academic economy, and – what is more – they occasionally advance our understanding of Aristotle. Yet whatever their value, you should have no truck with them when you are first starting on Aristotle.

For you will be interested in what *Aristotle* says, not in what Y thinks that X thinks that W thinks that Aristotle said. This is a trifling truth: if you are primarily interested in what W said about Aristotle, then you are starting to work on W, not on Aristotle. (Of course, if W is someone like Alexander of Aphrodisias or Thomas Aquinas, then the interest may be admirable – but it is still not an interest in Aristotle.) Moreover, you should try to find out what Aristotle says by reading *Aristotle*, not by reading what W says about Aristotle. And this is not a trifling truth – indeed, there will always be the temptation to deny that it is a truth at all (after all, W is a lot easier to read than Aristotle, and what he writes is shorter . . .). But a truth it is; and if you ignore this truth, you will find it horribly difficult to see Aristotle for yourself – you will be like a tourist who travels guide-book in hand and who sedulously absorbs M. Michelin's ideas about Paris while having only half an eye for the city itself.

For these reasons, the *Companion* offers a brief list of Selections for Further Reading (as well as a standard Bibliography);[1] and for its own part it is in principle a self-effacing work. Aristotle (it bears repeating) is difficult: everyone who reads him – even aged and eminent scholars – looks for a little help from the cribs and the commentaries. But when, for example, I turn to Sir David Ross's magnificent commentary on Aristotle's *Physics*, I do not do so in order to discover what the learned Sir David thought – I do so in order to discover what Aristotle thought. Generally speaking, I have little interest in finding out what Y's opinions are (unless Y is eminent and dead – or else a living friend or a living enemy). Rather, I read Y's commentary in order to find out what Aristotle was on about in this or that thorny passage. Y may, with luck (and sometimes quite by chance), help me to read Aristotle. But I am not, in a sense, reading Y: Y is transparent, and I read Aristotle through him. This is, I take it, the proper and the ordinary function of a commentary.

And it applies, by and large, to the *Companion*. So do not read the *Companion* in order to find out what, for example, Barnes thinks about Aristotle's metaphysics; do not wonder whether Barnes really means this or that; do not ask whether what *Barnes* says is true – ask rather whether what Barnes says is *true*. (Questions about Barnes are of consuming interest to Barnes, no doubt – but they should leave you perfectly cold.) In short, read the *Companion* to help you with *Aristotle*. Unlike a commentary, it will not – save incidentally – help you through particular patches of difficult text. Rather, it should provide a more general form of assistance, and it should be used in the way in which intelligent tourists use a guidebook to a city which they do not yet know but expect to admire and to love.

Why visit Aristotle at all? Why study Aristotle at all? (Reading and studying are different occupations; and the *Companion* is written for would-be students rather than for prospective readers.)

There are several different contexts in which this question might be posed. "Why study Aristotle – in fact, why should anyone do

1 Why a Bibliography at all? Perhaps some readers (not those for whom the body of the *Companion* is primarily intended) will find it useful; and in any event, the publisher demanded it.

philosophy at all?" "Why study Aristotle – why should philosophers study the works of their dead predecessors?" "Why study Aristotle – why should a student of the mighty dead not turn rather to Plato or to Descartes or to Kant?" I shall not say anything about the first of these questions – you will have already answered it for yourself.[2] But the third and the second questions invite a paragraph or two.

Why Aristotle rather than Plato or Descartes or Kant? Why indeed make a choice at all? Why not study the lot? The implacable goddess Time will not allow it: you need time to study, in any detail and to any purpose, the works of a considerable philosopher; and in half a dozen student years – or, come to that, in the course of a philosophical lifetime – no one is able to study more than a handful of these heroes. If one or two, which one or two? Any reasonable choice will be largely determined by individual taste and individual capacity. If, for example, you have no particular interest in the ancient world but a passion for the German Romantics and a smattering of German, then you will have one reason to prefer Kant to Aristotle. And there are similar personal reasons for opting for Aristotle.

But there is a little more to be said than that. For Aristotle holds a position of unparallelled importance in the history of philosophy – and he is a thunderingly good philosopher to boot. Compare him first to Descartes. Descartes's influence on the history of the subject is well known: after him, and in large part as a result of his work, philosophers took epistemological issues to be the primary and fundamental issues in philosophy. Descartes affected profoundly the way in which people looked at philosophy and the way in which philosophers did philosophy. Here is reason enough to read Descartes. Yet, by contrast with Aristotle, Descartes's philosophical range was limited; and – let me confess – I have always taken Hobbes to be a shrewd judge when he observed that "M.des Cartes' head does not lie for philosophy."

Compare Aristotle next to Plato. Plato had an influence second only to Aristotle,[3] and the range of his philosophical interests was vast. Moreover, his philosophical talents – the capacity to see where

---

2 For Aristotle's own answer to the question see pp. 196–197.

3 Someone – was is A.N.Whitehead? – observed that Western philosophy is a series of footnotes to Plato. A witty apophthegm, but false: substitute "Aristotle" for "Plato" and the aphorism will be, as it were, less false.

a problem lies, the ability to tell a promising line of inquiry from a dead end, the gift for producing relevant arguments – were surely greater than those of Descartes. Here is reason enough to read Plato. But Plato's philosophical views are mostly false, and for the most part they are evidently false; his arguments are mostly bad, and for the most part they are evidently bad. Studying Plato will indeed make you realize how difficult philosophy is, and the study has a particular fascination and a particular pleasure. But it can also be a dispiriting business: for the most part, the student of Plato is preoccupied by a peculiar question – How and why did Plato come to entertain such exotic opinions, to advance such outré arguments?

What the admen call "knocking copy" is in poor taste. And of course, these comparisons could have been more subtly done. And of course, Descartes and Plato are both First Division philosophers. Nonetheless, Aristotle is incontrovertibly their superior. And this surely is an excellent reason – not an unsurmountable reason, but still a very excellent reason – for studying Aristotle, if you are concerned to study the history of philosophy at all.

And why study the history of philosophy at all? Chemists do not, as a matter of course, study the history of chemistry, nor do physicists study the history of physics; and yet all philosophy students are supposed to spend a substantial proportion of their time on the history of philosophy. Why so?

For the last several decades it has been fashionable to recommend the study of the history of philosophy – and hence of Aristotle in particular – along the following lines. "As philosophers, we are not primarily interested in history or in interpretation: if we read Aristotle's works, we read them as works of philosophy – we read them with the same goal and in the same spirit as we read the latest productions of the Cambridge University Press. After all, Aristotle was a distinguished philosopher; and he was working on the same problems as we are working on: perhaps his insights will enable us to solve the problems ourselves; surely they will enable us to see more clearly what the problems are and how they might best be tackled. Again, Aristotle's occasional lapses may be philosophically instructive: by noting how he failed to see something, we may sharpen our own vision. Moreover, where Aristotle's philosophical interests do not after all intersect with our own, even here there may be philosophical value for us: if he wrestles with a problem which no longer seems to

concern us, or if he passes lightly over an issue which greatly exercises us, the differences between him and us may themselves force us
to reflect in a deeper fashion on our own preconceptions."

This line of thought offers a purely philosophical reason for studying Aristotle. It is certainly not a despicable line of thought, and its
proponents can point to cases in which reflection upon Aristotle has
led a modern philosopher to make important philosophical innova-
tions. (Two celebrated examples: Brentano's introduction of the concept of an intensional object and Lukasiewicz's invention of multi-
valued logic both depended on their studies of Aristotle's writings.)
But although I am content to allow that reading Aristotle – like
gazing into space or doodling on a piece of paper – may provide philosophical inspiration, I do not think that philosophers should be
urged to study Aristotle on the grounds that they may win a rich
philosophical reward.

On the one hand, if you study Aristotle seriously, you will quickly
become involved in the details of Aristotle's arguments and the problems of his text: you will become preoccupied with exegetical and
historical issues. (If such issues do not occupy your attention, then
you are not a student of Aristotle.) Roughly speaking – this at least is
my own experience – , the more you concentrate on Aristotle and
the more seriously you study him, the less you reflect on philosophical problems themselves and the less "pure" philosophy you
do.[4] On the other hand, the desire for philosophical profit does not
encourage a dispassionate study of Aristotle's texts. You will reasonably care more about what Aristotle *might* have said or *might* have
meant than about what he actually said and actually meant, and
much of the work which scholarly study demands will seem – will
be – irrelevant to your ends. After all, a misreading or a lazy reading
of a text may be more fruitful philosophically than a profound and
accurate study. (Brentano and Lukasiewicz both got Aristotle wrong.)
The philosophical justification for studying the history of philosophy is not a justification for studying the *history* of philosophy at
all: it is a reason for pretending that the subject has no history.

4 I do not say that you will do *no* pure philosophy – although this fate has
  befallen more than one scholar. But you will surely do less pure philosophy. Of course, not much pure philosophy is ever done: most things
  published in the journals are contributions to the history – the very
  recent history – of the subject.

Thus the purely philosophical reason for the study of Aristotle is not to be urged.[5] Then is the only possible motive for studying Aristotle purely historical? After all, Aristotle is an historical figure; in studying his thought you are doing history, like it or not; and historical curiosity is far from an ignoble motive.

I have heard it said that philosophers *ought* to feel such historical curiosity, that it would be *wrong* for someone to study philosophical issues and yet have no interest at all in the way in which past philosophers had addressed these issues. This asseveration – which is presumably meant to convey a moral truth – seems to me to be as plausible as the parallel claim that biologists ought to feel historical curiosity about the work of past biologists. That is to say, the asseveration seems to me to be wholly implausible. I have also heard it said that philosophers *necessarily* feel a historical interest in their subject; philosophy – unlike biology or truffle-hunting – is in an important sense inseparable from its history, so that to be a philosopher is *ipso facto* to have an interest in the history of philosophy. This metaphysical asseveration can hardly be evaluated until it has been articulated with rather more clarity and precision. But it seems fairly clear that, however articulated, the claim will turn out to be false – for it will surely have the consequence that neither Gottlob Frege not Ludwig Wittgenstein were philosophers. (And no philosopher will hold that *neither* of these great men did philosophy.)

Here is another asseveration. If you are a philosopher, then it is very likely that you will have an interest in the history of philosophy, or at least in the work of some of the more eminent figures in that history. If you are fascinated by philosophical questions, then you are likely to be fascinated by the way in which others have attempted to answer – and to formulate – philosophical questions. (And more particularly: if you are a philosopher working in a given tradition, then you are likely to be interested in the earlier representatives of the tradition.) This asseveration is not platitudinous; nor is it universally true. But I take it to be a truth, a general psychological truth.

"But suppose that I'm not an intellectual necrophiliac – suppose

---

5 And it has in fact led to much third-rate work: secure in the knowledge that my aim is a philosophical aim, I allow myself to get away with shoddy scholarship; assured by the thought that I am, after all, a historian, I expect to get by with sloppy philosophizing.

that I don't have a taste for Aristotle or for Plato or for Descartes or for any other dead thinker? Suppose that I find their works unrewarding or frustrating or simply tedious – what then?" I have met people who do not like oysters and champagne, and I know people who cannot abide the operas of Richard Strauss. They are, I think, unfortunate; but they are not delinquent – and I see no reason why they should be forced to eat or drink or listen to the stuff. If you have no taste, and can develop no taste, for Aristotle, then that is a pity. But it is not a sin: you should not study Aristotle through gritted teeth and with rage in your heart – you should not study him at all.

In 1831 Immanuel Bekker edited the Greek text of Aristotle's surviving works. 'Bekker's Aristotle' no longer provides the most authoritative and up-to-date text of Aristotle's writings (for almost every work there is a later and superior edition); but it remains the standard edition, inasmuch as scholars continue to refer to Aristotle by way of Bekker. Thus I might say: "Aristotle describes his scientific methodology at HA A 6, 491a9–14 . . ." The reference, "HA A 6, 491a9–14", gives first the title of the work in question ("HA" abbreviates "History of Animals"); then the book number (the "A" here is a Greek alpha and refers to the first book of the History); then the chapter number (the Arabic numeral "6");[1] and finally the Bekker code: page number, column number, line numbers (here, lines 9 to 14 of the left-hand column on the four hundred and ninety-first page).

Different scholars prefer different abbreviations (the abbreviations used in the Companion are listed below); some scholars refer to books by numbers rather than by Greek letters, and some do not refer to books at all; different editions of Aristotle's works have used different chapter divisions, and, again, some scholars do not refer to chapters. But Bekker will rarely let you down: virtually all later editions of the Greek texts print Bekker references in their margins; virtually all books and articles on Aristotle use the Bekker code; and most decent translations give Bekker numbers either in the margin or at the head of the page.

1 Scholars customarily speak of Aristotle's works as divided into books, and the books as divided into chapters; but what they understand as books correspond roughly to modern chapters, and what they mean by chapters correspond roughly to modern sections. A 6, in modern terms, is the sixth section of the first chapter.

Bekker's Aristotle contains several works which are not by Aristotle himself: written by later (and unknown) hands, they found their way – for uncertain and no doubt various reasons – into the corpus of Aristotle's writings. It is customary to stigmatize the spurious with square brackets. Thus a reference to the *Problems* will normally read "[Aristotle], *Prob*" rather than "Aristotle, *Prob.*"

Conversely, not quite all of Aristotle's genuine words are to be found in Bekker; for his lost works (that is to say, those of his works which did not survive antiquity and were unknown to the medieval manuscript tradition) have left scattered traces here and there – a reference, a description, a paraphrase, a quotation. Most of these "fragments" are short and insubstantial; they are standardly referred to by an Arabic numeral followed by the symbol "R³": the reference designates the number of the fragment in the third edition of Valentin Rose's *Aristotelis qui ferebantur librorum fragmenta*, published in Leipzig in 1886. (There are often more recent and better texts than Rose's; but it remains convenient to use Rose numbers as references.) Substantial fragments of two lost works survive – perhaps. First, there is a text, nearly complete, of the *Constitution of the Athenians* (which many scholars ascribe to the "school of Aristotle" rather than to Aristotle himself): it was discovered on an Egyptian papyrus at the end of the last century: references give the sections into which the first editor divided the text. Secondly, many scholars believe that most of the *Protrepticus* has been preserved, in paraphrase, by the philosopher Iamblichus in his own work of the same name.[2] Here it is convenient to key references to the fullest edition of the texts, Ingemar Düring's *Aristotle's Protrepticus*, which was published in Göteborg in 1961.

Everything in Bekker's Aristotle, together with a generous selection of the "fragments" is translated into English in *The Complete Works of Aristotle* – the revised version of the "Oxford Translation", edited by Jonathan Barnes and published in Princeton in 1984. There are many other good translations available; for most of Aristotle's works have been translated into English several times. Every translation traduces; and even the best translations contain errors. Readers who are not able to check an English version against the original Greek are not, however, entirely helpless: checking one English

2 Iamblichus lived from about A.D. 245 to about A.D. 325.

version against another will often suggest the possibility of error or infelicity, even if it will not reveal how the error should be corrected or the infelicity avoided.

In the following table the first column lists the contents of Bekker's Aristotle. Spurious items are marked with an asterisk. The second column indicates which Bekker pages the work occupies. The third column gives the abbreviation used in the *Companion*.

Some scholars use Latin titles for Aristotle's works; others prefer a modern language: here I have followed *The Complete Works* – English, with two Latin exceptions. Different scholars, as I have said, prefer different abbreviations; and the choice I have made here is a hotchpotch, sometimes shortening an English title and sometimes a Latin. These minor inconcinnities may be aesthetically displeasing; but they should not mislead.

Categories	1–15	*Cat*
de Interpretatione	16–24	*Int*
Prior Analytics	24–70	*An. Pr*
Posterior Analytics	71–100	*An. Post.*
Topics	100–164	*Top*
Sophistical Refutations	164–184	*SE*
Physics	184–267	*Phys*
On the Heavens	268–313	*Cael*
On Generation and Corruption	314–338	*GC*
Meteorology	338–390	*Meteor*
On the Universe	391–401	*Mund*
On the Soul	402–435	*An*
Sense and Sensibilia	436–449	*Sens*
On Memory	449–453	*Mem*
On Sleep	453–458	*Somn*
On Dreams	458–462	*Insomn*
On Divination in Sleep	462–464	*Div. Somn*
On Length and Shortness of Life	464–467	*Long. Vit*
On Youth, Old Age, Life and Death	467–470	*Juv*
On Respiration	470–480	*Resp*
On Breath	481–486	*Spirit*
History of Animals[3]	486–683	*HA*

3 Book 10, and perhaps other parts, spurious.

ABBREVIATIONS

An	On the Soul
An.Post	Posterior Analytics
An.Pr	Prior Analytics
Aud	*On Things Heard
Cael	On the Heavens

4 Book K = 11 probably spurious.
5 But some have argued for authenticity.

Cat	Categories
Col	*On Colours
Div.Somn	On Divination in Sleep
Econ	*Economics
EE	Eudemian Ethics
GA	Generation of Animals
GC	On Generation and Corruption
HA	History of Animals
IA	Progression of Animals
Insomn	On Dreams
Int	de Interpretatione
Juv	On Youth, Old Age, Life and Death
Lin.Insec	*On Indivisible Lines
Long.Vit	On Length and Shortness of Life
MA	Movement of Animals
Mech	*Mechanics
Mem	On Memory
Meteor	Meteorology
Met	Metaphysics
Mirab	*On Marvellous Things Heard
MM	*Magna Moralia
Mund	*On the Universe
MXG	*On Melissus, Xenophanes and Gorgias
NE	Nicomachean Ethics
PA	Parts of Animals
Phys	Physics
Physiog	*Physiognomonics
Plant	*On Plants
Poet	Poetics
Pol	Politics
Prob	*Problems
Resp	On Respiration
Rhet	Rhetoric
Rhet.ad Alex	*Rhetoric to Alexander
SE	Sophistical Refutations
Sens	Sense and Sensibilia
Somn	On Sleep
Spirit	*On Breath
Top	Topics
Vent	*The Situations and Names of Winds
VV	*On Virtues and Vices

JONATHAN BARNES

1 Life and work

I. ARISTOTLE'S PERSONALITY

Did Aristotle sport a beard? Ancient portrait busts show a stern and noble figure: a long face, a deep brow – and a luxuriant beard. On the other hand, an ancient biographer remarks that "he had thin legs and small eyes; he wore fashionable clothes, and rings on his fingers – and he shaved."[1] The evidence can readily be harmonized: no doubt the youthful Aristotle was a flashy character who followed the latest style, whereas the Aristotle who posed for the bust was sage and successful (and perhaps a trifle dull). But such harmonization is mistaken in principle; for it misunderstands both the bust and the biographer. Ancient philosophers were supposed to sport beards – the beard was a badge of their profession. Hence a bust of Aristotle was likely to have been given a fine beaver, whatever Aristotle himself may have looked like. Again, ancient biographies are not cordon bleu concoctions of fact – they are crude stews, the rare gobbets of fact swimming in a sauce of dubious inference and unreliable anecdote. We have little reason either to credit Aristotle with a beard or to believe that he was close-shaven.

The state of Aristotle's chin is no doubt of minor philosophical interest; but what goes for his beard goes equally for the rest of him: we know very little about his body and very little about his soul. Later sources offer us various pieces of information; but we are not told much, and most of what we are told it would be rash to believe.[2] Nor

1 Diogenes Laertius, *Lives of the Philosophers* V 1.
2 Diogenes' *Life* of Aristotle runs to fewer than 20 pages, of which fewer than ten are devoted to biography proper. The other surviving *Lives* of Aristotle are even shorter. – All the biographical material is collected in I. Düring, *Aristotle in the Ancient Biographical Tradition* (Göteborg, 1957).

I

should we be tempted to draw inferences of a personal nature from Aristotle's philosophical works: such inferences are rarely reliable, and Aristotle's writings are in any case uncommonly impersonal.

But a few personal documents do survive: a couple of poems, one of them in praise of Plato; snippets from letters, a few of which may just possibly be genuine; and Aristotle's will. The text of the will is apparently authentic; and although it is in several places difficult to follow and difficult to translate, the general drift is clear. I quote it here in full: it needs no commentary.[3]

All will be well; but should anything happen, Aristotle has made the following provisions:

Antipater[4] is to be executor in all matters and in perpetuity; but until Nicanor[5] arrives, Aristomenes, Timarchus, Hipparchus, Dioteles, and Theophrastus (if he is willing and able) are to take care of the children and of Herpyllis[6] and of the estate.

When my daughter comes of age, they are to marry her to Nicanor; and should anything happen to her (may it not do so, and it surely will not do so) before her marriage or after she has married but before there are any children, then Nicanor is to be responsible for administering the affairs of my son and the others in a fashion worthy both of himself and of us. Let Nicanor take care both of my daughter and of my son Nicomachus in whatever way he judges appropriate to their situation, as though he were both father and brother to them.

If anything should happen to Nicanor before this (may it not do so), either before he has taken my daughter or after he has taken her but before there are any children, then if he has made any arrangements, let these take effect. If Theophrastus wishes to live with my daughter, let the same provisions stand as with Nicanor; if he does not, then the executors are to consult with Antipater and administer the affairs both of my daughter and of my son in whatever way they think best.

The executors and Nicanor, remembering me and Herpyllis and how good she was to me, are to take care of everything – and in particular, if she wants to take a husband, they are to see to it that she is given away in a fashion not unworthy of us. In addition to what she has previously been

3 The will is found in Diogenes Laertius, *Lives of the Philosophers* V 11–16; see also below, pp. 195–196.
4 The Macedonian governor of Athens.
5 Aristotle's adopted son.
6 Aristotle's second wife.

given, they are to give her a talent of silver from the estate and three women servants, if she wishes, and the maid which she has, and the slave from Pyrrha. If she wants to live in Chalcis, she is to have the guest-house in the garden, if in Stagira the family house; and whichever of these she wants, the executors are to furnish with whatever seems proper to them and satisfactory to Herpyllis.

Nicanor is also to take care of the slave Myrmex, so that he is conveyed in a fashion worthy of us to his own people, together with those of his belongings which we received. They are to free Ambracis and to give her, on the marriage of my daughter, five hundred drachmae and the maid which she has. They are also to give Thale, in addition to the maid which she has (the one who was bought), a thousand drachmae and a maid. As for Simo, apart from the money which has already been given him for another slave, they are either to buy him a slave or to give him money. Tycho is to be freed on the marriage of my daughter, as are Philo and Olympius and his child. Do not sell any of the slaves who served me, but employ them; and when they come of age, set them free as they deserve.

They are to take care too that the statues which I commissioned from Gryllio are completed and set up – those of Nicanor and of Proxenus[7] (which I intended to commission), and of Nicanor's mother; as for the statue of Arimnestus which is already completed, set it up as a memorial to him since he died childless. They are to dedicate the statue of my mother to Demeter in Nemea or wherever seems best.

Wherever they make my grave they are to take and deposit Pythias' bones too, just as she instructed.[8] And Nicanor, if he is preserved (which I have prayed for on his behalf) is to set up statues in stone four cubits in height to Zeus the Saviour and Athena the Saviour at Stagira.

II. ARISTOTLE'S LIFE

He was born in 384BC, in the small township of Stagira in northern Greece. His father, Nicomachus, was a doctor, friend and physician to King Amyntas of Macedon. His mother, Phaestis, was rich in her own right.

In 367 he moved to Athens, where he became a member of the intellectual circle which centred on Plato. No doubt he had learned some philosophy as a boy in Stagira; perhaps he had read some of

7 Aristotle's uncle.
8 Pythias was Aristotle's first wife and the mother of his two children.

Plato's philosophical dialogues; and maybe he moved to Athens precisely in order to study philosophy with Plato. But there is no positive evidence for these easy suppositions. Nor do we know exactly what Aristotle found at Athens.

Plato was a celebrated figure – perhaps a controversial figure. His fame had attracted intellectuals from abroad; and the Platonic circle – "Plato's Academy" – included some of the most eminent philosophers and scientists of the age. The circle met, either at Plato's house or in the public gymnasium of the Academy. There were discussions. And there was teaching. For the Academy was also in some sense a school (and there was a keen rivalry between it and the establishment which the orator Isocrates had set up for the political education of the Athenian youth). Aristotle may properly be called a student at the Academy insofar as he received teaching there; and in addition the Academy may have had some of the features of a modern club – senior and junior membership, officers, regular meetings, dinners.[9] But we may not imagine the Academy as a University or a College: in particular, we may not think of formal syllabuses and formal lecture-courses, of examinations and degrees.

He stayed in Athens for the next twenty years, always associated with the Academy; and he surely spent much of his time in listening to philosophers and scientists, and eventually in writing and teaching himself. It is reasonable to suppose that the Academicians debated the matters which Plato discussed in his dialogues – ethics and political theory, psychology, metaphysics and epistemology and logic. In addition, we know that Plato encouraged the study of mathematics and of astronomy. And there is some reason to think that other, less abstract, sciences were not excluded.

Plato died in 347, and Aristotle left Athens. Why he left is uncertain, but political reasons have been hypothesized. Aristotle had Macedonian connexions, and the Athenians are reported (on admittedly dubious authority)[10] to have set up an inscription in his honour, thanking him in particular for intervening with the king of Macedon in their interest. But in 347 the northern town of Olynthus

9 But the earliest evidence for these features refers to the period after Plato's death.
10 An Arabic *Life* of Aristotle: see Düring, op.cit., p. 215.

had just fallen to the Macedonian army, and the anti-Macedonian party in Athens, led by the orator Demosthenes, was in the ascendent. Aristotle was not – then or ever – an Athenian citizen, and his situation may have been delicate.

However that may be, he went with Xenocrates, a fellow Academic, to Atarneus, on the coast of Asia Minor: Hermias, the "tyrant" of the place, had connexions with the Academy, and there appears to have been a small Academic community at Atarneus. Hermias welcomed Aristotle, and gave him and his friends "the town of Assos to live in, where they spent their time in philosophy, meeting together in a courtyard; and Hermias provided them with all they needed."[11] Aristotle was to marry Hermias' niece, Pythias; and when, in 341, Atarneus was taken by the Persians and Hermias tortured to death, Aristotle wrote a moving poem in his memory.

From Atarneus Aristotle moved to the city of Mytilene on the island of Lesbos. There he met Theophrastus, a native of the island, who was to become his most famous pupil. It is reasonable to suppose – there is circumstantial evidence in Aristotle's works – that he devoted part of his time in the eastern Aegean to the study of marine biology.

After Mytilene, a brief period home in Stagira. And then, in 343, Philip II, King of Macedon in succession to his father Amyntas, invited Aristotle to the court at Mieza – and to the tutorship of his son, Alexander.[12] Thus began the association between the most powerful mind of the age and the most powerful man. The coupling excited the romantic imagination, and numerous stories were spun. But what Aristotle said to Alexander the Great, and Alexander to him, we do not know. (It is in vain that historians look for Aristotelian influence on the bloody career of Alexander; and philosophers will find nothing – or virtually nothing – in Aristotle's political writings which betrays interest in the fortunes of the Macedonian empire.)

In 335 Aristotle returned to Athens. Plato's Academy was

11 The report comes from the Epicurean Philodemus' history of philosophy: Philodemus, or his source, is hostile to Aristotle – but this story may nevertheless be true.
12 Theophrastus too was invited, and so was Aristotle's nephew Callisthenes, whom Alexander later had put to death.

flourishing under a new head; but Aristotle preferred to set up an establishment of his own, and while the Platonists walked and talked in the Academy, Aristotle did the same in the Lyceum.

A dozen years later Alexander the Great died; and shortly afterwards, in 322, Aristotle left Athens. He did so, he allegedly said, "in order that the Athenians might not commit a second crime against philosophy"[13] – in order that they might not condemn him to death as they had condemned Socrates to death. It is a pretty story, and doubtless fabricated. Yet a second story, equally pretty, is perhaps true. A letter from Aristotle to Antipater, which may conceivably be genuine, contained this sentence: "As for the honour which was voted me at Delphi and of which I have now been stripped, I am neither greatly concerned nor greatly unconcerned".[14] We happen to know what the honour was; for an inscription, dating from about 330, has been discovered at Delphi in which Aristotle (and also Callisthenes) are "praised and crowned".[15] The inscription was found in fragments, at the bottom of a well. On Alexander's death, anti-Macedonian sentiment ran high and was vividly expressed. Aristotle had close and overt connexions with Macedonia. At Delphi they stripped him of his honour and chucked the honorific inscriptions down a well. And perhaps the atmosphere at Athens again encouraged Aristotle to remove.

At all events, he retired to Chalcis, on the island of Euboea, where his mother's family had estates. And there, within a twelvemonth, he died.

The Lyceum survived him, as the Academy had survived Plato. Theophrastus became the head of the school.

III. ARISTOTLE'S WRITINGS

So much for Aristotle's external life. What of the inner man? What can be said in the way of *intellectual* biography? what, in particular, is known of his philosophical personality and his philosophical development? Let us start by asking, crudely enough, what he *wrote*. Three of the ancient *Lives* of Aristotle contain catalogues of his writings; and I shall reproduce the list transmitted by Diogenes

13 Aelian, *Varia Historia* III 36.
14 Fragment 666 R³ = Aelian, *Varia Historia* XIV 1.
15 See e.g. Dittenberger, *Sylloge*³ 275.

Laertius. The original source of this catalogue is disputed (did it come ultimately from the Lyceum, or did it derive from a catalogue of the great library at Alexandria?); and its general level of reliability is uncertain. It is not complete – it omits some of Aristotle's most celebrated surviving works. It contains some things which were surely not written by Aristotle – all ancient book-lists have their spurious items. It includes a number of "doublets" – that is to say, the same work may be included twice, under two different titles. But with all its faults – and for the reason which Diogenes Laertius himself offers – , it is worth reading as a whole.[16]

He wrote a vast number of books, which I have thought it appropriate to list because of the man's excellence in all fields of inquiry: –

[A] On Justice, 4 books; On Poets, 3 books; On Philosophy, 3 books; On the Statesman, 2 books; On Rhetoric, or Grylus, 1 book; Nerinthus, 1 book; Sophist, 1 book; Menexenus, 1 book; Eroticus, 1 book; Symposium, 1 book; On Wealth, 1 book; Protrepticus, 1 book; On the Soul, 1 book; On Prayer, 1 book; On Good Birth, 1 book; On Pleasure, 1 book.

[B] Alexander, or On behalf of the Colonies, 1 book; On Kingship, 1 book; On Education, 1 book; On the Good, 3 books; Excerpts from Plato's Laws, 3 books; Excerpts from the Republic, 2 books; Economics, 1 book; On Friendship, 1 book; On being affected or having been affected, 1 book.

[C] On the Sciences, 2 books; On Eristics, 2 books; Eristical Solutions, 4 books; Sophistical Divisions, 4 books; On Contraries, 1 book; On Genera and Species, 1 book; On Properties, 1 book; Notebooks of Arguments, 3 books; Propositions on Virtue, 3 books; Objections, 1 book; Of things said in many ways or by addition, 1 book.

[D] On Feelings or On Anger, 1 book; Ethics, 5 books.

[E] On Elements, 3 books; On Knowledge, 1 book; On Principles, 1 book.

[F] Divisions, 16 books; Division, 1 book; On Questioning and Answering, 2 books; On Motion, 2 books; Propositions, 1 book; Eristical Propositions, 1 book; Syllogisms, 1 book; Prior Analytics, 9 books; Great Posterior Analytics, 2 books; On Problems, 1 book; Methodics, 8 books; On what is better, 1 book; On Ideas, 1 book; Definitions prior to the Topics, 1 book; Syllogisms, 2 books; Syllogisms and Definitions, 1 book; On the desirable

16 The text is found in Diogenes Laertius, *Lives of the Philosophers* V 22–27. I have translated the titles in the order in which they occur in Diogenes' text; but the groupings, indicated by paragraphing, are my own. (I should note that it is sometimes unclear what Greek text to print, and sometimes unclear how to translate the Greek text which is printed.)

and on accidents, 1 book; Pre-Topics, 1 book; Topics aimed at definitions, 2 books; Feelings, 1 book; Division, 1 book; Mathematics, 1 book; Definitions, 13 books; Arguments, 2 books; On Pleasure, 1 book; Propositions, 1 book.

[G] On the Voluntary, 1 book; On the Noble, 1 book.

[H] Theses for arguments, 25 books; Theses on love, 4 books; Theses on friendship, 2 books; Theses on the soul, 1 book.

[I] Politics, 2 books; Lectures on Politics (like those of Theophrastus), 8 books; On Just Acts, 2 books.

[J] Collection of Arts, 2 books; Art of Rhetoric, 2 books; Art, 1 book; Art (another work), 2 books; Methodics, 1 book; Collection of the Art of Theodectes, 1 book; Treatise of the Art of Poetry, 2 books; Rhetorical Enthymemes, 1 book; On Grandeur, 1 book; Divisions of Enthymemes, 1 book; On Diction, 2 books; On Advice, 1 book; Collection, 2 books.

[K] On Nature, 3 books; Physics, 1 book; On the Philosophy of Archytas, 3 books; On the Philosophy of Speusippus and Xenocrates, 1 book; Excerpts from the Timaeus and from the works of Archytas, 1 book; On Melissus, 1 book; On Alcmaeon, 1 book; Against the Pythagoreans, 1 book; On Gorgias, 1 book; On Xenophanes, 1 book; On Zeno, 1 book; On the Pythagoreans, 1 book.

[L] On Animals, 9 books; Dissections, 8 books; Selection of Dissections, 1 book; On Composite Animals, 1 book; On Mythological Animals, 1 book; On Sterility, 1 book; On Plants, 2 books; Physiognomonics, 1 book; Medicine, 2 books.

[M] On Units, 1 book; Storm Signs, 1 book; Astronomy, 1 book; Optics, 1 book; On Motion, 1 book; Memory, 1 book.

[N] Homeric Problems, 6 books; Poetics, 1 book.

[O] Physics (alphabetically ordered), 38 books; Additional problems, 2 books; Standard problems, 2 books; Mechanics, 1 book; Problems from Democritus, 2 books; On the Magnet, 1 book; Conjunctions of Stars, 1 book; Miscellaneous, 12 books; Explanations (arranged by subject), 14 books.

[P] Claims, 1 book; Olympic Victors, 1 book; Pythian Victors in Music, 1 book; On Music, 1 book; On Pythia, 1 book; List of Pythian Victors, 1 book; Victories at the Dionysia, 1 book; On Tragedies, 1 book; Theatrical Records, 1 book; Proverbs, 1 book; Rules for Messing, 1 book; Laws, 4 books.

[Q] Categories, 1 book; On Interpretation, 1 book.

[R] Constitutions of 158 States (arranged by type: democratic, oligarchic, tyrannic, aristocratic).

[S] Letters to Philip; Letters about the Selymbrians; Letters to Alexander (4), to Antipater (9), to Mentor (1), to Aristo (1), to Olympias (1), to Hephaestion (1), to Themistagoras (1), to Philoxenus (1), to Democritus (1).

[T] Poems, beginning: "Holy one, most honoured of the gods, far shoot-ing . . . "; Elegies, beginning: "Daughter of a mother of fair children . . ."

The bulk, as Diogenes insists, is impressive in itself: more than 150 items, running in all to some 550 books – the equivalent, per-haps, of about six thousand modern pages. More impressive than the bulk is the range.

As it survives, the catalogue is disorderly; but it preserves the vestiges of an original ordering, and the divisions which I have im-posed on the text are not wholly artificial. The list presumably be-gins, in Group [A], with what were – or were later taken to be – youthful works, at least some of them written in dialogue form. Group [B] has no evident homogeneity; but with Group [C] we meet a coherent set of logical titles. Group [F] and Group [Q] are also logical in content, logic thus accounting for more than one quarter of the items in the list. With Group [D], on ethical isues, we may connect the titles in Group [G] and perhaps those in Group [H] – ethics thus accounts for less than one-twentieth of the list. Group [E] belongs either to logic or else to philosophy of science ("phys-ics"); and in the latter case we may associate with it Group [O] and also Group [K], on the history of physics. Group [I] is politics, and Group [J] is rhetoric and poetics (add Group [N]); and Groups [L] and [M] deal with science. In Group [P] we find what may be called Aristotle's public works. Groups [R], [S], and [T] need no comment.

The surviving works, some thirty in all, run to fewer than 2,000 modern pages.[17] We therefore possess about a third of the matter which the catalogue knows as Aristotelian – and less than a third of Aristotle's total *oeuvre* inasmuch as the catalogue omits such major works as *On the Soul*, the *Parts of Animals*, and the *Generation of Animals*, and contains only a truncated version of the *Ethics*. [19] Cer-tain major areas of study we know only from the catalogue, apart from a few hints elsewhere. Thus Aristotle's historical works – on the lists of Olympic victors and of Pythian victors, and of the winners at the Dionysia in Athens – represent a considerable piece of scholarly re-search; and his 158 *Constitutions*, of which only one has survived,

17 The revised Oxford translation (above, p.xxii) contains 2383 pages, ex-cluding the fragments; but this includes a number of spurious works.
19 Nor does it contain the *Metaphysics* as such – but some of its titles may represent individual books or parts of our *Met.*

were a formidable exercise in descriptive political science.[20] Nonetheless, our modern corpus represents most of Aristotle's main interests and all of his main philosophical interests. The amount of space which the corpus allots to different subjects may not be proportional to the space and time which Aristotle actually devoted to those subjects; but it is reasonable to believe that the corpus does not wildly misrepresent Aristotle's interests and achievements.

Whence came our corpus? There was a story current in antiquity which told a romantic tale about Aristotle's library: Theophrastus inherited it on Aristotle's death; it then passed to Theophrastus's nephew Neleus, who took it to a city called Scepsis in Asia Minor, where he hid it away in a cave. Two centuries later the manuscripts were rediscovered, moulding and worm-eaten. They were transferred first to Athens and then to Rome, where the Peripatetic philosopher Andronicus eventually prepared an edition.

There is a modern story which carries the tale further. For two centuries after Theophrastus's death, Aristotelianism had little or no philosophical influence; for the essential documents were buried in Scepsis and not to be read. Then the edition of Andronicus returned Aristotle to the world: the sun rose, and the philosophical world was warm and light again. And the Aristotle which we read – "Bekker's Aristotle"[21] – derives directly from Andronicus.

The ancient story may be true, in whole or in part – it is hard to decide whether to be sceptical about Scepsis. But the modern story should be dismissed. The ancient story does not state or imply that Aristotle's *works* disappeared for two centuries: it says only that his *books* disappeared. Private individuals probably, and the Lyceum at Athens surely, preserved copies or reports of at least some of his works; and it is fanciful to believe that his thought was simply forgotten. It is true that, after Theophrastus, the Peripatetic school suffered a decline; but there is no reason to explain this by the Scepsis story – nor is it true that once Andronicus had done his work Aristotle immediately resumed his rightful position in the sky.

20 The *Constitution of the Athenians* is preserved not in the manuscript tradition, but on a papyrus which chanced to survive in an Egyptian rubbish-pit. Most scholars suppose that Aristotle did not write the *Constitutions* himself – he may have offered some general supervision, but they were surely the work of his pupils. There is little evidence for this supposition.

21 Above, p.xxi.

The edition of Andronicus, however, was real enough; and it is also reasonable to think that our Aristotle derives ultimately from his. What did Andronicus do? How did his edition – how does our edition – differ from what Aristotle actually wrote? The answer, roughly put, is probably this: Andronicus himself composed the works which we now read.

I do not mean that Andronicus forged the things, nor even that he wrote many actual sentences himself. Rather, he composed them in the sense of putting them together: "he divided the works of Aristotle and of Theophrastus into treatises, having grouped together the appropriate subjects."[22] We read Aristotle's *Topics* as a single work in eight books. The catalogue in Diogenes Laertius does not mention the *Topics*; but it does contain *On the desirable and on accidents* (1 book), which surely answers to our *Top* 3. Again, *On Genera and Species* (1 book) may correspond to *Top* 4, and *On Properties* (1 book) to *Top* 5. For *Top* 1–2 we perhaps look to *Definitions prior to the Topics* (1 book) and perhaps to *Pre-Topics* (1 book); and *Top* 6–8 might derive from *Topics aimed at definitions* (2 books) and *On Questioning and Answering* (2 books). Perhaps Andronicus grouped these items together and turned them into our *Topics*?

Any specific suggestions of this sort are, of course, wholly speculative; but it is reasonable to accept the general thesis which they speculatively illustrate. And acceptance of the thesis will affect the way in which we read Aristotle's treatises. The *Topics* does indeed form a more or less unified piece of work. But the unity was composed by Andronicus – and we cannot be sure that it had also been intended by Aristotle himself. In particular, we may not interpret the *Topics* – or any other treatise – on the assumption that it is an Aristotelian unity.

How did Andronicus dare to edit Aristotle? What was the nature of the material which he edited? I shall take a crabwise approach to these questions, starting from the question of Aristotle's literary merits.

Several ancient authors praised his style: most modern readers find it lacking in polish. There are, it is true, a few finished passages; but the rest is rough. The roughness is not unpleasing (and if you

---

22 So Porphyry, who cited Andronicus as a precedent for his own edition of the works of his master, Plotinus: see *Life of Plotinus* 24.

love Aristotle's thought, you will come to love his style), but it is undeniable: the syntax is spare, ornamentation is rare, transitions are abrupt, and connections opaque: the language rarely seems to have been chosen with any aesthetic aim, and often enough the intellectual aim is hard to discern – reading Aristotle, as the poet Thomas Gray put it, is like eating dried hay. Did Aristotle's ancient admirers really admire *this* stuff? Perhaps not; for their judgments of Aristotle's style probably referred to his "exoteric" and not to his "esoteric" works.

The distinction in Aristotle's works between the esoteric and the exoteric is an ancient one. Roughly speaking, the exoteric works were supposed to have been written for a broad public: they were serious, but they were not tough and technical – and they were no doubt written with style and elegance. None of these works has survived, and of them we can form only a partial and frustrating impression from the few fragments which have by chance been preserved. By contrast, the esoteric works were technical things, made for the use of philosophers and for use within the school: they were not "written up for publication" and they were not given a literary polish – indeed, they were not literary texts at all. All Aristotle's surviving works are esoteric in this sense.

Modern scholars have offered a further gloss on the esoteric. The surviving works, it is commonly said, are lecture-notes: they are the notes which Aristotle jotted down and then lectured from (and in some cases perhaps they are notes taken down by his pupils).[23] This idea fits snugly with the notion of the esoteric; for Aristotle's lectures, and hence any lecture-notes, will have been paradigmatically esoteric – things "within the school." The idea also explains why Aristotle's works are so abrupt and unliterary; for you do not think of your lecture notes as publishable prose. Again, it explains why there are relatively few illustrations and almost no jokes: such things get added in the lecture room – only bad lecturers write down their witticisms in advance.

Most interestingly, the idea explains the various inconsistencies and inconcinnities which have been discovered – or imagined – in

23 Several examples of this sort of thing survive from late antiquity; thus what we refer to as Ammonius's *Commentary on Aristotle's Prior Analytics* is in fact a record of Ammonius's lectures taken down and preserved by his pupils.

Aristotle's works. For lecture-notes generally serve for several years, their contents emended and adjourned with each successive delivery. By the time he died, Aristotle will no doubt have given his course of lectures on ethics a dozen times or more. His lecture-notes will have betrayed the fact: there will have been a basic layer of text, representing the first version of the lecture-course; but this basic layer will have been overwritten in numerous places and to different effects – some passages will have been deleted and replaced by paragraphs maintaining an entirely different thesis; other passages will have been modified in more subtle ways, the thesis or the argument being qualified to meet objections; other passages again will have received additions which reinforce rather than change or destroy the original text; and so on. And there will have been several layers of this sort of thing, the text of the first revision being itself replaced by a second revision . . . Moreover, Aristotle will not always have deleted the earlier material as it became dated; and his manuscripts – and therefore, ultimately, the texts which we read – will have contained "doublets": both X and Y will be printed, even though Aristotle intended Y to supplant rather than to supplement X.

The idea is seductive; but it rests on the perilous supposition that Aristotle taught and worked in much the same way as a twentieth century professor of philosophy might teach and work. Let us handle the idea with tongs.

Or perhaps we may embrace the seductive idea while spurning the perilous supposition? Consider, all thoughts of lecturing forgotten, the Aristotelian "doublets". These seem to me to be real enough: sometimes a passage X is indeed followed closely by a passage Y which says pretty well the same as X, in slightly different words. Now Aristotle is normally sparing with his ink – he does not repeat himself: the tempting hypothesis, then, is that X and Y are rival versions of the same sentences, and that one was written to replace the other. It is difficult to be sure about doublets: where some scholars see a palpable repetition, others – more ingenious – descry subtle and intended differences which show that both sets of sentences were intended to stand together. But for what it is worth, I myself find it hard not to think that *some* of the alleged doublets are actual doublets.

In that case, Aristotle certainly revised his texts. And once we allow that revisions took place, it is legitimate – and certainly irresistible – to look for other evidence of revision. For doublets can hardly be the only manifestation of second or third thoughts. Sometimes, for example, a sentence will seem to have been spliced inelegantly into the text: remove the sentence and everything reads more smoothly. So perhaps Aristotle added the sentence in a later revision. Often Aristotle will support a contention not by one argument but by a sequence of considerations. Such sequences easily lend themselves to expansion; and in some cases a turn in the wording or a quirk in the argumentation raises the suspicion that this or that consideration was added to the sequence after it had first been composed.[24]

These facts do not support the seductive idea that Aristotle's surviving writings were lecture-notes; but they do suggest that the writings were, by and large, working drafts – and this suggestion itself has all the explanatory powers of the seductive idea.

These thoughts have an important bearing on the topic to be discussed in the next section. Here let me return to Andronicus. We may reasonably suppose that he aspired to produce a systematic edition of Aristotle's thoughts. To hand he had various manuscripts, some of them perhaps Aristotle's own autographs, and others of them later copies. The texts were evidently not literary texts, but rather working drafts; and although some of the papers may have been grouped together into a book or a treatise, many of them were short and unattached. Andronicus made a selection (on what criteria?); some of the selected papers he grouped together as successive parts of a single work; and he edited a collection of treatises. Some of the items in the collection remained very slight, others were substantial. Some were internally cohesive, others relatively loose. Andronicus will hardly have modified the content of Aristotle's views; and it is plain that he did not tamper much with the style. But no doubt he did a small amount of editorial work: he probably added some cross-references, and he may have interpolated an occasional sentence to link one essay in a treatise to its successor.

All this is fascinating enough in its own right. It also has some philosophical importance. You cannot read Aristotle in the way in which you might read Plato or Descartes or Kant: when you pick up

24 The various books of the *Topics*, say, would have lent themselves to frequent revision of this sort, since for much of their length they simply assemble different argument-forms.

the *Metaphysics* or the *Nicomachean Ethics*, you are not picking up a finished philosophical text, comparable to the *Theaetetus* or the *Meditations* or the *Critique of Pure Reason*.[25] It is proper to assume that you are picking up a set of papers united by a later editor; and it is proper to assume that you are reading a compilation of Aristotle's working drafts. In any case, you should surely read Aristotle's drafts in the manner in which you would read the notes which a philosopher had written for his own use. The sentences are crabbed – sometimes telegrammatic: you must expand them and illustrate them. The arguments are enthymematic – or mere hints: you must supply the missing premises. The transitions are sudden – and often implicit: you must articulate and smooth and explain.

It is difficult to read a text in this way. It is also challenging – and fun. There are dangers: disciplined reading softens into imaginative interpretation – and then into free association. But the dangers can be avoided. And there really is no other way to take these texts.

IV. ARISTOTLE'S PHILOSOPHICAL DEVELOPMENT

Did Aristotle view all or most of his works as parts of, or contributions towards, some systematic whole? Was he a systematic worker, a systematic thinker, a systematic writer? Is there such as thing as "Aristotelianism"?

For centuries these questions were answered with a confident affirmative – and you were then given an outline of the Aristotelian system of thought. Twentieth-century scholarship has by and large preferred what seems to be a more sophisticated approach to the texts. It is a mere truism that Aristotle cannot have written all his works in the same week; and it is a fact that there are differences – perhaps even downright contradictions and inconsistencies – among the works and within the works. (Thus there are two quite different accounts of pleasure within what we call the *Nicomachean Ethics*. The question "Can you *prove* definitions?" is answered in contradictory ways in the *Topics* and the *Posterior Analytics*.) From the truism and the fact scholars inferred, safely enough, that Aristotle's thought must have changed in the course of his life; and they

25 *Rough* modern parallels might be found among the works of Hegel – or of Wittgenstein.

attempted, more audaciously, to write a history of his intellectual development. Instead of a static and systematic Aristotle, we have a dynamic figure.

The modern conclusion, that Aristotle's philosophical ideas must have developed and that the surviving works represent different strata of his thought, will no doubt seem blindingly obvious – surely every philosopher's thought develops and leaves traces of its development in his writings? And as an abstract thesis – as the formal claim that Aristotle sometimes changed his mind – it can scarcely be denied. Yet it has proved surprisingly difficult to make the abstract concrete and to add matter to the form – to describe the actual development of Aristotle's ideas.

The pioneer of "developmental studies" was the German scholar Werner Jaeger. His book *Aristotle – Fundamentals of His Development*, which was first published in German in 1923, determined the course of Aristotelian scholarship for half a century. Jaeger started from two facts about Aristotle's career: first, the fact that Aristotle was Plato's pupil and spent some twenty years as an apprentice in the Academy; secondly, the fact that after Plato's death, Aristotle immersed himself in empirical studies, and notably in detailed biological research. Thus Aristotle moved from Platonism to empiricism. As a young man in the Academy, he fell under the philosophical influence of Plato – how could he not have done? And for a while he embraced Platonism, transcendent ideas and all – how else might the young man have reacted? As he matured, he gradually came to find Plato's metaphysical notions less than satisfactory. Methodological reflection and the actual practice of philosophizing led him more and more in the direction of empiricism: of an empirical method, which gave observation the authority over theory, and of an empiricist epistemology, which insisted that all our concepts and all our knowledge must ultimately be based on the data of perception. This empiricism was confirmed during his scientific interlude in the eastern Aegean, where he was preoccupied by his zoological studies. When he returned to Athens and to philosophy, the empiricism stuck – and it marked the whole of his thought, most notably his political theorizing.

Holding in mind this general thesis, which postulates a move from Platonism to empiricism, Jaeger then scrutinized the surviving works. The thesis allowed him to date them (or their parts) relatively to one another: if A is more empirical than B then A came after B; if B is more Platonist than A, then B came before A. And once the works have thus been arranged in chronological order, the general thesis may be enlarged into a specific history: we may read Aristotle's writings in the order in which he wrote them, and hence reconstruct his intellectual biography in living detail.

Most scholars have taken Jaeger's work seriously. Some have accepted not only the general thesis but also most of the detailed story with which Jaeger himself supplemented it. Others think that the general thesis is roughly right, but prefer a different set of details: they disagree over the dating of this or that work, over the degree of empiricism to be found here and the degree of Platonism there. Yet others dislike not only Jaeger's detailed story but also his general thesis; but they nevertheless applaud his method and his principles: he was right at bottom – only his facts were false. We should rather imagine that Aristotle was an Angry Young Man, who vigorously contested his master's metaphysics and advocated a robust empiricism – and who later mellowed and reflected again on his master's contentions and discovered that Platonism was not so bad a philosophy after all. Not from Platonism to empiricism, but from empiricism to Platonism.

For my own part, I am mildly sceptical of the whole enterprise. It is entirely reasonable to think, on general grounds, that Aristotle's views changed: perhaps they matured or perhaps they fell off – or perhaps they simply changed. And in a few individual cases it may be possible to establish with some degree of probability that this particular bit of text was written before that particular bit of text. But I doubt if we are in a position to say much more than this; and certainly no intellectual biography thus far written has commanded – or has deserved to command – general support.

There are good reasons for scepticism. First, we know little enough about Aristotle's youthful attitude to Plato. To be sure, Aristotle was profoundly influenced by his master, and the surviving works are steeped in Plato's thought – there are innumerable allusions to Plato's writings and to Plato's ideas, some of them explicit and most of them implicit; there are passages in which particular Platonic texts are submitted to a sustained criticism (thus the *Politics* criticizes the *Republic* and the *Laws*); there are centrally Aristotelian texts for which Plato's views are evidently a main source of inspiration and of puzzlement (thus the last two books of the *Metaphysics* are largely moved by Platonic notions about mathematics); and – more vaguely but more importantly – whole areas of Aristotle's philosophical interests were shaped and determined by Plato's philosophical interests. Aristotle's debt to Plato is not in doubt. But it was not merely a youthful debt – for these loans were never repaid or repudiated; nor was its currency belief – for the passages in question do not show Aristotle up as a Platonist, as an adherent of Plato's main doctrines.

What matter in the present context are Aristotle's early writings: these survive only in a few fragments, and the fragments do not contain enough to show what sort of a philosopher the young Aristotle was; in particular, they prove neither that he was a Platonist nor that he was not a Platonist. (Indeed, it is usually difficult to be sure how accurately these "fragments" report Aristotle's own words; and even when it is reasonably plain that Aristotle wrote this or that particular sentence, it is likely that the sentence will be open to two or three incompatible and equally plausible interpretations.) It is still possible that some of these early works will be recovered – on a forgotten library shelf or in the sands of Egypt. But until that splendid event, we had better remain silent about the earlier part of Aristotle's career.

A second reason for scepticism concerns the dating, whether absolute or relative, of the surviving works. There is very little to go on. None of Aristotle's works was explicitly dated by its author,[26] nor does any external source date any of them for us. There are no diaries or letters to tell us about Aristotle's modes and habits of composition.[27] There are, it is true, several references in the works to historical events; and an historical reference of this sort offers us, in principle, a terminus post quem – that is to say, it fixes the *earliest* date at which the work containing it could have been written. Thus if the *Posterior Analytics* casually refers to a battle which took place in a certain year, we shall be inclined to infer that the *Posterior Analytics* was written between that year and Aristotle's death. But references of this sort are in fact surprisingly rare; and in any case, inferences from them – for reasons which should already by clear – are far from reliable. Even if we made all the possible inferences and

26 Aristotle *could* have dated his works – Epicurus dated many of his.
27 Contrast the case of Cicero, whose surviving letters tell us an enormous amount about how and when he wrote his philosophical works.

treated them all as reliable, we should not have got very far towards
establishing a chronology of Aristotle's works.

It might be said, with some justice, that only the *relative* chronology matters from a philosophical point of view: if we are concerned
to interpret Aristotle's philosophical views, then it may well be
important to know whether the *Eudemian Ethics* was written before
or after the *Nicomachean Ethics*; but it will be of far less interest to
know that one was written in this year and the other in that. Now it
may seem as if we possess a quantity of solid and objective evidence
for the relative dating of Aristotle's works. For Aristotle quite often
refers to his own writings – in the course of a discussion he will
quite often say, "I have already dealt with this point in such-and-
such a place" or else "I shall deal with this matter elsewhere." And
these internal cross-references should enable us to date the works
relative to one another: if A refers back to B, then B must have been
written before A; and if A refers forward to B, then B must have been
written after A.

But the cross-references are a disappointment and a delusion. If
we collect and compare them all, we shall find that they are
inconsistent – they imply that A was written before A. Moreover,
the vast majority of them are readily detachable from their contexts: they look for all the world like later additions to the text,
inserted either by Aristotle himself or by a later editor,[28] and then
the "chronology" which they suggest concerns not the order in
which Aristotle composed the works, but rather the order in which
he or his editor supposed that his audience would hear or read
them. Most scholars now agree that cross-references cannot be
used to date the texts in which they are embedded.

What other evidence might be called upon to support a relative
chronology? Sophisticated modern scholarship sometimes appeals
to what is called "stylometry." The "style" which stylometry mea-
sures is not self-conscious literary artifice; rather, it is concerned
with linguistic facts which no reader or author normally notices. (A
stylometrist might consider, say, the average length of sentences in
different works, or the average number of sentences which end with

28 *Rhet* refers back more than once to *An.Pr*; but each reference can be
    lifted from its context without leaving any scar; and so far as I know, no
    scholar has taken these particular cross-references to indicate an order of
    composition.

a participle, or the spread of particles and prepositions and conjunctions.) Suppose, then, that the "style" of A turns out to be markedly different from the "style" of B. (A's sentences are on average considerably longer than B's; A has a decided penchant for one or two particles which are rare in B; and so on.) Then one plausible explanation of this difference will be that A and B were written at different periods. And if a third work, C, can be shown to lie between A and B in these stylistic dimensions, then it will become tempting to hypothesize that C was written between A and B.

Stylometry makes use of computer searches and it employs subtle statistical tests. For these reasons it has attracted several cranks and repelled many scholars. But there is no doubt that it is, in general, a potentially serious business. Here, the question is whether it has a serious application to *Aristotle*'s works. And there are I think, reasons for giving the question a moderately pessimistic answer – reasons which I shall postpone for a paragraph or two.

Traditional scholars have traditionally appealed to "philosophical" rather than to "stylistic" arguments, arguments which tend to run somewhat on the following lines: Suppose that A is inconsistent with B, or that A addresses the same issue as B but in a different fashion – then A is later than B provided that A is more mature than B. Now in its most general form, this sort of argument is quite hopelessly crude. For the judgment that A is "more mature" than B is disquietingly subjective; and the assumption that as philosophers grow older they "mature" – and mature in a more or less linear fashion – needs only to be stated to be hissed off the stage. There is a restricted version of the argument which seems rather more promising. Suppose that A solves a problem which B left unsolved – then A is later than B. Or rather (to avoid any indeterminacy or subjectivity of judgment): Suppose that B says, "Here is a problem which I cannot solve, viz. . . . ," while A says, "I have now solved the old problem, thus . . . " In such a case we may surely date A after B. No doubt – but our "philosophical" argument now has virtually no practical utility; for there are virtually no Aristotelian texts which pair off in the way the restricted version of the argument requires.

Is there no hope for a *via media* between the hopelessly crude and the uselessly impractical? There is; and in a few cases it seems to me that tolerably plausible arguments are available. But these few cases are indeed few.

There is a third general reason for scepticism about chronological hypotheses. I have already rehearsed the plausible hypothesis that Aristotle's surviving writings are working drafts, papers which underwent various revisions and modifications at their author's hands. We might well wonder *when* Aristotle revised his stuff – at the end of a morning's work? After a week's reflection? Months, years, decades later? And we might equally wonder *how often* he made revisions. These are real enough questions – and, again, we cannot answer them except by speculation and conjecture. But the mere fact – or perhaps I should say the presumed fact – of revision has its consequences for the question of Aristotelian chronology.

Suppose that work A was begun in 350, heavily revised a couple of years later, lightly retouched in about 340, and finally rethought a decade later. Suppose that work B was begun in 345, revised carefully in 335, looked at again a year or so later, and then abandoned. Well, which was written first, A or B? If you are going to produce a chronology of Aristotle's writings, will you put A before B (on the grounds that the first version of A preceded the first version of B) or will you put B before A (on the grounds that the final – let us not say definitive – version of B was later than the final version of A)? Pretty clearly, you will say neither of these things; for pretty clearly, it is absurd to talk about chronology in these terms at all. If Aristotle's texts were subject to revisions of the sort I have sketched, then it makes no sense to ask whether A came before or after B – and hence it makes no sense to attempt to provide a chronology of Aristotle's writings.[29]

For these reasons, then, I incline to scepticism. But I do not, alas, want to advocate anything as exciting as a radical scepticism. Here and there, as I have said, we can indeed make chronological claims which have a certain plausibility to them; and some of these claims are not without philosophical significance. (For example, I believe that the core of the theory of demonstration which is expounded in

---

29 Of course, Aristotle's writings had a chronology; but its truths will include neither the sentence "The *Analytics* was written after the *Metaphysics*" nor the sentence "The *Analytics* was not written after the *Metaphysics*" (nor even one or other of the sentences "*Met* A was written before *Met* B" and "*Met* B was written before *Met* A"). The chronology is simply too fine for our traditional methods to reconstruct – and I suspect that it is too fine even for the sophisticated methods of stylometry.

An. Post was developed before the polished theory of syllogistic which is expounded in *An.Pr;* and I believe that this has some bearing on the way in which we should interpret some of Aristotle's views about the nature of science.) But claims of this sort will rarely be made with any confidence; they cannot yield a chronology of Aristotle's writings; and they will not amount to anything which we could call an intellectual biography.

V. ARISTOTLE'S SYSTEM OF THOUGHT

Less than a century ago, most scholars – as I have already said – would have unhesitatingly affirmed that Aristotle was a system-builder and that his thought formed a unified whole. That traditional orthodoxy was supplanted, and it was supposed instead that Aristotle's thought was a dynamic and developing affair. But there is a false antithesis in the air; for it is evident that development and system-building cannot be antithetical attributes, inasmuch as even the most rigid of systematic philosophers will have developed – he will not have been born with a silver system in his mouth. Thus the dynamic Aristotle and the systematic Aristotle should not be thought of as irreconcilable enemies: perhaps the youthful Aristotle was developing precisely into a mature system-builder.

Nonetheless, two facts might be thought to tell against the traditional supposition that there was an Aristotelian system. First, consider the fact that only a small proportion of Aristotle's work has actually survived. This does not, of course, show that Aristotle had no system–but it surely does make it difficult to believe that *we* can recover that system: we only possess a few of the pieces of the jigsaw puzzle, and they do not suffice to determine the original picture, or even its rough outlines. We might conjecture that Aristotle was a system-builder (or that he was not): we should be rash to venture any thoughts about the shape of his system.

This line of thought has a rare quality – it is too pessimistic. It assumes, in effect, that chance has determined which bits of Aristotle have survived and which perished; but this is not so. Our Aristotle – the collection of Aristotle's surviving works – owes its origin not to the ravages and the generosities of chance, but to the work of ancient scholars; for, as I have said, it is highly probable that our corpus is based on the selection made by Andronicus, a selection presumably made with the intention of providing a reasonably full and a reasonably balanced account of Aristotle's philosophy. If this is true, then it is reasonable to look for a system in our corpus if it was ever reasonable to look for a system in Aristotle's thought. Of course, our corpus may still be a distorted thing; for ancient scholars were no less blind and no less free from bias than their modern successors. But it is not merely hopeless to search for a system.

Secondly, consider again the character of Aristotle's surviving writings. If Aristotle revised his material every so often, if he actually went on rewriting and rethinking until his last days, then surely his thought was far too fluid and far too flexible to constitute a system. So, at least, many modern scholars have imagined; and they have therefore portrayed an unsystematic Aristotle.

The unsystematic Aristotle is customarily characterized by the word "aporetic" (or "aporematic"). "*Aporia*" is the Greek for "puzzle" or "difficulty," and Aristotle himself frequently uses the noun and its various cognates: he frequently surveys the *aporiai*, the puzzles or problems in a determined area – and then tries to solve them. An aporetic philosopher is a philosopher who supposes that puzzle-stating and puzzle-solving form the heart of philosophical activity: philosophers of this strain are not supposed to construct elaborate edifices, they are not expected to present their "system" of things; they are not even supposed to produce "theories"; rather, in this area and in that, detailed and diverse problems present themselves to a philosophical mind, and the philosopher's principle task, or perhaps his sole task, is to solve these problems – or to dissolve them.

Was Aristotle aporetic in this sense? Certainly, *aporiai* often buoy the course of his philosophical voyage – thus (to take the most prominent example) the third book (Book Beta) of the *Metaphysics* consists of a sequence of *aporiai* which certain philosophical notions seem to generate. Certainly, too, Aristotle's occasional remarks on philosophical methodology insinuate an aporetic attitude. Thus:

Here [i.e., in discussing *akrasia*, or lack of self-control] as elsewhere we must first set out what seems to be the case; then, having first discussed the puzzles, we must try if possible to maintain the truth of all the reputable opinions on the matter – or if not, then of most and the most authoritative. For if we resolve the difficulties and leave the reputable opinions intact, we shall have offered a sufficient proof of the matter.   (*NE* 1145b1–7)

You set out "what seems to be the case" – which includes all the "reputable opinions" on the matter; you then survey the puzzles which this material engenders; you try to resolve the difficulties without disturbing too many of the reputable opinions. And then? And then nothing: your philosophical task is over.

More generally, in reading through Aristotle's works, you do not gain the impression that you are gradually becoming familiar with a systematic construction. On the contrary, you seem to be led through a series of exhibition rooms, each stocked with problems and difficulties: the problems and difficulties can be looked at from this angle and from that; they are taken up and examined; different analyses are essayed; various attempts at a solution are offered. But – for the most part – nothing systematic seems to emerge, and sometimes nothing definitive emerges. Rather, Aristotle is still searching for the answer – and inviting us to search with him.

All this is true – up to a point; and it also helps to explain why Aristotle has had such a powerful attraction for a certain sort of modern – and aporetic – philosopher. But the truth in it is compatible with a modified version of the systematic view of Aristotle's enterprise. In some of his works – perhaps most notably in the *Metaphysics* – Aristotle is indeed predominantly aporetic. But elsewhere – in the *Prior Analytics*, say, or in the *de Caelo* – the discussion is less puzzlebound and less tentative, and there are straightforward passages of solid doctrine. And in most of his works, he is betwixt and between. On the one hand, it is clear that the surviving works are not concerned to present a perfected system of thought: the corpus is certainly not systematic in this sense. On the other hand, there is some reason to ascribe to Aristotle the conviction that, in principle, the problems with which he was grappling could be solved, the obscurities through which he was stumbling could be illuminated, and the knowledge towards which he – like every natural man – was stretching out his hands could eventually be grasped and organized and contemplated as a totality. There was a system *in posse* but not *in esse*; a virtual but not an actual system.

What would the system look like? Aristotle did not believe in a single unified science: the totality of knowledge – of genuinely scientific knowledge – divides into independent disciplines or sciences. Some of these sciences are theoretical, others practical, others productive – according to whether their goal is the discovery of truths, the performance of actions, or the making of objects. Among the productive sciences are poetics and rhetoric. The practical sciences include ethics and politics (we study ethics, Aristotle avers, not in order to know what sort of men are good but in order to become good men ourselves). The theoretical sciences subdivide into the theological, the mathematical, and the natural. The mathematical sciences are what they seem to be: Aristotle had a keen interest in them, but did not profess an expertise. The natural sciences include physics and chemistry and meteorology and biology and zoology and botany – subjects to which Aristotle devoted a major part of his time and of his writings. And finally there is 'theology', or the science of changeless items, which Aristotle claims as superior to all other studies and to which the essays in his *Metaphysics* are given.

Aristotle does not elaborate these ideas at any length; and there are some obscurities in them.[30] He is far more concerned to insist that the sciences are not unified: there is no single set of truths from which they all derive, no single set of concepts which gives structure to them all, no single method which they all must follow, no single standard of scientific rigour which they all must meet. In all this Aristotle was self-consciously pluralistic – and self-consciously anti-Platonic. Nonetheless, the sciences, or at any rate the theoretical sciences, do have something in common.

Aristotle, like Plato, was impressed by the progress made in the most successful of Greek sciences, geometry; and in particular he was impressed by the way in which geometry could be presented as a unified area of knowledge. And he required, in effect, that the features to which geometry owed its unity should be transferred, so far as possible, to the other theoretical sciences. In short, knowledge is to be systematized in the form of axiomatized deductive sciences. The constituent truths of each science divide into two classes: the first truths or principles, and the derived truths or theorems. The principles of a science – the axioms of geometry, for example – do not need proof: they are primary and self-explanatory. The theorems are proved from the principles: the proofs, which must take the form of valid deductive arguments or syllogisms, explain the theorems and ground our knowledge of them on our knowledge of the principles. A science has

30 Where, for example, should logic be located? Is it a theological science?

a finite and a unitary set of principles, and it constitutes a closed body of explained or self-explanatory truths.

Aristotle's own scientific works do not themselves present things in this rigorous way: they contain few formal deductions; they rarely identify first principles; they do not possess the orderliness and unity which a finished science would possess. Aristotle's *Parts of Animals*, say, is not a strongly systematic work. Nonetheless, Aristotle had systematic thoughts about the science to which *PA* contributes. And here and there in *PA* the system peeps through. So, more generally, with Aristotle's philosophy. Our corpus is not a strongly systematic body of work. Nonetheless, Aristotle had systematic thoughts about the nature of the enterprise to which he was contributing. And here and there in his works the system peeps through.

2   Logic

Aristotle claims a special kind of priority for his treatises on logic. In every other subject matter, he sees himself as continuing a line of work which began before him, and he presents his own theories as further developments of what he has received from his predecessors. When it came to the study of argument, however, Aristotle found himself in a different situation: "When it comes to this subject, it is not the case that part had been worked out in advance and part had not; instead, nothing existed at all." (SE 34, 183b34–36) Aristotle does not mean that no one before him argued, or even that no one before him tried to teach how to argue. What he does claim – and we have no reason to dispute this – is that he was the first to conceive of a systematic treatment of correct inference itself. As such, Aristotle was the founder of logic. This makes the extent of his logical theories all the more remarkable. His *Prior Analytics* contains the complete exposition of a theory of inference (ususally called the "syllogistic"), developed with a striking mathematical rigor. History's first logic has also been its most influential, with an unparalleled importance in post-Hellenistic philosophy, medieval Islamic philosophy, and especially medieval European thought: indeed, for many generations of philosophers, Aristotelian logic was identically logic. Not until the twentieth century was it finally supplanted as a result of the work of Frege and his successors. But even as modern mathematical logic dethroned Aristotle, it also provided the materials for a better understanding of his achievement: recent studies have revealed a strong kinship in methods and interests between Aristotle and present-day logical theory, even if his actual results are wanting by modern standards.

But if the syllogistic is the most brilliant part of Aristotle's achievement as a logician, it is by no means the whole of it. Many of his views on reasoning, argument, and language are relatively independent of it, and many of these are of great importance for the understanding of his other works. Even large parts of his treatises on argument know little of the syllogistic. There are still fewer traces in the works on natural science, ethics, or politics: if historical accident had deprived us of the exposition of the syllogistic in the *Prior Analytics*, we could read virtually all of these without being aware of the loss. By contrast, his views on definition, on demonstration, on dialectical argument, on necessity and possibility, on predication are ubiquitous in the treatises.

In this Chapter, I have tried to balance these concerns, giving roughly equal time to the syllogistic, because of its intrinsic significance, and to the remainder of Aristotle's logical doctrines, because of their importance in his other works.

Aristotle has no word for logic as a whole, nor did he leave us a single comprehensive treatise on logic. What we have instead is treatments of two species of reasoning and argumentation: *demonstration*, which produces scientific proofs, and *dialectical argument*, which is found in debates and exchanges between persons. Demonstration is the principal subject of the *Posterior Analytics*, while the *Topics* gives a method of use in dialectical argument. Other treatises are closely connected with each of these. The *Prior Analytics* describes itself as a preface to a theory of demonstration and has close ties with the *Posterior*, though the syllogistic presented in it claims to be the correct account of every kind of argument. Turning to dialectic, *On Sophistical Refutations* is an appendix to the *Topics*, ending with what is clearly intended as the final chapter of that work. Two other short treatises round out the logical works. *On Interpretation* gives a theory of the structure of propositions and their truth-conditions, much of which is presupposed by the *Prior Analytics*. The treatise we know as the *Categories* is more difficult to classify. An ancient tradition took it to be a preface to the whole of logic, giving a theory of the meanings of the terms of which propositions are composed. So interpreted, however, its latter half (Chapters 10–15) makes no sense (thus, there is an equally ancient tradition regarding this as spurious or out of place). But an even older tradition entitled it "Prefatory Materials for the *Topics*," implying that the *Categories* has something of the same relationship to the dialectical treatises as *On Interpretation* to the works on demonstration. On this basis, I am inclined to number the *Categories* among the dialectical works. To these may be added the *Rhetoric*, which says that its theory of oratory rests on the dialectical theory in the *Topics* (an assertion borne out by close parallels between the works). Six of these seven treatises (minus the *Rhetoric*) were known by the ancient commentators under the collective title *Organon* ("Instrument") and regarded as the works to be studied first in approaching Aristotle's philosophy. Neither title nor grouping is recognized by Aristotle, but cross-references among these treatises show that he saw them as closely connected.

There are also scattered discussions of argumentation in other works. The most extensive of these is *Metaphysics* IV, which undertakes to show that no one can reject the principle of non-contradiction and still engage in meaningful discourse. Briefer passages on argument and methodology are found in most of the treatises (several passages are discussed below; see also *NE* VI.3–6, *Met* I.1–2, *PA* I.1).

PART I. ARISTOTLE'S THEORY OF ARGUMENT

The two types of argument: deduction and induction

Argument is discourse that tries to prove a point: any argument purports to give reasons for accepting some proposition. Let us call the proposition an argument tries to support its *conclusion* and those propositions which it advances as that support its *premises*. Aristotle recognizes two kinds of arguments which support their conclusions in fundamentally different ways. The first of these is *deduction*:

A deduction is an argument in which, certain things being supposed, something else different from the things supposed follows of necessity because of their being so. (*An. Pr* I.1, 24a18–20)

What Aristotle defines here (and in essentially the same terms in *Top* I.1, *SE* 1, *Rhet* I.1) is the relation of logical consequence or implication: a deduction is an argument in which the conclusion follows necessarily from the premises. In modern terms, deductions are *valid arguments*. The principal subject of logical theory, modern as well as ancient, is just this relation of logical consequence.

A comment is in order on the word "deduction." The Greek word Aristotle uses is *sullogismos,* which in ordinary usage can mean "computation" or "reckoning." Plato uses it and its associated verb of the drawing of a conclusion. The English word "syllogism" is its historical descendant, and in fact the line of descent is not just from Greek but from Aristotle. However, this very history makes "syllogism" a bad translation of *sullogismos* in Aristotle. Logicians normally use "syllogism" to *mean* one of the specific forms of valid argument Aristotle discusses in *An. Pr* I.1–6, but Aristotle's definition of *sullogismos* comprehends a much wider class: pretty much any valid argument, or at least any argument with a conclusion different from any of its premises. If we translate *sullogismos* as "syllogism," the broad scope of this definition is obscured, and with it the nature of some of Aristotle's logical theorizing. In the *Prior Analytics,* Aristotle tries to show that any valid argument can be transformed into an argument using only those deductive forms nowadays called syllogisms. This is a substantive claim (and from the standpoint of modern logical theory, it is also demonstrably false). However, if we translate *sullogismos* as "syllogism," we render it true but trivial: "Every syllogism is a syllogism." (A related point might be made about his claim that no *sullogismos* can have only one premise. Aristotle thinks this is worth arguing for; but if, as the ancient commentators thought, it is simply part of the definition – implicit in the plural "certain *things* being supposed" – then the point is trivial and the arguments redundant.)

In addition to deductions, Aristotle (like modern philosophers) recognizes a second kind of argument: *induction* (*epagôgê*). An induction argues "from particulars to universal," that is, infers a general claim from a number of its instances, as in the following:

> Socrates has two legs.
> Plato has two legs.
> Aristotle has two legs.
> Therefore, all humans have two legs.

The conclusion of this argument introduces the term "humans" not found in the premises. How is this justified? Modern accounts of induction would say that the individual cases need a fuller description:

Socrates is human and has two legs.
Plato is human and has two legs.
Aristotle is human and has two legs.

Aristotle, however, may have thought instead that a further premise is presupposed:

Socrates has two legs.
Plato has two legs.
Aristotle has two legs.
Socrates, Plato, and Aristotle are human.

However we construe it, inductive arguments have one property that sharply distinguishes them from deductions: they can be rendered invalid by *adding* a premise of the right sort. Suppose that we add the following to our example:

Monosceles is human and does not have two legs.

A single one-legged human like Monosceles – a single *counter-example* – is sufficient to block the inductive inference from any number of cases to the generalization "All humans have two legs." A good inductive argument, then, must also suppose that there are no counterexamples. We could try adding still another premise saying this explicitly:

I. There is no other human who does not have two legs.

But this new premise is almost equivalent to the conclusion "All humans have two legs." We have thus saved the argument only by trivializing it. Instead, we might try:

II. Socrates, Plato, and Aristotle are all the humans there are.

The new premise, of course, is false, but if we add sufficiently many cases (i.e., one for each human being) and sufficiently many names to the list, we could in principle make it true. Such a reworking gives us a good argument but only by making it *deductively* valid. It also makes such arguments very hard to come by, since the number of cases required will be enormous, and the knowledge that these are all the cases would be difficult or impossible to come by. As a third possibility, we might add a premise of this sort:

III. Socrates, Plato, and Aristotle are all the humans we have observed.

With this premise, the argument is not merely a deduction, and it does capture an important use of inductions, namely, drawing conclusions about what we have not yet encountered from generalizations about what we have. Modern philosophy of science concentrates on precisely this type of inference: the "problem of induction" is explaining the reliability of arguments of the type "Every A observed so far is B; therefore, every A without qualification is B."

It is not easy to say which, if any, of these Aristotle favors, since what he has to say about induction is far briefer and much less systematic than what he says about deduction. He shows little concern with the modern "problem of induction," and thus it is unlikely that anything like III was at work. However, there are different texts which lean toward I and II respectively. In dialectical contexts, where arguments take on the form of contests between two opponents (see below), Aristotle says that a disputant who has accepted a number of instances of a generalization must either agree to the generalization or offer a counterexample. This leans toward a presupposed premise of Type I: if I cannot think of any non-two-legged humans, then I have in effect conceded that there are no humans who do not have two legs.

Elsewhere, Aristotle seems inclined to treat at least some inductions as relying on a premise of Type II. This is most evident in connection with inductions in which the cases concern species, not individuals, as in this example:

> Grapevines are deciduous.
> Oaks are deciduous.
> Elms are deciduous.
> (Various other cases, one for each broad-leaved species)
> Grapevines, oaks, elms, etc., are all the broad-leaved species there are.
> Therefore, all broad-leaved species are deciduous.

Here, the Type II premise is not nearly as intractable as in the earlier example. The number of different species is certainly much smaller than the number of individuals, and for Aristotle it is permanently fixed since species neither come to be nor pass away. But even if this is how Aristotle thinks of inductions in which the "particulars" are species rather than individuals, it is hard to imagine him extending this analysis to inductions such as our first example (and there is plenty of evidence that he counted such arguments as inductive).

In fact, Aristotle simply does not give us anything like a complete theory of inductive arguments, and any attempt to reconstruct one from his scattered remarks is bound to include speculation. Although he assigns induction a critical epistemological role as our means of coming to know generalizations, he never attempts to set out systematic rules for inductive arguments (although there are hints in that direction in *Top* VIII).

The language of the syllogistic

Deductions (and inductions) are composed of sentences which are capable of being true or false: *assertions* or *declarations* (*apophanseis*), as Aristotle calls them in *On Interpretation*. He regards such assertions as taking one of two forms. In an *affirmation*, something is "affirmed of" something else: "Socrates is human" affirms humanity of Socrates, "Horses are animals" affirms "animal" of "horses." In a *denial*, something is denied of something else: "Socrates is not walking," "Horses are not fish." Aristotle thus takes any assertion to consist of two parts: a *predicate*, which is either affirmed or denied of something, and a *subject*, of which the predicate is affirmed or denied.

We may distinguish between individual assertions, in which the subject is a concrete particular such as Socrates, and general ones, in which the subject is a general term or *universal*, such as horse. Individuals cannot normally serve as anything but subjects, whereas universals can also serve as predicates. We say "Horses are animals" and "Clydesdales are horses" with equal naturalness. But when we force "Socrates" into predicate position, what we have no longer seems to be predication, but instead a kind of identification: "That man is Socrates" amounts to "That man and Socrates are the same." A further distinction is that general predications accept determinations of quantity, such as "every," "some," "no": "Every horse is a mammal," "Some horses are not tame." With individual predications, such quantifiers seem ungrammatical.

Because of these and other differences, modern logicians regard "Socrates is human" and "Every Athenian is human" as having different logical forms, despite a superficial resemblance. "Socrates is human" is taken to be a predication with Socrates as subject, whereas "Every Athenian is human" does not contain "Every Athenian" as subject at all but instead says "For anything you take, if it is an Athenian then it is human." Aristotle also recognizes that general and individual predications are different, but he nevertheless takes both to have subject-predicate form. Modern logicians would disagree for fundamental reasons (which I will not pursue here).

Predications with universal subjects may be different in *quantity:* a predicate may be affirmed or denied of all of a subject ("Every human is rational," "No humans are Greek,") or only of some of it ("Some dogs are not vicious"). These distinctions complicate a fundamental relation between propositions, that of *contradiction.* In the case of an individual predication, there is a simple relationship between an affirmation and its corresponding denial: the proposition "A is B" affirms exactly what the proposition "A is not B" denies, and of these two, exactly one must be true and one false. What corresponds to this relationship in the universal case? As Aristotle shows (*Int* 7), the following schema gives the proper correspondences:

> "Every A is B" and "Some A is not B" are contradictories.
> "No A is B" and "Some A is B" are contradictories.

Note further that "Every A is B" and "No A is B" are not contradictories: they cannot both be true, but both can be false. "Some A is B" and "Some A is not B" are even further from being contradictories, since they can both be true (although for Aristotle they cannot both be false).

Sentences of these four types are *categorical sentences.* A convention – non-Aristotelian but nevertheless handy – dating from the Middle Ages designates each sentence type with a vowel: "a" for "belongs to every," "e" for "belongs to no," "i" for "belongs to some," "o" for "does not belong to some." Categorical sentences may then be abbreviated using the sequence "predicate-sentence type-subject," as follows:

> AaB = A belongs to every B (Every B is A)
> AeB = A belongs to no B (No B is A)
> AiB = A belongs to some B (Some B is A)
> AoB = A does not belong to some B (Some B is not A)

From the standpoint of modern logic, only a limited number of sentences can be represented in this form. Those involving sentential composition ("If either it rains tomorrow or we have no money left, then we shall not proceed with our journey unless we both receive unexpected assistance and any rain that falls is both brief and light,"), relational predicates ("Socrates was older than Plato," "Socrates is sitting between Plato and Aristotle"), and multiple quantification ("Everyone knows someone by whom he is not known") stoutly resist being put in categorical form. Modern logicians regard categorical sentences as merely one species of proposition. Aristotle, however, appears to hold that every declarative sentence can be analyzed in terms of categorical sentences. Therefore, in studying categorical sentences, he took himself to be studying *what can be said*, without qualification. This last point is essential in understanding Aristotle's theory of validity. In fact, this is a theory of validity for arguments composed of categorical sentences, but since Aristotle thought that all propositions could be analyzed as categoricals, he regarded the syllogistic as the theory of validity in general.

The theory of validity: arguments in the figures

At the foundation of Aristotle's syllogistic is a theory of a specific class of arguments: arguments having as premises exactly two categorical sentences with one term in common. Three forms of such combination are possible: the subject of one premise may be the predicate of the other, the premises may have the same predicate, or the premises may have the same subject. Aristotle calls these three configurations the "first figure", "second figure," and "third figure," respectively.

First figure		Second figure		Third figure	
predicate	subject	predicate	subject	predicate	subject
A	B	A	B	A	B
B	C	A	C	C	B

He then asks: What combinations of categorical sentences in each of these figures imply some conclusion containing just the two terms which the premises do *not* have in common? Working systematically through all 16 premise combinations in each figure, Aristotle either proves that a certain form of conclusion follows or proves that no conclusion containing just those terms follows.

Before we consider these proofs, some preliminaries (terminological and otherwise) are in order. Aristotle calls the term which appears in both premises the *middle* term; the other two terms, which appear as subject and predicate of the conclusion, are the *extremes*. He also makes a distinction between the *major* extreme and the *minor* extreme, which requires some explanation. In the first figure, Aristotle only investigates whether a conclusion follows which has as its predicate the extreme that is used as a predicate in its premise, and has as its subject the extreme used as a subject. In other words, a first-figure deduction has for him the form:

> A (predicated of) B
> B (predicated of) C
> Therefore, A (predicated of) C

Aristotle calls "A" (the predicate of the conclusion, and the extreme that appears as the predicate of one premise) the *major term*, and he calls "C" (the subject of the conclusion, and the extreme that figures as subject of a premise) the *minor term*. He also calls the premises containing these terms the major and minor premises, respectively. Within the first figure, then, major and minor terms have different roles in the *premises*. This distinction cannot be applied to the second and third figures, but Aristotle continues to call the predicate and subject of the conclusion, respectively, the major and minor terms. In stating forms, Aristotle's practice is to give the major premise first.

The next point is more than terminological. After defining "deduction," Aristotle distinguishes between "complete" (or "perfect") and "incomplete" (or "imperfect") deductions. A complete deduction is a deduction with the further property that it "needs no term from outside to make the necessity obvious": that is, it is an argument in which the conclusion not only follows from the premises but *obviously* follows. An incomplete deduction is still a deduction, but its validity is not obvious and requires proof: this consists of inserting additional steps of reasoning between premises and conclusion which "make the necessity obvious." Aristotle says that the following first-figure deductions are complete:

AaB, BaC;   therefore AaC   (*Barbara*)[1]
AeB, BaC;   therefore AeC   (*Celarent*)
AaB, BiC;   therefore AiC   (*Darii*)
AeB, BiC;   therefore AoC   (*Ferio*)[2]

Proofs by 'Completion'

Aristotle then turns to the second and third figures and uses these first figure syllogisms, together with certain other rules, to construct proofs for the deductions in them, all of which he regards as incomplete. These other rules involve *conversion:* to "convert" a categorical sentence is to interchange its subject and predicate. Aristotle notes that some forms imply their converses:

> *AeB* implies *BeA* ("No dogs are horses" implies "No horses are dogs")
> *AiB* implies *BiA* ("Some dogs are pets" implies "Some pets are dogs.")

Obviously, this relationship is symmetrical, since the converse of the converse of a sentence is that sentence. Neither *a* nor *e* sentences convert, but an *a* sentence implies the corresponding *i* sentence with transposed terms:

> *AaB* implies *BiA* ("All dogs are animals" implies "Some animals are dogs.")

Aristotle calls this "accidental conversion."

The following example illustrates how Aristotle's proofs for second- and third-figure forms work. His objective here is to show that combination *ae* in the second figure yields an *e* conclusion:

If M belongs to every N but to no X, then neither will N belong to any X. For if M belongs to no X, then neither does X belong to any M; but M belonged to every N; therefore, N will belong to no N (for the first figure has come about). And since the privative converts, neither will N belong to any X.   (*An.Pr* 1.5, 27a9–12)

---

1 The curious names following these combinations are medieval mnemonics for the forms; though not Aristotelian, they are commonly encountered in the literature and worth knowing.
2 The vowels indicate the types of premises and conclusion, in order. Thus, *Celarent* indicates premise-combination *ea* and conclusion *e*; knowing that this is in the first figure lets us reconstruct the form.

The proof given in this text may be presented formally as follows:

1. MaN		If M belongs to every N
2. MeX		but to no X,
To prove: NeX		then neither will N belong to any X.

3. MeX	(2, premise)	For if M belongs to no X,
4. XeM	(3, e-conv)	then neither does X belong to any M;
5. MaN	(1, premise)	but M belonged to every N;
6. XeN	(4,5,Celarent)	therefore, X will belong to no N (for the first figure has come about).
7. NeX	(6,e-conv)	And since the privative converts, neither will N belong to any X.

This proof can be read as a schema for constructing a completed deduction from premises of the forms MaN, MeX to the conclusion NeX. Aristotle's letters have a role much like the figure in a Greek geometrical proof and the letters which label its parts.[3]

Sometimes, Aristotle must use another pattern of proof, namely

3 The medieval name for this form, *Camestres*, also encodes this proof. The letter "s" (*conversio simplex*) means "apply e-conversion or i-conversion to the proposition whose vowel precedes"; e-conversion is used at step 4 on the e premise, and at step 7 on the intermediate result XeN. The initial letter "C" is the first letter of *Celarent*, indicating the first-figure form, which will be appealed to in the proof (step 6). The letter "m" (*movere*) means "interchange premises," indicating that the premises must be reversed in order to obtain the first figure (Aristotle never supposes that the order of the premises affects the validity of a deduction, although he does generally *state* premises in a fixed order). In other names, "p" after a vowel indicates that conversion of an *a* to an *i* (*conversio per accidens*) must be used.

completion through impossibility. He adds the denial of the desired conclusion to the premises and, from this and one of the original premises, deduces the contradictory (or contrary) of the other premise. This shows that the original premises and the denial of the conclusion cannot all be true; therefore, if the premises are true then the denial of the conclusion must be false (i.e. the conclusion must be true). An example (second-figure *Baroco*, from *An.Pr* I.5, 27a37–b1):

1. MaN	premise	If M belongs to every N
2. MoX	premise	but does not belong to some X
To prove: NoX		it is necessary for N not to belong to some X.

4. NaX	(denial of NoX)	For if it belongs to every X
5. MaN	(premise 1)	and M is also predicated of every N,
6. MaX	(4,5, Barbara)	then it is necessary for M to belong to every X;
7. MoX	(premise 2)	but it was assumed not to belong to some.

The proof ends here: line 6 is the contradictory of premise 2, and thus the assumption of NaX leads to an impossibility. The "impossibility" is an impossibility *given the premises:* if the premises MaN and MoX are both true, then the further assumption NaX leads to the impossible pair MaX, MoX.

Disproofs by counterexample

Establishing that certain forms of premises always yield a conclusion is half Aristotle's task. To have a complete logical theory, he must also show that these are *all* the concluding forms. To show that an argument is invalid, it suffices to show that its conclusion *might* be false when its premises are all true. The standard logical technique for doing this is the *counterexample:* describing a possible situation in which the argument has true premises and a false conclusion. But Aristotle's concern is with argument forms, not arguments, and an argument form is valid only if all its instances are valid. Therefore, a counterexample to an argument form will be any argument of that form with true premises and a false conclusion. Aristotle could proceed through all possible combinations of premise and conclusion forms and give counterexamples for the invalid ones. Instead, he shows that certain premise pairs "do not syllogize" by showing that no matter which of the four possible conclusion forms we try, the result is always invalid. He does this with an ingenious and efficient technique that is best explained on the basis of an example. To argue that the combination AaB, BeC in the first figure does not syllogize, he says:

For nothing necessarily follows as a result of these being so. For the first can belong both to all and to none of the last, so that neither a particular [conclusion] nor a universal [conclusion] is necessary; and since nothing is necessary through these, there is no deduction. Terms for belonging to all are animal-man-horse, for belonging to none animal-man-stone.   (*An. Pr* I 4, 26a3–9)

Here is how this works. Suppose that animal, man, and horse are the terms (in order of appearance) in a pair of premises of the forms AaB, BeC: the premises are then "Animal belongs to every man" and "Man belongs to no horse," and these are evidently true. The same also holds for the terms animal, man, and stone. In the first case, however, "Animal belongs to every horse" happens to be true, while in the second "Animal belongs to no stone" is true:

Case I	Case II
Animal belongs to every man	Animal belongs to every man
Man belongs to no horse	Man belongs to no stone
Animal belongs to every horse	Animal belongs to no stone

These two cases show that it is possible for there to be sets of true propositions of these two forms:

Case I	Case II
AaB	AaB
BeC	BeC
AaC	AeC

Now, suppose that there is a valid *form* of argument in the first figure with premises AaB, BeC. Its conclusion must have one of four possible forms: AaC, AeC, AiC, AoC. But Case I shows by counterexample that it cannot be either AeC or AoC (since AaC is inconsistent with each of these), and Case II likewise is a counterexample to it being AaC or AiC. Aristotle refers to this type of argument by counterexample as "proof by terms".

With these techniques, Aristotle establishes that the following, and only the following, are the valid forms of deduction in the three figures:

First figure:	AaB, BaC; therefore AaC	*Barbara*
	AeB, BaC; therefore AeC	*Celarent*
	AaB, BiC; therefore AiC	*Darii*
	AeB, BiC; therefore AoC	*Ferio*
Second figure:	MaN, MeX; therefore NeX	*Camestres*
	MeN, MaX; therefore NeX	*Cesare*
	MeN, MiX; therefore NoX	*Festino*
	MaN, MoX; therefore NoX	*Baroco*
Third figure	PaS, RaS; therefore PiR	*Darapti*
	PeS, RaS; therefore PoR	*Felapton*
	PiS, RaS; therefore PiR	*Disamis*
	PaS, RiS; therefore PiR	*Datisi*
	PoS, RaS; therefore PoR	*Bocardo*
	PeS, RiS; therefore PoR	*Ferison*

Aristotle does not actually show the invalidity of other premise-conclusion combinations for concludent premises, e.g., he gives no counterexample to AaB, BaC; therefore AeC. There is another point he does not treat systematically. A first-figure premise pair might imply a conclusion having the major term as *subject* and the minor as *predicate*:

A (predicated of) B
B (predicated of) C
Therefore, C (predicated of) A

There are, in fact, five valid forms of this type (medieval logicians classified them as a fourth figure apart from Aristotle's three). Aristotle recognizes all of them, at various places in the *Prior Analytics*, as a sort of appendix to the first figure. However, he does not give systematic proofs for their validity, and he does not give counterexamples to reject inconcludent combinations (Theophrastus filled this gap, treating them systematically as "indirect" first-figure forms).

In the short compass of *Prior Analytics* I.4–6, then, Aristotle has given a masterly treatment of his subject: for every combination of premise types in the three figures, he has either given a proof to show that a certain form of conclusion follows, or he has shown by counter-example that no conclusion follows. Moreover, his methods allow him to assert that in a way, the first-figure forms are sufficient for all deductions from premises in these figures. But Aristotle goes further. The first-figure deductions *Darii* and *Ferio* can be completed by arguments through impossibility using *second*-figure forms. *Darii*, for example, goes like this:

1.	AaB	(premise)
2.	BiC	(premise)
3.	Suppose AeC	
4.	BeC	(1,3 *Camestres*)
5.	BiC	(premise 2)
6.	AiC	(denial of 3: proof through impossibility)

Therefore, says Aristotle, since *Camestres* in turn was proved from first-figure *Celarent*, we can give an extended proof of *Darii* from *Celarent*. Similarly, *Ferio* can be derived from *Celarent* by way of *Cesare*. These results illustrate an important point of kinship between Aristotle and modern logicians: he wants to study the overall structural properties of his deductive system – to do *metalogic*, in modern terms – rather than simply to see which actual arguments are valid and which invalid.

Metalogical concerns dominate the remainder of the *Prior Analytics*. Having shown that every "deduction in the figures" can be completed using only the first-figure universal forms, he then turns to the more general question whether this holds for *every* deduction. Some scholars interpret him as at least attempting to prove the *completeness* of the syllogistic in a well-defined, and quite modern, sense: whenever any set of categorical sentences implies a conclusion, then it is possible to construct a chain of two-premise inferences, using the forms of the syllogistic, from those premises to that conclusion. (Whether or not Aristotle successfully states or proves this result, it can be shown to be true.) Moreover, Aristotle does try to show that any valid argument whatsoever can be reduced to syllogistic inferences. This depends on showing that every argument either consists entirely of categorical sentences or can be recast in them. He argues in *An Pr* I.23 that any argument must try to establish a categorical conclusion, and thus must have categorical premises; in *An Pr* I.32–44, he considers how to put various types of apparently non-categorical arguments into his three figures. On the whole, however, this part of his project is much less convincing, and he acknowledges himself the difficulty of "reducing" certain arguments, particularly arguments through impossibility.

Problems in interpreting the syllogistic

Modern logical theory rejects the syllogistic as a general theory of validity because its theory of propositional forms is too limited. However, it is possible to interpret the syllogistic as a fragment of a more general logical theory such as predicate logic. One way to do this is to translate the categorical sentence types into predicate logic as follows:

AaB = For any x, if x is a B then x is an A
AiB = For some x, x is a B and x is an A

The translations of AeB and AoB are then the negations of these:

AoB = For some x, x is a B but x is not an A
AeB = For any x, not both: x is a B and x is an A

But on these translations, Aristotle's conversion rules do not work. The difficulty is that the translations of AiB and AoB assert the existence of something, whereas the translations of AaB and AeB do not. Even if nothing is a B or an A, it can be true of everything that *if* it is a B *then* it is an A. As a result, the conversion AaB, BiA fails. The upshot is that third-figure *Darapti* and *Felapton* become invalid.

It is possible to regard this as showing merely that these translations are inadequate, but they bring an important point to the fore: Aristotle tacitly employs certain assumptions about the *existential import* of terms. The simplest way to preserve his results is to suppose that *all* terms have existential import (in which case the syllogistic can be interpreted as a theory of the relations of non-empty classes). This has intuitive support: if I say "All my daughters are brilliant," you will conclude that I have daughters.

A difficulty of another sort is making sense of the relation "belongs to" itself. The problem is that terms in the syllogistic all can appear both as subjects and as predicates (Aristotle insists on this in *An. Pr* I.27). What can terms be, if they are to function in this way? From a modern standpoint, the most satisfactory response is that they designate *classes:* we can then interpret AaB as "A contains B," AiB as "A overlaps B," and AeB and AoB as the negations of these. Such an interpretation sometimes fits with Aristotle, but sometimes it does not. In particular, he appears to take seriously the parallel between "Some people are snub-nosed" and "Socrates is snub-nosed": each ascribes the property of being snub-nosed to its subject. But it is absurd to suppose that a class has the property "snub-nosed."

Modal propositions and the modal syllogistic

On Interpretation also extends its treatment of relations of contradiction to modally qualified propositions, that is, to categorical sentences with "necessarily" and "possibly" attached to them. It will be useful to compare his results with modern modal logic. Logicians today generally take "necessarily" and "possibly" to be interdefinable in a simple way: "necessarily" = "not possibly not," and thus "possibly" = "not necessarily not." Modern logicians also suppose that "necessarily p" and "possibly p" are in a simple way stronger and weaker than "p": "Necessarily p" implies "p", and "p" implies "possibly p." Aristotle's views are more complicated. He accepts that "Necessarily p" implies "p," and he often says that the necessary is "what cannot be otherwise." However, he distinguishes two senses of "Possibly p." In his preferred sense, "Possibly p" is equivalent to "p is neither impossible *nor necessary.*" On such an analysis, the denial of "Possibly p" is "*Either* necessarily p *or* necessarily not p." Moreover, "p" does not imply "Possibly p," but "Possibly p" implies and is implied by "Possibly not p." He does, in addition, recognize that "Possibly p" can be used to mean "Not necessarily not p," but he treats this as a secondary or aberrant usage (in *An. Pr* I.13–22, it is sometimes called "possibility not according to the definition").

When these distinctions are applied to the categorical sentences, matters become very difficult indeed. How, for instance, should we interpret "Possibly no horses are white"? Aristotle takes it to assert, of *every* horse, that it is possibly not white, and therefore possibly white; thus, "Possibly AeB" implies "Possibly AaB" (and the converse also holds). In the same way, "Possibly AiB" and "Possibly AoB" imply each other. Aristotle tries to work up a general modal syllogistic in *An. Pr* I.8–22; the result is far less satisfactory than his nonmodal or "assertoric" syllogistic. Some of his claims are notoriously difficult to understand. The most widely discussed of these is the problem of the "two Barbaras." Aristotle holds that "Necessarily AaB; BaC; therefore, necessarily AaC" is valid, but that "AaB; necessarily BaC; therefore, necessarily AaC" is not. The first of these inferences is remarkable in that it derives a necessary conclusion from premises not all of which are necessary. Many subsequent logicians have held that this is unacceptable – among them Aristotle's lifelong associate Theophrastus, who dropped the offending rule from his own modal syllogistic in favor of the simpler rule that the modality of the conclusion is always the weakest of the modalities of any premise. Various commentators have also pointed out that the offending rule seems to commit Aristotle to contradictory results concerning other combinations of premises. In recent years, interpreters have expended enormous energy in efforts to find some interpretation of the modal syllogistic that is consistent and nevertheless preserves all (or nearly all) of Aristotle's results; generally, the outcomes of such attempts have been disappointing. I believe this simply confirms that Aristotle's system is incoherent and that no amount of tinkering can rescue it. (Of course, this still leaves us with the knotty problem of why Aristotle should have developed such a system.) Fortunately for the student of Aristotle, the modal syllogistic is largely self-contained: hardly anything in Aristotle's other works, even including the *Analytics,* appears to take notice of it.

The problem of future contingent statements

Although it is not closely connected with the syllogistic, it is appropriate to mention here the problem about necessity and possibility which Aristotle discusses in *On Interpretation* 9. As noted above, one of the principal subjects of that work is the determination of the denials of each form of assertion. The denial of a proposition p denies exactly what p affirms. Now, it seems that p and its denial exhaust between them all the logical possibilities; either p or its denial must be true. But if p is true, then its denial is false; and if p's denial is true, then p must be false. This is the *principle of excluded middle*; for any proposition p, either p or its denial must be the case.

Aristotle usually takes this to be one of the securest of principles. However, in *Int.* 9 he raises a puzzle about its application to future-tense statements about contingent matters, that is, things which might either happen or not happen. Is the sentence "There will be a sea battle tomorrow" now true or false? On Aristotle's principles, it appears that either it or its denial "There will not be a sea-battle tomorrow" must be true. But Aristotle takes it as equally obvious that the past is unchangeable, so that all truths in the past tense are necessary truths. Suppose, therefore, that someone said yesterday, or ten thousand years ago, that there would be a sea battle tomorrow. If the utterance was true *then*, in the past, then it is *now* a necessary truth about *tomorrow* that there will be a sea battle; similarly, if it was false when uttered, then it is now a necessary truth that it was false, and therefore it is necessary that there *not* be a sea battle. And, says Aristotle, surely it makes no difference whether anyone actually *did* utter such a sentence: the same argument holds if we suppose only that someone *might* have done so. The upshot is that whatever happens could not possibly happen except as it does. This threatens to undermine our concepts of deliberate action, for it seems that we cannot by taking thought have any effect on what occurs, or even on what we do. From relatively simple logical principles, then, we have reached a kind of fatalism.

It is much easier to state Aristotle's problem here than to explain his solution: the literature on this brief chapter during the past forty years is enormous. Some conclude that in order to preserve deliberation, Aristotle restricts the law of excluded middle and holds that future contingent statements are neither true nor false: it is not *now* either true or false that there will be a sea battle tomorrow. It has also been proposed (and denied) that he gets himself into this problem only by mistakenly inferring "Either necessarily p or necessarily not p" from "Necessarily (either p or not p)."

Demonstrative sciences[4]

Aristotle's *Posterior Analytics*, especially its first book, is concerned with knowledge in a precise sense, for which he uses the word *epistêmê* (one of several Greek words for knowledge). An *epistêmê* in this technical sense is a body of knowledge about some subject, organized into a system of *proofs* or *demonstrations*: a good modern equivalent is "science," provided we drop its connotations of reliance on experimental method. Aristotle's model for a science was the mathematical disciplines of arithmetic and geometry, which in his time were already being presented as systematic series of deductions from basic first principles.

The central concept of the *Posterior Analytics* is the *demonstration (apodeixis)*, which Aristotle defines as "a deduction that makes us know." Demonstrations, then, are a species of deduction. Broadly speaking, Aristotle supposes that deductions have an epistemic power: if I know that the premises of a deduction are true, then that knowledge together with my grasping of the deduction can bring it about that I also know its conclusion. Aristotle generally associates this power of epistemic transmission with deduction (he thinks that it also holds for belief). It would seem, then, that an account of knowledge that arises from demonstration would simply be an account of what it is to know the premises of a demonstration; knowledge of the conclusion would follow automatically. However, Aristotle thinks of scientific knowledge as knowledge in a specific sense: to know something scientifically is *to know the cause or reason why it must be as it is and cannot be otherwise* (*An. Post* I.2). From this it follows obviously that nothing can be known scientifically except that which cannot be otherwise, and that scientific knowledge must consist in knowledge of causes; less obviously, it also follows that scientific knowledge of that which has no cause is impossible.

This conception seems to rule out any knowledge of merely contingent facts. If we suppose (as Aristotle does) that most of what happens in the world of particular sensible objects is contingent, we

4 See also chapter 4, pp. 109–113.

might expect that science so conceived will be very impoverished. In fact, Aristotle does hold that there is no real scientific knowledge of individuals or individual facts *as individuals*. However, science of individuals is possible to the extent that they fall under unchanging universals.

To have scientific knowledge of *p*, then, is to know the cause why *p* is true, that is, to know the answer to the question "Why is it that *p*?" This answer will take the form "Because *q* and *r*, from which *p* follows." For such an answer to be adequate, the premises *q* and *r* must at the very least be true and the conclusion *p* must follow from them. A demonstration must therefore be a valid argument with true premises which are known to be true. Aristotle, however, imposes still further conditions. First, the premises must be truths of a special sort: Aristotle says they must be primary (*prôta*) and unmiddled (*amesa*). Second, the premises must stand in an appropriate relationship to the conclusion: they must be *prior* to it; "better known" or "more intelligible" than it; and the cause or explanation of it. Controversy exists about the interpretation of any of these expressions; here is one possible account among many.

There are several ways in which one proposition might be said to be prior to another. A might be prior to B epistemically if A is more obvious or more certain than B; or A might be prior to B causally, if A caused B and not conversely; or A might be prior to B in a logical sense if A is in some way naturally fitted to serve as a premise from which B follows. In fact, all these senses enter into Aristotle's conception of the priority of the premises of demonstrations to conclusions. It is plausible to hold that a demonstration can produce knowledge of its conclusion only by transmitting it from the premises, and therefore the premises must have a higher epistemic status than the conclusion: they must be "more intelligible." Since Aristotle thinks that this is necessarily asymmetric, so that the process of demonstration always flows downhill, it follows that demonstrations cannot form a circular system in which everything serves both as premise and as conclusion. Instead, as Aristotle takes pains to argue, the very possibility of demonstrative knowledge requires that there be some starting points or principles (*archai*) known in a way that does *not* depend on demonstration. These principles are then the primary propositions, since they are prior to everything else.

Which propositions are primary in this sense? Aristotle draws on the syllogistic for part of his answer. Any true proposition which can be demonstrated must be demonstrated by deduction from other truths, and if this demonstration is syllogistic in form, then it must have a middle term. Conversely, if there are truths which *cannot* be demonstrated, then there must be no such true premises and consequently no such middle term: such a truth would be "unmiddled." This designation takes on a special appropriateness in the case of *a* propositions. AaB is demonstrable only if it can be deduced from other propositions AaC, CaB; in this case, Aristotle thinks of the middle term C as falling between the extremes A and B and serving as the cause that links them. Unmiddled truths would in this way be prior to anything else, and thus primary in this sense.

On either understanding of priority, primary propositions will not have explanations. This, for Aristotle, is a point of great importance. Since scientific knowledge is by definition knowledge of causes, and since these first principles have no causes, the ultimate foundation of scientific knowledge must be something other than scientific knowledge. To use a modern term, Aristotle's picture of science is *foundationalist* in the sense that he thinks demonstration is possible only if there are first truths known without demonstration.

Posterior Analytics I spells out many of the details of the structure of demonstrative sciences, the criteria which the premises of demonstrations must meet, and the nature of the first principles. But this entire account remains a mere theoretical possibility unless we have some reason to believe that the principles themselves can become known to us. Aristotle tries to supply such a reason at the very end of the treatise (II.19), when he promises to tell us, "concerning the principles, how they become known and what the state is that makes them known" (99b17–18). The brief account that follows is one of the most perplexing in the entire corpus.

Aristotle begins his account with a puzzle. On the one hand, it cannot be the case that we have a sort of innate knowledge of the principles, since these principles are generally not known to most people, or to anyone prior to philosophical inquiry: it would be absurd to suppose that we had within ourselves the highest type of knowledge without being aware of it. On the other hand, if the knowledge of principles is indeed the first knowledge of all, then it would seem that if we lack it we can never acquire it; for we always acquire knowledge, says Aristotle, on the basis of previous knowledge, so that we must already have some knowledge to acquire any other knowledge. How, then, can we make the principles known to ourselves?

The answer begins by noting that we do have an innate or inborn ability, perception, by means of which we acquire knowledge. Our sensory abilities are (for Aristotle) unlearned: we do not learn how to see colors or hear sounds. Instead, the capacities to have these perceptions arise in us naturally, and the perceptions themselves are produced by the actions of external objects on us. In a way, then, a certain kind of knowledge of colors is innate in our sense organs, though it takes an external colored object to make it actual. Aristotle then describes a series of more complex types of experience, beginning with simple perception of what is present, proceeding to memory of what has been perceived, and finally reaching an awareness or recognition of a universal present in a series of perceptions. Each advance depends in some way on repetition: many perceptions lead to a single persistent memory, many memories of the same thing lead to an "experience," and many experiences eventually lead to the recognition by the soul of a universal present in them all. The "state" which has, or constitutes, this knowledge is named *nous*: interpreters clash strongly over whether to render this *mind, intellect,* or *intuition,* and even whether to regard it as naming a mental faculty, a condition, or something else.

The account just given appears to be an account of the acquisition or formation of universal concepts, although it is quite controversial both how it is supposed to work and how it solves Aristotle's problem. On one interpretation, he supposes that the soul has an innate ability, analogous to a perceptual ability, to recognize universals after seeing many of their instances: "the soul is so constituted as to be able to undergo this," he says. This might be taken as saying that all the universals are already present in the soul and only require actualization by sensory experience; thus, some interpreters have held that Aristotle's theory is ultimately a kind of Platonic innatism, and *nous* an intuitive knowledge of self-evident first principles. But Aristotle's emphasis on the role of experience leads others to conclude that his conception is fundamentally empiricist. In either case, there is an apparent gap between what this process would lead to, namely, the grasping of universal *concepts*, and what is needed for scientific knowledge, namely, coming to know the *truth* of propositional first principles. If, as is often held, the first principles take the form of definitions, then, perhaps this gap can be bridged by supposing that knowing a concept is equivalent to knowing its definition. But it is no easy matter to reconcile this with Aristotle's claim elsewhere that definitions alone cannot establish that anything is the case.

Definition and division[5]

Although scientific knowledge consists in knowledge of demonstrations, Aristotle also has much to say about another formalized type of expression: *definitions*. He defines "definition" as "an account which signifies what it is to be something" (*logos hos to ti ên einai sêmainei*). As accounts of a thing's nature, definitions are the products of scientific and philosophical inquiry, not of lexicography (we may follow a later tradition and call these *real* definitions). The finding of definitions was, evidently, a major preoccupation of Plato's Academy (Aristotle himself traces this preoccupation back to Socrates). Aristotle also takes definitions to be important, but he is careful to distinguish defining from explaining. Although definition is not the subject of any extant Aristotelian treatise, it is prominent in many places, especially *Posterior Analytics* II and the *Topics*.

Generally, Aristotle assumes that definitions must have a certain form which we find already present in Plato's later dialogues (*Sophist, Philebus*). Plato employs the following procedure of "Division" for finding definitions. To determine what X is, first determine the largest kind or class G under which X falls. Then, divide G into its largest parts (usually into two: say, G_1 and G_2) and determine which of these parts X falls into. Suppose it is G_1; divide G_1 in turn into $G_{1,1}$ and $G_{1,2}$ and locate X in one of these. The procedure continues until some subdivision is reached which is identical to X. X's nature is then given by the entire division, which can be represented as an inverted tree:

$$
\begin{array}{c}
G \\
\diagup \; \diagdown \\
G_1 \quad G_2 \\
\diagup \; \diagdown \\
G_{1,1} \quad G_{1,2} \\
\diagup \; \diagdown \\
G_{1,1,1} \; G_{1,1,2} = X
\end{array}
$$

5 See also chapter 4, pp. 124–127.

In this process, each division is a matter of subdividing some kind (*genos*) into parts on the basis of a relevant difference (*diaphora*). The kind "animal," for instance, might be subdivided into "terrestrial animal," "aquatic animal," and "flying animal"; the differences are then "terrestrial," "aquatic," and "flying." Combining the kind with the difference defines each part. This is ultimately the pattern for an Aristotelian definition. To define a thing is to determine what kind it falls under (its *genus*) and what characteristic differentiates it within that kind (its *differentia*). In a formula: an Aristotelian definition consists of genus plus differentia.

But Aristotle sharply criticizes Plato's understanding of the method of division. In *An. Pr* I.31, he says that the Platonists wrongly suppose Division is a kind of proof. Instead, says Aristotle, all that a Division could prove is a triviality. Suppose that we wish to define "human." We start with the genus "animal" and divide this into, say "immortal animal" and "mortal animal." From this, a sort of deduction can be extracted: Every human is an animal; every animal is either mortal or immortal; therefore, every human is either mortal or immortal. But what we want to know is, which is it? The Divider simply asserts "Mortal"; but that is exactly the thing that needs to be proved. Yet despite these criticisms, Aristotle elsewhere spells out a procedure for finding, or even establishing, definitions that is hard to distinguish from Division (see *An. Post* II.13, *Top* VII.3).

In *An. Post* II.2–10, Aristotle again considers the relationship between demonstration and definition, now asking whether it is possible to give a demonstration (in the narrow sense) of a definition, or to reach the knowledge produced by demonstration but using a definition. In general, he argues that these are impossible. However, there is a class of definitions which, he says, are a kind of condensed demonstration. For instance, suppose that the cause of the noise called thunder is the extinction of fire in clouds. A demonstration explaining why it thunders then might go: "Wherever fire is extinguished, there is a noise; in the clouds, fire is extinguished; therefore, there is a noise in the clouds." This answers the question "Why is there thunder?" i.e., "Why is there that noise in the clouds?" With a certain change of form, however, it becomes an answer to the question "What is thunder?" "Thunder is the extinction of fire in the clouds."

The exact role played by definitions in a demonstrative science is debatable. If definitions cannot be demonstrated, then it would seem that they could only appear in sciences as principles, and Aristotle does say that at least some of the principles are definitions. In other places, he seems to imply the more difficult view that *all* principles are definitions.

Words said in many ways[6]

Aristotle also pays attention to the project of distinguishing the different meanings of words (a tradition with a Sophistic ancestry, e.g., Prodicus). This is recorded in the discussions of equivocation in *Top* I.15 and in the "philosophical lexicon" of *Metaphysics* V. These distinctions may not themselves play a role in demonstrations, but they are a major part of the underpinning of much of his argumentation. He recognizes that sophistical fallacies (and more serious philosophical errors) often turn on the equivocal use of a term, and a thorough understanding of uses is a crucial instrument for defense against these.

The predicables

We noted above Aristotle's preference for definition by genus and differentia. These notions are in fact part of a more elaborate system of classifying relationships among terms, which we find presupposed (though never quite fully explained) in the *Topics* and elsewhere. If A is the genus of B, then evidently B is a kind, but not the only kind, of A. This means that the genus of a thing "says what it is": if animal is the genus of horse, then what a horse is is an animal. A thing's differentia, however, does not say what it is but only gives a mark of it. For instance, if the differentia of mammals within the genus animal is "hairy," this differentia does not by itself say what an animal is: in answer to the question "What is that?" asked of a mammal, e.g., a horse, it would be quite odd to say "hairy." Aristotle develops this into a general distinction of predicates. Some of the predicates that apply to a thing say what it is: Aristotle says that these are "predicated

6. See also below, chapter 3, pp. 72–77.

in the what-it-is"; modern convention calls these "essential predicates." Some predicates, then, are essential, and others are not, and the essential predicates of a thing include its definition and its genus.

But definitions can be characterized in another way. The definition of A should apply to whatever A applies to and to nothing else: in Aristotle's word, A and its definition must "counterpredicate" with one another. This is a necessary but not sufficient condition for being a definition, since some counterpredicating terms do not give the nature of that with which they counterpredicate ("able to laugh," for instance, does not define "human"). Aristotle therefore distinguishes between a thing's definition, which not only counterpredicates but also explains its nature, and its *proprium* or *unique property* (*idion*), which merely counterpredicates.

We have so far noted four relationships a predicate may have to a subject: unique property, genus, differentia, definition. All these share the characteristic that they are *necessarily* associated with their subject. Others are accidental or incidental in the sense that they may belong as well as not belong. For instance, a given horse may at one time be awake and at another asleep; and some horses are male while others are female. "Awake," "asleep, "male," "female" are therefore *accidents* of "horse."

These five predicate-subject relationships – definition, unique property, genus, differentia, accident – form the background for Aristotle's discussions of definitions. Commentators later called these the "predicables," and they became one of the most familiar bits of Aristotelian jargon, especially in later antiquity and the early Middle Ages. The way Aristotle presents this structure in the *Topics* suggests that it is not his own invention, although he has clearly developed it in his own way. Frequently, it also creaks at the joints. For instance, he gives two different definitions of "accident" in the *Topics:* "what can belong as well as not belong to one and the same thing" and "what belongs but is not definition, unique property, or genus"; though he treats these as equivalent, it is far from obvious that they are. Aristotle's views on differentiae are also problematic and perhaps inconsistent (in the *Topics* this predicable receives only a kind of secondary recognition).

The Categories[7]

Closely related to the predicables is another set of categories: *the*
"Categories," perhaps the single most heavily discussed of all Aristotelian notions. It is not an easy matter to describe these in
neutral terms. Interpreters are strongly divided about just how
they are to be understood. Perhaps the best course is to begin with
two texts:

> we should distinguish the categories of predications in which the four predi-
> cations mentioned are found. These are ten in number: what-it-is, quantity,
> quality, relation, location, time, position, possession, doing, undergoing. An
> accident, a genus, a peculiar property, and a definition will always be in one
> of these categories.   (*Top* I.9, 103b20–25)

> Of things said without any combination, each signifies either substance or
> quantity or qualification or a relative or where or when or being-in-a-
> position or having or doing or being-affected. To give a rough idea, examples
> of substance are man, horse; of quantity: four-foot, five-foot; of qualifica-
> tion: white, grammatical; of a relative: double, half, larger; of where: in the
> Lyceum, in the market-place; of when: yesterday, last year; of being-in-a-
> position: is-lying, is-sitting; of having: has-shoes-on, has-armor-on; of do-
> ing: cutting, burning; of being-affected: being-cut, being-burned.
>   (*Cat* 4, 1b25–2a4; trans. Ackrill)

These lists can be viewed in at least three ways. First, the passage
from the *Categories* appears to be listing *types of predicate*, that is,
types of expression that can be predicated of something else. On this
interpretation, the categories arise out of reflection on the most
general types of question that can be asked about a given thing:
What is it? How much? What kind? Where? When? and so on. Answers appropriate for any particular one of these questions will
make no sense as responses to any other.

A second interpretation, more closely tied to the predicables, is
that the categories are *highest genera*. A given thing will fall under
many genera, some higher and some lower: horses fall under the
genus mammal and also under the genus animal. If we look for
progressively higher genera under which a thing falls, we should
expect the process eventually to stop with some highest genus: the

7 See also below, chapter 3, pp. 78–80.

categories are these highest genera. Thus, substances or entities, such as people and horses, are one kind of thing; qualities such as whiteness are another kind of thing; relations such as double another; and so on for each category.

A third interpretation is that the categories are *kinds of predication:* each category gives one possible relationship between predicate and subject. On this view, some predications say of their subject "what it is," others what it is like, others how much it is, and so on. This fits well with the meaning of "category," which is simply the Greek word for predication (*katêgoria*), and it seems a plausible construal of the *Topics* passage. Texts can be advanced to support each of these three interpretations (with still further nuances). It would be quite out of place for me to plump for one or the other here.

The names of most of the categories are, in Greek, interrogative or indefinite expressions: "what is it?" (*ti esti*); "how much?" (*poson*); "what kind" (*poion*); "in relation to what" (*pros ti*); "where?" (*pou*); "when?" (*pote*). Various abstract nouns have traditionally been used in translation ("quantity," "quality," etc.), and these are both convenient and in wide use, but they are not quite translations. The term "substance" (*ousia*) is a different sort of case. This is an important philosophical term for Aristotle with a meaning something like "entity" or "reality." In the *Metaphysics*, Aristotle supposes that asking "What is being?" or "What exists?" amounts to asking "What is substance?" or "What are the substances?" (For more on this point, see the Chapter on Aristotle's metaphysics.) In the *Topics* passage, the first category is identified instead with the phrase "what is it" (*ti esti*).

Now, the categories figure in an important doctrine in the *Metaphysics* and elsewhere concerning being (or "being") and, perhaps, certain other notions of wide applicability, such as goodness. Aristotle says that "that which is" is not really a genus. Instead, what "is" or "exists" means depends on the category of the thing which is being said to exist. Thus, existence is one sort of thing for a substance or entity like a horse, another sort of thing for a quality such as white, and so on. Similarly, Aristotle sometimes says that "good" has meanings which vary with the category of its subject. He also holds that the primary sense of "is" when it is used "without qualification" – that is, when it means "exists" – is the sense it has in connection with things in the category of substance or entity. Things from other categories can be only in a way that depends on substances: a quality, for instance, can only be if it is the quality of a substance which is.

We do not find this doctrine in the *Organon*, although we do find the categories put to work in many ways in arguments. Perhaps the most important of these is in an argument in the *Posterior Analytics* to support the thesis that a demonstrative science must rest on indemonstrable first premises. In *An. Post* I.3, Aristotle rejects the possibility that any scientific truth whatever can be deduced from other truths, so that there is an infinite regress of "demonstrations" – and thus no real demonstration. He later defends this rejection with an argument (in *An. Post* I.19–22) intended to show that such an infinite regress of premises simply cannot happen. Making sophisticated use of results following from the syllogistic, he first argues that if there were such an infinite regress, then there would have to be subjects having infinitely many predicates; then he appeals to the categories to argue that there can be no such subject. In the *Topics*, the categories are used in many argumentative strategies, for example, two things can be shown to be in different genera, or two uses of a word to have different meanings, by showing that they fall under different categories. In *An. Pr* I.25, the categories seem to make an appearance as highest genera. The full list of ten categories is found only in the two passages quoted above from the *Topics* and *Categories*. Many other lists of categories are found, but with eight, six, five, or even four members: substance, quantity, and quality are invariably present, others come and go, and "having" and "position" are unique to the *Categories* and *Topics*.

Dialectical argument

Demonstration is one major venue in which arguments are used; the other argumentative practice Aristotle discusses is *dialectical argument*. The *Topics* claims to present us with a dialectical method. In order to understand the method, we must have some idea what it is a method for. In fact, scholars have divergent views about just how dialectical argument is to be defined. The view I present here is rather heterodox; I will try to indicate what some of the major alternatives are.

Aristotle's *Topics* was not written for us; it was written for an audience of Aristotle's contemporaries who already knew what dialectical argument was. Thus, Aristotle takes a certain understanding of his subject for granted. If I want to learn how to be a better cook, I will look for a manual that tells me how to cook better; I do not need to be told what food is or what "cook" means (if I did, I could hardly want to get better at it). But if I actually do not know what cooking is, a cookbook is probably not going to tell me. I believe that our situation with respect to the *Topics* and dialectical argument is a little like this. Aristotle takes a familiarity with dialectical practice for granted; we must instead try to reconstruct it. A good place to begin is with the century or so before Aristotle.

The word "dialectical" comes from a verb, *dialegesthai*, which means "argue." Arguments are verbal disputes in which each party attacks and defends positions; arguments can be won and lost. Here we already have an important distinction from demonstrations, in which attack and defense play no part. Dialectical argument differs from demonstrative reasoning in that it is intrinsically a kind of exchange between participants acting in some way as opponents. Within this broad description, certain types of argumentation became especially associated with the term "dialectic" in the century before Aristotle. The philosopher Zeno introduced a style of argument that refuted opposing opinions by deducing absurd consequences from them. In a different spirit, Socrates took his philosophical mission in life to be a kind of testing or examining of the beliefs of others through questioning. Socrates' goal was to reveal to his fellow citizens that they knew less than they thought they did, and thereby to encourage them to search for wisdom. To this end, he would engage someone in conversation, asking him his opinion about some subject or other. He would then ask a series of further questions until he had led his respondent into admissions inconsistent with those he had made earlier. To the charge that he had tricked or misled his interlocutors, Socrates would always respond that he himself expressed no opinions whatever: all his arguments were constructed from the interlocutor's responses. Therefore, his refutations were built on that interlocutor's beliefs, or at least expressed beliefs.

Plato took up philosophy under Socrates' inspiration, and the majority of his written works take the form of dialogues in which

Socrates questions various interlocutors. These depictions of dialectical exchanges are more than a device of presentation for Plato: he gives the name "dialectic" to the method of philosophy itself. Interpreters differ widely about just what Plato has in mind when he speaks of philosophical dialectic, and I will not attempt to resolve that issue here. It is significant, however, that in his *Republic*, the last stage of the education he proposes for his philosopher-rulers is a training in "dialectic" which includes the subjecting of opinions to critical scrutiny in a way reminiscent of Socrates. In fact, Plato appears to have instituted formal argumentative contests as part of the program of his Academy. Book VIII of the *Topics* clearly presupposes structured contests, with rules and judges, and Aristotle assumes that his readers know a good deal about the nature of these encounters – making things worse for us, who would benefit very much from a little more explanation. In these contests, one participant took the "Socratic" role and asked questions, while the other responded to them. The answerer chose, or was assigned, a thesis to defend; the questioner's goal was to refute the thesis. In order to do this, the questioner would try to get the answerer to accept premises from which such a refutation followed. However, the questioner could only ask questions which could be answered by a "yes" or "no"; questions like "What is the largest city in Lacedaemonia?" were not allowed.

This argumentative sport – we may call it "gymnastic dialectic" – may have been pursued largely as a form of education, training its participants in such logical skills as the evaluation of arguments and the detection of the consequences of a given proposition. However, formal dialectical exchanges could well have served loftier goals. Exploring the consequences of different views is a critical part of evaluating them, and institutionalized debates could have been a good means by which to pursue that sort of exploration. Perhaps debates served the same purpose as the exchanges in today's scholarly journals and conferences. In this connection, it is significant that Aristotle usually begins his own treatment of a subject by reviewing the opinions of his predecessors and noting the inconsistencies which can be deduced from them (he then presents his own position as a response to these puzzles).

But dialectical argument can be taken to include more than these rule-governed exchanges. Arguing with others by asking them questions and drawing conclusions from their answers is hardly something Socrates had to invent. It is, for instance, a natural way to proceed in a forensic setting, and Athens had very active law-courts. Generally speaking, the practice of arguing with others on the basis of their own opinions, and securing premises by asking questions, may be described as "dialectical argument." We see this confirmed by one of the features which Aristotle says distinguishes dialectical arguments from demonstrations: those who demonstrate do not ask questions, those who argue dialectically do. I would propose, then, as a definition of dialectical argument in its most general sense, *argument directed at another person which proceeds by asking questions.*

Now, people are generally likely to answer in accordance with what they believe; therefore, dialectical argument can be described as based on the opinions of the person at whom it is directed. In this respect, too, it differs from demonstration, which must deduce from first principles and not from what people think: indeed, Aristotle says, it will typically be the case that the first principles are unfamiliar to most people or even rejected by them. Thus, says Aristotle, the premises of dialectical arguments must be "accepted" (*endoxos*).

Most interpreters take the term *endoxos* to apply to a special class of propositions and suppose that the essential feature of dialectical arguments is that they reason from these *endoxa* (common beliefs, reputable views). Thus, the following passage is often supposed to be a definition of the *endoxa:* "accepted things are what seem so to everyone, or to most people, or to the wise – either to all of those, or to most of them, or to the most famous and celebrated" (*Top* I.1, 100b21–23). I am inclined instead to think that this passage lists different *kinds* of *endoxa.* Aristotle's purpose in the *Topics* is to spell out a method for success in dialectical argument. Since dialectical premises must be secured by questioning, it is important to know what one's opponent is likely to accept or reject. We can do that most effectively if we have lists of things that people of different sorts accept: things that everyone accepts, things that the wise accept, etc. As evidence for this interpretation, note that Aristotle repeats the above list of types of proposition in *Top* I.10, 104a8–11, but this time expressly as *kinds* of *endoxa.*

What a dialectical method should do is make us able to deduce the conclusion we want from premises conceded by the opponent we are faced with. This can be accomplished if we can find premises that have two properties: (1) the desired conclusion follows from then, and (2) the answerer will concede them. Having various inventories of what various classes of people believe – what everyone believes, what most people believe, what the wise believe, etc. – would be useful for telling which premises an opponent would accept: I need only determine which class my opponent falls into and choose the relevant inventory. Aristotle compares this to the art of medicine, which studies what is healthful for this or that *type* of person but not what is healthful for Socrates or Plato: likewise, dialectic as an art studies what is credible to types of person.

Of course, it is of no use to put forward just any premises acceptable to an interlocutor: we must be able to find premises from which the desired conclusion follows. For this purpose, Aristotle provides (in *Top* II–VII) a collection of argumentative rules he calls *topoi:* "locations" or "places." The term probably comes from ancient systems for memorizing lists of items by associating each item with a standardized set of imaginary places; in any event, these are what give the *Topics* its name. Each of these rules is a device for discovering premises from which to deduce a given conclusion. They rest on a classification of conclusions according to form: each gives premise-forms from which a given form of conclusion can be deduced. However, there is nothing approaching a systematic classification of all valid arguments, nor is Aristotle concerned to prove that the rules he offers are correct.

Overall, the dialectical method of the *Topics* requires the joint application of the "locations" and the inventories of opinions. To find my argument, I first look up a location appropriate to my desired conclusion and use it to discover premises that would be useful; then I consult the relevant inventory of opinions to see if those premises are found there. If they are, I have my argument; all that remains is to cast it into the form of questions and present them to my opponent. Assuming that my inventories of opinions are properly constructed and that I have correctly estimated what type of person my opponent is, I can reasonably count on my premises being accepted. For broader contexts of application, this is probably all that can be asked of a method of argumentation (I might after all meet up with an especially cantankerous adversary or with someone who holds bizarre opinions). In the context of gymnastic dialectic however, there may well have been some standards governing the respondent's behavior. For example, Aristotle indicates that a respondent who has conceded a string of instances of the form "This F is G" must then, when asked "Is every F G?," either agree or provide a counterexample; otherwise, the questioner could call a foul. It is plausible that the respondent was also judged for answers in conformity with a certain type of person (or perhaps a certain philosophical position). So construed, gymnastic exchanges would have been a particularly vivid form of philosophical exercise.

Dialectic is a competitive activity, and Aristotle gives due emphasis to the importance of strategy. It makes a difference which questions I ask first: if my opponent sees where I am going, he may try to avoid giving me the premises I need. Therefore, it might help if I put the premises forward in a confusing order, perhaps mixing in any number of irrelevant premises to conceal my argument until it is too late. Aristotle discusses these and many other devices, some verging on the deceitful, in *Topics* VIII. However, this should not distract us from one of the fundamental characteristics of dialectical arguments as he conceives them: they are supposed to be valid. In a dialectical deduction no less than in a demonstration, the conclusion is a necessary consequence of the premises. It is therefore no surprise that Aristotle says his dialectical method is of value in philosophical inquiries, at least to the extent that it provides the critical tools needed to bring to light the puzzles and problems in the generally accepted views about a subject.

Some interpreters have seen a much larger role for dialectic in philosophy and scientific theory. As noted above, Aristotle needs an account of how we can come to know the indemonstrable first principles of sciences. *Topics* I.2 has been read as claiming that dialectic has some power to reach these principles, and passages in other works suggest that generally held opinions may function as an important kind of starting point for inquiry. A much-discussed sentence in the *Nicomachean Ethics* (VII.1, 1145b2–7) says that at least in the sphere of ethics, a sufficient measure of the correctness of an account is that it solve all the puzzles in the commonly held opinions about a subject and nevertheless retain as many of those opinions as possible. This is yet another subject about which scholarly opinion is deeply divided.

Sophistical Refutations

Aristotle regularly distinguishes dialectical argument from "contentious" or "sophistical" argument, which is a kind of verbal combat that aims at winning by any means, foul or fair. Sophistical arguments only *appear* to be good dialectical arguments: either they appear to be deductions but are not, or they rest on premises which appear to be acceptable but are not. The first sort of fault is now usually called *fallacy:* invalid but apparently valid argument. The second sort may initially sound paradoxical: how can it only *seem* to me that I agree with a premise? But many of the examples of sophistical arguments show nicely how this is possible:

> Whatever you have not lost, that you still have? – Yes.
> Well then, have you lost horns? – No.
> Therefore, you must have horns.

The problem with this argument is not that it is invalid, but that its first premise – despite its initial appearance of innocence – is not true: after we hear the argument, we want to amend it to "Whatever I *once had and* have not lost, that I still have."

On the evidence of Plato's *Euthydemus,* there evidently were practitioners of this sort of contentious argument in ancient Athens, although it is a little difficult to see when and why they engaged in their trade. Aristotle catalogs a variety of fallacies and deceptive premises in *On Sophistical Refutations* and diagnoses their flaws. Modern textbook treatments of fallacy still follow much of his classification to a remarkable, if not embarrassing, extent.

Rhetorical Arguments[8]

The art of rhetoric, says Aristotle, should really be seen as an "outgrowth" of the dialectical art and the "political study of character": rhetoric combines the argumentative procedures of dialectic with a study of the types of audiences one might encounter and the premises each type will find persuasive. In effect, this simply results from the difference between dialectical argument and oratory. Those arguing dialectically must depend on a respondent's answers for their

---

8 See also below, chapter 9, pp. 268–272.

premises, but they know when their respondents have assented or dissented to a premise. Orators, however, do not ask questions but make speeches, and they must therefore be able to judge on their own whether their premises are agreeable to their audiences. Consequently, they must make a careful study of what will be persuasive to which type of audience.

As with his dialectical art, Aristotle's rhetorical method is heavily influenced by his historical circumstances: thus, he must deal with the special features of forensic speeches, speeches made to a deliberative assembly, public encomia, etc. These details, together with his treatment of style, fall outside the sphere of logic. When it comes to the construction of arguments, however, Aristotle makes it clear that rhetorical arguments are, for him, just arguments in another type of dress. There are, to begin with, two principal types of rhetorical argument: *example*, which he treats as the rhetorical equivalent of induction, and *enthymeme* (consideration or reason), the rhetorical counterpart of deduction. Just as deductions receive the bulk of attention in the *Topics*, so the study of arguments in the *Rhetoric* primarily concerns enthymemes, and here the dependence on dialectical theory is especially clear: *Rhet* II.23 is a highly condensed listing of *topoi* mostly traceable to the *Topics*. The views concerning the nature of dialectical argument expressed at various places in *Rhet* I.1–2 also recall those expressed in *SE* 11.

In conclusion

The syllogistic is history's first serious attempt at a comprehensive theory of inference; in developing it, and in using it in the *Posterior Analytics*, Aristotle gives us the first essays at metalogic. And his modal syllogistic, for all its problems, is also the first attempt at a theory of necessity and possibility. These theories, in turn, have implications for Aristotle's views on argumentation – demonstrative, dialectical, rhetorical – and on his conception of philosophy. To work all these ingredients into a harmonious whole, an all-encompassing and all-purpose theory of argumentation, would have been a truly gigantic task (one might say that logicians are still at work on it today, and still in piecemeal fashion). Aristotle himself probably took such a comprehensive theory as an ideal – perhaps yet another point in which he sets the model for his successors – and he thought he had some ideas about the direction in which it should be developed, but his logical works give more the impression of research in progress (often with notes that certain points need further study) than of finished system. Perhaps the fairest verdict on his achievements is the one he offers himself at the end of *On Sophistical Refutations*, even though he probably wrote these words before composing the *Analytics* and *On Interpretation:*

And if it should seem to you after reflection that our study, arising out of these things as from its beginning, compares well with our other inquiries which have been developed out of material handed down, then it remains incumbent on all of you our hearers to pardon its shortcomings and give much thanks for its discoveries.   (*SE* 34, 184b2–8)

3   Metaphysics

I. WHAT IS METAPHYSICS?

The word "metaphysics" is not Aristotelian, and Aristotle's *Metaphysics* was given its title by a later editor.[1] But there is a subject, vaguely and variously called "wisdom," or "philosophy," or "primary philosophy," or "theology," which Aristotle describes and practises in his *Metaphysics*; and the subject deals with many matters which we might now characterize as metaphysical. The *Metaphysics* is, for most of its length, a work of metaphysics; and Aristotle makes remarks on metaphysical issues elsewhere in his works, notably in the *Categories*, which some would indeed classify as an essay in metaphysics.

What were Aristotle's metaphysical contentions, and what is Aristotle's *Metaphysics*? The latter question is the easier. The work, as we now have it, divides into fourteen books of unequal length and complexity. Book Alpha is introductory: it articulates the notion of a science of the first principles or causes of things, and it offers a partial history of the subject. The second book, known as "Little Alpha," is a second introduction, largely methodological in content. Book Beta is a long sequence of puzzles or *aporiai*: possible answers are lightly sketched, but the book is programmatic rather than definitive. Book Gamma appears to start on the subject itself: it characterizes something which it calls "the science of being *qua* being" – and it then engages in a discussion of the principle of non-contradiction. Next, in book Delta, comes Aristotle's "philosophical lexicon": some forty philosophical terms are explained and their different senses shortly

1 The Greek phrase *"ta meta ta phusika"* means "What comes after the *Physics"* – but what precisely the editor had in mind by this is disputed.

set out and illustrated. Book Epsilon is brief: it returns to the science of being *qua* being, and also passes some remarks on truth.

Books Zeta, Eta, and Theta hang together, and together they form the core of the *Metaphysics*. Their general topic is substance: its identification, its relation to matter and form, to actuality and to potentiality, to change and generation. The argument is tortuous in the extreme, and it is far from clear what Aristotle's final views on the subject are – if indeed he had any final views. The following book, Iota, concerns itself with the notions of unity ("oneness") and identity. Book Kappa consists of a resumé of Gamma, Delta, and Epsilon and of parts of the *Physics*. In book Lambda, we return to the study of beings and of first principles: the book contains Aristotle's theology, his account of the "unmoved movers," which are in some sense the supreme entities in his universe. Finally, Books Mu and Nu turn to the philosophy of mathematics, discussing in particular the ontological status of numbers.

This crude summary indicates clearly enough that our *Metaphysics* has no consecutive story to narrate. There are indeed cross-references from one book to another and there are linking passages between consecutive books. But these texts give only a specious and superficial appearance of unity. There are two introductory books, neither of which genuinely introduces the material which is treated in the rest of the work. The list of puzzles in Book Beta suggests a programme of study – or even a sequence of chapters; but the programme is not adhered to in the later books: some of its constituent puzzles are discussed at length, others are merely glanced at or else ignored. The philosophical lexicon, which is oddly positioned, discusses many terms which have no importance in the rest of the work; and it ignores several terms which are of considerable importance. Book Kappa, which many scholars rightly think was not written by Aristotle at all, has no place in the collection. Book Mu, which repeats certain paragraphs from Alpha almost verbatim, shares a subject with Nu; but the two books do not form a whole.

A close reading of the *Metaphysics* does not reveal any subtle or underlying unity: the work is a collection of essays rather than a connected treatise. The collection was presumably made by Andronicus for his edition of Aristotle's works. Why these particular essays were collected and why they were placed in this particular order are questions to which no reasonable answer is apparent.

The *Metaphysics* is a farrago, a hotch-potch. This in itself might make us wonder whether we shall be able to extract any coherent set of metaphysical theories from its constituent essays and ascribe them to Aristotle; and we might also wonder if we can discover or characterize any single science or discipline or subject to which the various essays, in their various ways, contribute. Indeed, as soon as we ask the most elementary question, namely "What is Aristotelian metaphysics? what study does Aristotle suppose himself to be undertaking in these essays?", we find ourselves in a perplexity. For the texts appear to offer us three or even four answers: the answers are certainly different one from another, and it looks at first glance as if they are actually incompatible with one another.

Book Alpha invites us to study causes or explanations of things, and in particular it describes "the science we are searching for" as "a science which investigates the first principles and causes" (A 2, 982b8). In Gamma we are introduced to the study of being *qua* being:

There is a science which investigates being *qua* being and the attributes which belong to this in virtue of its own nature.   (Γ 1, 1003a21–22)[2]

Aristotle makes at least one thing perfectly plain: this science is not limited to a certain sort or type of being – it ranges over absolutely everything that there is. And yet Book Epsilon then appears to restrict our study to theology and its objects to those items which are divine:

If there are any immovable substances, then the science which deals with them must be prior, and it must be primary philosophy. (E 1, 1026a29–30)

(The context shows that the "immovable substances" are divinities.) Finally, Book Zeta appears to restrict our subject matter in a rather different way:

The question which, both now and in the past, is continually posed and continually puzzled over is this: what is being? that is to say, what is substance?   · (Z 1, 1028b2–4)

This eternal question defines the nature of Aristotle's inquiries, at least for a large part of the *Metaphysics*, and it thus implicitly offers a fourth account of the study or science of metaphysics.

2 For a corrected translation, see below, p. 69.

The science of first principles, the study of being *qua* being, theology, the investigation into substance – four compatible descriptions of the same discipline, or rather several different descriptions of several different disciplines? Perhaps there is no one discipline which can be identified as Aristotelian metaphysics? And perhaps this thought should not disturb us: we need only recall that the *Metaphysics* was composed by Andronicus rather than by Aristotle. But the four descriptions do have at least one thing in common: they are dark and obscure. The first thing to do is to dispel some of the darkness. I shall begin with "being *qua* being."

II. THE STUDY OF BEINGS *QUA* BEING

Here, first, is a paragraph from Book Gamma, the first sentence of which I have already quoted. (The translation here differs in one small but vital respect.)

There is a science which investigates beings *qua* being and the attributes which hold of them in virtue of their own nature. This is not the same as any of the so-called special sciences; for none of these deals generally with beings as being – rather, each cuts off a part of being and investigates the attributes of this part (this is what the mathematical sciences, for example, do).

(Γ 1, 1003a20–26)

The science is in some sense wholly general or universal, for it is contrasted with the special sciences, each of which "cuts off" a portion of reality and studies it. (In *An. Post*, Aristotle remarks that the sciences are defined and individuated by the kind of item which they study: thus arithmetic is the science which deals with units and their properties.) Our science, on the other hand – or metaphysics as, for convenience, I shall continue to call it – deals with beings in general.

The word "be" in this context bears the sense of "exist": metaphysics studies beings inasmuch as it studies items which exist. It studies existents, or entities, *qua* existent. (This is denied by some scholars, who suppose rather that the word "be" is here being used in some more generous sense.) In the previous section I wrote, ". . . being *qua* being" in my translation of Γ 1; and metaphysics is in fact standardly characterized in the modern literature as the science of being *qua* being. But this characterization is false and misleading: it is misleading inasmuch as the first occurrence in it of the word "being" will naturally be read as an abstract noun ("we are going to study being or existence"); it is false inasmuch as the Greek phrase, although it is in the singular (*to on*), is here properly rendered by an English plural (beings, items which exist). Our science studies beings, not being; it studies the things which exist.

But so, in a sense, does every science – what else, after all, is there to study? Our science is marked off from the other sciences not insofar as it studies entities, but rather insofar as it studies them "*qua* being" or "*qua* existent." The phrase "*qua* being" does not here modify the noun "beings," as though the words "beings *qua* being" served to pick out a particular *kind* of being. This would be absurd in itself and directly contradictory to what Aristotle says about the universality of the science. "Beings *qua* being" is not a phrase at all (no more than "Aristotle slowly" is a phrase in the sentence "I read Aristotle slowly"). Rather, "*qua* being" goes with the verb "investigate": it indicates the manner or mode in which entities are to be investigated.

What is it to investigate beings *qua* being? What, more generally, is it to study Fs *qua* G? The word "*qua*" means something like "insofar as they are": to study Fs *qua* G is to study Fs insofar as they are G: that is to say, to study those features of Fs which belong to them insofar as they are G. Thus you might study Fs *qua* G while I study them *qua* H: perhaps you study medieval manuscripts *qua* works of art, whereas I study them *qua* witnesses to ancient texts – we shall both be interested in the same items (we shall visit the same libraries and handle the same documents), but you will concentrate on one aspect of them and I on another. According to Aristotle, natural scientists study physical objects *qua* moving bodies, while geometers study them *qua* three-dimensional solids.[3] In phrases of the form "to study Fs *qua* G," the term replacing F fixes the *domain* of the study, and the term replacing G fixes the aspect or the *focus* of the study.

Metaphysicians, then, in studying beings *qua* being, take entities in general – everything which exists – as their domain and focus on the fact that items in the domain *exist*. And when Aristotle says that our science "investigates beings as being and the attributes which

3 See below, p. 85.

hold of them in virtue of their own nature," the word "and" is, as the grammarians say, epexegetic: it stands for "i.e." To study beings *qua* being simply is to study those attributes which hold of entities in virtue of the fact that they are entities.

And what sort of features are attributes of entities *qua* being? Aristotle urges that unity or oneness is such a feature, on the grounds that everything – everything which exists – is *one* thing. And if our science treats the notion of unity, then it must discuss its opposite, plurality – and hence also otherness, difference, and contrariety.

And similarly with all other such items. Since these are essential features of units *qua* unit and of beings *qua* being – and not *qua* numbers or lines or fire – , it is plain that it belongs to this science to investigate their essence and their properties.   (Γ 2, 1004b4–7)

One line may be different from another line; but being different is not something peculiar to lines, and lines are not different insofar as they are lines: they are different insofar as they are entities.

Book Iota discusses the concept of unity or oneness, together with various related notions. It is clear that in this book at least Aristotle is involved in the practice of the science which he describes at the beginning of Gamma. Gamma itself contains an extended discussion of the principle of non-contradiction. Why?

We must say whether it belongs to one science or to different sciences to inquire into the truths which in mathematics they call axioms and into substances. Plainly, the inquiry into these belongs to one science, namely the science of the philosopher; for these truths hold of everything that there is, and not of some special kind of thing apart from others – all men use them, for they are true of beings *qua* being.   (Γ 3, 1005a19–24)

By the term "axiom" Aristotle probably mean to designate those primary truths which are common to all sciences ("all men use them"): thus the principle of non-contradiction, in particular, and the laws of logic, in general, are axioms, and are indifferent to any particular subject matter. That is to say, axioms hold of absolutely everything – and so they are studied by metaphysics.

Thus metaphysics is in effect the study of "topic-neutral" concepts and of "topic-neutral" truths, of entirely abstract concepts which can be applied to any subject matter whatever, and of entirely general truths which are true of any subject matter whatever. Very roughly speaking, metaphysics, as Book Gamma describes it, is logic. We might have a few doubts about Aristotle's characterization of the subject. (For example, why restrict logic to *entities?* Does not the principle of non-contradiction hold of, say, fictional characters no less than of real characters? Or again, is the word "*qua*" appropriate? No doubt each entity is *one* thing – but is it one thing *qua* being, or insofar as it exists? Is it in virtue of being an entity that my cat is *one* cat rather than a whole litter?) But these doubts are peripheral; and we might reasonably think that we have a decent grasp of what the science of beings *qua* being would actually look like.

III. EXISTENCE

And we shall perhaps be content to allow that there *is* such a science: how doubt the existence of logic? Yet it was just here that Aristotle himself had doubts. For metaphysics, construed as the science of beings *qua* being, seems to be a science without a subject:

It is not possible that either unity or existence should constitute a kind of things; for the differentiae of any kind must each of them exist and be one, and it is impossible for a kind to be predicated of its differentiae.

(B 3, 998b21–24)

"Existence is not a kind of things" – or, in the traditional version, "being is not a genus." Now sciences are defined by their subject-kind; but if there is no such thing as the class or kind of entities, then there is nothing for metaphysics to be about – and hence there is no such thing as metaphysics. Metaphysics purportedly studies every entity (or, if you prefer, everything). But there is no such totality as the totality of entities; there is no such beast as everything.[4]

Aristotle's argument in Book Beta may seem less than compelling; but he also has another reason for denying that entities form a kind or that (in the traditional phrase) "being is a genus." The reason turns on the thought that "things are said to be in various ways" – on the thought that the verb "be" (or "exist") is homonymous. Aristotle

4 Quantified sentences ("Everything is F", "Some things are G") are intelligible only insofar as the domain of quantification is specified – only insofar as you can tell what the sentences are talking about. And to say that they are talking about *everything* is not, on Aristotle's view, to specify a domain at all.

was keenly sensitive to homonymies, and he was much exercised by them in his philosophical writings. The *Categories* opens with some reflections on homonymy and synonymy; there is a chapter on the subject in the first book of the *Topics*; the philosophical lexicon in *Met* Delta is devoted to distinguishing the different uses of certain philosophical terms; the *Sophistical Refutations* analyses, inter alia, fallacies based on ambiguities; and Aristotle not infrequently observes that this or that philosophical theory goes wrong because it fails to take note of a crucial homonymy. Moreover, he theorized about the subject, distinguishing different types or kinds of the phenomenon.

Ambiguity, as we normally understand it, is multiplicity of senses: a word is ambiguous when it has more than one meaning. Aristotle sometimes talks in these terms; but his most common way of invoking the phenomenon of homonymy is by saying something of the form "Fs are so-called in several ways" or "Things are called F in several ways." Thus the theory of the "four causes" might be introduced by a remark to the effect that causes are so-called in different ways.

In making this remark, does Aristotle mean that the word "cause" – or rather the Greek word *"aitia"* – is ambiguous? If so, then he is not rehearsing a theory of four causes at all: there are not four distinct types of cause – rather, the word "cause" is used in four different senses. (To speak of four types of cause would be like speaking of three types of mole: the rodent, the jetty, the spot.) And this does not sit well with most of what Aristotle says about causes. Rather, he seems to hold that there are four *types* or kinds of cause, so that he is committed to the view that the word "cause" or *"aitia"* (as it is used in sentences pertinent to the theory) has a single meaning and is not ambiguous. But although the word "cause" has only one (pertinent) sense, what it is for x to be cause of y may be different from what it is for z to be cause of w – x is cause of y, perhaps, insofar as x is the object which *produced* or made y, whereas z is the cause of w insofar as z is the *matter* or stuff of which w is composed. In general, Fs are so-called in several ways if what it is for x to be F is different from what it is for y to be F.

I shall use the word "homonymy" rather than "ambiguity" when discussing Aristotle's reflections on the different ways in which certain terms are used. Aristotle seems to treat what we call ambiguities as special cases of homonymy; but this would be an error.[5] Again, and perhaps more clearly, not all homonymies are ambiguities.[6] Thus Aristotle holds that "we say homonymously of the necessary that it is possible" (An.Pr 32a20). He does not mean, absurdly, that one *sense* of the word "possible" is "necessary"; he means that, in some cases, what makes an item possible is precisely the fact that it is necessary.

Things are said to be in various ways; indeed, there are different groups of different ways in which things are said to be. The homonymy which concerns us here is explained in the following passage from Book Zeta, which itself refers back to Book Delta:

Things are said to be in many ways, as I said earlier in my remarks on homonymy: being signifies what a thing is (i.e. this so-and-so), and quality and quantity and each of the other things predicated in this way.

(Z 1, 1028a10–13)

This text has been subjected to a variety of interpretations. If it is taken in a straightforward way, then Aristotle is maintaining that the verb "exist" is homonymous between its occurrences in, say, the sentences "Cats exist" (where it applies to a "this so-and-so" or a substance) and "Colours exist" (where it applies to a quality). You can truly say of cats that they exist; and you can truly say of colours that they exist (so that in a sense cats and colours are both entities). But cats do not exist in the way in which colours exist: what it is for a cat to exist is different from what it is for a colour to exist. In this way, cats and colours do not fall under a common kind – they are not both members of the kind *entity*.

And thus the very enterprise of metaphysics seems to be threatened. Suppose that we decide to inquire into keys. After lengthy

5 Aristotle holds that "sharp" is homonymous between "The knife is sharp" and "The note is sharp". This is presumably a case of ambiguity (the word "sharp" has two different senses). It is a case of homonymy? Is it one thing for a knife to be sharp and another thing for a note to be sharp? No doubt it is -- but only in the way in which it is one thing for a knife to be sharp and another thing for butter to be soft; and this latter fact does not induce homonymy. – We do not find a clear and unified account of homonymy and its relation to ambiguity in Aristotle's works; nor yet in the commentaries of his modern interpreters.
6 Indeed – see the last note – there is reason for thinking that *no* homonymies are ambiguities.

researches, we conclude that there are several interestingly different species of key – the metal devices for locking and unlocking doors, the hieroglyphs on the edges of maps, the scale which fixes a certain piece of music, and so on. An Aristotelian critic observes that "keys are not a kind," for keys are so-called in different ways – it is one thing for a piece of metal to be a key, another for a set of symbols to constitute a key, and so on.[7] The critic's observation is apposite; and it reveals the absurdity of our original enterprise: there is no such thing as *the* study of keys – there are several distinct studies, each of which might be called a study of keys, and we cannot begin to study keys without first specifying in which way we are taking the word. If entities are like keys, there is no such thing as metaphysics.

At some point in his career Aristotle was perhaps led by the argument I have just rehearsed to deny that there could be a science of metaphysics. However that may be, he certainly came to believe that he could answer the argument and rescue metaphysics. His answer depends on finding a middle way between homonymous and non-homonymous terms. In the first chapter of the *Categories* he distinguishes between "homonyms" and "synonyms": two items are homonyms if there is a word which applies to each of them but in different senses; two items are synonyms if there is a word which applies to each of them in the same sense. Thus Sirius and Rover are homonyms inasmuch as the word "dog" applies to each of them, but means an animal in the one case and a star in the other; Rover and Fido are synonyms inasmuch as the word "dog," in its animal sense, applies to each of them.

To homonyms and synonyms the *Categories* adds what Aristotle calls "paronyms": two items are paronyms if a derivative of a word which applies to the one applies to the other. I and my countenance are paronyms inasmuch as "man" applies to me and "manly" applies to my countenance. Paronyms are, in a sense, halfway between homonyms and synonyms. But this halfway house offers no rest to metaphysics. Rather, Aristotle discovers a different resting place,

7 Or is "key" merely ambiguous? – I had originally spoken of moles here – but evidently "mole" is a mere ambiguity. Perhaps "good" would be a better example? Good things do not constitute a kind inasmuch as it is one thing for an argument to be good and quite another for, say, a dinner to be good; and yet the word "good" is not ambiguous between cases of this sort. Hence there is no science of good things . . .

which is best introduced in terms of one of his own illustrative examples.

Take the word "healthy": an athlete, a sport, a complexion, and a diet, say, may all properly be called "healthy." Milo is healthy, and so is wrestling – but they are not healthy in the same way: what it is for Milo to be healthy is not what it is for wrestling to be healthy. (Milo and wrestling are not synonyms with regard to "healthy.") But the two ways of being healthy are surely not unconnected one to the other – Milo and wrestling, as Aristotle elsewhere puts it, are not merely "chance homonyms." Rather, the way in which wrestling is healthy is parasitical upon the way in which Milo is healthy; for what it is for wrestling to be healthy is for it to tend to produce or conserve health in its practitioners – wrestling is healthy insofar as it makes people like Milo healthy. In general,

everything healthy is so-called with reference to health – some things by preserving it, some by producing it, some by being signs of health, some because they are receptive of it; and similarly, things are called medical with reference to the art of medicine – some things are called medical by possessing the art of medicine, others by being well adapted to it, others by being instruments of the art of medicine.   (Γ 2, 1003a34–b2)

The different healthinesses all point toward one sort of health: all the items to which the word "healthy" applies are healthy *with reference* to some one item.

Or, as some modern scholars like to put it, the word "healthy" has a *focal* meaning, its different senses focusing on some one item. A word has focal meaning if it is used in several ways, one of which is primary and the others derivative, the accounts of the derivative way containing the account of the primary way. "Healthy," when applied to Milo, is used in the primary way – it means, say, that Milo has a body in excellent functioning shape. When applied to Milo's complexion or to his diet, the word is used in a derivative way: it means that his diet is the sort of diet which makes the dieter healthy (i.e., which makes the dieter's body function excellently), and that his complexion is the sort of complexion typically manifested by someone healthy (i.e., by someone whose body is in an excellent functioning condition).

"Exist" or "be," according to Aristotle, is in this respect just like "healthy": the word has a primary use, and it has various derivative uses, each of which contains in its account the account of the primary use. And now metaphysics can be defended against the objection that "being is not a genus." There can be no *one* science of keys; for keys are homonyms. But existing items are not homonyms in the way in which keys are; for the word "exist," as it is applied to different types of item, is not *simply* homonymous: its uses, though indeed different, are all tied together inasmuch as they are all connected to one central, focal, primary use. Just as a student of medicine, interested in health, will consider diets and complexions as well as bodies, and will not thereby find that his science falls apart into several distinct disciplines, so a metaphysician, interested in entities, will consider everything to which the word "exist" applies and will not thereby find that his subject has dissolved.

So too there are many ways in which things are said to exist, but they all refer to a single starting-point. . . . Then just as there is one science which deals with all healthy items, so too in the other cases. For it is not only when items all fall under one common notion that they are investigated by a single science: rather, this is so also for items which are related to a single common nature – for they too in a sense fall under a common notion. It is clear, then, that it is the task of a single science to study all the things that exist *qua* existent. (Γ 2, 1003b5–16)

Aristotle's conception of focal meaning has rightly been hailed as a genial discovery. But it is not yet clear how – or indeed, whether – it applies to the verb "exist;" nor whether it is in principle adequate to preserve the science of metaphysics.

IV. ENTITIES

Let us call things which exist in the primary way *substances*, things which exist in a derivative way *accidents*. This, I suppose, corresponds pretty well to the way in which these terms are normally used in discussions of Aristotelian metaphysics. (Substances are things which "stand under" or support other entities; accidents are items which "happen to" or depend upon other entities.) Every entity is either a substance or an accident.[8] If there is only *one* way in

8 Perhaps there are accidents of accidents, doubly parasitical entities? No doubt there are (time, according to Epicurus, is an accident of accidents, namely of changes which are themselves accidents of the items which change). But an accident of an accident is an accident.

which things exist – if, in other words, existence does not have focal meaning (and is not merely homonymous) – then all entities are substances.

In Zeta 1, it will be recalled, the discipline of metaphysics seemed to be implicitly determined by reference to a central question –

the question which, both now and in the past, is continually posed and continually puzzled over is this: what is being? that is to say, what is substance?

(Z 1, 1028b2–4)

The question "What is being?" is an ontological question, a question about *existence:* "What is being?" means "What is existent?" – or better, "What items exist?" In Zeta 1 Aristotle reduces the question of being to the question of substance, the question of what exists to the question of what exists in the primary way; for he assumes that once we have established the category of substances, the accidents will look after themselves. But here I shall proceed more cautiously, looking first at the general question about existence.

Then what beings are there, what items exist? How might we set about answering this daunting question? One way might be to enumerate all the items which exist, one by one: Sirius, Australia, the President of France, that box of matches on the desk in front of me . . . Surely we shall never complete such a list – and evidently we shall never know that we have completed it. The list will be infinitely long if it contains numbers. (And if we are asking, quite generally, what there is, it will be difficult to reject out of hand the suggestion that there is a prime number between 6 and 8 – so that the number 7 will be on our list of entities.) The list will surely be indeterminately long, since it will contain future entities. If this were the inquiry to which Aristotle's eternal question invited us, then we should prudently decline the invitation.

But instead of enumerating entities, we might try to enumerate *kinds* of entity. It is far from clear that we could ever complete this list either, or know that we had completed it; but the task no longer seems utterly hopeless, and for two reasons. First, we need not suppose that the list will be infinitely long. Secondly, the items on the list will fit together in a way which will make the task easier.

For it will become plain that some of the items so to speak include others. Cats will be on the list – there are surely such things as cats. So too will mammals; for mammals undeniably exist. And also, for the same reason, animals. But cats are a sort of mammal, and mammals are a sort of animal; so that these three items can be arranged in a hierarchical structure. More generally, among the heap of items which we have collected, some will be species or kinds of others, some will be subspecies or subkinds of these species or kinds, and so on. We shall be able to draw a tree, the nodes corresponding to the items on the list and the branches indicating relations of subordination.

If we assume that the number of items on the list is finite, then there will be at least one highest node on the tree, at least one item which is itself subordinate to no other item. These items constitute the most generic kinds of being: there *must* be at least one such item, there *may* be any number of them. In the Aristotelian tradition, these highest kinds of being are customarily called "categories."[9] Sometimes Aristotle writes as if he knows that there are exactly ten categories, which he can enumerate. Sometimes he seems more cautious. In any event, he is pretty sure that the number of categories is small; and he knows at least some of its members.

Why a plurality of categories? – why not one single category? After all, the items on the list are all *things:* is not the class of things the single highest kind? But this class would be the same as the class of all *entities*, and we know that there is no such thing as the class of all entities. (If "be" is homonymous, then so too is "thing.") There will be at least as many categories as there are senses of "exist"; indeed, the opening sentence of Zeta 1[10] suggests that there are precisely as many categories as there are senses or ways of being.

Suppose, then, that our inventory of the world – our ontological catalogue – is completed and structured in the way I have suggested. At least one of the categories which it shows will be a category of substances; and it seems compelling to suppose that exactly one category will be a category of substances, the others being categories

9 The Greek word *"katēgoria"* means "predicate": Aristotle itemises the things which exist by itemising *predicates* – but this plainly comes to much the same thing as itemising *kinds* of entity. On the categories see further pp. 55–57 – here I simply adopt, without argument, one of several possible interpretations of Aristotle's theory.

10 Quoted above, p. 74.

of accidents. Let us now tackle the business of explaining the existence of accidents in terms of the existence of substances, on the assumption that "exist" has a focal meaning.

Take a typical accident, something which falls into the category of quality. Take folly. Folly exists, there is no denying it; and it seems eminently plausible to think that folly is an accident. For folly is surely an accident of fools, or, more precisely, of foolish human beings. That is to say, folly exists if and only if certain existent substances are foolish. The existence of folly is thus derivative from or parasitical upon the existence of foolish substances. Plainly, what has just been said of folly will apply equally, mutatis mutandis, to wisdom. Plainly, what can be said of folly and of wisdom can be said of qualities in general: qualities are accidents, their existence deriving from or focussing upon the existence of substances in this way – a quality Q exists just insofar as some substance is Q-ish.

Similar analyses are available for other categories of entity. Thus fatherhood exists, and it exists insofar as one substance has sired another. Fatherhood is a relation; and in general a relation R will exist just insofar as one substance stands R-ishly to another. Relations are accidents, their existence focussing on the existence of substances. And so on. Thus it seems that all derivative entities can be dealt with, if not at one blow, then at nine blows, one blow for each derivative category. What is it for Fs to exist? To answer the question, you simply place Fs in their category, C, and apply the general account of what it is for Cs to exist.

Aristotle points to this path, but he does not march along it himself; and it is a curious fact that the categories are not mentioned in the most extended of Aristotle's descriptions of the focal meaning of "exist."

Evidently there are many differences among things: some are characterized by the mode of composition of their matter, e.g. things, like honey-water, which are mixtures; others by being tied together, e.g. bundles; others by being glued, e.g. books; others by being nailed, e.g. boxes; others in several of these ways; and others by position, e.g. thresholds and lintels, which differ insofar as they have a different position; others by time, e.g. dinner and breakfast; others by place, e.g. the winds; others by the features proper to sensible objects, e.g. hardness and softness, density and rareness, dryness and wetness; and some things by some of these qualities, others by all of them, and in general some by excess and others by defect. Clearly, then, the word "is" has as many significations: a thing is a threshold because it lies in such-and-such a position, and its being means its lying in that position; being ice means being solidified in such-and-such a way.

(H 2, 1042b15–28)

What is it for there to be ice? – It is for water to be solidified in this particular way. What is it for there to be thresholds? – It is for a stone or wooden slab to be placed thus and so. What is it for there to be flocks of sheep? – It is for several individual sheep to live together in such-and-such a fashion. And so on.

There are difficulties with this text which I ignore. But the way in which it deals with derivative entities – with accidents – does seem to be different from, and rather more subtle than, the relatively mechanical ascent to the categories. Nonetheless, the method behind the text from Eta is not utterly different from the method implied by the ascent to the categories. Roughly speaking, in order to discover what it is for Fs to exist, we need to ask what sort of things Fs are; and the answer to this question will give us the clue we need. Ice is solidified water – so for ice to exist is for water to be solidified. Breakfast is the first meal of the day – so for there to be breakfasts is for people to eat something prior to eating something else. A kir is a mixture of white wine and crème de cassis – so for there to be kirs is for wine and cassis to be suitably mixed. The method of the categories had us ask what sort of things Fs are, i.e., what category they belong to; the method of Eta has us ask for something more specific, namely a definition of what it is to be an F.

Each method could be characterized as a method of "reduction," and the notion of focal meaning could be construed precisely as a reductive device. But if we speak of reduction in this context, we should beware of at least two errors to which the word might beckon us.

First, Aristotle is not concerned with what is sometimes called "eliminative" reduction. An eliminative reduction sets out to show that there are (really) no such things as Fs by reducing apparent Fs to real Gs. ("There are really no such things as propositions; for propositions reduce to sentences – anything you want to say when you use the word "proposition" you can say by means of suitable paraphrases using the word "sentence." Propositions disappear from a well-ordered ontology.") There is no suggestion in the *Metaphysics* that Aristotle wanted to *eliminate* any unwanted entities. He is offering an analysis of what it is for something to exist: the analysis presupposes that the items exist – it cannot insinuate that they do not exist (nor even that they do not "really" exist).

It is worth stressing in particular that the appeal to focal meaning does not eliminate what we think of as *abstract* entities. Here is a crude way of distinguishing between Plato and Aristotle in point of ontology: Plato believed in the existence of abstract entities – Aristotle was more hard-headed and denied that there were any such things. This is not merely crude – it is false. Plato believed that justice exists, and Aristotle believed that justice exists: Aristotle, here, was no more parsimonious than his master. Where he differed from his master was in the mode or manner of existence which he allotted to justice: for Plato, justice enjoys the eternal and independent existence which belongs to the Forms; for Aristotle, justice exists insofar as some substances are just. Justice has a parasitical existence, not an independent existence; but this is not to say that justice does not exist at all. The phenomenon of focal meaning allows us to assign a derivative existence to certain items – it does not encourage us to deny them existence: on the contrary.

Nor – and this is the second error to avoid – should we hastily suppose that Aristotle's reductions are open to a charge made against many ontological reductions. Consider the following argument. "Colours are parasitical entities – they reduce to, or are parasitical upon, physical bodies. For there cannot be any colours unless there are physical bodies: any colour must be the colour *of* some body or other." This is a bad argument. (Quite apart from the dubious claim that colours are always colours of some physical body.) Let us allow that every colour must belong to some body, and let us allow that this shows that colours depend on bodies. Does it follow that colours are parasitical on bodies? Evidently not: for all that *this* argument says, bodies may also depend upon colours. Indeed, if it is true that every colour is the colour of some body, it seems equally true that every body is the possessor of some colour. If the former truth establishes the dependence of colour on body, the latter establishes the dependence of body on colour. Hence the former truth cannot establish the parasitical nature of colours.

Aristotle's reductions are not open to this sort of objection; for focal meaning establishes an asymmetry which mere dependence does not. If Fs are reduced to Gs by way of focal meaning, then an account of what it is for Fs to exist will include the account of what it is for Gs to exist. But if this is so, then it cannot also be true that an account of what it is for Gs to exist will include the account of what it is for Fs to exist. For then the account would be viciously circular: the account of what it is for Gs to exist would include the account of what it is for Gs to exist.

Nonetheless, Aristotelian reductions do face a standard difficulty for reductive exercises. The difficulty is this: How on earth can we establish that Fs reduce to Gs? Return to the case of folly. Aristotle supposes, first, that folly exists only so long as fools exist; and he supposes, secondly, that for folly to exist simply is for fools to exist. Why accept either supposition? The first supposition at any rate demands some supporting argument. ("There's such a thing as honour, you know – but alas, no one is honourable any more.") The second supposition also requires a speech in its favour. ("I allow that boxes exist if and only if half a dozen pieces of wood are nailed together thus and so. But why ever think that what it is for boxes to exist is for wood to be nailed thus and so? There is a gap between the symmetrical "if and only if" and the asymmetrical claim about existence: Why should we jump the gap?")

Aristotle's most sustained exercise in ontological reduction occurs in his treatment of the objects of mathematics, in Book Mu and Book Nu of *Met.* Here Aristotle offers us his "philosophy of mathematics;" but it is worth observing that his interests are not quite the same as those of modern philosophers of mathematics. One difference is evident: Aristotle is not here concerned to analyse mathematical concepts and mathematical operations, nor – more generally – is he concerned with the technical development of the mathematical disciplines. Books Mu and Nu are not in this respect comparable to Frege's *Grundgesetze* or to Russell and Whitehead's *Principia.* Another difference is perhaps less obvious: Aristotle implicitly supposes that the problems he is concerned with are raised by and can be solved for "mathematical" objects as such – he does not entertain the thought that arithmetic and geometry, for example, might demand quite different approaches. (Here the difference from Frege is particularly marked.) Nonetheless, there is a recognizable and an important overlap between his interests and the interests of the modern heroes of the subject.

The general problem is stated in the first chapter of Book Mu.

If the objects of mathematics exist, then they must exist either in sensible objects (as some say), or separately from sensible objects (and this too is said by some people); or if they exist in neither of these ways, then either they do not exist or else they exist in some other way. Hence the subject of our discussion will not be whether they exist but how they exist.

(M 1, 1076a32–36)

The last sentence of this extract seems a non sequitur inasmuch as Aristotle has just mentioned the possibility that mathematical objects do not exist at all. But in fact Aristotle does not take this possibility seriously: he does not doubt that mathematics is a genuine science, or rather a set of genuine sciences, and that it therefore has a subject matter, or rather a set of subject matters; and, trivially, these subject matters must exist (otherwise mathematics would be a fancy, not a science).

. . . it is true to say, without qualification, that the objects of mathematics exist, and that they have the character which mathematicians ascribe to them.   (M 3, 1077b32–33)

The serious question is not: Do the objects of mathematics exist? It is rather: In what way do mathematical objects exist? And, in particular: Are mathematical objects substances, or are they rather accidents and derivative entities? (Here, and plainly, Aristotle is no eliminative reductivist.)

Almost the whole of Aristotle's discussion is negative, and indeed polemical. He considers at length the view of Plato and his colleagues, who contended that mathematical objects were substances of some sort; he brings a sequence of objections against their view; and he concludes, as it were by default, that mathematical objects must be derivative entities. Suppose, for example, that numbers are items separate from the perceptible objects which we count:

then, on similar principles, there will be, apart from perceptible objects, the items with which astronomy deals and those with which geometry deals. But how is it possible that a heaven and its parts – and indeed anything which moves – should exist apart from the perceptible heavens? Again, the objects of optics and of harmonics will exist apart, and there will be sounds and sights apart from perceptible and individual sounds and sights.

(M 2, 1077a2–6)

The considerations which purport to introduce separate and substantial numbers will also introduce separate and inaudible sounds; but separate sounds are evidently absurd – hence the argument for separate numbers will not work.

Many of Aristotle's particular arguments, including the argument I have just quoted, are excellent – they are, in other words, sound ad hominem arguments. But precisely because they are ad hominem arguments, they do not suffice to prove Aristotle's positive contentions: at best, they show that the Platonist philosophy of mathematics is muddled or ill grounded; they do not, and they cannot, show that mathematical objects are not substances. And for this reason they will carry relatively little weight with any modern philosopher who is inclined to what is now called Platonism about mathematical objects.

Aristotle's positive view is expressed most plainly in the following short passage:

There are many statements about things considered merely as items in motion, and it is not therefore necessary for there to be either something moving separately from perceptible objects or some separate substances in the perceptible objects. In the same way, in the case of items in motion, there will be statements and sciences which treat them not *qua* moving but only *qua* bodies, or again only *qua* planes, or only *qua* lines, or *qua* divisibles, or *qua* indivisibles having position, or only *qua* indivisiblees.

(M 3, 1077b24–30)

Insofar as there is a positive argument for this positive view, it relies on an analogy with the non-mathematical sciences. Medicine, Aristotle remarks, "has the healthy as its subject," but this does not imply that there exist healthy items separate from perceptible objects – on the contrary, medical scientists are concerned with ordinary perceptible objects (with animal bodies) and not with anything apart from ordinary perceptible bodies. They treat perceptible bodies *qua* healthy (or perhaps rather *qua* subject to health and disease): the object of their attention is one particular aspect of physical bodies, but the ontology which they presuppose does not require any substantial items other than these physical bodies. If you study Fs *qua* G, then Fs form the domain of your inquiry, and the ontology presupposed by any inquiry consists precisely of the items within its domain.

So too with mathematics: the mathematical sciences are concerned with certain aspects of perceptible objects – with their countable aspect, in the case of arithmetic – and a mathematician does not presuppose an ontology which requires any other substantial items. Thus the presumed analogy between medicine and mathematics reveals the actual presuppositions of mathematics; and since the objects of mathematics are simply those objects whose existence is presupposed by mathematics, the Aristotelian conclusion follows.

And what is it to study perceptible objects *qua* bodies, say, or *qua* divisible? When we study Fs *qua* G, we are studying those features of Fs which hold of them insofar as they are G: we are studying those features of perceptible objects which hold of them insofar as they are bodies, or insofar as they are divisible.[11] (Is mathematics, for Aristotle, the study of *abstract* objects? Yes and no: yes, inasmuch as Aristotle will from time to time refer to the objects of mathematics as abstract, as "spoken of in virtue of abstraction"; no, inasmuch as the only sort of abstraction involved is the abstraction introduced by the *qua* locution – and *that* is not anything which we would normally regard as abstract.)

There might seem to be a difficulty in studying perceptible objects *qua* lines, say, or *qua* indivisible. You can study Fs *qua* Gs only if Fs actually are Gs. But bodies are not lines, nor are they indivisible. This is true for the case of lines: perceptible objects surely are not lines. But Aristotle has merely expressed himself with a certain degree of laxity, and he has something like this in mind: a wall, for example, has length, height, and breadth; its length is the distance from this point to that point; and a geometer who talks about lines is talking about such things as the length of the wall – geometry studies perceptible objects not *qua* lines but rather *qua* bounded or determined by lines. As for indivisibility, perceptible objects indeed are "indivisible", in the pertinent sense. A sheep is "indivisible" inasmuch as you cannot divide it *into*

11 Why of *perceptible* objects? *All* objects, perceptible or not, can be counted, as Aristotle knew, and so are potential objects of arithmetic. Are Aristotle's restrictive references to perceptible objects simply a carelessness? Or does he mean to suggest that perceptible objects are the *primary* items to be counted, non-perceptible objects being countable only insofar as they are referred to countable perceptible objects?

sheep – it is *one* sheep. To study perceptible objects *qua* indivisible is to study them *qua* one so-and-so, *qua* units – and it is arithmetic which so studies them.

When a mathematician speaks, he talks about ordinary perceptible objects; when an arithmetician remarks, say, that the cube root of 27 is 3, his remark refers to sheep and goats, to cats and carpets. One way of putting the point – a way which Aristotle himself does not use – is this. Number words have both an adjectival and a substantival use. We can say both "Two chickens are too few for six diners" and also "Six is thrice two" (or 3 × 2 = 6); both "If you take half of these eighteen eggs of mine and buy another three, you'll have a dozen eggs" and also "Half eighteen plus three is twelve" (or 18/2 + 3 = 12). The substantival use of number words is the use which they have in arithmetic; and it is this use which insinuates that numbers are separate or independent substances. (What are arithmeticians talking about when they say that 7 × 7 = 49? Numbers, trivially. But not, it seems, perceptible objects – for where in the sentence 7 × 7 = 49 will you find any reference to perceptible objects?) The adjectival use of the number words, on the other hand, does not point to any substantial numbers. If I say "Three cats are too many for one house," I am pretty clearly talking about *cats:* the phrase "three cats" does not even appear to comport *two* references, one to cats and one to some other substance. Aristotle's point is in effect this: the adjectival use of number words is primary; this use is the only use which arithmeticians need; and this use leaves arithmeticians talking about cats and carpets.

If arithmeticians, in talking about numbers, are actually talking about cats and carpets, then presumably the existence of numbers is nothing over and above the existence of cats and carpets; the existence of numbers refers to, or focusses upon, the existence of perceptible objects. Aristotle characterizes the objects of arithmetic as units rather than as numbers: a number simply is a number of units, and the number 666 exists just insofar as 666 units exist. Units, or "ones", are the items which arithmeticians overtly talk about when they write, say, "1 + (1 − 1) = 1" – and hence what they covertly talk about when they write, say, "666 − 555 = 111." Then what is it for units to exist? The substantival use of "one" gives way to the adjectival use, and units exist just insofar as here is one cat and there is one dog and . . .

Is the adjectival use of number words primary? Do arithmeticians talk only about perceptible objects? These questions lead to
the heart of the philosophy of arithmetic, and they are far from
easy to answer. One thing is plain: Aristotle himself did not have
the resources to answer them properly. His negative and polemical
remarks, as I have said, cannot constitute a proof of his position;
the positive considerations with which he supports it are less than
demonstrative; and he does not even try to reconstruct arithmetic
on the basis of his thesis about the objects of the science. How,
after all, can we construe or reconstrue a sentence such as "$3^3 - 2
= 5^2$" as a sentence about *cats*? (And most sentences in arithmetic
are far more remote from cats than that sentence is.) Until such
questions have been faced, Aristotle's ontology of arithmetic remains at best an attractive hypothesis, a mere starting point for
serious reflection.

Finally, let us leave the particular case of arithmetical objects and
consider accidents in general. Metaphysics was threatened by the
idea that "being is not a genus." The focal meaning of "exist" was
introduced to parry the threat. Has the threat been parried? Well, the
threat suggested that, there being no such thing as the totality of
entities, it is not possible to say anything about *all* entities. Does the
phenomenon of focal meaning allow us to speak intelligibly and
truly about *all* entities?

It might seem obvious that we can say things about *all* healthy
items ("Everything healthy involves hard work") or about *all* medical items ("Everything medical is monstrously expensive"): the
focal meaning of "healthy" and "medical" seems to create the
space for such generalizations. Hence why not "Every entity is
. . ."? But it is not at all clear that the universal sentences involving
"healthy" and "medical" are acceptable. (They *seem* acceptable –
and so too does "Every mole is a physical object.") And for Aristotle they are surely not acceptable: a scientific sentence must say
one thing, it must be univocal; and terms with focal meaning induce homonymy. The sentence "Everything healthy involves hard
work" does not, in Aristotle's jargon, say one thing: it says many
things, and although those many things are linked one to another,
linkage is not fusion.

Hence focal meaning will not restore to metaphysics universal
truths of the form "Every entity is . . ." and metaphysics must be

saved in some more subtle way. Presumably the way is this. There will be trouble-free sentences of the form "Every primary entity is. . . ," and there will be trouble-free sentences of the form "Every entity is . . ." and "Everything is . . . ," provided that the entities in question are specified as substances and the quantifying pronoun "everything" is restricted to the domain of primary entities. These sentences we may regard as, so to speak, the focal sentences of the science of metaphysics. One of these sentences will be some version of the principle of non-contradiction, perhaps "Every substance is such that there is nothing which both holds and does not hold of it."

Since derivative entities are all related focally to substances, we can apply the focal sentences of metaphysics to these derivative entities. Movements are derivative entities: for movements to exist is for certain substances to be in motion. Now surely the principle of non-contradiction must in some fashion apply to movements – surely every movement is such that there is nothing which holds and does not hold of it? No movement can be both rapid and not rapid. We cannot take this last sentence simply as an *instance* of the principle of non-contradiction which was formulated in the last paragraph; for that principle was restricted to substances. But perhaps we can derive the sentence about movement from the principle? Thus to say of a movement that it is rapid is simply to say that some substance is moving rapidly. Hence if a movement, M, were to be both rapid and not rapid, then some substance would be moving both rapidly and non-rapidly. But if a substance is moving non-rapidly, it is not the case that it is moving rapidly. Hence if M were both rapid and not rapid, then some substance would have something, namely *moving rapidly*, which both held and did not hold of it. But this is excluded by the principle of non-contradiction.

But can derivations of this sort be carried out for all (or for most) basic metaphysical sentences? And if so, is this enough to preserve the discipline of metaphysics from fragmentation? And do the derivations provide plausible ways of dealing with derivative entities?

V. SUBSTANCES

Aristotle spends relatively little time on accidents, the objects of mathematics apart. He devotes the central books of *Met* to primary entities or substances. These books contain some of the most dense and the most difficult paragraphs Aristotle ever penned. It is not merely that the detail of his arguments is often uncertain: the general drift of his thought, the general thesis or theses towards which he was tending, the overall metaphysical position which he was inclined to accept – these things themselves are subject to scholarly dispute. This section merely sketches a simplistic version of one interpretation of Aristotle's remarks about substances.

Recall, once again, the leading question of Zeta 1:

> the question which, both now and in the past, is continually posed and continually puzzled over is this: what is being? that is to say, what is substance?
>
> (Z 1, 1028b2–4)

"What is substance?" What question or questions are we being asked here? and why is the issue so difficult?

We can distinguish at least three pertinent questions. The *first* asks what it means to call something a substance, what the predicate ". . . is a substance" means. This question is not at all difficult, for substances are, by definition, ontologically primary items – Fs are substances insofar as the account of what it is for Fs to exist does not include any reference to what it is for anything else to exist.[12] A *second* question supposes the first question answered and proceeds to ask what Fs must be like in order to be ontologically primary in this way. Substances are, trivially, basic entities – but what qualifies an entity as basic, in what does its primacy consist? A *third* question supposes the second question answered and asks what items – what sorts of item – turn out to possess these qualifications. Does it emerge that Anaxagorean stuffs, or Platonic Forms, or Democritean atoms are substances and the primary items in the universe? Or do all these early answers turn out to be mistaken, leaving room for a brave new Aristotelian world?

Why is the second question so difficult? Why can we not readily determine what characteristics an item must possess in order to qualify as a substance? Aristotle finds the question difficult in part because he finds himself pulled in apparently opposite directions. On the one hand, it seems evident to him that substances must in some sense be *individual* items: a substance must be a "this," a particular

12 See above, p. 77.

and individual object, rather than a "such-and-such," a general or common item. On the other hand, it seems equally evident to him that substances must be knowable, and in particular *definable* items: it must be possible to say what a substance is – and it is only common items which are definable and of which you can say what they are. Hence a tension – or rather, the threat of a simple inconsistency. Substances are individuals: Mozart is a substance, man is not. Substances are definable: man is a substance, Mozart is not.

A considerable part of Book Zeta is devoted to evading the inconsistency. Aristotle's argument is unusually tortuous; but in the philosophical lexicon in Book Delta he affirms, without apparent embarrassment, that

things are called substances in two ways: a substance is whatever is an ultimate subject, which is no longer said of anything else; and a substance is a this so-and-so which is also separable.   (Δ 8, 1017b23–25)

Let us consider the second way in which things are called substances (and let us not ask how the second way connects with the first).

A substance is a "this so-and-so," a *tode ti*. Aristotle's Greek is as odd as my English, and Aristotle presumably coined the phrase himself. The point is this: a substance is whatever may be referred to by an appropriate phrase of the form "This so-and-so" or "This F"; and this mode of reference is the mode which picks out the substance *as* a substance. We can immediately see the force of the expression; for surely the demonstrative adjective "this", answers to the first of Aristotle's demands on substances, while the dummy predicate "so-and-so" or "F" answers to the second. The demonstrative indicates that substances are individuals; the predicate indicates that they must be definable; and the combination of the demonstrative and the predicate unites into a consistent whole the two apparently inconsistent requirements.

Not any phrase of the form "This F" will pick out a substance. The demonstrative secures individuality, but it admits individuals which are not substantial. How does the demonstrative ensure individuality? An individual is something which, in Aristotle's jargon, is "one in number"; it is *one* item which can be identified and distinguished from other items and reidentified again as the same item. And the demonstrative "this" is precisely a device for picking out items of this sort. But demonstrative phrases as such do not exclude non-substances. For example, I might say something like "This vice is more attractive than that" or "This hangover is even more painful than yesterday's was." "This vice," "This hangover" – and yet there is no temptation to suppose that vices and hangovers are substances. For a vice to exist is for someone to be vicious; for there to be a hangover is for someone to be hung over – vices and hangovers are paradigmatic accidents.

Hence the second clause in the definition in Delta: substances must be separable. Aristotle does not explain what he means by "separable" in this context, but he *should* mean this: the so-and-sos which are substances must be ontologically basic in the sense we have already examined – they must be "separable" in the sense that their existence can be explained without invoking the existence of anything else. Hence "This vice" does not designate a substance: the phrase is of the form "This F," but the Fs which it invokes are not separable – for them to exist is precisely for something else to be so-and-so.

What, however, of phrases like "This pale object," "This polite man," "This policeman" ... ? Are pale items and polite men and policemen substances? Surely they are not: for policemen to exist is for there to exist men who follow a certain profession. Surely they are: this man is a substance, and this policeman *is* this man – therefore this policeman is a substance.

Aristotle does not like the latter conclusion – in his view policemen are not substances – and he attempts to escape it by appealing to a distinction between accidental identity and essential identity. The argument turns on an application of what is sometimes called Leibniz's Law: if x is identical with y, then if x is F, y is F. (If this man is identical with this policeman, then if this man is a substance, ...) Aristotle accepts the Law only in a restricted form: if x is *essentially* identical with y, then if x is F, y is F. Now this man is only accidentally identical with this policeman – and therefore the argument for substantial policemen fails.

There are grave difficulties with Aristotle's view: it is not clear how we are supposed to distinguish essential from accidental identity, and the restriction of Leibniz's Law to one sort of identity is implausible. In any event, the problem about policemen is better solved in another fashion. Let us say that a term "F" is a substance-term just in case the existence of Fs is not parasitical upon the

existence of anything else. Then (for the reason already given) we
may say that "policeman" is not a substance-term. Hence although
policemen are indeed substances, and the phrase "This policeman"
does indeed designate a substance, it does not designate a substance
by way of a substance-term. The canonical way of designating substances is by a phrase of the form "This F" where "F" is a substance-
term. The canonical phrases designate substances *as substances;*
other phrases do indeed designate substances, but they do not designate them as substances. (Proper names such as "Socrates" may, of
course, designate substances; that is to say, Socrates is a substance.
But a proper name does not designate a substance as a substance.)

It would be foolish to claim that thus far all has been plain – or
that it has been plainly faithful to the detail of Aristotle's text.
Nonetheless, it is time to turn to the third of the three questions
which I distinguished at the beginning of this section. What items –
what sorts of items – turn out to be substances? The earliest Greek
thinkers had (or so Aristotle believed) taken stuffs, and in particular
elemental stuffs, to be substances: perhaps just one stuff (as Thales
supposedly reduced everything to water), perhaps indefinitely many
stuffs (as Anaxagoras imagined), perhaps the "four elements", earth
and water and air and fire (as Empedocles discovered). Aristotle denies that stuffs are substances.

He has at least two arguments for rejecting the candidacy of
stuffs, one of which is unsurprising. The unsurprising argument
has it that a stuff is not a "this" (Θ 7, 1049a25–30). A mass term
like "bronze" or "bakelite" does not pick out an individual item:
bronze and bakelite are not particular objects, with particular
shapes and sizes and identifiable features. Mass terms, on their
own, do not in any case look like names of substances. But what
about phrases such as "This bronze" – or rather "This piece of
bronze"? (In general, "This piece of S," where S is a mass term.)
Surely this piece of bronze is a substance – at any rate it seems to
be an identifiable and reidentifiable individual. Indeed, "This piece
of bronze" does, or at least may, pick out a substance; but it does so
in the sort of way in which "This policeman" picks out a substance – it does not pick out a substance *as* a substance.[13] Just as

13 Note that you cannot *count* pieces of bronze except insofar as you count,
say, statuettes which happen to be pieces of bronze.

"This policeman" is not a substance-phrase, so "This piece of bronze" is not a substance-phrase.

There is a second argument against stuffs:

> it is plain that of the things which are thought to be substances, most are rather powers – . . . earth and fire and air.   (Z 16, 1040b5–8)

Stuffs, Aristotle urges, are essentially "powers," and powers are derivative entities. A stuff such as bronze, in other words, is to be conceived of as a set of capacities or potentialities:

> E.g., a box is not earthen nor earth, but wooden; for wood is potentially a box and is the matter of a box (wood in general of boxes in general, and this particular wood of this particular box).   (Θ 7, 1049a22–24)

Wood is a stuff, and stuffs are essentially stuffs *of* something – wood is, among other things, stuff of boxes. And to say that wood is stuff of boxes is simply to say that wood has the potentiality or capacity to become a box: anglice, you can makes boxes out of wood.

This particular capacity of wood is specialized, and it is a derivative capacity. For the capacities of stuffs are interdependent, some of them being derivative capacities and others basic. Ultimately, according to Aristotle's physics,[14] any capacity of any stuff depends on the fundamental capacities of the four elemental stuffs.

However that may be, it is plain that powers or capacities are accidents rather than substances: for there to be a power is simply for something to be able to do something; there is a capacity to Φ just insofar as something, some substance, is capable of Φ-ing. (As Aristotle himself puts it, capacities are posterior in definition: "I mean by "capable of building" that which can build" – Θ 8, 1049b14–15.) Thus stuffs are accidents. For bronze to exist is for certain substances to be brazen; that is to say, it is for certain susbtances to have certain powers or capacities – the power to be moulded into different shapes, the power to be hammered without breaking, and so on.

In Aristotle's texts, capacities or powers are standardly contrasted with actualities: *dunameis* contrast with *energeiai*. So that he will sometimes say that stuffs are potential, whereas substances are actual. Of course, substances have their potentialities too – this piece of brass is a substance (it is currently a candlestick) and it has the

14 See below, pp. 151–152.

potentiality to become a statuette. The point is not that substances are not potentially anything; rather, it is that in designating something by a substance-term you do not thereby ascribe any particular powers or capacities to it.

The distinction between *dunamis* and *energeia* (or between potency and act, as a scholarly jargon quaintly has it) is at bottom the commonplace distinction between being *capable* of doing or being something and *actually* doing or being it. I *can* (now) speak a sort of French, I have the capacity – the "potency" – to do so; but I am not (now) *actually* speaking French. When I do speak French, then I "actualize" my capacity for speaking French – that is to say, I actually do something which I can do. Book Theta contains Aristotle's longest discussion of capacity and actuality. Much of it is clear and sound and (as it will now seem) evident enough.[15] But Theta contains at least one characteristically Aristotelian thesis which is both perplexing and apparently relevant to our present concerns.

Capacities are accidents, derivative entities. Book Theta urges that actuality is prior to capacity, and prior in various ways. In particular,

> actuality is prior in time, in this sense. Actual members of a kind are prior to potential members of the same kind, though individual members are potential before they are actual. I mean that the matter and the seed and that which is capable of seeing – items which are potentially but not yet actually a man and corn and a seeing thing – are prior in time to this particular man who now exists actually (and to the corn and to the seeing thing); but they are posterior in time to *other* actually existing things, from which they were produced. For the actual is always produced from the potential by the actual. (Θ 8, 1049b18–25)

This is now *actually* a fine oak tree. It was once, when it was only an acorn, *potentially* an oak tree; so that in its history, potentiality preceded actuality. But that acorn was produced by an *actual* oak tree; so that before any potential oak tree there was an actual oak tree. And if, in general, actuality is prior to potentiality in time, then in some sense substances must be prior in time to stuffs.

15 Perhaps it is worth insisting that many things which seem patent to us now were once wrapped in mystery; and they only seem patent to us now because earlier thinkers laboriously unwrapped them.

But this last conclusion is surely absurd (and I should in justice add that Aristotle nowhere draws it). And Aristotle's position rests on a false principle – a principle which nonetheless enjoyed an astonishingly long life. It rests on the principle of "generation (or causation) by synonyms": if x makes y F, then x itself must be, or have been, F; if x heats y or makes y an oak tree, then x must itself have been hot or an oak tree. (Why? – well, how *could* x transmit heat to y if x had no heat to transmit, i.e., if x was not itself hot?) Far from being a logical or conceptual truth, the principle is open to easy empirical refutation. In any case, Aristotle does not manage to point to any general priority of actuality over potentiality: if he is right, then before every potential F there was an actual F – and equally, before every actual F there was a potential F.

Here, and elsewhere, Aristotle asks capacities and actualities to produce more power than they can provide. (They are asked to do tough philosophical work in the *Physics*,[16] for example, where they are adduced in order to define change or motion, and in *On the Soul*,[17] where they help to define the soul itself.

Plato did not take stuffs to be substances. In his view (as Aristotle construes it), it is universal items which are substances: Plato's substances are his Ideas or Forms – abstract items such as beauty and largeness and humanity and identity. Aristotle rejects this view – indeed, a considerable part of his metaphysical effort is put to showing that universals are not substances. The fundamental argument is this:

It is impossible that any universal term should be the name of a substance. For primary substances are those substances which are peculiar to an individual and which do not hold of anything else; but universals are common, since we call universal that which is of such a nature as to hold of more items than one.   (Z 13, 1038b8–12)

There are some odd touches to the argument (thus substances are apparently supposed to *hold of* individuals rather than simply to *be* individuals); but the general line of thought seems clear enough. Universals are items which are introduced by *predicates* – by expressions, as we would put it, such as " . . . is beautiful," " . . . is large," " . . . is human," " . . . is self-identical"; and such items,

16 See below, pp. 119–120.
17 See below, pp. 170–175.

which we might call beauty and largeness and so on, are plainly not individuals.

Aristotle, as I have already remarked, does not deny that universals exist; on the contrary, he is clear that they do exist. But their existence is derivative: beauty exists insofar as certain substances are beautiful; the existence of beauty focusses on the existence of other items.

Equally, Aristotle does not deny that forms exist: Plato had a mistaken notion of form, but he was not simply wrong in supposing that forms exist. Indeed, forms are an important and pervasive feature of Aristotle's metaphysical landscape. And although the Aristotelian concept of form introduces numerous problems which I cannot discuss here,[18] I shall briefly touch on two points.

First, the term "form" frequently rides tandem with the term "matter". Originally, indeed, matter and form are introduced as twins: substances[19] are in a sense composite entities, their component "parts" being matter and form. And originally, matter and form are simply stuff and shape: a bronze sphere – Aristotle's standard example – is an item composed of a certain stuff, namely bronze, and a certain shape, namely sphericality.[20] (Of course, the bronze and the sphericality are not literally *parts* of the bronze sphere, and the unity of the bronze sphere is not like the unity of, say, a table, which is put together from a top and four legs.)

Aristotle puts stuffs and shapes to good use in his account of change.[21] But matter and form soon forget their origins, and the words are used to pick out different aspects of things which, on the face of it, have little enough to do with stuff and shape. Thus the genus to which an animal belongs may be called its matter, its form being given by its differentia; and the contrast between body and soul is taken as an example of the contrast between matter and

18 Thus there is a close connexion between form and *essence,* and also between form and *species* (indeed the standard word for form is *"eidos"*, which also means "sort" or "species").

19 Or at any rate ordinary perceptible substances.

20 We often refer to the item by the phrase "This sphere". Aristotle sometimes says that forms are substances: he means that a phrase of the type "This F", where "F" is a form-word, will typically designate a substance.

21 See below, pp. 119–120.

form.[22] Here – or so it seems to me – Aristotle makes so broad a use of "form" and "matter" that their analytical powers are entirely lost.

Secondly, there is a long controversy over the question of whether Aristotle admits forms of individuals. In particular, it has been asked whether Aristotle's criterion for individuating substances invokes matter or form: Does Socrates differ from Callias inasmuch as the two men are constituted by different parcels of skin and bones, or do they rather each have a distinct form? The relevant texts perhaps present no clear and consistent thesis, but the following dull answer is as good as any: in a sense Socrates and Callias have the same form, and in a sense each has his own form.

If both Socrates and Callias have scarlet fever, do they have the same illness? Plainly, in a sense they do (they both have scarlet fever), and in a sense they don't (Socrates may recover before Callias does, so that his bout of fever ends while Callias' bout persists). Do Socrates and Callias both have the same form? Yes: they are both men, and the phrase "this man" may designate either. No: Socrates may die before Callias, so that this particular instance of the form of man perishes, while that one persists. Socrates' individual form is the form of man, and this is also the individual form of Callias. Socrates' individual disease is scarlet fever, and this is also the individual disease of Callias.

If substances are neither stuffs nor universals, then what are they? According to Aristotle, ordinary middle-sized physical objects are paradigm substances; and paradigm among the paradigms are natural objects – horses and hydrangeas, goats and geraniums, ducks and dahlias. The things we see about us – the items which, as Aristotle puts it are "most familiar to us" rather than "most familiar by nature" – are the fundamental furniture of the world. Neither technical science nor subtle metaphysics is needed to answer the eternal question "What is substance?": the answer is in front of our noses.

Things are more complicated – and less clear – than this last sentence suggests. But the complexities will not be worth worrying about unless Aristotle's answer at least has a plausible face. And there is at least one rather obvious objection to it: Why count middle-sized objects as substances? Why not take the fundamental

22 See below, pp. 170–175.

particles of science – not, to be sure, the elemental *stuffs*, but the elemental *parts* of everyday objects? Surely atoms are more basic than aardvarks and asters? And surely Aristotle, who was familiar with Democritean atomism, must have seen that they were?

Aristotle, however, maintains that the physical parts of a body are *less* basic than the body itself.

> The definition of an acute angle includes that of a right angle; for if you define an acute angle you invoke right angles (an acute angle is an angle less than a right angle). Similarly with circles and semicircles: semicircles are defined in terms of circles. And so, too, a finger is defined by reference to the whole body – a finger is such-and-such a part of a man. Hence the parts which are of the nature of matter and into which, as its matter, a thing is divided, are posterior to it. (Z 10, 1035b6–12)

Parts are essentially parts *of wholes*; fingers are essentially fingers *of bodies*. In order to explain what it is to be a finger we must make reference to bodies; and for there to be fingers is precisely for bodies to be in such-and-such a condition. Fingers are not fundamental.

This argument might be questioned at various points. But in any case we might wonder whether it can have any force at all against the Democritean proposal to take atoms as substances. For a Democritean need not claim that atoms stand to macroscopic entities as fingers stand to bodies. Indeed, a Democritean is far more likely to suggest that atoms stand to macroscopic entities as sheep stand to flocks and bees to swarms: the flock is posterior to the sheep, the swarm to the bee – and macroscopic objects to their constituent atoms.

Against this suggestion Aristotle has, implicitly, a new argument: to see what it is, we must introduce essences. The essence of something is "what it is" or "what it is to be it"; and to state the essence of something is to say what it is or to give its "real definition." More precisely, the essence of something consists of those of its characteristics on which all its other characteristics in some fashion depend. There are many things true of dandelions: they are green-leaved plants, they have yellow flowers, they have a tap-root, they flower annually, and so on. Of these features some are explanatorily fundamental – the non-obvious features which botanists seek to discover. The fundamental features constitute the essence of the dandelion: it is because dandelions are, in their essence, such-and-such, that they have yellow flowers and long tap-roots. Moreover, if we are to have genuinely scientific knowledge that dandelions have yellow flowers or that they flower annually, then we must derive these items of knowledge from our knowledge of the essence of the plants.[23] We might question this final point about scientific knowledge; but there is nothing particularly mysterious about the notion of real essence in itself – and in particular, Aristotle's conception of essence does not commit him to an "essentialism" of the sort which certain modern philosophers find repugnant.

One of Aristotle's terms for essence is *"ousia"* – which is also his standard word for substance. This is an ambiguity which translators find tiresome. But it is not a casual ambiguity; for Aristotle holds that there is the closest link between substance and essence. Chapter 6 of Zeta begins thus:

We must inquire whether a thing and its essence are the same or different. This is of some use for the inquiry into substances; for a thing is thought to be not different from its substance, and the essence is said to be the substance of each thing.   (Z 6, 1031a15–18)

The suggestion, in effect, is this: if "F" is a substance term, then "F" picks out the essence of what it applies to. This is a hard doctrine, but here what matters is one of its implications.

The implication is this: if substance is linked to essence, then substance terms not only designate the metaphysically basic entities – they also pick out the entities which are primary with regard to knowledge. What is first in being is also first in knowledge. This is a thesis which Aristotle explicitly maintains:

There are several senses in which things are said to be primary, and substances are primary in every sense – in definition, in knowledge, and in time.   (Z 1, 1028a31–33)

Priority "in definition" is the sort of primacy which focal meaning introduces. Priority in knowledge amounts to this: any knowledge which we may have about anything must depend on knowledge of its substance (that is to say, on knowledge of its essence).

Now it was quite plain to Aristotle that knowledge of *atoms*, however subtle and thorough it might be, could not possibly be basic

23 See above, pp. 47–51; below, pp. 109–113.

in this way.[24] The science of botany considers plants. Its epistemically basic items are plants of various species. Botanists do not consider atoms, and their science is not founded on a set of axioms which refer to atomic structures and atomic operations. The axioms of botany refer to plants. Atoms are not epistemically prior. Hence atoms are not substances.

This same argument confirms Aristotle's positive view that animals and plants are substances; for they are the epistemically basic objects of zoology and botany. What other Aristotelian substances are there? Parts of animals and plants are not substances; nor are combinations of animals or plants – a flock of geese is not a substance, nor is a field of cowslips. Certain other natural items are also substances: the heavenly bodies, certainly; and certainly also the "unmoved movers" which move the heavenly spheres.[25] Perhaps certain terrestrial features – rivers and mountains and the like? Perhaps the products of art as well as the products of nature?

The train of thought over the last few pages has been fragile. It has also ignored many pertinent texts, and it has treated no text with the scrupulous attention which the texts of the *Metaphysics* demand. So let me end the section with a banality: Aristotle's thought on these issues is certainly less clear and certainly more complex than the sketch I have just given, even if that sketch is not wholly misguided; and Aristotle's thought is certainly more exciting and more philosophically subtle than the dull pages which you have just read.

VI. GODS AND CAUSES

Metaphysics, construed as the study of substances, will consider what substances are and what items are substances; it will investigate certain general characteristics of substances – their unity, the fact that they are definable and have essences, the possibility of analyzing them in terms of form and matter, the sense in which they are actual as opposed to potential; and in conducting these investigations it will discuss numerous problems central to what we think of

24 Aristotle believes in any case that atomism is a *false* theory; but it is important to see that he could have *accepted* atomism without giving up his view of substances.
25 See below, pp. 104–105.

as metaphysics – and numerous issues raised, in particular, by the metaphysical views of Plato. But will such a study be the *same* study as the study of beings *qua* being?

Aristotle thinks that the two studies are one; for he says explicitly that it belongs to a single science to investigate axioms and substances, and this science is the study of beings *qua* being (Γ 3, 1005a20). He does not say why the study of substances and the study of beings *qua* being are one and the same. But presumably the focal meaning of "exist" must provide the key. Since entities form a logical hierarchy, some of them dependent on others, and since this dependence is, precisely, an ontological dependence, then what is true of accidents must depend upon and be derivable from truths about substances. Hence, in studying substances we shall thereby be studying, virtually or potentially, all other entities as well.[26] Conversely, the only coherent way to study beings *qua* being will be to select a certain *type* of being and focus on that – and evidently we shall select primary beings or substances as the focus of our researches. Hence, in studying beings *qua* being we shall thereby be studying substances.

This is an unsatisfactory argument. In studying *certain* aspects of substances, you are not studying beings *qua* being, nor are you studying substances *qua* being – you are studying substances *qua* substance. It is, for example, *qua* substance that items are analysable into matter and form; so that a study of matter and form cannot be part of the science which studies beings *qua* being. Perhaps the study of beings *qua* being must begin with or focus upon substances; but then it will study substances *qua* being and not *qua* substance.

Matters do not improve when we turn to the other two characterizations of metaphysics which were set out in the first section of this chapter: the study of first causes, and theology. It may seem easy enough to connect these two characterizations to one another; for we need only suppose that the gods, the subject matter of theology, are identical with the first causes, the subject of the science of first causes. And indeed Aristotle says something rather like this:

The science which it would be most proper for gods to possess is a divine science, and so too is any science which deals with divine items. But the present science [i.e., the study of first causes] alone has these two features:

26 See above, pp. 88–89.

the gods are supposed to be among the causes of all things and to be first principles, and either the gods alone or the gods above all others can possess this science.   (A 2, 983a6–9)

But things are less simple than this text may suggest; and it is in any event far less easy to connect theology and the study of causes with the science of substance and the science of beings *qua* being.

What exactly does the study of first causes study? Aristotle claims to have given us the answer in the first two chapters of Book Alpha (A 2, 983a23–24); but he has told us little, and even when we supplement his remarks from such passages as Lambda 1–4 we get only a sketchy account. Nonetheless, we may reasonably suppose that the study will include both the philosophical analysis of the different types of causation or explanation which we find in the *Physics*,[27] and also the philosophical investigation of the concepts which these types of causation or explanation involve.[28] In addition, the study will need to explain what makes a cause a *first* or primary cause.

(First causes are first not in a chronological sense: Aristotle is not interested in tracing the chain of causes back through time; nor indeed does he believe that there *are* first causes in this sense. Rather, the causes are first in the sense of being ultimate. I may explain why vines are deciduous by pointing out that they have broad leaves – but then I shall wonder why broad-leaved plants are deciduous. I may explain that in broad-leaved plants the sap coagulates at the joint of the leaves – and then I may wonder why coagulation should explain deciduousness. And so on. But eventually – or so Aristotle supposes – the explanations come to a stop and there are "unexplainable explanations": see, e.g., *An.Post* I 24, 85b27–86a3. These are the *first* causes of things.)

But Aristotle's science of first causes ought presumably to contain more than these analytical exercises: the exercises are surely preparatory, and the substantive task of the science must be to determine what the first causes of things actually are. Or is there any such science? Aristotle himself normally insists on the independence of the sciences one from another, and he argues against the Platonic idea that all scientific knowledge can somehow be arranged under a

27 See below, pp. 120–122.
28 Among them, matter and form – hence a connexion with the study of substance.

single superscience (see *An.Post* I 7, I 32). The first principles of geometry will surely fall within the domain of geometers, the first principles of botany within the province of botanists, and so on – what room is there for a separate science of first principles? Even if we concede that, in a certain sense, a geometer cannot consider the principles of geometry *qua* geometer,[29] we have no reason at all to think that some *other* science or study can consider these principles along with the principles of all other sciences.

What, next, does Aristotelian theology study? Theology is the subject of part of Book Lambda; and it is also, indirectly, the matter of the last two books of the *Physics*. It is, of course, the study of the gods or of things divine; but Aristotle has a refined view of the gods.

Our remote ancestors have handed down remnants to posterity in the form of myths, to the effect that the heavenly bodies are gods and that the divine encompasses the whole of nature. But the rest has been added by way of myth to persuade the vulgar and for the use of the laws and of expediency. For they say that the gods are anthropomorphic and like some of the other animals – and other things which follow from and are similar to this. But if you distinguish among what they say and accept only the first part – that they thought the primary substances to be gods –, then you would think that they were divinely inspired.   (Λ 8, 1074b1–10)

Zeus and Athena, the personal gods of the Greek pantheon, are to be dismissed – they are mythical elaborations. But they are elaborations of an important truth, which our ancestors discerned.

What is the important truth? Aristotle holds that all movement requires a mover: if **a** is in motion, then there is something which is moving **a**. Hence, on pain of a regress, there must be unmoved movers: **a** is moved by **b**, **b** is moved by **c**, . . . and, eventually, **y** is moved by **z**, which is itself motionless. (All the movements here are simultaneous: we are not chasing motion back through time, asking what *started* **a** off; we are asking what, now, is moving **a**.[30]) Hence if there are any objects in eternal motion, there must be some eternal unmoved movers. (Really? Why not a never-ending sequence of different movers?) Now,

29 See *An.Post* I 12, 77b5–9. Of course, a geometer cannot *prove* the first principles of geometry – but then no-one can. Of course, non-geometers might *discuss* the principles of geometry – but then so can geometers. (And why should they not do so *qua* geometers insofar as their geometrical expertise will be relevant to their considerations?)
30 Compare the chains of causes, above p. 103.

there *is* something which is always moving with an unceasing motion, which is motion in a circle – this is clear not only to reason but also to observation. Hence the first heavens must be eternal. There is therefore something which moves them. And since what both moves and is moved has an intermediate status, there must be a mover which moves them without being moved, eternal and a substance and actual.

(Λ 7, 1072a21–26)

Certain celestial movements are eternal, hence there must be as many unmoved movers as there are eternal celestial movements. Astronomical theory indicates that the movements are either 55 or 49 in number. There are, then, either 55 or 49 eternal unmoved movers (Λ 8, 1074a15–16).

These movers are substances. They must be incorporeal, partless, and indivisible. They cannot therefore impart movement by pushing and shoving. Rather, they cause movement in the way in which objects of desire cause movement (Λ 7, 1072a26–32). As ultimate objects of desire, they must be good. In addition, they are capable of thought – indeed, they think constantly. (But *what* they think is a difficult question: Λ 9.) They are, as objects of desire, ultimately responsible for all the goodness in the world. They are also, perhaps, providential in the sense that thanks to them, most of the natural world is arranged "for the sake of the good."[31] And, further, they are perhaps in some fashion creators and conservers of the world.

The last two contentions are controversial. Even without them, Aristotle's theology is hard enough to swallow – a cruel critic will urge that it is composed of five parts bad argument and five parts nonsense. However that may be, we might reasonably wonder what theology of this sort has to do with metaphysics.

First, how does theology, so conceived, connect with the study of first causes? The gods are indeed first or ultimate causes – they are ultimate causes of motion, and they are also in some fashion final causes. In studying theology you will surely spend some time on the causal aspects of divine activity. But this is not to identify the study of first causes with theology. I have already argued that, if he is to be consistent, Aristotle should deny the existence of *any* science of first causes: a fortiori theology cannot be such a science. And in any case, is there any reason in the world to think that the ultimate

31 On Aristotle's teleology see below, pp. 127–135.

explanation of why vines drop their leaves in autumn will invoke quasi-astronomical divinities?

Secondly, how are to we connect theology with the study of substance, and with the study of beings *qua* being? Theology seems to be a part of physics, or at any rate of a sort of hyperphysics – and it is, I suppose, neither accidental nor inappropriate that we read Aristotle's longest essay on the subject in his *Physics*. How, then, can theology be identified with the study of beings in general? Modern scholars have been particularly exercised by this issue, and there is a large literature given to the question of whether Aristotle professed a "general" or a "specific" metaphysics – whether he thought that metaphysics was about all beings or only about divine beings.[32] One answer, which was once popular, is demonstrably wrong: Aristotle did not change his mind, holding first the one view, then the other.[33] For in Book Epsilon he makes it quite clear that he holds both views at once – he sees that there is a difficulty in his position, and he thinks he has a solution. Here is the solution:

> ... if there are no substances other than those formed by nature, then natural science will be the primary science; but if there are immovable substances, the science which investigates them must be prior and it must be primary philosophy; and it is universal inasmuch as it is primary. And it will be its task to consider beings *qua* being – both what they are and the attributes which belong to them *qua* being.   (E 1, 1026a27–32)

The study of the immovable substances is theology. Immovable substances are primary, and so theology is primary. Because it is primary, it is universal and considers everything. Hence it considers beings *qua* being.

This argument was the model for the argument earlier in this section which attempted to show that the science of substances might study beings *qua* being. Aristotle's own argument in Epsilon 1 seems to me to have all the faults of the earlier argument – and a few more of its own. Even if the primacy of divine substances were the primacy of focal entities, the argument would fail. And the primacy

32 For reasons which escape me, the equally grave difficulties raised by the other two characterizations of the subject have not stimulated so much scholarly activity.

33 First the "Platonic" view which took metaphysics to be theology, then the "Empiricist" view which construed the subject as logic? See above, pp. 16–17.

of focal entities cannot be attributed to divine substances. The un-moved movers are no doubt primary in various ways; but they are surely not the focus for the existence of anything else – in particular, they are not the focus for the existence of other substances. Aristotle cannot imagine that for horses to exist is for the unmoved movers to be in such-and-such a state: the view is ludicrous in itself – and it has the unAristotelian consequence that horses are not substances, that the unmoved movers are the only substances there are.

The argument in Epsilon does not work. Nor will any other argu-ment. For it is plain that theology and logic are distinct subjects.

What, finally, of the connections between the study of causes and the study of substances, and between the study of causes and the study of beings *qua* being? At the beginning of Lambda, Aristotle remarks that

substance is the subject of our inquiry; for the principles and causes we are seeking are the principles and causes of substances.   (Λ 1, 1069a18)

This is a non sequitur; and it is, in any case, plain that the study of first causes is not the same as the study of substances. At the begin-ning of Epsilon, Aristotle asserts that

we are seeking the principles and the causes of the things which exist – and evidently of them *qua* being.   (E 1, 1025b2–3)

This is not evident at all; indeed, it might seem to be evidently false.

In Gamma, Aristotle offers us more than a bare assertion. Here is his argument:

Since we are seeking the first principles and the highest causes, it is plain that there must be something to which these belong in virtue of its own nature. And if our predecessors, who sought the elements of existing things, were seeking these same principles, then these elements must be the ele-ments of beings not accidentally but in virtue of the fact that they are beings. Hence it is of beings *qua* being that we must grasp the first causes.

(Γ 1, 1003a26–31)

We are seeking the first causes *of beings*; these first causes must be first causes of something *qua* that thing: hence the causes are causes of be-ings *qua* being – and in studying beings *qua* being we shall study them.

It is an argument – but it is a baffling argument. To say that x is a cause of y *qua* F presumably means that x explains why y is F; so that a cause of something *qua* being will be a cause which explains why the thing exists. No doubt there are numerous causes which explain why numerous things exist; and let us grant that there are *first* causes among them – items which explain why other things exist and whose existence itself is inexplicable. Even so, the old question returns: why suppose that these items have anything in common? Why not suppose – as Aristotle normally does suppose – that the first causes of existence in botany will be different from the first causes of existence in geometry? And even if all these causes do have something in common, why think that they are to be studied by the science of beings *qua* being? If x is cause of y *qua* beautiful (if x makes y beautiful), it does not follow that the study of beautiful objects *qua* beautiful will study x. No more need we infer that the study of beings *qua* being will study the causes of beings *qua* being.

Aristotle might have offered a different argument. He might have argued that *all* entities are causes or effects, explanatory or explained, so that the notions of cause and effect and of explanation are "topic neutral." They are thus part of the subject matter of logic – or of the study of beings *qua* being. It is, I think, true that a science of beings *qua* being would, for these reasons, say something about causes and explanations. But it would not say anything specifically about *first* causes; and in particular, the science would neither be limited to nor include a study of the first causes or explanations in the sciences.

The four characterizations of metaphysics do not cohere: there is no one science which they all describe, and hence there is (in a sense) no such thing as Aristotelian metaphysics. Does this matter? Or has the preceding account of Aristotle's attempts to describe what he was doing been merely pedantic? A just critique (perhaps), but a trifling critique?

In one way the criticisms are trifling; in two ways they are not. They are trifling inasmuch as they do not touch upon any of the major arguments or contentions in the *Metaphysics*. They are not trifling inasmuch as they claim to expose a muddle which is not a trifling muddle. And they are non-trifling inasmuch as they show clearly that we can – if we wish – prize apart (say) the theological material in Book Lambda from (say) the material on substance in Books Zeta and Eta,[34] for the two parcels of material belong to two different sciences.

34 "Why should anyone want to prise them apart?" – "Because much of Zeta and Eta is rather good, and most of Lambda is embarrassingly bad." (But were I to write this *in propria persona* I would lose the respect of my friends.)

4 Philosophy of Science

THE STRUCTURE OF ARISTOTELIAN SCIENCE

"All men by nature desire to know" says Aristotle at the beginning of the *Metaphysics*. But knowledge proper, for him, consists of understanding, *epistêmê*, and understanding involves science.[1] Indeed, *epistêmê* (as a concrete noun) can mean, in Aristotle's terminology, a science: an organized body of systematically arranged information. That systematic arrangement takes the form of exhibition as a chain of syllogistic deductions, preferably in the paradigmatic universal affirmative mood Barbara ("All Bs are Cs, all As are Bs, so all As are Cs"), where each of the premises (and hence the conclusion) is a necessary truth.[2] Indeed, at the beginning of the *Posterior Analytics*, Aristotle lays out the conditions of demonstrative argument: the premises must be

> true, primary, immediate, more intelligible than, prior to and explanatory of the conclusion. . . . The premises must be (a) true, since what is false cannot be known, e.g., the commensurate diagonal. They must be (b) primary and (c) indemonstrable, since otherwise they will not be known without demonstration; for to know that of which there is a demonstration (other than incidentally) is to have that demonstration. They must be (d) explanatory, (e) more intelligible and (f) prior: explanatory since we only have scientific knowledge when we know the explanation; prior since they are explanatory; and already known not only in the sense that they are understood, but in that they are known to be true.   (1: *An.Post* I 2, 71a21–33)

(a) is of course uncontroversial. (b) and (c), as Aristotle suggests, amount to the same thing: for a proposition ("all As are Bs") to be

---

1 See also above, Chapter 2, pp. 47–50.
2 The interpretation of Aristotle's modal operators is tricky: see further Chapter 2, pp. 44–45.

primary is for there to be no further propositions of which it is a deductive consequence, and which serve to explain why it is the case. That means (in Aristotle's terms) that there is no middle term C such that all As are Cs and all Cs are Bs (where A's being C explains its being B) – and that is what it is for a proposition to be immediate. Equally, (d) and (f) are linked: some property F is prior to G in this sense just in case something's being G is explained by its being F. Finally, by "more intelligible" Aristotle means more basic in the order of being: in the next paragraph he distinguishes between propositions that are more intelligible to us (i.e., more immediately and directly available) and those that are more intelligible in themselves (i.e., those which form the foundation of the structure of science: cf. *Met* 7 3, 1029b3 ff.; *NE* 1 4, 1095a30 ff.), which concern him here.

To have scientific knowledge, then, is to have explanatory understanding: not merely to "know" a fact incidentally, to be able to assent to something which is true, but to know *why* it is a fact. The proper function of science is to provide explanations, the canonical form of which is something like "Xs are F because they are G." The holding of one property for a class of objects (mortality of men, say) is to be explained in terms of the dependence of that property on some other property (e.g., being an animal): men are mortal because they are animals. Moreover, this fact can be exhibited syllogistically: all men are animals; all animals are mortal; so all men are mortal. However, for the syllogism genuinely to be explanatory, more needs to be the case than simply that it exhibits a true set of facts of class-inclusion. All mammals are mortal, and all men are mammals, but men are not mortal because they are mammals. Why not? Aristotle viewed the world, or at least the natural part of it, as being hierarchically organized into genus–species divisions (indeed, he more or less invented the notion of genus–species division).[3] The

3 Care is, however, required here: Pierre Pellegrin (1986: bibliographical references for the notes to this chapter are found on pp. 165–167) has established that Aristotle's usage of the terms "genus (*genos*)" and "species (*eidos*)" is, even in the biological works, logical in character (that is, the genus is simply the wider, inclusive class in any particular case: what the terms *refer* to in any particular instance will be determined by the context); moreover, Aristotle clearly does not offer anything like a Linnaean taxonomy, and perhaps is not interested in so doing (Balme, 1961); nonetheless, it is a mistake to infer from this that Aristotle is altogether uninterested in taxonomy or that he never uses "*eidos*" to refer to species.

world divides (realistically, and not as a matter of mere convention) into natural kinds, and those kinds stand in relations of greater and lesser resemblance to and distinction from one another.

The basic form of explanation may be laid out as follows. For any kind K (explanation in the strict sense stops for Aristotle at the species-level), the fact that Ks are Fs is explained by their being a sub-class of a more general class C, of which it is true that everything in C is F, but there is no class C' of which C is a proper subset such that everything in C' is F. Thus the explanatory level for any property is the highest level in the hierarchy at which it is still true to say that everything at that level has the property in question.[4] However even this is not quite enough. Explanation is, for Aristotle (quite properly), intensional: how you pick out the explanatory factors matters to the propriety of the explanations. Thus for an explanation of the fact that Ks are F, we require not merely to pick out the widest class which includes K which is such that all its members are *F:* we need to pick it out under the appropriate, perspicuous description. Thus, if two classes C_1 and C_2 are co-extensive, and Ks are F in virtue of their belonging to C_1, they will not, strictly speaking, be F in virtue of their belonging to C_2.

At *An.Post* 2 17, Aristotle considers an example. Take a property such as deciduousness; this belongs to vines and figs, but of course it has a broader extension simply than that of those two species. But (or so at least Aristotle thinks) all broad-leaved plants are deciduous (vines and figs being broad-leaved species); but moreover (again in Aristotle's view) *only* broad-leaved plants are deciduous. Thus "all broad-leaved plants are deciduous" is a convertible universal, or, as we might say, "broad-leaved" and "deciduous" are co-extensive. And, Aristotle holds, vines, figs, etc., are deciduous *because* they are broad-leaved, i.e., broad-leavedness is the explanatory middle-term linking the set of distinct species with the property of deciduousness (ibid. 16, 98a35 ff.). This can be laid out as a syllogism in the canonical scientific form of Barbara:

---

4 Actually, Aristotle is not entirely consistent in this. *An.Post* 2 18, 99b9 ff., says that if D is B because it is C, and all Bs are As, then D will be A because it is B. Cf. *Met.* 2 2.

[A]   (i) all broad-leaved trees are deciduous;
       (ii) vines are broad-leaved;
hence
       (iii) vines are deciduous.

But [A] is not the only sound syllogism that can be formulated with this material: given the (alleged) co-extensiveness of broad-leaved-ness and deciduousness, we might equally construct

[B]   (i) all deciduous trees are broad-leaved;
       (ii) vines are deciduous;
hence
       (iii) vines are broad-leaved;

and for Aristotle at most one of [A] and [B] can be fully explanatory.

In *An.Post* 1 13 he had considered the relationship between the planets' proximity to the earth and their failure to twinkle. All and only nearby objects fail to twinkle – but are the planets non-twinklers because they are near or near because they are non-twinklers? At most one can provide the proper direction of explanation (Aristotle not unreasonably plumps for the first option); and hence at most one "syllogism of the reasoned fact" can be constructed from this material, even though it necessarily yields two factual syllogisms.

Analogously, Aristotle considers that, of [A] and [B], [A] alone is genuinely explanatory. But the deciduousness case is further complicated by the fact that Aristotle takes the explanation advanced by [A] to be at best provisional; there is a further reason why broad-leaved trees are deciduous, namely that in them sap coagulates at the junction of the leaf-stem, which causes the stem to break off. Indeed, deciduousness *is* such coagulation (*An.Post* 2 17, 99a28–29): this is a definition (the latter being one of the two classes of per se predication: A is predicated of all B, and A belongs in the definition of B: *An.Post* 1 4, 73a35 ff.; cf. 2 16, 98b20 ff.). Thus we now have:

[C]   (i) all sap-coagulators are deciduous (since deciduous
            = $_{df.}$ sap-coagulator);
       (ii) all broad-leaved trees are sap-coagulators;
hence
       (iii) all broad-leaved trees are deciduous.

[C] justifies premiss [A](i), and drives the conclusion of that argument. The business of proper explanation of why some property holds universally of some class of things consists in finding the real, Lockean definition of that property (i.e, spelling out its real structure: cf. *An.Post* 2 10), and showing how that definition collects the class of things in question within itself. Vines are thus deciduous because they are a sub-class of the proper class of broad-leaved trees, and broad-leaved trees are deciduous because in them sap coagulates at the leaf-stems.[5]

SCIENTIFIC EXPLANATION: THE ACCIDENTAL AND FOR THE MOST PART

Since, for realists like Aristotle, the structure of scientific explanation must properly mirror the composition of the reality it explains, an Aristotelian science should consist of a sequence of explanatory deductions of the sort sketched above. Hence we might expect to find an Aristotelian science (of biology, in the *Parts of Animals, Generation of Animals*, and *Historia Animalium*,[6] for instance; or of dynamics in the *Physics*; or of cosmology in *de Caelo*) to be laid out, in Spinozist fashion, more geometrico.

But anyone anticipating such Euclidian delights will be sorely disappointed. Aristotle's scientific treatises seem either to be collections of more or less informal arguments, or, more depressingly still, farragos of weird, wonderful, and frequently quite incredible "facts" about the denizens of some particular domain (*HA* has usually been thought to be an example of the latter form, although, as we shall see in the following chapter, it may well be more systematic than it seems at first glance). Indeed, one can trawl the whole of Aristotle's considerable scientific oeuvre without netting a single instance of a fully worked-out syllogism. What one is to make of that fact is controversial:[7] the fact remains. Aristotle's commentators sometimes trouble to reformulate his arguments in syllogistic form – but Aristotle himself does not do so.

Moreover, many of his scientific claims (especially in biology)

5 On Aristotle's preoccupation with causal definitions, see Lennox, 1987.
6 I prefer the Latin designation for this treatise, which is not (in any modern sense) a history; Barnes (1982, 9) proposes *Zoological Researches*, which is certainly less misleading, although it perhaps suggests too great a systematicity.
7 Barnes, (1969 and 1981) offers two rather different resolutions.

actively resist any such formulation, not being couched in the appropriate form for a premiss in the canonical mood of Barbara. Often, indeed, they are not even universal, much less necessarily so: most, but not all, men have beards (cf. *An.Post* 2 12, 96a8–11). Indeed, all natural (as opposed to accidental) happenings occur either invariably or for the most part (*Phys* 2 8, 198b34 f.; cf. *Met* 6 3, 1027a14 ff.), which makes them, for Aristotle, susceptible of teleological, final-cause explanations. But while things in the heavens are invariable, immutable, and absolutely necessary, those in the sublunar world, the domain of Aristotelian physics, are not; here generalities tend to hold only for the most part. And such generalities ("most men have beards") cannot be squeezed into the canonical form of Aristotelian natural science as outlined above.[8]

Indeed, they can be accommodated only in a strictly limited number of valid deductions, in spite of what Aristotle sometimes suggests:

every deduction is either through necessary or through for-the-most-part propositions; and if the propositions are necessary, so too is the conclusion, while if for-the-most-part the conclusion too is such

(**2**: *An.Post* 1 30, 87b22–25; cf. *An.Pr* 1 27, 43b31 ff.)

The issue is complex. Valid syllogisms are constructible which contain one "for the most part" premiss, where "for the most part" is construed as a sentence-forming operator on sentences; the analogue to Barbara where the minor premiss is majority quantified and the major universal yields validly a majority quantified conclusion. But it is important to note that it does so only if "for the most part *p*" is not taken to entail "not invariably *p*" (i.e., only if "for the most part *p*" is compatible with "always *p*"); yet Aristotle apparently accepts, conversationally at least, the entailment from "for the most part" to "not always" (e.g., at *Met* 6 2, 1026b26 ff.). By contrast, the case in which the major premiss is majority quantified while the minor is universal does not yield a valid majority quantified conclusion (it does not even yield an existential conclusion: consider the premiss-pair "most Catholics are encouraged to marry" and "all Carmelites are Catholics"); and evidently nothing

8 See also below, Chapter 9, pp. 270–272.

whatever follows from two majority quantified affirmative premisses in the first figure.[9]

At all events, the prospects for producing a logic of "for the most part" useful in systematizing the vaguer parts of the Aristotelian sciences looks bleak indeed. And Aristotle sometimes rather suggests that, in a fully worked-out science, such irritating vaguenesses may be replaceable by more restricted universally quantified propositions:

that there is no science of the accidental (*kata sumbebêkos*) is clear: for all science is either of that which is always or of that which is for the most part. For how else could one learn or impart it to another? Things must be determined as either occurring always or for the most part, e.g., that honey-water is for the most part beneficial to fever-patients. But one will not be able to state when what occurs contrary to this happens, e.g., 'at the new moon' – for then it will be the case on the day of the new moon either always or for the most part – but the accidental is the opposite of this.

(3: *Met* 6 2, 1027a20–27)

The last sentence appears to hint at the possibility that the troublesome sentences of the form "for the most part xs are F" may, in the final version of the science, give way to sentences of the form "all xs, given conditions C, are F," where the content of C is specifiable independently in a non-circular manner. But this is a hint only, and Aristotle never follows it through. Moreover, there are reasons for thinking that Aristotle could not subscribe at least universally to such a position. For the reason why certain things happen only for the most part and not invariably is, for him, due to their involving matter.

Matter (which should not be thought of as simply analogous to

9 Although, interestingly, an existential conclusion does so follow in the third figure: "most As and Bs; most As and Cs; so some C is B" is valid, as (for a particular negative conclusion) is the equivalent majority analogue to the mood Felapton. In the first figure, the analogue to Celarent with a majority-quantified minor premiss yields a (negative) majority-quantified conclusion; and there are two valid second-figure moods, analogous to Camestres and Cesare, which do so too. But evidently this is a thin logical basis upon which to erect a significant and useful majority-logic for science (effectively it means that, in any deductive sequence, only one significant premiss, that which provides the ultimate subject for the conclusion, can be majority-quantified).

stuff or material: matter is that in which form is realized, and that which remains constant, at least in one sense, through change: *Met* 7 7, 1032b29–1033a22; cf. *Phys* 1 7) is properly to be found only in the sublunary world (I ignore here Aristotle's notions of the "intelligible matter" of mathematical objects, and the "topic matter" possessed by the heavenly bodies: *Met* 8 1, 1042a33 ff.; 4, 1044b8). And it is because natural objects are compounds of matter and form (or, better, have their forms realized in matter) that they are subject to change, growth, alteration, and decay. Moreover, matter in some sense resists the imposition of form; it is by nature recalcitrant, and from time to time the best efforts of form to actualize itself will fail (*Phys* 2 8, 199a11): thus Aristotle explains cases of natural deficiency and deformity (*GA* 4 3, 767b13 ff; 769b10 ff.; 4 4).

But these cases are not themselves, in Aristotle's view, generally susceptible of regular explanation: there will be *particular* reasons in each case why the form fails to come to fruition, but not necessarily, or even generally, of such a kind to be explained in terms of some further explanatory generality (*GA* 4 4, 770b9–17). This is where the accidental gets a hold in Aristotle's scheme of things, and it is this which Aristotle is concerned to show in *Metaphysics* 6: purely accidental collocations (of both events and descriptions) cannot be given a scientific (i.e., principled) explanation.

This is not necessarily to imply that accidental collocations of events of the type that fall outside the realm of science cannot be necessitated in some way, or even that they do not in some sense have causes.[10] It is worth here quoting a crucial passage at length.

that there are principles and causes which are generable and destructible without there being for them any *process* of generation and destruction is obvious; for otherwise everything will be of necessity, since what is in the process of being generated or destroyed must have a cause which is not accidentally its cause. Will this occur or not? Yes, if such and such happens, but not if it does not. And this will occur if something else does. And so if time is constantly subtracted from a limited temporal extent, we will clearly arrive at the present. This man, then, will die by violence if he goes out; and he will do this if he is thirsty; and he will be thirsty if something else happens. . . . For instance, he will go out if thirsty, and he will be

10 *Pace* Sorabji (1980) chapter 1, who argues that coincidences can be necessitated but not caused – but the issue turns precisely upon what one is prepared to accept as being a cause.

thirsty if he eats something spicy; and this is either so or not; so he will either of necessity die or not die. . . . Everything, then, that is to be will be of necessity; e.g., it is necessary that someone who is alive must some time die, since something has already occurred [sc. to necessitate it], namely the existence of contraries in the body. But whether he dies by disease or by violence is not yet determined, but depends on the happening of something else. Evidently then the process goes back to a particular starting-point, but this does not itself indicate anything further [in the past]. This, then, will be the starting-point of what happens by chance, and will have nothing else as the cause of its coming to be.

(4: Met 6 3, 1027a29–b14)

Much ink has been spilled over this, the nearest Aristotle ever comes to discussing something that we might recognize as the hypothesis of determinism; and commentators have been radically divided as to what precisely Aristotle is asserting here.[11] But it seems clear enough that Aristotle's primary concern is with explanation; and that he claims, among other things, that chance happenings are those for which there is no proper explanation. But it is equally clear that this does not mean that we cannot in some sense give an account of them.

Consider the example Aristotle sketches, of someone who will die by violence (set upon by robbers at a well) if he goes out to fetch water; and he will do that if he develops a thirst as a result of eating curry. We may say, then, that his taste for hot food caused his death – but it is not in any real sense an *explanation* for his death. He didn't die because his system could not tolerate curry, and no general connection exists between a partiality for Indian cuisine and untimely violent death. Or, to put it in Aristotle's language, there is no explanatory middle-term connecting curry-eating and murder. Thus it is not the case that our vindaloo-enthusiast's death can be given an explanation that stretches back indefinitely in time (note that this fact is perfectly compatible with its *causal* determination as we might understand it).

This emphasizes the crucial fact that for Aristotle explanation is general. He is not really concerned with the particular causes of individual events, but with the general patterns which run invariably (or at least for the most part) through the structure of the world. And

---

11 Compare the treatment of Sorabji (1980) chapter 1, with that of Frede (1985).

those patterns are, for him, to be explained in terms of processes – this is the point of the distinction made at the beginning of 4. In the case of coincidences, cases where two causal sequences intersect and give rise to a new set of events (such as my just happening to be at the well when the robbers were there, or, to use another Aristotelian example, my happening upon someone who owes me money while out shopping: *Phys* 2 5, 196b33 ff.), nothing in either process considered in and of itself should lead the scientist to predict their intersection, and hence to predict the novel turns of events. Thus, again in Aristotle's language, although there is a cause for my getting my money back, that cause does not itself have a causal (in the sense of explanatory) history – if it did, processes being the natural unfoldings of events according to a regular pattern, it would have been predictable.

A corollary of this is that chance and fortuitous events lack proper final causes, although chance events have in a sense an accidental final cause (this is what distinguishes them from the merely fortuitous: *Phys* 2 4–6), the final cause they would have had, had the action been undertaken with the outcome in mind: if I happen upon buried treasure while digging my garden, then "in order to discover treasure" is, for Aristotle, the accidental final cause of my happy discovery. Now, given Aristotle's teleological bent, which we shall examine further below, and given (relatedly) that for him the fundamental facts about the world are the working-out of regular causal processes toward a determinate end, it is perhaps unsurprising that he is concerned not so much with the lawlike regularities of the sort beloved of modern philosophers of science, but with the natural relations between types of property, and their propensities to express themselves as fully worked-out forms, a process whose theoretical underpinnings are provided by the *Physics*.

PHYSICS AND THE EXPLANATION OF CHANGE

The *Physics* is concerned with the world of change. In a distinction that was to form the backbone of the medieval world-picture which persisted at least until Galileo, Aristotle considered the universe to divide into two distinct parts. There is the domain of the heavenly bodies where perfection and eternal existence rule – nothing in that divine realm really alters. By contrast, in the region below the orbit of the moon (hence "sublunary"), change and decay are the norm.

Physical and physiological processes play out in regular, ordered, consecutive patterns, but the patterns are of flux and alteration; no denizen of the sublunary world can live for ever: the best it can hope for is a kind of etiolated immortality that derives from perpetuating the species (*GA* 2 1, 731b32 ff.)

If this picture is even to be coherent, Aristotle must first rehabilitate the concept of change itself against its pre-Socratic detractors, notably Parmenides. For although Aristotle dismisses the Eleatics as making no contribution to the understanding of nature (*Phys* 1 2, 184b27 f.), he nonetheless devotes two chapters (*Phys* 1 2–3) to refuting their views on the basic principles of things. Indeed, in his opinion, it is unclarity as to their nature and number that has vitiated all previous scientific inquiry. People have failed to see that, while in one (material) sense Parmenides was right to say that "nothing can come to be from nothing," in another (formal) sense he was wrong – and therein lies the solution to the general paradox of change. Absolute generation ex nihilo is indeed impossible (*Phys* 1 8, 191b9 ff.) – but that does not prevent the transfer of form from one object to another, in some cases merely altering it, in others effectively bringing it into existence (*Phys* 1 7, 190a31 ff.), although not actually creating the matter itself of which the thing is now made (*Met* 7 7, 1032b30 ff.). Thus Aristotle appeals to two types of principle – that of the material substrate which underlies any and every change;[12] and the contrarieties of form[13] in virtue of which that change can be analyzed and explicated (*Phys* 1 6–8).

12 It should be stressed that "matter" here is a logical concept and does not denote anything like basic "stuff"; rather, the matter for any change in an object (or collection of objects) is whatever level of description of it which is such that, at that level, no change takes place. Hence clay is the matter for the vessel, since the clay is there before the pot is made (and after it is destroyed); however, the clay itself is a composite of matter and form, since it is earth and water in a particular ratio and elaborated in a particular way. Thus what is matter for change (or decompositional analysis) at one level may itself be further analyzed, and changed, in virtue of its own matter/form relations at a more basic level: see *Met* 8 4, 1044a15 ff.

13 Strictly speaking, Aristotle differentiates between cases in which the change takes place from one form to its contrary, and those in which the movement is from privation to form, or *vice versa*, as in the case of someone becoming sick or recovering (*Met* 7 7, 1032b2 ff.);, but this refinement does not matter for our purposes.

For Aristotle, the world divides into two classes of things: those which exist by nature, and those which exist for other reasons (*Phys* 2 1 192b8–9; cf. *Met* 7 9). The paradigm cases of things existing by nature are living things – plants, animals, and the heavenly bodies; but their elements – earth, water, air, and fire (and the fifth element, the "ether" which makes up the heavenly bodies: *Cael* 1 2–4) – are also natural in this sense. Non-natural things include artifacts like beds and houses. This distinction is causal: natural objects are such as to contain within themselves their own principle (*archê*) of growth, movement, and rest (*Phys* 2 1 , 192b13–14; cf. *Met* 5 4, 1015a13 f.). By contrast, artificial objects have no such internal principles – or rather, insofar as they do, they do not have them *qua* the thing that they are, but only derivatively, in virtue of the nature of the material from which they are made (cf. *Met* 8 3, 1043b14 ff.).

Aristotle instances an example from Antiphon: if we planted a bed we should not expect it to sprout baby beds – if anything, it would produce a tree (*Phys* 2 1, 193a9–17). This shows that it is not its *nature* to be a bed. Being a bed is a matter of having an artificial structure imposed upon a natural material (in this case wood) by an alien artificer. By contrast, in the case of natural objects, there are no such artificers: in them, agent and patient coincide (ibid. 1, 192b23–27; cf. 8, 199b30–32; cf. *Met* 7 7–9). Such things have a principle of growth and propagation innate to them, a principle which seeks, so far as is compatible with the material exigencies of the environment, to realize itself in the completion of an adult instance of the species to which it belongs (and also to propagate further instances of that species).

Having thus refurbished the concept of change itself and supplied it with a formal analysis in *Physics* 1, and having distinguished the various senses of "nature" in *Physics* 2 1, Aristotle turns, in the rest of the book, to an investigation of the causal principles of things. His predecessors were, he thinks, excessively concerned with their material aspects (*Phys* 2 2, 194a19–21; cf. *Met* 1 3, 983b6 ff.), emphasizing them to the exclusion of other equally, perhaps more, important factors in explanation. To remedy this, Aristotle develops his doctrine of the Four Causes in *Phys* 2 3, and 7.

The Four Causes are four ways of answering different but equally crucial questions about why things are how they are. If we cannot answer these questions, Aristotle holds, we cannot really know the objects of which we speak. *Epistêmê* involves knowing the fundamental structure of things, of why they are the sorts of things they are; and to this end, Aristotle distinguishes four general classes of explanation:

(i) in one way the cause is said to be the existing thing out of which something comes to be, e.g., the bronze of the statue, or the silver of the phial, and the genera of these things. (ii) Another is the form or the template (*paradeigma*): this is the formula (*logos*) of the what-it-is-to-be, and its genera. . . . (iii) Furthermore, that from which the primary origin (*archê*) of change and rest, e.g., the responsible deliberator, or the father of the child, and in general the agent of the thing produced, and the changer of the thing changed. (iv) Moreover there is the end (*telos*). This is that for the sake of which, e.g., health of walking; for why does he walk? In order, we say, to be healthy, and in so saying we think that we have given the reason (*aition*).

(**5:** *Phys* 2 3, 194b23–35)

So Aristotle introduces the material, formal, efficient, and final causes. He notes the possibility of causal intermediaries ("like tools or drugs": ibid. 195a1), through which various actions or productions are brought to completion, although he does not (as a later tradition was to) classify them as causes.

The remark concerning genera simply points to the fact that you may refer to the explanatory item in question in a variety of ways. You may designate the statue's matter as bronze, or generically as metal; but in that case (unless you are specifically concerned with some feature the statue has in virtue of its simply being metallic) your designation will be explanatorily misleading.

Indeed *aitia* can be picked out in more specific or more general ways (ibid. 195a29): we may say that the doctor caused health, or that some skilful person did (ibid. 195a30–31). And we can refer to something as *aitios* under a description which is incidental (*kata sumbebêkos*) to the fact of its responsibility, e.g., when we say that Polycleitus is the cause of the sculpture (since the sculptor happens to have that name) or more generally still a man, or even an animal (ibid. 195a33-b1):

in the class of incidentals some are closer and some are further away [sc. from the explanatorily appropriate designation], as for instance if "the pale and cultured individual" was said to be responsible for the statue.

(**6:** ibid. 195b1–3)

Furthermore, at least in the case of agency, we may specify the cause as either potential ("the builder") or actual ("the builder in the act of building": ibid. 195b4–6). Finally, the same distinctions apply to the end result: we can consider it as a particular statue, or as simply as a statue, or in general as a likeness (ibid. 195b7–9). Aristotle's discussion is here driven by considerations of ordinary usage, but he takes them to indicate important extra-linguistic facts.

The concern with how we pick out the causal factors underlines the fact that it is explanation which is at issue; but on the other hand his willingness to allow generic and incidental references to those factors indicates that Aristotle is sensitive to the extensional nature of causal (as opposed to explanatory) talk, as well as the fact that he is concerned with both explanation and cause. Hence if my sole interest is in indicating what is as a matter of fact the cause of some outcome (the production of a sculpture), I can do so without worrying about whether or not my designation correctly describes it *as* the author of the result in question: I can call him "that man over there" if I so wish. If on the other hand I wish to indicate what it is in virtue of which the result came about, I must refer to him as the bearer of the explanatory property in question, or to the property ("the art of sculpture") itself (*Phys* 2 3, 195a33–b3; cf. *Met* 7 7, 1032a26 ff.).

Thus Aristotle's scheme incorporates the matter, which is the locus for the change and the potential bearer of form (and of its privation); the form, or structural organization which is realized in the matter; the agent, or efficient cause, which brings that information about; and (in some cases at least) the goal, or final end, toward which that process tends. At *Phys* 2 7, Aristotle remarks that

the last three often coincide – for the what-it-is [i.e., the form] and that for the sake of which [the final cause] are one, while that from which the primary motion comes is the same as them in species: for man generates man, and so too generally in the case of things which cause movement being themselves moved.   (7: *Phys* 2 7, 198a25–28; cf. *Met* 7 8, 1033b29 ff.)

But how easily do the different types of explanation sit with one another? And crucially, what sense can be made of the Aristotelian invocation of teleological explanation in nature? These questions become most pressing in the context of Aristotle's philosophy of biology, and to this we now turn.

ARISTOTLE'S BIOLOGICAL METHOD

Aristotle collected and organized a vast body of data regarding the comparative morphologies and modes of life of animals, and he has traditionally been revered as the founder of taxonomic biology. That assessment (at least in its naïve form) has recently been challenged[14] by a new interpretation which contends that properly understood Aristotle is not at all concerned with systematic animal taxonomy of a proto-Linnaean sort but rather with "moriology," a science of animal parts and their relations. Thus Aristotle's purpose in dividing animals into classes is to exhibit what type of structures (and associated functions and activities) typically go together, and hence (ultimately) to isolate the causes of the variousness of animal structure.

With this revisionist assessment I am in broad agreement. One consequence of adopting it is the temptation to re-think the traditional assessment of the purpose (and hence the order of composition) of Aristotle's biological corpus. It has usually been assumed that the vast, seemingly unruly rag-bag of information about animals' structures and behaviours that forms the *Historia Animalium* was conceived by Aristotle simply as a large data-base, a repository of facts (intermingled, it must be said, with fantasies) about the biosphere designed to provide the raw material for the later, organized works on animals' parts and generation which were intended to structure that data, and to provide thoroughgoing explanations of how and why animals are constructed the way they are.

HA is not, indeed, organized as an exhaustive enumeration of the various species' attributes, and it is something of a scrap-book, continually amended, extended, and refined. But for all that, it is not a hopeless jumble. We do not, certainly, find many cases of complete accounts of animals, but that is not (so the new orthodoxy has it) because of *HA*'s provisional and unfinished nature. Rather the isolated cases of more or less complete descriptions of animals (e.g., the ape at *HA* 2 8 and the chamaeleon at *HA* 2 11) represent not occasional instances of completed taxonomical description, but rather the earliest stage of information-gathering,

14 Most particularly by Pierre Pellegrin (1986, 1987), developing some earlier suggestions of David Balme (1961).

prior to the general descriptions of individual animals being broken down into their causally interesting parts. Thus the description of the dissection of the blind mole to reveal its hidden eyes at *HA* 4 8, 533a1–11 is described not in the interests of providing a complete account of the mole's structure and morphology, but simply in order to show that this unique case (the only one of a viviparous quadruped lacking one of the five senses) is the result of an imperfection in the working-out of nature – in some sense, the mole does indeed have eyes, but they are vestigial and useless. A complete description would, then, not merely have been surplus to requirements – it would have got in the way of the point Aristotle is trying to make.[15]

Moreover, the exordium of *HA* proclaims it as being concerned with animals' parts and their relationships. Animals are composed of non-uniform parts or organs, such as heads, feet, and hands; while these in turn are made up of uniform tissues, such as flesh, sinew, and bone (*HA* 1 1, 486a9–14; cf. *PA* 2). Organs may be identical in form (as one man's nose is, in this sense, with another's, differing only in such non-essential features as relative size: ibid. 16–19), or morphologically similar, as in the case of the parts of differing species within the same genus (such as the bills of different bird species: ibid. 486a20–b17); or they may exhibit the even more remote relationship of analogy, as hand to claw, hair to feather and scale, etc. (ibid. 17–21; cf. 3 9–10).[16] Furthermore, animals may be compared and classified with regard to similarities and differences in their modes of behaviour, especially reproductive and nutritive behaviour (*HA* 1 1–3, 487a11–489a19).

DIVISION, DIFFERENTIATION, AND DEFINITION[17]

What matters then, for Aristotle, is not animal species' differences as such, nor their complete descriptions per se, but rather those

15 Aristotle not infrequently points to peculiarities and uniquenesses among animal species, e.g., his remark that "of fishes the so-called scarus is the only one known to chew the cud like a quadruped" (*HA* 8 2, 591b24). On these issues, see Balme (1961, 1987).

16 Animal analogies were first noticed by Empedocles: fragment 31 B 82 Diels-Kranz.

17 See also Chapter 2, pp. 51–53.

differences which point to their causal relations with one another
(these include whether the creature in question is blooded or blood-
less, viviparous or oviparous, footless or footed). But Aristotle is at
pains to explain (in *PA* I 2–3) that simply dividing creatures according to certain differential characteristics provides no proper solution
to the question of what their essential characteristics are. His principal target here is Plato's practice of dichotomous division (most
completely, and tediously, expounded in the *Sophist*), in which by
going down a branching tree of successive bipartite divisions we
hope to arrive at the complete classification of the species in which
we are interested. But in any such division, one branch will generally be characterized in negative terms, and for Aristotle there can be
no specific forms of negations such as featherless or footless: the
animals that fall into these categories do so by exclusion and not
because they form a proper, coherent class (*PA* I 3, 642b22–25). The
purpose, then, of division is to isolate genuine kinds – and that will
frequently involve making more than two cuts at the same level.

Moreover, some divisions, although not involving privative terms,
mistake the actual order of things: thus people who divide animals
into terrestrial and aquatic alone have to divide the bird kingdom
between the two groups – but this does violence to the real structure
of things, in which birds form a proper group (*PA* I 2, 642b9–13);
equally to divide according to the attributes *winged* and *wingless*
will artificially carve up such families as ants (*PA* I 3, 642b32,
643b1). The appropriate method is to start with commonly recognized groups, such as birds and fishes (ibid. 643b9–12), and see what
combination of characteristics or differentiae sets them apart from
one another.

The aim is ultimately to arrive at a definition of the species which
states its essence by spelling out the genus (or larger kind) to which
it belongs, plus the specific differentia which marks it off securely
from the others.[18] But here, as elsewhere in Aristotle, definition is
not simply a matter of marking the extension of a particular class –
for that can be done on the basis of attributes which are, although

18 Note that this does not amount to providing a taxonomy in a Linnaean
   sense, a hierarchically organized system beginning at the level of the
   kingdom and working down through phylum, order, family, and genus to
   species: see further Pellegrin (1986).

unique and proper to the class in question, not yet part of its essence (Aristotle's favourite example of such properties is geometrical: the angle-sum of the triangle is not, he thinks, part of the essence of triangularity, but simply an inevitable entailment of it: e.g. *An.Post* 1 4, 73b24 ff.; the same principle holds good in biology as well). Rather, one must isolate that attribute or set of attributes which make the thing the thing it is; and these attributes will be causal of the other features of the animal in question. The purpose of division is to arrive at explanatory classifications of the differing animals which will explain why they possess the derivative properties they have.[19]

Division must, however, proceed by way of progressive subdivisions of differentiae: you cannot divide into feathered and featherless, and then subdivide the feathered class into tame and wild, for tameness is not a form of having feathers (*PA* 1 3, 643b18–22; cf. *Met* 7 12). A proper series of subdivisions, then, will divide first into a general class ("footed") and then into a proper subdivision of it ("two-footed" or "cleft-footed": *PA* 1 3, 643b27–644a11). Of course, in the latter case, "two-footed" and "cleft-footed" cross-divide: not all two-footed creatures are cleft-footed, and vice versa; consequently, what makes an animal two-footed cannot be what makes it cleft-footed, nor the other way round. The two traits are not causally linked to one another, and if they are to have explanations, those explanations must reside in other facts. Moreover, there are some cases in which what is apparently the same property will be given different explanations for different species (Aristotle's example is longevity: caused in quadrupeds, at least so he alleges, by the lack of a gall-bladder, but in birds "by constitutional dryness, or some distinct characteristic": *An.Post* 2 17, 99b4–7). In fact, in *PA* 1 2–3 at least, Aristotle comes close to rejecting the process of successive division as being able to provide a satisfactory definitional result (he explicitly rules out dichotomous division as necessarily inimical to exhibiting the proper structure of things); the final definition of an animal kind will, he thinks, generally involve specifying a variety of distinct differentiae arrived at by distinct diairetic procedures, and no one of which is necessarily more basic than or prior to any of the others.

19 See Lennox (1987); Matthen (1987).

Thus do we arrive at an account of the nature of each species, and of the relations in which it stands (via a consideration of its causally basic parts) to the others. It still remains, however, to explain what that nature is, and to account for its regular reproduction and persistence in the natural world: and that explanation, for Aristotle, must involve both teleological and mechanistic components.

TELEOLOGY AND NECESSITY

Aristotle was Plato's pupil, but he was no slavish adherent of Platonism. In Plato's world, eternal and unchanging Forms are represented in an imperfect manner in changeable material, under the influence of a divine Artisan (*Timaeus*, 27d–39e; 48e–57d). The Artisan is introduced in order to account for the regularity the world exhibits, and its evident (at least to Plato) goodness. Thus Plato is a teleologist, and his teleology is *directed*, in the sense that it appeals to the conscious will of a designing artificer; and this teleology lies at the heart of the debate between mechanists (most prominently the atomists) and those who, like Plato, felt that no mechanistic explanations were adequate to account for the structure and regularity of the world.

The choice seems stark: either account for the world as the necessary outcome of undirected, random processes – or introduce some organizing intelligence into the system. Indeed, this was how the young Aristotle saw it. Cicero (*On the Nature of the Gods* 2 95 = fragment 12 R3) reports Aristotle's cave-image: if people who had spent their whole lives as troglodytes were to emerge into the upper world, they would be bound to think it the product of intelligence. It is only our familiarity with it that breeds contempt for its wondrous organization. However, as he grew away from the Academy and abandoned the notion of independently existing, separable, eternal Forms owing nothing to their imperfect earthly instances, in favour of the notion of form immanent in matter that is (in some sense at least) posterior to the individuals whose form it is, Aristotle came to reject directed teleology as well. In his surviving mature works there is no trace of the divine Artisan. Aristotle is no atheist, however – and his God does play a role in the continuing unfolding of the world-order. But God is neither the creator of that order, nor its continuing efficient cause.

Aristotle, then, repudiates the divine Artificer. But neither does he rely on pure mechanical necessity to explain the world; rather he espouses a form of non-intentional teleology. Natural processes are goal-directed; we cannot understand them other than in terms of the end-states to which they (other things being equal) tend. But these tendencies are internal nisuses possessed by natural objects in virtue of their specific forms – they do not grow or move naturally in response to the edicts of some divine dictator. Rather the form itself is an internal structural principle striving to actualize itself as the fully mature individual.

Final causes are invoked by Aristotle in two distinct ways in his biology. First, he appeals to teleology to explain those things that occur always or for the most part (relative to some suitable background conditions). It is the regularity that requires a final-cause explanation: Aristotle's basic notion is that no description of the physical world that concentrates solely on material and efficient principles can account for the order and repeatability of natural physical processes. That does not entail that there is (except metaphorically) design or intentionality in nature. Rather it involves seeing particular physical processes (the maturation of a tree or infant, for instance) as being in a sense explanatorily basic. The mere material collocations allowed by the atomists, and (on one view) Empedocles, cannot account for this constantly repeated patterning. You misrepresent nature if you concentrate on the efficient and material aspects of its causal explanation at the expense of purposive considerations.

Secondly, and more importantly for our purposes, Aristotle treats the relation of part to whole in animals' structures as being essentially teleological – animals have the parts they have in order to be able to perform the functions for which they are designed. At times, indeed, Aristotle's invocation of nature's purposiveness invites the conclusion that he does after all presuppose a Nature which consciously entertains its goals:

Nature, like an intelligent human being, always assigns each organ to something that is capable of using it. . . . the most intelligent should be able to use efficiently the greatest number of tools: and the hand appears to be not so much a single tool as a tool of tools, as it were. Thus Nature has given the tool which is most widely useful, the hand, to the creature which is capable of acquiring the greatest number of skills.   (8: *PA* 4 10, 687a19–23)

Aristotle is criticizing Anaxagoras for holding that humans are the most intelligent of creatures because they have hands: Anaxagoras, Aristotle thinks, reverses the proper teleological direction of explanation.

Aristotle is pointing to the basic fact (as we would see it) of the functional well-adaptedness of most animals; and first impressions notwithstanding, his invocation of Nature's design is only metaphorical. While he insists on numerous occasions that nature does nothing in vain (e.g., *Cael* 1 4, 271a33; *PA* 2 13, 658a9; *GA* 2 5, 741b13, etc.), that should be interpreted both as a heuristic (a highly useful one) to the discovery of function, and as a reformulation of Nature's general end-directed nature, but not as a claim regarding any consciously entertained goals.

But there remain serious difficulties standing in the way of a satisfactory account of how the different modes of explanation, mechanical-efficient on the one hand, and teleological on the other, are to be reconciled, at least in the case of non-directed teleologies. Aristotle himself seems to see no problem here: indeed, the mutual compatibility of the two types of explanation and the desirability of effecting a suitable marriage between them is a central feature of his methodological preface to *PA:* 1 1, 639b11–642b4. Moreover, he regularly asserts, in particular contexts, the compatibility and the desirability of both types of explanation. Thus deers' antlers fall off because of their weight, but the shedding is also to their advantage (*PA* 3 2, 663b12: quoted as text **12** in Chapter 5). Equally, humans have hair on their heads of necessity (because the moisture of their brains naturally produces residues that form hair), but also for the sake of protection (ibid. 2 14, 658b2–6), a passage which immediately follows the claim that nature "invariably brings about the best arrangement out of those that are possible" (ibid. 658a24). Animals' teeth fall out of necessity (since their roots are thin and easily work loose), but for the sake of the better, since they blunt easily and are then useless and must be replaced (*GA* 5 8, 789a8 ff.). And fish eggs grow after they are laid of necessity because they contain a yeasty substance, but for the sake of the better "since it is impossible for them to reach their full size in the uterus on account of their great number" (ibid. 3 4, 755a22 ff.).

But if it is indeed the case that material-efficient factors uniquely determine the production of human hair, how can its usefulness as protection be anything other than fortuitous? How, in any genuine sense, can it be for the sake of protection? If antecedent material factors necessitate (i.e., are sufficient for) a particular result, how can a final cause also play a role in the outcome, other than by being at least a necessary condition for those material factors themselves?[20] But the latter option, at least in non-intentional cases,[21] does not appear to very attractive. What real explanatory work, then, can be done by appealing to ends that is not already done by the simple specification of materials involved?

A teleology may of course be merely heuristic in character (as is the case when we describe a thermostat or engine-governor in teleological terms); but Aristotle's conception of the role of teleological explanation necessitates a much richer construe than that – after all, he thinks no explanation of the natural world is adequate unless it invokes the teleological dimension. So what are we adding to our picture of stags' antler-shedding by pointing to the role it fulfills in the life of the stag? Or, in the case of the generation of an organism, what is left out of account if we refer solely to the structure of the semen and the menses and their interaction? The problem, then, is how to interpret the teleological components of Aristotle's natural philosophy in such a way that they both do some real explanatory work (since Aristotle insists that final causes are causes) and do not merely collapse either into heuristics or into some modified material account.[22]

The issue is, of course, one of reduction: why, and in what sense, do Aristotelian natural purposes resist being reduced to their material components? Reductionisms come in a variety of forms. They

20 These issues are raised in Balme (1972), 79 – and see in general 76–84, 93–101, and Barnes (1975), 221–22.
21 In cases where direct intentions are involved, it clearly makes sense to say that the agent's conception of the goal figured in his acting in a certain way in order to try and bring it about – but it is worth noting that even in these cases the appeal to ends need not be an irreducible one.
22 Not everybody sees the problem that way, however. Some commentators (Wieland (1975), and Nussbaum (1978), 59–99) have tried to interpret Aristotle's teleology as being merely of the heuristic kind – on this view Aristotle merely wants to say that nature acts as if it is purposive, as though it sets up goals. But this seems inadequate to the texts as they stand: on this issue see Balme (1987c), esp. 280–81.

may be ontological: we may assert, as Anaximenes apparently did, that heat really is rarefaction, or mean molecular kinetic energy, or whatever. Or they may be methodological or theoretical (we may be concerned with whether it makes better sense to consider theories as being in some sense reducible to other, more basic theories). Aristotle is concerned to resist any form of ontological reductionism: Aristotelian final causes are themselves things in the world[23] – no merely material account of the world's structure can conceivably account for that structure. And that fact allows us to reject as an interpretative possibility one weaker sense in which our explanations might in a sense be teleological, although not irreducibly so, namely that they are more intuitively satisfactory answers to 'why' questions (since they wear their explanatory value on their sleeves, as it were); for such essentially epistemological versions of teleology are, at bottom, merely heuristic.[24]

Why, then, can we not specify properties of the purely material components of living organisms in virtue of which they develop and exhibit the structural capacities that they do? Let us turn to an important methodological passage at the beginning of Book 2 of *Parts of Animals*.

The order of generation is the opposite of that of being: things prior in generation are posterior in nature, and the primary thing is last in generation (for a house does not come to be for the sake of the bricks and stones, but they for the sake of the house). . . . Everything generated makes its generation from something and to something, namely from one principle to another, from the primary motive principle, which already has within it a certain nature, towards a form, or some other end. For instance, man begets man, a plant a plant, each from their appropriate matter. Thus matter and generation are prior in time, but the substance and form are prior in formula.

(9: *PA* 2 1, 646a25–b1)

Aristotle is discussing the various levels of matter involved in the construction of animals. At the lowest level we have the elements earth, water, air, and fire; above them lie the uniform substances composed from them; above them the non-uniform organs; and finally the creature itself (ibid. 646b2–10). But in the order of being,

23 This is well brought out by Cooper (1987), 269–74.
24 For a defence of the attribution of such a teleology to Aristotle, see Sorabji (1980), 165–66.

the fully realized form is prior to its component parts (*PA* 1 1, 640a33 ff.: this is a perfectly general Aristotelian thesis: compare *Pol* 1 1–2, 1252a1-53a38; and cf. *Met* 7 11): the parts exist for the sake of the form.

That claim can be interpreted in at least two ways. First, and more weakly, one might think (a) that the concept of a part only made sense in the context of a completed whole -- we cannot talk of parts without presupposing their contributory role to the whole of which they are parts. But that is a piece of linguistics, with no obvious immediate metaphysical implications: perhaps we cannot describe things as parts unless we implicitly refer to what they are parts of – but that does not mean we cannot refer to them at all. Aristotle clearly needs something rather stronger than that to justify any metaphysical claim about the priority of whole to part: perhaps (b) that there could not have been parts (however designated) unless there were to be the wholes of which they are parts. That is a metaphysical thesis, assigning priority in a recognizable way to the fully realized wholes (cf. *Met* 7 11). But (b), precisely because it allots a quasi-causal, genuinely explanatory role to the whole, risks falling foul of the incompatibility argument outlined above: *how* can the whole be so contributory in a non-directed teleology?

It has been suggested[25] that final causes are "irreducible potentialities for form", irreducible just in that they cannot be attributed to the matter of which things are made up. It seems clear that Aristotle needs to think something of the sort[26] – but it is quite unclear whether it can be rendered at all plausible. If suitable material-efficient conditions really do necessitate their outcomes, they must do so however they are described: the intensionality of explanation is irrelevant here. A description of those conditions which fails to mention their habitual outcomes may be explanatorily misleading, but it will not be causally false. Only if we can make sense of the notion that, had the final cause not been the way it is, then precisely these material-efficient conditions would have failed to bring about the result, does it seem as though the final cause genuinely has a role to play. Yet that is precisely what the thesis of material sufficiency denies.

25 By Gotthelf (1976).
26 *Contra* Nussbaum (1978), 55–99, and Sorabji (1980), ch. 10.

What is certainly the case is that the materials, simply placed together in a heap, will not on their own, for Aristotle, bring about the formation of complex organisms – but that is where the organizing efficient cause (in animals the semen) comes in. It is that which sets up motions in the menstrual fluid, and sets in train the complex sequence of embryological events (*GA* 2 1–2; 4 1–3). The only role finality can play here is as part of the explanatorily appropriate specification of the nature of the efficient cause (certain types of efficient cause are self-generating: man begets man, and plants, plants: **9**, above; *PA* 1 1, 640a20; cf. *Phys* 2 7, 198a27; *Met* 7 7, 1032b24). The processes of nature are, in a sense, goal-directed (we need to see how the various stages of growth and organogenesis contribute to the final functioning of the whole), but that does not require that their explanation be teleological in any strong sense.

On the other hand, it is crucial to Aristotle's account that it is form which is transmitted in the process of generation: the bringing about of a new natural substance is the creation of a new individual nature with its own internal principle of motion and change:

> when it is separated from both [its parents], the thing which has come to be must manage for itself, just like a child setting up home apart from its father: thus it requires a principle.   (**10**: *GA* 2 4, 740a6–8)

That principle must be something capable of organizing and arranging what would otherwise simply be inert matter – and it must in a sense be already there, not of course as the fully actualized individual, but as the complete and self-sufficient potentiality for the development of that individual, since there is now no other efficient cause (the father) in contact with the matter from which that individual is to be made. One may think of form in this sense as being a blueprint, akin to the genetic code embodied in the DNA, with the crucial proviso that Aristotle has no account, developed or otherwise, of the mechanical processes by which the form realizes itself – and that in itself contributes to his anti-reductionism.

But what is the relationship between individual natures and the material elements which make up animals' bodies? First of all, matter imposes constraints on what nature can achieve. Bones, which are necessary for the structural integrity of the animals which possess them, are also of necessity brittle: the stuff of which they are made cannot fail to be otherwise. Thus the matter of which animals are produced has its own necessary properties which cannot be avoided or circumvented by nature. But crucially for Aristotle, those elemental properties are not enough in themselves to account for the emergence of form: matter on its own, then, is insufficient to explain the regularity and repeatability of large-scale formal complexes such as animals. Aristotle never directly argues for this; but he no doubt regarded the failure of purely mechanistic theories, paradigmatically those of the atomists, to provide rationally satisfying accounts of such stabilities solely in terms of the basic particulate properties, as total and irremediable. Thus there is a gap between what can and should be explained in a reductionist manner on the basis of the elemental properties, and the overall explanandum; and this is a gap plugged for Aristotle by his notions of nature, form, and the final cause.

Aristotle distinguishes clearly between several senses in which things may be necessary. First, they may be absolutely and naturally necessary, such as the necessity of unimpeded heavy objects to fall; secondly, and relatedly, there is the necessity of enforced motion. But finally, and most importantly for our purposes there is the species of necessity which Aristotle describes as hypothetical. His example is the building of a wall – we cannot explain how the wall comes to be simply by referring to the properties of its materials

so that stones descend to form the foundations, while the brick rises because of its lightness, with the timber at the top since it is the lightest.

(11: *Phys* 2 9, 200a2–5; cf. *PA* 1 1, 642a1 ff.; *GC* 2 11, 337b30 ff.)

The materials are necessary for the building in the sense that it can't be constructed without them – but they do not themselves necessitate its construction. No true description of the material *as material* will be such as to entail the growth and development of complex structures from that material. Similarly, if something is to be a saw, it must be realized in a material capable of taking an edge (Aristotle thinks this restricts it to iron: ibid. 200a11 ff.), but merely producing a lump of iron will not make a saw.

But appealing to the hypothetical necessity of certain materials or types of materials is not for Aristotle an alternative to teleological

explanation – it is part and parcel of it.[27] The end in question makes
it the case that, given the physical properties of available materials,
only a small class of them can as a matter of fact be pressed into
service in realizing the end (you cannot make a saw of wool or wood:
Met 8 4, 1044a 26 ff.), but that is of course quite distinct from their
actually *necessitating* the end. Democritean atomism errs in thinking that structurally complex, regular outcomes can be accounted
for solely on the basis of the second type of material necessities; the
interplay of atoms in the void cannot provide a satisfying model for
the emergence of a structured and regular world.

Herein lies Aristotle's reason for rejecting a picture of the universe
as the macroscopic outcome of fundamentally random (although
causally determinate) microscopic processes, and consequently for
rejecting full-scale reductionism in favour of a world-picture in
which complete individuals and their form and functioning are basic
to any persuasive account of the world: no satisfying account can in
principle be given, he thinks, for the pure emergence of form from a
random background.[28] Such an account will naturally be expressed
in terms of nisus and tendency, of the development of form and the
interplay of informed substances – as such it will not lend itself to
the sort of mathematization favoured by contemporary scientific
models. Which takes us to our final topic.

THE NATURE OF ARISTOTELIAN SCIENCE: REASON AND EXPERIENCE

It is often observed that ancient science (apart from mathematical
astronomy, harmonics, and optics, and with the luminous exception of Archimedes) is in general qualitative in form, avoiding the
precision of rigorously expressed equations. Thus Aristotle will express principles of proportion (the velocity of an object moving with
its natural motion is directly proportional to its size and inversely
proportional to the resistance of the medium through which it
passes: *Phys* 4 8, 215a24 ff.: see further Chapter 5, pp. 144–148), but

27 As Cooper (1987), 253–57, emphasizes; see also Balme (1972), 79–80.
28 Strictly there are two distinct problems, one concerning the emergence
    of form, the other the maintenance of it, although since for Aristotle the
    world and its contents are (in terms of their kinds) eternal, there is no
    issue of the *original* emergence of form.

these are never fleshed out by reference to precise physical quantities. Moreover, the notion of the constant, so crucial to the modern expression of physical quantities in the form of equations, is entirely alien to the ancients.

Allied to this deficiency (as it is usually perceived) is the fact that ancient science appears, to modern eyes at least, excessively aprioristic and hence insufficiently empirical. Evidence is adduced, if at all, in a haphazard and uncontrolled fashion, with little apparent concern for the methodological niceties of the relation between theory and observational and experimental evidence. Indeed, while there are scattered reports of specifically designed experiments, there is little or no sign of any experimental *method* in ancient science at all. The extent and applicability of such objections is a matter of scholarly debate,[29] and we need to establish how far, if at all, they apply to Aristotle. Much of the succeeding chapter is concerned with this issue; but we should here at least sketch out the terrain and say a little about Aristotle's claims to being a scientific empiricist.

Aristotle regularly extols the virtues of observation. At the end of the exordium to *Parts of Animals* (*PA* 1 5), he makes a passionate plea for the seriousness and importance of biological research: it may not treat of the highest or most divine beings, but while inquiry into the latter is hampered by want of direct evidence,

concerning perishable things – plants and animals – we are much better placed, since we live among them; and anyone who wants to take sufficient trouble may grasp many things about every kind that exists.

(**12**: *PA* 1 5, 644b28–32)

We should not shrink from biological research simply because some creatures seem loathsome to us, and their internal structures repulsive (ibid. 645b15 ff, 26 ff.). And at the end of *Generation of Animals*, he takes Democritus to task for having made an unsound induction from too few instances concerning the shedding of milk-teeth: Democritus thinks that all mammals shed them, since they are formed prematurely as a result of suckling – but, as Aristotle observes, some mammals retain their original teeth:

29 Lloyd (1987), ch. 5, argues against the orthodox view that ancient science was in general insufficiently quantitative.

Democritus erred in his generalisation about this through not having examined what happens in all cases; but it is essential to do this.

(13: *GA* 5 8, 788b10–19; cf. ibid. 3 5, 765a2 ff.; 6, 756b13 ff.)³⁰

Furthermore, in a number of places (e.g., *GA* 2 4, 740a2 ff.; 5, 741b15 f.)
he asserts (not wholly accurately) that the fact that the heart is the
first organ to develop in the embryo is something which is apparent
both to reason and to the senses (he carried out some fairly detailed
observations of the development of the chicken embryo: *HA* 6 3,
561a6–562a20; see Chapter 5, pp. 162–163). That there must be some
such first organ which is then responsible for the subsequent development of the creature is, he thinks, obvious a priori; the animal has to
develop its own internal principle of change and growth soon after the
semen has set up its distinctive form-producing motions in the menstrual fluid, for only thus can the animal function independently (see
9 above). But that this first directing principle is the heart is learned
from observation, and in general theory must be adequate to the empirical data (*GA* 3 10, 760b28–33: Chapter 5, **13**).

On the other hand, Aristotelian science is often berated for its
excessive apriorism, as evidenced in such ubiquitous notions that
right is superior to left, front to back, top to bottom (*IA* 4–5,
705a26–707a5), ideas which he even tries to apply to the cosmos as
a whole (*Cael* 2 2), and in the belief that the male is superior in all
respects to the female. There can be no doubt that these assumptions did play a guiding role in his science: his entire theory of
sexual generation is predicated on the belief that the female is an
inferior form of the male, lacking his innate heat and consequent
ability to concoct blood into something with the life-inducing properties of semen; by contrast, the female supplies only the matter, in
the form of the menstrual fluid, for the offspring. And equally there
can be no doubt that they frequently led him astray:³¹ witness the
curious case of Aristotle's (admittedly tentative) postulation of the
existence of animals on the moon in order to make room for fire-
dwelling creatures to parallel those whose natural elements are

30 It should be noted, however, that some of the counter-evidence that
   Aristotle adduces here is (as a matter of empirical fact) false.
31 Lloyd (1983), 94–105, documents the cases in which Aristotle's commitment to the natural superiority of the male led him to overlook, suppress, or attempt to finesse awkward contrary evidence.

earth, water, and air (*GA* 3 11, 761b16 ff.). But if Aristotle is prone to see what he wanted and expected to see (what scientist is not to some degree?), he still insists on the vital importance of a theory's empirical adequacy, in sharp contrast with Plato's extravagant flights of geometrical fancy in the *Timaeus*.

These assumptions function in a sense as regulatory methodological principles, the most important of them being his oft-repeated refrain that nature does nothing in vain. We must seek for organization and purpose in even the most apparently unpromising natural subjects; in so doing we will be led to marvel at nature's providentiality, and be able to discern the causal links which tie natural products together:

> absence of the fortuitous and purposiveness are particularly to be found in the works of nature; and that for the sake of which they are put together, the goal for which they come to be, has its place in what is beautiful.
>
> (**14:** *PA* 1 5, 645a24–27)

The search for form and finality in nature has often been ridiculed, from Bacon onward; but it needs to be stressed that Aristotle's conception of natural teleology is by no means a naïve and jejune one: on the contrary, as has been stressed earlier, he is drawn to it among other things by what he takes to be the evident and spectacular failure of the dominant purely mechanistic paradigm of his time, Democritean atomism, to provide anything like a remotely satisfying account of how structure and regularity can emerge from what is at bottom nothing more than a buzz of atoms in the void. And even if we, with our sharper and more refined conceptual tools, can aspire to succeed where Democritus failed, nonetheless it cannot be denied that, as a methodological principle at least, the idea that nature constructs things for a purpose is heuristically valuable in what is, for Aristotle, the core enterprise of science, namely, the search for the causes and principles of things.

And that enterprise itself cannot get off the ground without factual, empirical input. In order to ask why something is the case, we need first to know *that* it is the case, and then search for the explanatory syllogism whose middle term will illuminate the fact (*An.Post* 2 1–2; cf. *Met* 7 17); and that process (at least if it is successfully carried out) will lead us ultimately to definitions of substances, real definitions, by reference to the properties expressed in which we can understand and explain the facts at issue. Moreover, the definitions themselves, being real and not merely lexical, must express the way things actually are in relation to some really existing non-arbitrary natural kind: we cannot simply sit in our armchairs and stipulate them into existence; the definitions will tell us (in the case of natural things at least) what they are and (in the case of artifacts) what they are for (*Met* 7 17, 1041a20–32). And while Aristotle's account (*An.Post* 2 19) of how we come to appreciate the definitional first principles which will yield the deductive structure of natural science is notoriously compressed and unclear, it is at least evident that the process is, in a broad sense, an empirical one: we simply come to see, as a result of repeated perceptual engagement with the form of the kinds in question, what the kinds of things are. The world presents us with the kinds it contains; this is one reason for Aristotle's insistence (in the methodological preface to *PA*) that biological classification should begin from the obvious natural divisions in things (*PA* 1 2 642b11 ff.; 1 3, 643b9 ff.). Thus, while Aristotle may on occasion be convicted of allowing his a priori presuppositions to stand in the way of properly empirical research, nonetheless he is consistent in his commitment to the methodological slogan enunciated and approved at the beginning of *PA* (1 1, 639b3 ff., 640a14 ff.), that a natural scientist should begin by grasping the phenomena, and only then proceed to try to uncover their causes.

5 Science

The previous chapter dealt with the basic structure of Aristotle's conception of science, and with its motivation. Here we turn to aspects of that structure as it is realized in practice in Aristotle's physics, cosmology, meteorology, and biology. Let us begin with the *Physics*. Having rehabilitated and analyzed the nature of change and generation in Book 1, and having explored the notions of explanation, chance, co-incidence, and necessity in Book 2, Aristotle turns to the specific problems with natural explanation which occupy most of the remainder of the *Physics*. Thus *Physics* 3–4 contains a set of essays on the related issues of Change, Infinity, Place, Void, and Time; Books 5 and 6 deal with problems of change and the continuum (Aristotle argues fiercely that space and matter must be at least potentially infinitely divisible – and hence has to counter Zeno's paradoxes: *Phys* 6 9); while Books 7 and 8 discuss the sources of motion and change. I shall here deal only very briefly with some of the issues raised.

FINITUDE, MOTION, AND NATURAL PLACE

Aristotle is, in a variety of senses, a finitist. He rejects the idea that there can be actualized infinite sets of things, including, it appears, the natural numbers (Aristotle argues that mathematicians do not require it: *Phys* 3 7, 207b28 ff.). This causes him some difficulties with time, since he holds the world to be without beginning, and hence must (in some sense) allow that there have been infinitely many days prior to this one – moreover, there must have been an infinite number of rotations of the heavenly bodies. However, "time and motion are indeed infinite, as is thought; but the parts that are

taken do not persist" (1: *Phys* 3 8, 208a20–21); there exists *now* no
infinite collection of present moments. His rejection of infinity extends to the natural world. It is impossible, he thinks, for the universe to be infinite in extent, and for it to contain an infinite amount
of matter, as the atomists hold. His reasons for this are various, but
they are intimately connected with the notion of natural places (cf.
Phys 3 5, 205b24ff.), which we shall examine below.

Nonetheless, the infinite must in a sense exist, otherwise we shall
be committed to the quantization of matter and space, which Aristotle takes to have even worse consequences:

> to suppose that the infinite does not exist in any way at all leads clearly to
> many impossible results: time will have a beginning and an end, a magni-
> tude will not be divisible into magnitudes, number will not be infinite.
>
> (2: *Phys* 3 6, 206a9ff.)[1]

Thus he allows the number-series to be in a way infinite, by intro-
ducing the notion of a potential infinity. For any number you can
always take one larger than it, although it doesn't follow for Aristotle that there must exist an actual infinite set of numbers. People
have erred, he says, in assuming the infinite to be that which includes everything – rather, the infinite is such that no matter how
much you have of it, you can always take something more (*Phys* 3 6,
206b33–207a14.; cf. 206b16ff.; *Cael* 1 5, 271b33ff.).

One reason why, for Aristotle, the universe must be finite in extent is that, were it infinite, we could make no sense of the natural
motions of things. The natural motions, discussed and justified at
Cael 1 2–4, are intimately linked with the concepts of place and of
weight and lightness. They are those motions proper to objects in
virtue of their being the type of thing (elementally) they are – all the
elements (earth, water, air, and fire) have internal, irreducible
nisuses to move toward their natural places, which are determined
absolutely: the heavy tend toward the centre of the cosmos (which
coincides, in Aristotle's cosmology, with the centre of the earth:
Cael 2 14, 296b9 ff.), while the light tend toward the extremities
(determined by the innermost of the heavenly spheres). Thus the

---

1 It would undermine geometry as well (*Cael* 1 5, 271b9ff.), presumably
  because there could, for instance, be no right-angled isosceles triangles
  (since their sides are incommensurable, yet ex hypothesi in a quantized
  world all magnitudes are commensurable).

natural place for an element will be that region of space which is closest to the defining position which is capable of containing all of the element in question: in the case of earth, a sphere of finite extent centred on the centre of the cosmos.

The elements will, other things being equal, occupy their natural places; and they will fail to move to them only if they are in some way prevented from so doing. Aristotle treats weight and lightness as being conceptually on a par – lightness is not simply the privation of weight. Rather they are both positive, albeit contrary, properties (*Cael* 3 1–2; 4 1–4), since it could not be the case that some of the defining characteristics of fire, for instance, were negative – fire cannot be that which lacks weight. Aristotle further argues that if fire moves upward by extrusion, as the atomists say, that is, simply by being forced, as the least massive object, relatively upward, then it would still have weight – but then the greater the mass of fire, the slower it should move upward, which is contrary, Aristotle thinks, to the phenomena (*Cael* 1 8, 277a33 ff.): here, then, he appeals to (admittedly controvertible) empirical evidence to refute an opponent's theory.

These internal tendencies are absolute, not relative, a fact which drives Aristotle's argument against there being a multiplicity of worlds – fire here must tend to the extremity *here*, but how could fire there behave? If it really were fire, it must have precisely the same tendencies as fire here, and hence tend to the extremities of *this* cosmos; but then, contra hypothesem, there would be only one cosmos (*Cael* 1 8, 276a18–277a12; 4 3, 310b12 ff.).

Natural motions must, for Aristotle, be simple – and there are only two (generic) kinds of simple motion, rectilinear and curvilinear (*Cael* 1 2, 268b11 ff.), of which the former has two proper species, up and down. This yields three possible basic or natural motions, to which Aristotle assigns his three most basic elements: Ether for the circular motion of the heavenly bodies, Fire for upward motion, and Earth for downward motion. Indeed, Aristotle will on occasion speak of these as the three elements. Elsewhere, however, he seeks to make conceptual room for Water and Air, the remaining two of the canonical four sublunary elements, as in some sense intermediate between Earth and Fire (although whether successfully or not is controversial).

But natural rectilinear motion must, for Aristotle, be potentially completable, that is to say, there must be some point at which the motion naturally comes to an end, which is where the object in question is naturally supposed to be: its natural place. Thus the idea of natural rectilinear motion requires that of natural place; and natural place can be made sense of only in a finite universe, since there can be no centre of an infinite space, nor, trivially, can there be an extremity to it (*Phys* 3 5, 205a19–20). Moreover, an infinite universe must contain an infinity of stuff (otherwise stuff would be infinitely rarely spread out through the cosmos, and hence could not form worlds); but then an infinite body could not have a natural motion, since there can be no differentiation between heavy and light in such a universe, and no proper distinctions of direction (ibid. 205b24–206a7).

Moreover, in *Cael* 1 5–6, Aristotle applies similar considerations to the case of the heavenly bodies. These, located above the sublunary world, are not subject to change or decay (consequently there is no real distinction of matter and form in them);[2] and they move (at least according to *de Caelo*)[3] in virtue of a natural principle of circular motion. Since circular motion is (in a sense) infinite, there is no place where they naturally come to rest, and so they continue uninterruptedly forever. But there can be no such thing as a circle of infinite radius (*Cael* 1 5, 271b26–272a7) and hence no such thing as motion in an infinite circle. Thus the heavens are limited in extent (Aristotle does not consider the possibility that the universe might be infinite in virtue of its consisting of a never-ending sequence of concentric circles).

Evidently the success of all of this turns on the intuitive acceptability of the notion of natural place; why should we believe in any such thing? Aristotle's answer is, I think, twofold. First of all, such a supposition seems plainly supported by empirical evidence: heavy things do fall, and, insofar as they are free to do so, fall on a vertical

---

2 Except in the etiolated sense that they have "topic matter," i.e., can move from place to place (*Met* 8 1, 1042a33 ff.; 6, 1045a34 ff; cf. 12 2, 1069b23–26), but this does not affect their ontological composition.

3 Elsewhere (*Met* 12 7, 1072b3 ff.), the heavenly bodies are said to move the way they do in emulation of the Prime Mover, the highest being whose example of perfect contemplative activity inspires everything else in the universe to imitate it to the best of its ability (cf. *Phys* 8 5–6, 9); I shall have nothing more to say about this aspect of Aristotle's cosmology.

trajectory toward the centre of the earth (of course this last can be known only by extrapolation – but it is a perfectly reasonable extrapolation). Similarly, fire rises, and if there is no wind, it rises straight upward; while the same goes for bubbles of air in water, and so on. And it is but a small step from these observations to the conclusion that, unless they are interfered with by some external force, natural objects will always move in accordance with these internal tendencies (thus the theory involves, albeit in a jejune way, the sort of conceptual idealization essential to all general scientific theories).

But not only does empirical evidence support the theory; the theory itself is elegant (at least at first sight), and general – it promises to account for a wide variety of phenomena on the basis of a small stock of primitive concepts. Moreover, it does not involve action at a distance (except perhaps insofar as the elements need to know which way to go: Aristotle never explains how they can do this), that supremely counter-intuitive notion which made Universal Gravitation so difficult to swallow. And that serves to underscore another aspect of Aristotle's science – it is commonsensical. It tries to explain the general structure and functioning of the world in terms of processes whose operations are evident to all; it involves no theoretical arcana. Of course, in a sense, that is what hamstrings it and prevents it from fulfilling Aristotle's own aspirations of providing a complete, and completely intelligible, guide to reality. But what is impressive, to my mind at least, is how much Aristotle is able to accomplish within his self-imposed constraints, and how cohesive that final result turns out to be.

DYNAMICS

Let us now turn from the general concepts deployed to Aristotle's particular dynamical theories. At this point it is worth quoting the main texts in full:[4]

a given weight moves a given distance in a given time; a weight which is greater moves the same distance in less time, the times being inversely

4 They are discussed more fully in Carteron (1975). [Bibliographical references: pp. 165–167.]

proportional to the weights. . . . Furthermore, a finite weight travels any finite distance in a finite time.   (3: *Cael* 1 6, 273b30–274a3)

Let A be the mover, B the thing moved, C the distance, D the time; then in the same time the same force A will move 1/2B twice the distance C, and in 1/2D will move 1/2B the whole distance C – for thus the ratio will be preserved. Again, if a given force moves a given object a certain distance in a certain time and half the distance in half the time, half the motive power will move half the object the same distance in the same time. . . . But if E moves F a distance C in a time D, it does not necessarily follow that E can move twice F half the distance in the same time. . . . in fact it may well cause no motion at all.   (4: *Phys* 7 5, 249b29–250a16)

We see the same weight or body moving faster than another for two reasons, either because there is a difference in what it moves through . . . or because, other things being equal, the moving body differs from the other owing to excess of weight or lightness. . . . A then will move through B in time C, and through D (which is less dense) in time E (if the size of B equals that of D) in proportion to the density of the impeding body.   (5: *Phys* 4 8, 215a24–b4)

Text 3 asserts a basic principle of proportionality: velocity is directly proportional to the weight of the body in motion. Aristotle is here thinking of natural motions – but what he says goes also for those he categorizes as forced, where an external agent compels a body to move. Moreover, for any body of finite weight, its velocity too must be finite. This latter claim is pressed into service repeatedly by Aristotle in his various proofs of the conceptual impossibility of a (homogeneous) body of infinite size: if such a body were to exist, then no matter how rarified it was, it would still be, in total, infinitely heavy, and hence would have to move with infinite velocity; but then consider the same infinite magnitude minus a finite proper part of itself – the resulting magnitude will still be infinite, yet it would be smaller than the original. As it is infinite, it will move with infinite velocity; yet as it is smaller than the original its velocity should be less than infinite (there being no degrees of infinity), by the proportionality principle; hence a contradiction lurks in the supposition that a body may be infinitely large. Aristotle rehearses this and corollary arguments at length in several places (*Cael* 1 6, 273b27–274a29; *Phys* 6 2, 233a32–b14; etc.).

Text 4 introduces further considerations involving motive force and marks a critical exception to the general smooth proportionalities involved. If a force of given strength S suffices to move an object of given weight W (in a given time t), then any fraction f of S will suffice to move $f.W$ (in t). And if S can move W in t, then for any n, $S.n$ will move W in t/n. But it is crucially not the case that, if S can move W in t, then for any n, S/n can move W in $t.n$. Forces have thresholds of operation – if they did not, it would be possible for a single man to haul a ship (albeit very slowly) if fifty men can haul it (*Phys* 7 5, 250a16 ff.). This latter consideration is of great importance, since it betrays the extent to which Aristotle is constrained by evident phenomenal facts. The a priori temptation to extend the proportion-principles to include decreased forces operating on the same weights must have been strong – but Aristotle resists it in the face of devastating (at least to him) empirical counter-evidence. Thus forces are not all treated as continuous and divisible magnitudes – below the threshold of operation, no force is exerted at all. But lacking (as we would see it) the notion of inertia[5] as well as adequate concepts of momentum and force, he can give no further specification of this exception to the general principles – Aristotle cannot formulate general principles of masses immovable by given forces under certain conditions, much less quantify them.

It is also worth noting that he does not differentiate between cases such as that of the ship-hauling, which we would analyze in terms of frictional impediment to the initial force, and that of a weight-lifter unable to raise a certain mass from the ground, which involves a contest between the opposing forces of gravity pulling the mass downward and the muscular force of the lifter. Moreover, Aristotle does not, as we do, think in terms of forces applying *accelerations* to masses.[6] All of these divergences are crucial in differentiating Aristotelian from modern dynamics – and they underscore the conceptual

5 At least in a modern theoretical sense: Carteron (1975), n. 41, points out that we can find "traces" of the inertial concept in Aristotle, but rightly stresses that it is simply the commonsensical empirical observation that objects once given a shove often tend to keep on moving – but certainly not (in idealized circumstances) indefinitely. Moreover, Aristotle could never in any case sufficiently effect the divorce between the notions of force and motion which the modern concept requires.

6 Aristotle is not, of course, unaware that bodies in free-fall (and free-rise) do accelerate (*Phys* 5 6, 230b21–26; *Cael* 1 8, 277a27–b8), but that acceleration is never adequately incorporated into, or explained on the basis of, his basic dynamic principles.

and explanatory inadequacies of the Aristotelian scheme, inadequacies cruelly exposed by Galileo.[7] Even so, Aristotle's principles represent a bold attempt to bring physical phenomena within the grip of generally mathematical ratios. The desire to discern order in the world, and to try to give an account of that order in at least weakly mathematical terms, is the characteristic drive behind the entire project of scientific explanation.

Text 5 adds a refinement to the picture so far discerned: the medium through which objects move will impede their progress, and that impediment itself obeys certain proportional principles. Aristotle does not, of course, go as far as to try and specify coefficients of resistance for different media – indeed, his account is merely a sketch. But it suggests room for further refinements and ways in which, by increasing the complexity of the different factors to be taken into consideration in accounting for the relative speeds of objects, to account for some of the empirical problems the theory as it stands must inevitably encounter. But that suggestion was not taken up, either by Aristotle or his successors.

Moreover, Aristotle also knows that the extent to which a given body will cut through a medium (and hence its speed in fall) is determined to some degree by its shape: broad, flat objects move less freely through water than their narrow counterparts (*Cael* 4 6, 313a14–b21), but he offers no systematic account of these phenomena beyond remarking that "bodies possessed of breadth stay where they are, because they cover a large quantity, and the larger quantity is not easily cleft [since] in every kind the smaller quantity is more fissile and easily cleft"; and this "explanation," while accounting for the propensity of certain thin metal discs to float, is powerless to explain the phenomenon Aristotle himself noted a few lines earlier, namely the buoyancy of metal dusts. In short, Aristotle is a long way from having any adequate account of the phenomena he describes – there is no hint even of any crude analogue to the concept of surface-tension in his works, and once again he assumes that phenomena which we would take to be explained by quite different physical facts (the floating of iron filings

7 Although earlier physicists had already questioned large parts of the system. Philoponus, for instance, had already established (in the 6th century A.D.) that heavier objects did not necessarily move more rapidly in free-fall.

on water, and of dust in the air) are taken to be susceptible of a unified explanation.

But even given these very real shortcomings in Aristotle's dynamics (and hydrostatics: the deficiencies of the latter were unmasked in Galileo's 1612 discourse "On Bodies that Rest in, or Float upon, the Water"), nonetheless they represent an admirable attempt to account for a variety of diverse phenomena from within an economical and (relatively) conceptually clear framework which is yet responsive to the empirical facts (indeed, as we saw, this concern with empirical adequacy is in fact responsible for some of the roughnesses of the theory), and they were not (in general) bettered for the best part of two millennia.

THE IMPOSITION OF MOTION

It is one thing to account for the relations that hold between force, velocity, and mass; it is another to explain the mechanisms by which that force is imparted, and by which the motion of objects is maintained. And, as Carteron (1975), 168–69, well brings out, because Aristotle is unable conceptually to isolate the notion of force from the substance in which it inheres, he finds himself driven toward the position that an agent can act upon its object only while it is contact with it (cf. *Phys* 7 2, where all species of motion are reduced to pushing and pulling). There can be for Aristotle no action at a distance. Furthermore, compatibly with the fundamental distinction between natural and forced motion, all motions must ultimately originate in the action of some agent for whom that action is proper and natural to it. Thus a rod may move a stone, and a man's hand move the rod; but the man's hand is moved by the man, and nothing moves him – he is a proper locus of the initiation of motion (*Phys* 8 5, 256a6–9; cf. 12–14, 22–25, 30–33); one may describe both the proximate and ultimate causes of the stone's motion as causes with no impropriety – but only the latter is properly the cause (256a9–13). Here there is no real problem with explaining the mediation of the causal activity, since every item of the chain is in contact with some other.

But what can Aristotle make of the case of projectile motion, where the activity continues after the agent has apparently stopped acting (it is worth stressing that, for Aristotle, an efficient cause of some event is, canonically at least, supposed to be operating at the time of the event)? And what is the proper analysis of the ultimate agent in the chain? I shall have little to say about the latter problem, that of the Prime Mover (or movers), for which Aristotle's argument (or arguments) is notoriously problematic (*Phys* 8 5–10; *Met* 12 7) and difficult to interpret, and is, in any case, strictly speaking outside the realm of science. But the explanation of the continued motion of projectiles once they leave the thrower's hand does demand a brief review. It is of course a case of forced motion, and as such cannot (on Aristotle's general principles) be continuous and eternal – it is consequently no problem for him that such motions ultimately come to an end. It is, however, difficult to explain why they continue at all. At *Phys* 8 10, 266b27–267a22 Aristotle confronts the problem:

if everything that moves is moved by something, how can some things which are not self-movers yet continue to move when the mover is not in contact with them, such as projectiles?   (6: *Phys* 8 10, 266b29–31)

Aristotle rejects the possibility that the agent also moves something else (the surrounding air), which then continues to impart motion to the projectile, on the grounds that this simply pushes the problem a stage back – there will still be motion in the air after the thrower's hand stops moving:

we must thus say that the first mover makes the air (or water, or whatever else can both move and be moved) such as to be able to cause motion, but that this does not cease to cause motion and to be moved at the same time, but stops being moved as soon as what moves it ceases moving, but still continues to cause motion, and so it moves something else consecutive with it. And the same thing is true for the latter. It stops in cases where the motive force engendered in the consecutive object is always less, and it comes to an end when the former can no longer make the latter a mover, but only moved.
          (7: ibid. 267a2–11; cf. *Cael* 3 2, 301b18–30; *Meteor* 2 8, 368a7 ff.)

Thus successive parcels of air are endowed with the capacity to maintain movement in the missile, but with decreasing force. This solution is ingenious (it has been unjustly derided in some quarters); Aristotle does not say (*pace* Alexander of Aphrodisias: cf. Simplicius, *Commentary on the Physics* 1347.6 ff.) that each successive parcel is made into a *self*-mover.[8] Why cannot the impetus (as a later age was to call it) simply be impressed directly into the projectile, as Philoponus was to hold? Perhaps because Aristotle thought that the material of the projectile was not of the appropriate type to be a motion-causer, unlike air and water.[9] Force, then, is not something that any and every body is fitted to receive (except insofar as they have elemental motive tendencies – the projectile, after the exhaustion of the force in its intermediate movers, can still fall downward).[10] Rather, certain bodies have an innate tendency to receive the motion-causing capacity, which they can then impart to others.

THE STRUCTURE OF THE PHYSICAL WORLD

We have already seen, in brief, how Aristotle conceived of the Universe as a sequence of concentric spheres, the outermost containing the heavenly bodies being composed of an incorruptible and immutable element he called "ether" whose natural motion is circular. The astronomical system he adopted was basically that of Eudoxus, the great mathematician of the Academy who had shown how it was possible to "save the appearances" of the apparently randomly moving planets by viewing their behaviour as the product of superimposed uniform spherical motions. Eudoxus's scheme was purely mathematical – Aristotle, however (in contrast with the majority of instrumentally minded astronomers down to Copernicus), attempted to give the structure a physical interpretation which involved the postulation of counter-spheres interposed between the spheres of the

8 Which would multiply difficulties elsewhere in the account: self-movers are such as to be the cause of their own motion and rest, so if something is made into a self-mover, it will continue to possess the capacity for initiating motion in itself and other things, as a human being does, at least as long as it retains its substantial form; cf. Carteron (1975), n. 38.

9 This raises further questions, such as why should air be a more suitable motion-causer than the projectile itself? Perhaps because we can see, in other circumstances, air (in the form of wind) doing work. This is as it stands inadequate, but I cannot pursue the issue here.

10 There is no reason to assume, however, as some unsympathetic critics have done, that Aristotle is committed to the view that the projectile moves laterally until the impressed force is exhausted, and only then begins to fall.

Science

heavenly bodies in order to balance their forward motions, and to explain how a sequence of nested spheres need not become progressively more and more rapid the further into the sequence one goes (the most detailed, albeit still sketchy, account is given at *Met* 12 8). Thus, for Aristotle, the heavens are a physical system of interlocked spheres, held together and moving like a vast astrolabe under the power of their own inherent, natural, never-ending circular nisus.

Of more interest from our point of view, however, is Aristotle's account of the structure and explanation of phenomena in the sublunary world of change and decay, which is largely to be found in his *Meteorologica*. *Meteorologica*, as its name suggests, is concerned with atmospheric phenomena – but not exclusively so. Book 4 presents, in part at least, Aristotle's theory of chemical combination, and has more in common with *GC* 2, a fact that was already noticed in antiquity.[11] It is worth briefly reviewing some aspects of the theory contained in these books, as it represents a refinement upon the traditional four-element physical chemistry adopted by Aristotle elsewhere. First of all, primary now are the four qualities Hot, Cold, Wet, and Dry (*GC* 2 2, 329b17–330a29): and the four elements are composed of combinations of them (Earth = Cold/Dry, Water = Cold/Wet, Air = Hot/Wet, Fire = Hot/Dry: *GC* 2 3). These primary "powers" (*dunameis*), as Aristotle sometimes (e.g. *PA* 2 1, 646a14–15) prefers to call them, are themselves the basis of further physical properties, such as heaviness and lightness, condensation and rarefaction, roughness and smoothness (ibid. 646a18–21), as well as others such as malleability, ductility, and brittleness (*Meteor* 4 8–9).

Aristotle's theory is thus reductive; moreover, he distinguishes between the pairs Hot/Cold and Wet/Dry on the grounds that the former are active principles involved in change, while the latter merely form the passive substrate (*Meteor* 4 1, 378b10–27) in which the change takes place. The elements (earth, etc.) are the first level of actual ontological existence (there being no such thing as the Hot in separation), although even then the actual physical stuff we call earth is itself a compound of elemental Earth and Water (*GC* 2 3, 330b22–30). Cold is responsible for solidifying and compacting objects, Heat sometimes for their solidification and sometimes for

11 And has led some moderns to question its authenticity, albeit on insufficient grounds: see Düring (1944), 19–22.

their dissolution, according to whether they are uniform or non-uniform in character.

While it is undeniable that this scheme involves a priori elements, nonetheless Aristotle's willingness to abandon strict parallelisms and contrarieties (e.g., in the case of Heat's dual action by contrast with that of Cold) indicates the extent to which he strives to make the theory at least compatible with empirical phenomena – it is of course a fact that heat solidifies some things (clay, for example: *Meteor* 4 7, 384b19ff.; 9, 385b9). Moreover, Aristotle's theory attempts to give the causes for the various distinctive chemical and physical changes in terms of the basic properties of the basic elemental constituents, whether singly or in combination; and he develops a clear conception of the difference between real combination (which occurs in the formation of uniform parts) and mere juxtaposition or mixture (*GC* 1 10; 2 7; cf. *Sens* 3, 440a31–b25), even if his conceptualization of such a distinction is quite different (necessarily so, given his continuous physics) from our own. Furthermore, his view that solidification and liquefaction are the two basic chemical processes leads to the conclusion that there are, properly speaking, only two states of matter, solid and liquid, a fact which causes him serious problems in his discussion of phenomena that we would classify as gaseous, the so-called "exhalations," a fact which leads us naturally to the earlier portion of *Meteor*, where the exhalations play a critical role.

In *Meteor* 1–3 Aristotle deals with, in order: meteors (*Meteor* 1 4), the Aurora Borealis (1 5), comets (1 6–7), the Milky Way (1 8), rain, cloud, and mist (1 9), dew and hoar-frost (1 10), snow (1 11), hail (1 12), winds, rivers, and springs (1 13), climatic and coastal changes (1 14), the source and saltiness of the sea (2 1–3), winds again (2 4–6), earthquakes and volcanoes (2 7–8), thunder and lightning (2 9), hurricanes (3 1), haloes (3 2–3), rainbows (3 4–5), and mock-suns (3 6).

That may well seem a pretty heterogeneous collection of phenomena, conflating meteorology proper with astronomy, seismology, and geology. Aristotle describes its subject-matter as

everything which occurs naturally, but in a less orderly manner than that of the first element [i.e., ether] of bodies, in the place bordering most closely on that of the motion of the stars, e.g., the Milky Way, comets, meteors, everything we assign as being common attributes of air and water, as well as the kinds, parts, and attributes of earth, from which we will examine the causes of winds and earthquakes, and whatever occurs as a result of their movements . . . , as well as the fall of thunderbolts, typhoons, firewinds, and the other recurrent phenomena which occur to their bodies as a result of condensation.   (8: *Meteor* 1 1, 338b27–339a6)

Aristotle's concern in *Meteor* is with things which, although in some sense explicable, are not part of the perfect domain of the heavenly spheres. Most such phenomena are meteorological at least in his sense, namely that they are concerned with the interrelations of air and water, since most alteration takes place in those elements. But even in cases of apparent alterations of the earth, their causes are, Aristotle thinks, to be assigned to phenomena associated with the atmosphere (*vide* his explanation of earthquakes: see p.156). Thus, first appearances notwithstanding, the collection of phenomena analysed in *Meteor* 1–3 does, at least within Aristotle's own theory, possess some considerable causal integrity.

Comets are included in the sublunary world because they exhibit little regularity, and because they apparently grow and die. Some ancients (notably the Pythagoreans: *Meteor* 1 6, 342b30–35; and the mathematician Hippocrates of Chios: ibid. 342b35–343a20) held that comets were in fact planets with very long periodicities (as some, of course, indeed are); but Aristotle rejects these views, largely on inadequate and parochial grounds (ibid. 343a21–b8). He thinks such explanations are too far-fetched to be taken seriously – which is a pity, since they are (at least partially) correct, and at least insofar as regularity is concerned respect Aristotle's own division between the immutable ether and the sublunary world of change (their growth and diminution, if more than merely apparent, of course remain obstacles from Aristotle's perspective to assigning them to the superlunary realm; but Aristotle's own account of the phenomena is in any case divided, since he holds – wrongly – that some comets apparently move in accordance with the sphere of fixed stars).

Aristotle has already (*Meteor* 1 3) elaborated his theory of the two "exhalations," hot and dry, and hot and moist,[12] which he thinks

12 Some commentators, notably Ross (1923), 109–10, think that the second exhalation, *atmis*, should be characterized as cold and moist – but this has less MSS authority. The version I choose makes one exhalation effectively comprise the air, the other the fire-sphere (cf. *GC* 2 3, 330b4), in apparent conflict with *Meteor* 1 3, 340b24–30. This conflict can, I think, be resolved.

arise from the earth, which nourish respectively the upper and lower parts of the atmosphere, the air and the fire-sphere. Aristotle is at pains here (as he is not elsewhere) to emphasize that the fire-sphere is not *literally* made of fire "for fire is an excess of heat and a kind of boiling" (ibid. 340b23); rather it is that part of the upper air (in a general sense) which is highly inflammable; it is moved by being in contact with the innermost celestial sphere (ibid. 341a2); and there is a constant interchange (the mechanics of which are never adequately specified) between the air- and fire-spheres (ibid. 341a7–9). The sun generates heat not because it is itself naturally hot (it is not made of fire), but rather by friction (ibid. 341a13–37): Aristotle remarks that "moving bodies are often seen to melt" and that "the air about something being moved by force becomes particularly hot."

Here, then, primitive observations are pressed into service in order to demonstrate the plausibility of the theory; but they do no more than that. Only if the possibility of a fiery sun has already been eliminated (as Aristotle, on the basis of his general theory of the composition of the Universe, believes it has been) need we even cast around for alternative explanations of the sun's power to heat.[13] The observations adduced in no sense *demand* the account given – at best they are weak indications of it.[14] But Aristotle is well aware of this: in a key methodological passage at the beginning of *Meteor* 1 7, he writes that "we consider that we have given an adequate demonstrative account

13 In Aristotle's defence, however, it should be observed that he does indeed *argue* for his preferred account of the structure of the Universe (in *Cael* 1 1–4 and elsewhere), and he gives reasons why the sphere of the heavens cannot be made of either fire or air: it is, by common astronomical consent, enormously greater in size than the terrestrial sphere – but then if the predominant elements were either fire or air, and these are transmutable with the other elements, then they (or whichever predominates) would simply have annihilated earth and water (*Meteor* 1 3, 339b30–340a18; cf. *GC* 2 6; *Phys* 3 5, 204b12–23). Again, crucial and questionable assumptions are made – but at the very least Aristotle is not offering his views ex cathedra – and the resulting total theory is commendable in its pretensions to completeness and general coherence.

14 The term Aristotle tends to use in these contexts for his empirical evidence, that it is a *sêmeion* or sign of the truth of the general theory, is borrowed from forensic (and medical) contexts. A sign in this sense is something that points toward the truth of a conjecture without entailing it.

of things unavailable to sensation when our account is consistent with what is possible" (9: *Meteor* I 7, 344a5–7). The phenomena (or perhaps rather the possible phenomena) do not entail the theory – they simply have to be consistent with it. That remark prefaces Aristotle's own account of comets: the "hot and dry exhalation" (i.e., the fire-sphere), which is contiguous with the innermost celestial sphere, is carried around with it, and sometimes ignites as a result of this motion (again the precise mechanics are left, perhaps deliberately, vague), causing meteors on the one hand (when the combustion is rapid) and comets on the other (when the combustion is slow and steady, and there is enough combustible material: ibid. 344a13–20). The progress of a meteor is likened to that of a flame running through a string of chaff (25–29), while "if this fire were not to run through and exhaust the fuel, but were to stand at the point where the inflammable material were densest, then the end of its progress would be the beginning of its orbit" (ibid. 344a29–32). Again, analogies from everyday experience are invoked in order to render less mysterious a remote phenomenon – and they are ingenious. They are of course of no probative value – but I do not think Aristotle envisioned them as having any. On the other hand, some of the alleged empirical data regarding the incidence of comets (notably that they are more prone to occur in windy and dry weather, which is taken to be an "indication" of their association with the hot and the dry: ibid. 344b19–25) are simply false. Aristotle's empiricism, admirable as it may be in conception, is flawed in practice, as we shall see again in biological contexts.

I have dwelt at length on a relatively small section of *Meteorologica* because I think it exemplifies the structure and method of Aristotle's scientific inquiry, and serves to point up both its strengths and its weaknesses. Aristotle is concerned with scientific explanation as a unifying phenomenon – the basic physical postulates (the five elemental types, the circular motion of the outer spheres, the existence of exhalations from the earth) are limited in number and pressed into service with much ingenuity to account for the phenomena in question (the Milky Way, for example, is explained as being a similar phenomenon to that of comets, albeit a permanent one: *Meteor* I 8). Moreover, they are supported, if weakly, by empirical observation – vapours are indeed seen to rise from the earth and the sea.

Finally, they are extended as explanatory postulates into areas which are at first sight remote from them. Aristotle's account of earthquakes, which seemed in 8 to sit rather oddly with the other phenomena, invokes the exhalations once more. Earthquakes are caused by exhalations trapped within the earth (those that escape easily are the cause of winds): *Meteor* 2 8. Aristotle is aware that certain areas are more prone to quakes than others, and attempts to account for this, consistently with his general theory, in terms of their differential geological structure. On the other hand, false "data" are also adduced and integrated into the theory: earthquakes generally occur in times of calm weather (366a5 ff), although in seasons (spring and autumn) which are prone to wind (366b2 ff.); the sun becomes misty and dim prior to them (367a22 ff.); they are likely to happen during eclipses of the moon (367b19 ff.).

I have concentrated so far on parts of the *Meteorologica* where Aristotle's accounts of the phenomena in question are, as a matter of fact, false. I shall conclude, for a variety of reasons, with a brief examination of a passage in which Aristotle's positive proposals are more successful: his account of the origins, nature, and dynamics of the sea (*Meteor* 2 2–3). It is plausible, he thinks, that the sea is in some sense the source of all water, since it is the largest bulk of that element – moreover, it is stable, unlike the rivers that flow into it. Furthermore, it surrounds the earth, albeit imperfectly, like an envelope, as the other spheres do (*Meteor* 2 2, 354b3–15);

but another difficulty stands in the way of this view: if this body is the source of all water, why is not drinkable but salt? The reason for this will constitute the resolution of this difficulty, and will ensure that our basic assumptions regarding the sea are correct.   (10: *Meteor* 2 2, 354b19–23)

The movement of the sun is responsible for periodically drawing up "the finest and sweetest" part of the water each day (cf. *Meteor* 1 9),[15] leaving the heavier brine behind (*Meteor* 2 2, 354b28–33, 355a33–35, 355b19); the whole system is self-regulating, and an equal amount of water evaporates from the sea as flows into it, although the evaporation is less perceptible than the inflow since it takes place across the entire surface of the water (355b21–33); and

15 Cf. the Hippocratic *Airs, Waters, Places*, with which much of *Meteor* may be fruitfully compared, ch. 8; once again, no mechanical explanation for its action is essayed.

Plato's *Phaedo* (111c ff.) theory that waters flow both in and out of the earth is shown to be both unnecessary and explanatorily inadequate (*Meteor* 2 2, 355b33–356a34).

The next chapter takes up the issue of the sea's saltiness.[16] If the Universe is eternal (as Aristotle believes) then the sea must always have been there. Consequently, those theories which hold that the world is gradually drying out must be false, and hence the hydrological system of the world must be (in its broad outlines) stable (*Meteor* 2 3, 356b4–357a3). Aristotle proceeds to examine and find wanting various theories of the sea's saltiness (including Empedocles' "poetical metaphor" that the sea is "the sweat of the earth": (ibid. 357a25–28, which he tartly dismisses as "not conducive to understanding"). Aristotle's preferred explanation involves, unsurprisingly, the exhalations, in this case the dry one (ibid. 357b24–26), and the general claim that residues are salty (ibid. 358a3–12). "Something similar," Aristotle alleges, "occurs in combustion: what the heat does not master, which in bodies becomes residue, in combustibles becomes ash" (ibid. 12–14). Thus residues (such as sweat and urine) are by nature salty; the dry exhalation is such a residue; and it mixes with the moist in clouds, and subsequently falls as rain, containing salt (16–25). And this process ensures that the sea is continually becoming more salty, since the salt part is left behind, a fact which Aristotle claims to have observed experimentally (ibid. 358b16–18).

This is a remarkable mélange of pointed observation and theoretical fancy, of partially correct solutions to problems vitiated by wholly false accounts of their mechanism and explanation: as such, it is typical of Aristotle's science. Before turning to his biology, let us briefly consider a passage appended to this discussion, and intended in support of it:

that saltiness consists in a mixture of something is clear not only from what has been said, but also [from the fact that] if someone places a jar made of wax in the sea, having bound its mouth so as to prevent the sea getting in, the water which percolates through the wax walls becomes fresh: for the earthy part which causes the saltiness in the mixture is separated off as though by a filter. This is also the cause of its weight (for brine weighs more

16 On this passage see Bourgey (1975), 177–78, for a sage and sane assessment of Aristotle's aims and achievements here.

than fresh water), and of its density; for their densities vary so much that vessels laden with the same weight almost sink in rivers but ride well at sea and are seaworthy. . . . An indication that the mass of a mixed substance is denser is that whenever one makes water highly salty by mixing salt with it, eggs will float on it.   (11: *Meteor* 2 3, 358b34–359a14)

That passage reports acute observations and two experiments, or sketches for them. Each is well designed in the sense that were things to turn out experimentally as alleged, they would be extremely strong evidence for the truth of the contentions they are intended to support. The second, of course, is true. But the first is empirically quite false – wax cannot act as a filter of this sort.[17] For all that, Aristotle was proud of it: he repeats the claim at *HA* 8 2, 590a22–27.

THE NATURE OF ARISTOTLE'S BIOLOGY

That makes a pleasing – if adventitious – bridge to my last subject. Aristotle wrote more about biological matters than about any other science; and he collected a vast dossier of material on the peculiarities (and resemblances) of different animal species, as well as reflecting theoretically on the appropriate ways to classify them in order to be able better to explain their structures. And those explanations are, for Aristotle, at least in part teleological: Aristotle insists throughout his biology that efficient, material, and final causes must all be taken into account in the course of giving a complete explanation of things (see Chapter 4, pp. 120–122). Consider the shedding of stags' antlers:

deer are the only animals in which the horns are solid throughout, and are also the only animals to shed them, on the one hand for the sake of the advantage gained by the increased lightness, but on the other hand from necessity because of their weight (12: *PA* 3 2, 663b12–15)

PA 3 2, from which 12 is excerpted, is in effect a short essay on the relationship between horns, teeth, claws, and various other features of animals (notably their size and speed). The argument is

17 It is hard to determine what Aristotle is thinking of here – wax jars are hardly everyday objects; indeed, it is difficult to see how you could construct a jar from wax. Moreover, I know of no material suitable for jar-construction which does have such filtering properties.

function-driven: these things are required by animals for defence. Horns are restricted to viviparous animals (ibid. 662b26); and among these no many-toed creature has horns, since nature has already supplied them, in the form of claws and teeth, with adequate weaponry (ibid. 662b29 ff.). Even so, Aristotle recognizes that in some cases horns are useless (nature already having provided their owners with other means of defence) and even a disadvantage (PA 2 16, 659a19; 3 2, 663a11; 4 12, 694a20); and here he invokes material factors to account for their existence. Horns occur only in large animals, in which heavy, earthy materials predominate (PA 3 2, 663b24 ff.), indeed are available in excess – but Nature makes use of that excess to furnish them with means of defence (ibid. 663b30 ff.). In cases where the excess does not go to make horns, it produces either tusks or extra teeth: "thus it is that no animal that has horns also has front teeth in both jaws" (ibid. 663b34–664a11).

Thus nature is circumscribed in what it can achieve by material constraints, but within those constraints it always strives to produce the best available design-solution. How it does so is not Aristotle's concern – he does not seek a mechanism by which natural forces could contrive (for the most part) such beneficial ends, as modern biologists do in the combination of random genetic mutation and natural selection. Rather, he expressly eschews such a possibility by making nature itself, in the role of the formal and final causes, an irreducible part of the explanatory system of the world.[18] Matter itself cannot effect results, being ultimately inert: it needs something else in order to amount to anything.

In the case of animals, that extra something is the form that is injected into the matter of the female menses by the male sperm: GA is devoted in large part to the detailed working-out of the theory that the male supplies form in the semen, while the female supplies the embryological matter, and to anticipating and answering objections to it, as well as to the refutation of other popular theories of the time, notably that of pangenesis, part of whose refutation takes the form of pointing out that acquired

18 See on these issues Gotthelf (1976); Balme (1987a); Cooper (1987); Sorabji (1980), ch. 10; for a general discussion of the relationship between teleology and mechanism, see Hankinson (1989).

characteristics are not in general inherited (*GA* 1 17–18).[19] Crucial among the observable facts for which Aristotle's theory must show that it can account is that of the inheritance of characteristics from both sides of the family, and for throwbacks, and Aristotle devotes much ingenuity to the task of showing how offspring can resemble their mothers (*GA* 4 3). The role of the semen is essentially to limit, determine, and mould the otherwise indeterminate tendencies of the raw material (*GA* 2 1; 2 3; 2 4, 740b29–741a3; 4 4, 772a2–35; 4 10, 778a6–9). Aristotle is here following a Platonico–Pythagorean tradition of treating matter as essentially indeterminate, requiring the quantitative and qualitative definition given to it by form (cf. *Met* 7 3, 1029a7–30), but he goes much further than any of his predecessors in his attempt to put flesh on that skeletal notion, and to turn it into a theory capable of essaying an explanation of the complex and mysterious processes involved in the transmission and sustenance of life.

It is worth remarking in passing, however, that one of the pieces of supposed empirical support for his view that the male supplies only form and no matter in generation is his belief that insects copulate by the female inserting a part into the male, and not vice versa (*HA* 5 8, 542a1 ff.). Why he should have thought this (utterly false) claim should support that account is utterly obscure; but apart from that, he describes it (again utterly falsely) as being easily observable (*GA* 1 16), a fact which prompts two related questions: (1) How empirical was Aristotle's biology? and (2) How far are reports of "observations" moulded by prior commitments to theory?[20]

OBSERVATION AND ERROR

Let us return to the raw material of Aristotle's biology, the observations recorded in *HA*, and to a lesser extent in the other zoological

---

19 He also argues that pangenetic theories cannot account for the facts of resemblances because those facts are essentially matters of morphology, not simply of there being the appropriate sort of matter available (e.g., granted that my nose-matter comes originally in embryo from my father's nose, what can account for my having inherited its distinctive and impressive Roman profile?).

20 These issues have already been broached in the Chapter 4.

treatises. Not, as we have seen, that this means abandoning the theoretical – Aristotle's observations are, in a sense, theory-driven. On the other hand there is little doubt that he at least made the effort to observe and record the peculiarities of animal species in an objective and unprejudiced manner; on occasion, however, he falls short of his ideal and is sometimes too credulous in his acceptance of tall travellers' tales. For example, he records that an animal known as the *bonasos* (usually translated "European bison") is able to defend itself by ejecting its own coruscating dung over large distances, as well as building protective stockades of excrement "which it can eject in prodigious quantities" (*HA* 9 45);[21] and this is not an isolated instance – in the discussion of animals' defence equipment at *PA* 3 2, 663a14–16, Aristotle once more draws attention to the bison's defensive offensiveness.[22] Equally, he thinks that camels have a severe incest-taboo, telling a story of a camel-keeper who was bitten to death by an enraged male upon its discovering that it had been duped into mating with its mother (*HA* 9 47). Less anecdotally, recall the error regarding insect-copulation.

Aristotle is aware of the possibility of parthenogenesis (*GA* 2 5, 741a32 ff.), although he reserves judgment on the issue, acknowledging a lack of reliable data – the most he is prepared to say is that in some cases no male of a species has yet been identified, and he is well aware that that, on its own, is not conclusive. Congruently, while devoting a great deal of time to studying and reporting the habits of bees (*HA* 5 21–22; 9 40, 623b7–627b22), he frankly admits that the data he has gathered are insufficient to prove his contentions concerning their generation (*GA* 3 10, 760b29 ff.: in fact he thinks, wrongly, that they reproduce asexually). But it is worth reproducing his closing remarks as testimony to his admirable circumspection (as well as his commitment to empiricism):

as far as theory [*logos*] and what seem to be the facts about them are concerned, this seems to be how things stand with regard to the generation of

21 The authenticity of the late books of *HA* has been doubted, but not, I think, with good reason, apart from the case of Book 10.
22 David Balme, however, writes: "I confess I was still blaming Aristotle for swallowing the story about buffaloes projecting their dung at enemies, until in 1983 I saw a picture on television of hippopotamuses doing just that" (Balme (1987b), 17); I am not sure that is much of a vindication of Aristotle, however.

bees. But the facts have not been sufficiently ascertained, and if ever they are, then perception must be believed over theories, and theories only so long as they show themselves in agreement with the phenomena.

(13: *GA* 3 10, 760b28–33)

Perhaps Aristotle's most influential mistake was his theory of spontaneous generation. Aristotle held that some species do not reproduce themselves at all, but are rather perpetuated when fortuitous material circumstances occur (*HA* 5 1, 539a23 ff.): all testaceans, he thinks, come into being this way (*HA* 5 15; *GA* 1 23, 731b9 ff.; 3 11, 763a25–b7; etc.), as do anemones and sponges (*HA* 5 16), the grey mullet (*HA* 5 11, 543b18), and eels (*HA* 6 16; *GA* 2 5, 741a38 ff.: this view persisted into the 19th century). Here again he has been misled by the evidence – but it is important that his idea is indeed based upon evidence: he can find no trace of reproductiveness in the species in question, and hence infers, reasonably (if falsely), that they do not reproduce (in the case of eels at least his observations were accurate: eels do not develop reproductive organs until their migration to the Sargasso Sea). Equally, his view that the testicles are not (directly) essential to sperm-production (*GA* 1 3–4), and hence fertility, is bolstered by his belief that recently castrated bulls are still capable of impregnating cows (*GA* 1 4, 717b3 ff; *HA* 3 1, 510b3). And while he dismisses as being "silly and extremely wrongheaded" the view that hyenas may have both male and female genitalia (a view no doubt deriving reasonably from the correctly observed fact that the female spotted hyena has a peniform clitoris: Peck (1942) 565–66), he correctly notes that the striped hyena "has beneath its tail a line similar to the female genitalia" (*GA* 3 6, 757a2 ff.).

Yet his treatises abound with examples of accurate and detailed observation. He noticed, for example, the hectocotylization of one of the octopus's tentacles, and guesses at its function (*HA* 4 1, 524a3–20), a phenomenon not rediscovered until the last century; and he was aware of the fact that certain fish were externally viviparous, the embryo being attached to the parent by a cord, notably the "smooth dogfish" (a kind of selachian: *HA* 6 10, 565b1 ff.; cf. ibid. 565a4 ff.), again a set of observations not repeated (and vindicated) until the 1840s.

He was particularly interested in the differential development of eggs – and it is in this context that he reports a famous sequence of observations of the different states of development of the eggs of a domestic hen on each day after laying until hatching (*HA* 6 3, 561a6–562a20). The observations are carefully done and recorded; yet this is not the description of anything that would count for us as an experiment, since it involves no mechanism of control. What we have, once more, is intelligent and directed observation. Elsewhere, he describes the effects of gentle heating on egg whites and egg yolks (*HA* 6 2, 560a20–b3; *GA* 3 1, 752a1–8): first, the different whites agglomerate into a single albumen (and similarly with the yolks), and then the white hardens, while the yolk becomes runnier.[23] That is an experiment of sorts, but the conclusion Aristotle draws from it (that yolk and white differ in their innate heat), is patently under-determined by the data presented.

One other case illustrates this tendency to interpret experimental data in the light of a preconceived theory. Aristotle is extremely interested in the role and function of the heart: he repeatedly claims, not quite accurately, that it is the first organ to develop in the embryo (*Juv* 468b28; he says he observed it in the egg experiment), and relates this to his view of the heart as the primary bodily organ (*PA* 3 4, 666a18–24), a view partly at least arrived at by a priori means:

thus in embryological development, all the parts are present in a way potentially, but the first principle has made the most progress, and for this reason the heart is the first organ to be distinguished in actuality. This is evident not only to the senses (for things are actually thus) but also to reason.

(**14:** *GA* 2 4, 740a2–6)

Aristotle's view is certainly based upon direct observation; but the conclusion he draws – that the heart is the seat of sensation, cognition, indeed life itself – far outruns its empirical, evidential base. Questions (1) and (2), then, demand nuanced, not to say ambivalent, answers. On the one hand, Aristotle goes further than any of his predecessors in the pursuit of hard empirical data, in line with his own methodological precept of collecting "first the phenomena, then the causes" (*PA* 1 1, 639b8–11; 640a14–15), and his uncompromising call to overcome whatever natural distaste careful examination of animals' insides may occasion, and to get one's hands dirty in the cause of science (*PA* 1 5); but he is also, no less than his Hippocratic and pre-Socratic predecessors, prone to hasty generalization

23 See Bourgey (1975), 180: Bourgey describes this and examples like it as "real experiments."

from insufficient evidence despite the warnings he himself issues against it (*GA* 5 8, 788b10–19: Chapter 4, text 13; cf. ibid. 3 5, 765a2 ff.; 6, 756b13 ff.).

Finally I should say a few words about Aristotle's classificatory practice in the difficult cases, cases where, in his own terms, animals equivocate or are ambivalent between one genus and another.[24] One example of such a species is the seal: it is by nature a land animal, yet spends most of its time in the water (*HA* 6 12, 566b26–567a12). Aristotle is of course struck by the fact that seals are mammals, and yet, unlike most of their kind, they do not live on land: they are, he thinks (in a sense rightly), imperfect quadrupeds (*HA* 2 1, 498a31 ff.). They may therefore be expected to exhibit peculiarities – and Aristotle searches for them with diligence. Thus they have no ears, in common with other marine mammals like whales and dolphins (*HA* 1 11, 492a27 ff.). But Aristotle does not merely note these peculiarities – he tries to account for them in terms of the constraints imposed upon them by nature in the form of their chosen habitat. Whales and dolphins do not have gills (and hence cannot breathe under water); but they are supplied instead with blow-holes, which enable them, although basically of mammalian morphology, to live in the sea (*PA* 4 13, 697a15–b14). Let me close by quoting Aristotle's account of a particularly severe taxonomical problem-case, the Libyan ostrich:

> it has some of the attributes of a bird, some of a quadruped. It differs from a quadruped in being feathered, and from a bird in being incapable of flight, and in having feathers which resemble hair and are useless for flight. Again, it agrees with quadrupeds in having upper eyelashes, and the parts around the head and the upper section of the neck are bare, so that its eyelashes are more hairy; but it agrees with birds in being feathered in all its hinder parts. Moreover, it resembles a bird in being a biped, and a quadruped in having a cloven hoof – for it has hooves, not toes. The explanation for these peculiarities resides in its bulk, which is that of a quadruped rather than a bird, since in general a bird must be of small size (for a massive body can only with difficulty be raised aloft).   (**15:** *PA* 4 14, 697b14–26)

That passage epitomizes both the strengths and the weaknesses of Aristotle's classificatory biology.

24 On equivocation, or "dualizing" (as he prefers to call it), see Lloyd (1983), 44–53.

CONCLUSIONS

What, then, are we to make of Aristotle the scientist? Different
people have championed violently different assessments: I can do no
better than to quote the opening lines of the entry on the subject in
Medawar and Medawar (1983), 26–27:

"Aristotle 'was a man of science' in the modern sense. He was a careful
collector and observer of an enormous range of facts . . . much of his work is
still regarded with respect by scientists who care to study it." Those two
sentences by the humanist Goldsworthy Lowes Dickinson betray an almost
majestic incomprehension of the character of science and of Aristotle's
influence on science in the modern sense,

an influence which the Medawars take (in Baconian fashion) to be
entirely pernicious. Later, after indulging in a little knockabout fun at
the expense of Aristotle's less impressive observations and claims,
they remark that "the biological works of Aristotle are a strange and
generally speaking rather tiresome farrago of hearsay, imperfect observation, wishful thinking, and credulity amounting to downright gull-
ibility," and conclude, "we do not believe that anyone who decides
not to read the works of Aristotle the biologist will risk spiritual
impoverishment."

Whiggish, hindsight judgments of that sort are easy to make; and
no doubt people like Lowes Dickinson have gone overboard in their
praise for Aristotle's achievement. But we must not lose sight of the
fact that Aristotle was a man of his time – and for that time he was
extraordinarily perspicacious, acute, and advanced. Whatever their
failings as "science" (construed in a 20th-century manner), his scientific treatises are among the most remarkable products that the history of natural investigation has ever produced: and anyone who
does not appreciate that is spiritually impoverished indeed.

BIBLIOGRAPHICAL REFERENCES

Balme, D.M. 1961. "Aristotle's Use of Differentiae in Biology." In Mansion,
    ed., 1961; reprinted in Barnes, Schofield, and Sorabji, eds., 1975; Gotthelf
    and Lennox, eds., 1987.
———. 1972. Aristotle's de Partibus Animalium I and de Generatione Ani-
    malium I. Oxford.

————. 1980. "Aristotle's Biology Was Not Essentialist." *Archiv für Geschichte der Philosophie* 62, 1–12; reprinted in Gotthelf and Lennox, eds., 1987.

————. 1987a. "Teleology and Necessity." In Gotthelf and Lennox, eds., 1987.

————. 1987b. "The Place of Biology in Aristotle's Philosophy." In Gotthelf and Lennox, eds., 1987.

Barnes, J. 1969. "Aristotle's Theory of Demonstration." *Phronesis* 14, 123–52; reprinted in Barnes, Schofield, and Sorabji, eds., 1975.

————. 1975. *Aristotle's Posterior Analytics*. Oxford (2nd rev. ed., 1993).

————. 1981. "Proof and the Syllogism." In Berti, ed., 1981.

————. 1982. *Aristotle*. Oxford.

Barnes, J., Schofield, M., and Sorabji, R.R.K., eds. 1975. *Articles on Aristotle Volume 1: Science*. London.

Barnes, J., Mansfeld, J., and Schofield, M. eds. Forthcoming. *The Cambridge History of Hellenistic Philosophy*. Cambridge.

Berti, E., ed. 1981. *Aristotle on Science: The Posterior Analytics*. Proceedings of the VIII Symposium Aristotelicum. Padua.

Bourgey, L. 1975. "Observation and Experiment in Analogical Explanation." In Barnes, Schofield, and Sorabji, eds., 1975.

Carteron, H. 1975. "Does Aristotle Have a Mechanics?" In Barnes, Schofield, and Sorabji, eds., 1975.

Cooper, J. 1982. "Aristotle on Natural Teleology." In Schofield and Nussbaum, eds., 1982.

————. 1985. "Hypothetical Necessity." In Gotthelf, ed., 1985.

————. 1987. "Hypothetical Necessity and Natural Teleology." In Gotthelf and Lennox, eds., 1987.

Düring, I. 1944. *Aristotle's Chemical Treatise: Meteorologica Book IV*. Göteborg.

————. 1961. "Aristotle's Method in Biology." In Mansion, ed., 1961.

Frede, D. 1985. "Aristotle on the Limits of Determinism: Accidental Causes in *Metaphysics* E 3." In Gotthelf, ed., 1985.

Gotthelf, A. 1976. "Aristotle's Conception of Final Causality." *Review of Metaphysics* 30, 226–54; reprinted with additions in Gotthelf and Lennox, eds., 1987.

Gotthelf, A., ed. 1985. *Aristotle on Nature and Living Things*. Bristol.

Gotthelf, A., and Lennox, J.G., eds. 1987. *Philosophical Issues in Aristotle's Biology*. Cambridge.

Hankinson, R.J. 1989. "Galen and the Best of All Possible Worlds." *Classical Quarterly*. 39, 206–27.

————. Forthcoming. "Causation and Explanation." In Barnes, Mansfeld, and Schofield, eds., forthcoming.

———. Forthcoming. "Determinism and Indeterminism." In Barnes, Mansfeld, and Schofield, eds., forthcoming.

Hussey, E. 1983. *Aristotle's Physics, Books 3 and 4*. Oxford.

Kahn, C.H. 1985. "The Place of the Prime Mover in Aristotle's Teleology." In Gotthelf, ed., 1985.

Lennox, J.G. 1987. "Divide and Explain." In Gotthelf and Lennox, eds., 1987.

Lloyd, G.E.R. 1979. *Magic, Reason, and Experience*. Cambridge.

———. 1982. *Early Greek Science: Thales to Aristotle*. London.

———. 1983. *Science, Folklore, and Ideology*. Cambridge.

———. 1987. *The Revolutions of Wisdom*. Berkeley.

———. 1991. *Methods and Problems in Greek Science*. Cambridge.

Mansion, S., ed. 1961. *Aristote et les problèmes de méthode*. Proceedings of the II Symposium Aristotelicum. Louvain.

Matthen, M. 1987. "Individual Substances as Hylomorphic Complexes." In Matthen, ed., 1987.

Matthen, M., ed. 1987. *Aristotle Today*. Edmonton.

Nussbaum, M.C. 1978. *Aristotle's 'de Motu Animalium'*. Princeton.

Owen, G.E.L. 1961. "*Tithenai ta phainomena*." In Mansion, ed., 1961; reprinted in Barnes, Schofield, and Sorabji, eds., 1975.

Peck, A.L. 1942. *Aristotle: Generation of Animals*. London/Harvard: Loeb Classical Library.

Pellegrin, P. 1986. *Aristotle's Classification of Animals*, trans. A. Preus. Berkeley.

———. 1987. "Logical Difference and Biological Difference: The Unity of Aristotle's Thought." In Gotthelf and Lennox, eds., 1987.

Schofield, M., and Nussbaum, M.C., eds. 1982. *Language and Logos*. Cambridge.

Solmsen, F. 1960. *Aristotle's System of the Physical World*. New York.

Sorabji, R.R.K. 1980. *Necessity, Cause, and Blame*. London.

———. 1988. *Matter, Space, and Motion*. London.

Wieland, W. 1975. "The problem of teleology." In Barnes, Schofield, and Sorabji, eds., 1975.

STEPHEN EVERSON

6   Psychology

To pillage even Aristotle's psychological writings in search of a theory of the mind is to run an obvious risk of anachronism. Although they contain discussions of many of the staple topics of contemporary philosophy of mind – such as perception, memory, belief, thought and desire – there is still reason for caution. His subject matter in the *De Anima* and the collection of shorter works known collectively as the *Parva Naturalia* is the nature of the *psuchê* (plural: *psuchai*) and its capacities – and so, although in a certain technical sense of "psychological" they can be said to contain his psychological theory, it is not obvious that they also articulate his theory of the mind.

To attribute such a theory to someone is already to suggest his acceptance of a particular view of the taxonomy of science, according to which certain creatures are naturally marked out in virtue of enjoying consciousness and intentionality. The subject matter of Aristotelian "psychology," however, is demarcated in a quite different way from that studied by the contemporary psychologist. While the latter focuses on conscious and intentional states, Aristotle is rather concerned to give an account of all those activities which are characteristic of living things. It is no accident that the biological works as well as the more obviously psychological treatises contain material which is important for understanding Aristotle's theory of the *psuchê*. What determines the scope of his psychology is not the recognition of a distinction to be drawn between the mental and the physical, but rather that between the living and the dead. Since the states and events which concern the contemporary psychologist are indeed characteristic of living creatures, they will also interest the Aristotelian psychologist – but so, however, will growth and nutrition. A theory which includes, and requires, an explanation of the behaviour of plants cannot be straightforwardly classed as a psychological theory.

Important as it is to take note of these considerations, it is also important not to be bounced by them into the thought that it is merely anachronistic to attempt to elicit an Aristotelian theory of the mind from his work. Certainly, they prevent one from identifying the *psuchê* and the mind and leave Aristotle without a term to denote the latter – but one does not need to believe in the existence of minds in order to produce a theory of the mind, otherwise the vast majority of contemporary psychologists and philosophers of mind would also be barred from this. To say that something has a mind is to say no more than that it has thoughts or sensations, and a theory of mind is just a theory of these. In attempting a theory of the *psuchê*, Aristotle is implicitly committed to providing a theory of mind: while Aristotelian "psychology" may not be a theory of the mind, it must include such a theory. To be complete, it must provide an explanation of all the capacities which are possessed by living things – hence Aristotle's discussions of nutrition and respiration – and so it must include an account of those capacities which are possessed by humans. In providing an analysis of perception and belief, thought and desire, which is such as to furnish the materials for the explanation of human (and animal) behaviour, Aristotle is engaged in psychological enquiry in a quite straightforward sense. It would be senseless to acknowledge that he provides an analysis of cognition and desire as part of an attempt to explain human behaviour and yet doubt whether he offers a theory of the mind.

Where the fact that Aristotle's theoretical interest is focused on the *psuchê* rather than the mind should lead to interpretative caution is when we come to attribute explanatory intentions to him. Contemporary philosophical psychology is dominated by the concern to show how material substances can enjoy consciousness and intentionality. This is natural enough when the subject matter of psychology is precisely identified as such in virtue of its involving consciousness or intentionality. Aristotle is duly concerned with the question of the relation between the *psuchê* and the body, but we cannot assume from the start that he thinks that those psychic activities which involve consciousness and intentionality present special problems, at least in this respect. To be successful in its own terms, that theory must provide an analysis of those states which feature in the explanation of human behaviour. We should not assume from the start that it will also attempt to meet the objectives of the contemporary philosopher of mind.

The interests of the psychologist, ancient or modern, are wide-ranging. Not only will he want to elucidate the general relation between the mind, or *psuchê*, and the body; he will also want to provide specific analyses of the states and events which enter into psychological explanations. A developed theory of the mind will include (among much else) theories of perception and action, belief, desire, and imagination: a theory of the *psuchê* will add accounts of nutrition and growth. I shall not attempt here to provide even an outline of what Aristotle has to say about all these topics. Rather, I shall concentrate on elucidating his basic psychological claim – that the *psuchê* is the "form" of the living body – and exploring the consequences he draws from this for what is required of psychological science. It would be neither possible nor desirable to do this without making reference to what he has to say about particular psychic capacities, but I shall not attempt any systematic exposition of his accounts of these. It is worth stressing the point that, since what Aristotle's views actually are is usually a matter of high, or at least intense, controversy, it should not be thought that my reading of a passage of text is uncontentious simply because it is given here as support for a claim which is more obviously controversial.

PSUCHÊ AS FORM

The first book of the *De Anima* is largely a prolegomenon to the exposition of Aristotle's psychology in Books II and III. *An* I.1 contains some opening reflections on the subject matter and proper method of the psychologist and then the following chapters are taken up with a critical appraisal of the claims of Aristotle's predecessors.[1] It is not until II.1 that Aristotle offers his own

1 This is not to diminish the importance of *An* I for the understanding of Aristotelian psychology. The discussion of previous accounts of the *psuchê* is very much a critical one and is revealing of Aristotle's own views, both substantial and methodological. That some translations should exclude most of Book I is very much to be deplored.

characterization of the nature of the *psuchê*. He moves into this by considering the nature of living creatures: "Every natural body which has life is a substance, and so a substance in the sense of being a composite" (412a15–16). By describing living things as "composites," Aristotle is placing them in terms of a distinction that is central to his whole metaphysics – that between different types of "substance":

There are three kinds of substance [*ousia*]: matter, which in itself is not a this; secondly, shape or form, which is that precisely in virtue of which something is called a this; and thirdly that which is compounded of both.

(412a6–9)[2]

Natural bodies, including living bodies, fall within the third class of substances: they have both form and matter. It thus makes sense to ask about any plant or animal, as of any inanimate substance, what is its form and what its matter. It turns out that to specify the form of a living substance is to cite its *psuchê*, as *psuchai* just are the forms of those natural bodies which are (potentially) alive (412a19–21).[3] Living bodies are a subclass of natural bodies and, on Aristotle's view, Greek already had a term to pick out the forms possessed by the members of that subclass – and that term was *psuchê*.

It should be noted immediately that the bodies which have *psuchai* as forms are themselves individuated substances, and each is individuated in virtue of having its *psuchê*. "Body" here is a count noun, not a mass noun. Any individual body must, in principle, be identifiable as a token of a particular *type* of thing – as, for instance, that oak or that house or that person. When Aristotle says (at 412a8–9, cited above) that it is in virtue of its form that a body is called a "this," he is recognizing that nothing is a "bare particular." Every "this" is a "this such," and the form is not the *this* but the *such* (*Met* VII.8, 1033b20f.). Every particular, that is, is a particular F or G or H or whatever, where "F", "G", "H" here stand in for such general

2 Unless specified otherwise, translations of Aristotle are adapted from J. Barnes, ed., *The Complete Works of Aristotle: The Revised Oxford Translation* (Princeton: Princeton University Press, 1984).

3 Too much stress should not be put here on the notion of potentiality: at *An* II.1, 412b25–26, Aristotle says that what is potentially living is what has a *psuchê*. To be potentially alive is consistent with being actually alive – and it may even be the case that everything which is potentially alive is actually so.

nouns as "oak," "house," and "person."⁴ To specify the form of a body is to say what kind of thing it is, and to define the form is to state what it is to be that kind of thing.

The individual body is a composite of its form and its matter and is not to be identified with either. The matter, as Aristotle says at 412a7–8, is not in itself (*kath'hauto*) a this; and, we can add, since the body is a this, the body and its matter are not identical. The "in itself" qualification here is not unimportant. In identifying a particular object, say a plant, one is thereby identifying a collection of matter, but that collection is delimited by its being the matter of a plant, by having that form, and not in virtue of its being the matter it is. The point could be put the other way round. Anything which is identified as a particular must thereby be delimited, and if it is delimited, then it will have a form. To do the work required of it in this respect, form need not be a metaphysically rich notion – the form of some objects can simply be a certain shape. The particular thing may be (to use one of Aristotle's examples) a bronze sphere, and the form of this will be a sphere or being spherical. For other objects, the form will be more complex, and its specification may, for instance, require reference to particular functions or activities.

In elucidating how the form/matter distinction is to be employed in the case of living substances, Aristotle draws a parallel between an axe and the eye:

Suppose that a tool, e.g., an axe, were a natural body, then being an axe would be its essence, and so its *psuchê*; if this disappeared from it, it would have ceased to be an axe, except in name. . . . Next, one should apply this to the parts [of the living body]. Suppose that an eye were an animal – sight would have been its *psuchê*, for sight is the substance of the eye which corresponds to the account, the eye being merely the matter of sight; when sight is removed the eye is no longer an eye except homonymously – no more than the eye of a statue or painted figure.   (412b11–22)

4 These are what are called "sortal" terms – terms which supply "a principle for distinguishing and counting individual particulars which it collects" (P.F. Strawson, *Individuals* [London: Methuen, 1959], p. 168). For contemporary discussions of these issues in an Aristotelian spirit, see especially D. Wiggins, *Sameness and Substance* (Oxford: Blackwell, 1980) and E.J. Lowe, *Kinds of Being* (Oxford: Blackwell, 1989). [See also above pp. 90–93.]

An individual axe has both form and matter. Its form is that of being an axe and, if eyes and axes are parallel, then what it is to be an axe will be to possess a certain capacity, presumably that of chopping (or cutting, cf. 412b28). Whatever something is which is not able to be used for chopping things, it is not an axe. Similarly, whatever something is which is not capable of vision, it is not an eye. Of course, we can call toy axes "axes," and we can call dolls' eyes "eyes," but these are merely "homonymous" axes and eyes – that is, they are axes and eyes in name only.[5] What it is to be an eye (proper) is to possess the capacity for vision: whatever material something is made of, it will not be an eye unless it has that capacity.

What Aristotle says about the eye is intended to exemplify his general account of the *psuchê*. By this stage in *An* II.1, he has in fact provided three different characterizations of the *psuchê*. It is described first, at 412a20–21, as "the form of a natural body which potentially has life"; as "the first actuality of a natural body which potentially has life" (412a27–28), and finally, at 412b5–6, as "the first actuality of a body which has organs." These are intended to be equivalent. As form, the *psuchê* stands to the matter as "actuality" to "potentiality." There are, however, two levels of actuality in respect of the capacities of a living thing. The first actuality is achieved by a creature once it possesses the capacity in question, and the second when the capacity is exercised. Thus, while "waking is actuality which corresponds to cutting and seeing [i.e., second actuality], the *psuchê* is actuality corresponding to sight, that is the capacity of the organ [*organon*][6] [i.e., first actuality]" (412b27–413a1). Further, a living body which has achieved first actuality is thereby a body which has organs (412a28–b1). To achieve first actuality is to possess certain capacities, and this requires that the body have the relevant organs. Every capacity (except that of *nous*) needs an organ (*GA* IV.1, 766b35) – and for something to be an organ is just

---

5 Homonyms are defined at the beginning of the *Categories:* "When things have only a name in common and the definition of being which corresponds to the name is different, they are called homonymous" (1a1–2). It is quite consistent with two things being homonymous that there is an explanation for their sharing the name. [See above pp. 72–76.]

6 Or possibly, "the *psuchê* is actuality corresponding to sight and the capacity of the tool." The Greek term *organon* can denote tools as well as organs.

for it to possess some capacity. For a body to be alive, then, it must have bodily parts which are such as to support the capacities which are constitutive of its kind, and every such body has a *psuchê*.

It is not accidental that Aristotle's final characterization of the *psuchê* should make reference to organs, since the effect of treating the *psuchê* as the form of the living body is to shift the explanatory weight from the *psuchê* to its capacities. These are instantiated hierarchically. All living things have the capacity for nutrition, some (i.e., animals) have in addition the capacity for perception and desire, and some (i.e., humans) possess all the capacities, including the capacity for abstract thought (*nous*).[7] This variation across species is something the psychologist must explain: "we must ask in the case of each, What is its *psuchê*? i.e., What is the *psuchê* of plant, human, animal?' (*An* II.3, 414b32–33).

It turns out that the *psuchê* is not something which can be defined, since, strictly, only things with essences are definable.[8] *Psuchai are* essences; they do not have them:

It is now evident that a single account [*logos*] can be given of *psuchê* only in the same way as it is for figure. For, as in that case, there is no figure apart from triangle and those that follow in order, so here, there is no *psuchê* apart from those just mentioned [i.e., those of plants, animals and humans].

(414b20–22)

The form of a particular triangle is triangularity, and that of a particular square is squareness. Both triangularity and squareness are types of shape, but in specifying the essence of any particular figure, it is the specific shape which is required and not the notion of shape in general. A geometrician who restricted himself to the level of shape and eschewed the notions of triangularity, etc., would make no progress at all. Similarly, not everything which has a *psuchê* has the same capacities; living things are not alive in virtue of sharing some one thing – the *psuchê* – which itself has an essence. The genuinely explanatory psychological work will be done by investigating particular

7 Cf. *An* II.3, 414a29–b19. Matters are somewhat more complicated than this: some animals (but not all) have the capacity for locomotion; some do not have all the five senses; and only some have the capacity for *phantasia*, i.e., the ability to store and use the images gained through perception.

8 One can give a *logos* of it, but not a *horismos*. Cf. *Met* VII.4–5.

types of living thing and not living things in general: "It is absurd to look for the common account which will not express the peculiar nature of any existing thing and will not apply to the appropriate indivisible species, while omitting to look for one that will" (414b25–28). So, he concludes the chapter, "it is evident that the way to give the most adequate account [logos] of psuchê is to give the account of each [of its capacities]" (415a12–13).[9]

CAPACITIES AND THEIR OBJECTS

The rest of the De Anima is duly taken up with Aristotle's accounts of the individual capacities of the psuchê, beginning in II.4 with that of nutrition. Characteristically, his first step is to determine the proper method for providing an account of a psychic capacity:

If one is to say what each of these is, for instance what the capacity for thought is, or for perception or nutrition, one should first say what is thinking and perceiving; for activities and actions are prior in account to capacities. And if this is so, and if, even before these, one should have investigated their correlative objects, then for the same reason one should first determine these, i.e. about food and the objects of perception and thought.

(II.4, 415a16–22)

The first move here is straightforward enough. One will only be able to understand what the capacity to φ is if one understands what it is to φ. It is much less obvious why the psychologist should need first to make reference to the objects of a capacity in order to give an account of it. A clue to the motivation for this can perhaps be found in a remark made at the beginning of An II.2: "It is not enough for a definitional account to make clear the that [i.e., the thing itself], as most do, it should also contain and exhibit the cause (hê aitia)" (413a13–16).[10] The need to make reference to a capacity's objects is explicable if these are what actualize the capacity.

To see why this is so, it is helpful to consider the role of the psuchê as the "cause and principle" (aitia kai archê) of the living body (II.4,

9 Thus answering the question left open in An I.1, whether the psychologist should seek to define the psuchê or its attributes first (402b16–25).
10 So, in the Posterior Analytics II.10, 93b38ff., Aristotle gives the example of thunder, which is to be defined as a noise in the clouds caused by the quenching of fire, rather than just as a noise in the clouds.

415b8). It is standard Aristotelian doctrine that there are four ways in which one can cite a "cause" (aition) of something: one can specify its matter (the material cause), specify what sort of thing it is (the formal cause), say what the thing is for (the final cause), and say what brought it about (the efficient cause).[11] The psuchê can be cited as the cause of the living body in all these ways except the first (415b8ff.). Thus, as well as being the formal and the final cause of the living body, it is also the principle or source of its changes (415b10–12).

The psuchê is also the primary source of change of position but this capacity is not found in all living things. But alteration (alloiôsis) and growth are also due to the psuchê. For perception seems to be a kind of alteration and nothing perceives which does not share in psuchê.   (II.4, 415b21–26)

In what sense, however, can the psuchê be the cause of perception? In An II.5, Aristotle compares what can perceive with what is combustible: the latter never catches fire of its own accord, but requires an agent which has the capacity to ignite it (417a8–9). This is surely right: if the causes of perceptual activity were internal to the subject, perception would not fulfill its purpose. The whole point about perception is that it makes the subject sensitive to the things around him, and this requires that it must be an external object rather than the subject's own psuchê which is the cause of his perceiving.[12]

While this is true, it is not to the point. The force of Aristotle's claim is that how a substance can be affected by other objects depends on the nature of that substance. This is clear from the description of the relation between food and what is fed at An II.4, 416b9–15:

Since nothing except what is alive can be fed, what is fed is the animate body and just because it is animate. Hence food is essentially related to what has psuchê. Food has a power which is other than the power to increase the bulk of what is fed by it; for in so far as what is animate has bulk this is increased, but in so far as it is a "something in particular", that is a substance, the food acts as food; for it preserves the substance.

Here Aristotle contrasts two different effects which the ingestion of matter can have on what takes it in. The first is simply to increase its bulk. All that is required for this to happen is that both what

11 See Phys. II.3. [See above pp. 120–122.]
12 For Aristotle's discussion of the purpose of the perceptual capacity, see An III.12 and Sens. 1.

ingests and what is ingested have mass. Sometimes the substance can also be nourished by what it takes in. For this to occur, the substance must be animate and to describe the change intelligibly one must describe what is changed not as a collection of matter but as a living creature. It is only because the substance has a *psuchê* that it is able to be fed by food – just as only animate substances are able to perceive – and so Aristotle can legitimately claim that the *psuchê* is the principle or source of nutrition and perception.

Correspondingly, not just anything which is ingested even by a living body will nourish it. What is distinctive of food is that it is capable of feeding animate substances. Food is thus a causal notion: something counts as food just if it possesses this capacity, which is why food is non-accidentally related to what is animate (416b10–11). The objects correlated with the capacity of nutrition are thus those things which are such as to actualize that capacity.

Nutrition and perception are entirely parallel in this respect. In *An* II.5, Aristotle says that "what bring about the activity of perception, i.e. the objects of vision and hearing and the other objects of perception [*aisthêta*], are external" (417b19–21). Just as he begins the discussion of nutrition by looking at its objects, so when he turns to provide accounts of the individual senses, he says that "one should speak first about the objects of perception in dealing with each sense" (418a7–8). At the beginning of his treatment of vision, he accordingly specifies the object of vision as what is visible, which is "colour and something which can be described in words but has no name" (418a26–28).[13] These are what are visible *kath'hauta* (singular: *kath'hauto*), in virtue of being what they are:

Whatever is visible is colour and colour is what lies upon what is *kath'hauto* visible; *kath'hauto* visible not in account but because it has in itself the cause [*to aition*] of its own visibility. Every colour is such as to change what is actually transparent; and that is its nature.   (418a28–b2)

What unifies the objects of vision is that they are such as to act on what is transparent and hence to affect the organ of sight. As with the objects of the nutritive capacity, the class of visible objects is determined by reference to the causal powers of its members.

Aristotle's talk of objects which are perceptible *kath'hauta* signals

13 The latter type of thing turns out to consist of what appears fiery or shining in the dark (II.7, 419a2–5).

a distinction which is important for the employment of perceptible objects within his account of perception. For, as the nutritive capacity and its objects are non-accidentally related, so "the substance [ousia] of each sense is relative" to its objects. The objects to which it is related are those which are proper to it (idion), and these are perceived kath'hauta. Each sense has a range of objects which is specific (idion) to it, and it is these which are strictly (kuriôs) perceptible. Other things can be perceived than these, but they are only accidentally perceptible – perceptible not in virtue of being what they are, but in virtue of being accidents of the proper sensibles.[14] Thus, if the agent of my present perception is that white object, and the white object is the son of Diares, then the son of Diares is accidentally perceived:

Something is called an accidental object of perception as when the white object is the son of Diares: for this is an accident of what is perceived. That is why nothing is affected by the [accidental] object of perception as such.

(II.6, 418a20–24)

The son of Diares is seen, but not because he is the son of Diares: he is seen because he is also a white object and, in virtue of this, is able to act on the eye. The distinction between things perceived kath'hauta and those perceived accidentally thus rests on the distinction between kath'hauta and accidental agency in Physics II.3. The proper sensibles are the kath'hauta causes of the changes in the sense organs: those things which form accidental unities with these are only accidental sensibles because they can only be accidental causes of those changes. By effecting the distinction between what is perceptible kath'hauto and what is accidentally perceptible, Aristotle is able to acknowledge, without giving up his method of defining the senses by reference to the agents of their actualization, that we perceive a much wider range of things than the proper objects of the five senses.

MATERIAL EXPLANATION

All the capacities of the psuchê except nous have organs – that is, each is possessed by some determinate part of the body. Aristotle

14 The third class of perceptible objects, the "common sensibles" (change, rest, shape, magnitude), are also perceptible kath'hauta (An II.6, 418a8–11), but they are only accidentally perceived by the individual senses.

takes it to be a requirement for a satisfactory psychology that it should explain why particular bodies, or parts of bodies, are such as to possess the capacities they do. In *An* I.3, he ridicules those who attempt to characterize the *psuchê* without paying any attention to the body of which it is the form:

[Plato's] view, along with most theories of the *psuchê*, involves the following absurdity: they join the *psuchê* to a body, or place it in a body, without giving any specification of the cause [*aitia*] – that is of the bodily conditions.

(407b12–16)

Such theorists think that it is sufficient merely to describe the characteristics of the *psuchê* – but their failure to discuss the relation between *psuchai* and their bodies manifests a misunderstanding of the nature of the *psuchê*. "They do not try to determine anything about the body which is to receive it, as if it were possible, as in the Pythagorean myths, that any *psuchê* could be clothed in any body – an absurd view, since it is apparent that each body has its own particular [*idion*] form and shape" (407b20–24). Aristotle, having placed the *psuchê* as the form of the living body, feels able to provide proper explanations of the relation between a living body's capacities and its material constitution.

In the first book of the *De Partibus Animalium*, Aristotle discusses what is generally called "hypothetical necessity":

For just as there is a necessity that the axe be hard, since one must cut with it, and, if hard, that it be of bronze or iron, so too since the body is an instrument [*organon*] (for each of its parts is for the sake of something, and so is the body as a whole), therefore there is a necessity that it be *such* a thing and made of *such* things if that end is to be.   (642a10–13)[15]

For something to be an axe, it must have the capacity to cut things up, and this places constraints on what it can be made of. *If* it is to have this capacity, its head *must* be made of a hard material: a

15 Translation from D.M. Balme, *Aristotle's De Partibus Animalium I and De Generatione Animalium I* (Oxford: Clarendon Press, 1972). For discussion of hypothetical necessity, see J.M. Cooper, "Hypothetical Necessity and Natural Teleology," in A. Gotthelf and J.G. Lennox, eds., *Philosophical Issues in Aristotle's Biology* (Cambridge: Cambridge University Press, 1987), 243–75; and D. Charles, "Aristotle on Hypothetical Necessity and Irreducibility," *Pacific Philosophical Quarterly* 69 (1988): 1–53.

toolmaker cannot create an axe out of just anything. Similarly, if the body is to have organs which are able to fulfill their constitutive functions, these also need to have particular material constitutions.

In the case of the sense organs, for instance, their distinctive capacity is that of receiving "the perceptible forms without the matter" (An II.12, 424a17–19). This formulation is reasonably obscure, but in fact amounts to no more than that a sense organ must be capable of becoming like its objects – that is, of taking on the relevant property of what is affecting it.[16] This has definite consequences for the possible material constitution of perceivers. In An III.13, Aristotle argues that an animal body cannot be simple – that is, be composed of only one element – since every animal must possess the sense of touch, and the organ of touch cannot be simple.[17] The reason for this is that "touch is as it were a mean between all the objects of touch, and its organ is receptive not only of the differentiae of earth, but also of the hot and the cold and all the other objects of touch" (435a21–24). Thus, plants and such parts of the body as bones and hair, all of which are made of earth, are not capable of perception.

Each sense is sensitive to at least one determinate range of properties, and these are its proper objects (cf. An II.11, 422b23ff; PA II.1, 647a5ff.), which, as we have seen, are able to act on it in virtue of being what they are. Each range is limited by a pair of contraries (hot/cold, white/black, sharp/flat, etc.) between which there are intermediates. For the relevant sense organ to be sensitive to its objects, it must be constituted by matter which is capable of taking on the properties in the range. The organ of touch cannot be composed only of earth, otherwise it would not be able, for instance, to become hot. The organ of sight must be able to take on the colours of its objects, and this means that it must be made of something transparent, since

16 It should be noted that this claim, though correct, is certainly controversial. The strongest evidence against it is An II.5 – this is discussed below, p.

17 D.S. Hutchinson, "Restoring the Order of Aristotle's De Anima" (Classical Quarterly 37 [1987]: 373–81), argues convincingly that what are standardly treated as being the last two books of the An (III.12 and 13) were originally placed between II.4 and II.5. This is an attractive suggestion both because it would result in a better argumentative structure in Book II itself and because, as they stand at the moment, III 12 and 13 are arbitrarily appended to the work as a whole.

the effect which colour produces *kath'hauto* is to change what is transparent (*An* II.7, 418a31–b2).[18]

This explains why eyes have the material constitution they do:

> It is true that the eye (*hê opsis*) is composed of water, yet seeing occurs not because it is water but because it is transparent – something common to both water and air. But water is more easily confined and condensed than air and this is why the pupil, i.e., the eye proper, consists of water.
>
> (*Sens* 2, 438a12–16)

The explanation of the material constitution of the eye here exactly parallels the example of the axe in *PA* I.1. *If* there is to be an organ of sight, it *must* contain transparent matter and so must contain either air or water. Because water is better suited to this role, eyes contain water rather than air.

For something to be an eye, it must have the capacity for vision. To have that capacity, it must contain water, since this is the only element with the requisite combination of transparency and condensability. If to specify something's essence is to state those properties which it cannot lose without ceasing to be that thing, it would seem that there is as much reason to include the material composition in the essence (and hence the form) of the eye as there is its constitutive capacity. The fact that the material constitution of a living body is necessitated by its form thus puts some pressure on a rigidly maintained distinction between form and matter.

This is perhaps apparent in the discussion in *An* I.1 of what sort of definitions should be given by the psychologist. Aristotle draws a contrast there between the method which is proper to the study of geometrical objects and that which is required for the understanding of natural bodies. While the former is concerned with those properties which "are inseparable in fact, but are separable from any particular kind of body by abstraction" (403b14–15), the physicist treats of "all the actions and affections of this sort of body and this sort of matter" (403b11–12). Neither geometrical forms nor the forms of living things can exist uninstantiated, so the difference between them must be that whereas one does not have to think of squares and cubes as being instantiated in any particular *kind* of matter, this is not the case for living things.

18 Cited above, p. 177.

The affections of the *psuchê*, Aristotle has told us at 403a5, are *logoi enhuloi* – "enmattered accounts" – and he takes this to place constraints on their proper definition:

Thus the definitions will be of this sort: 'Anger is a certain change of this sort of body (or part or capacity) brought about by this for the sake of that'.

(I.1, 403a25–27)

We have already seen that, in defining the affections of the *psuchê*, Aristotle gives priority to identifying the causes of the relevant changes, and here he insists that reference must also be made to the body as well. That "this sort of body" here is not proxy for a reference to a form is confirmed by what follows. He contrasts the definitions of anger which would be offered by the dialectician and the physicist: the former would define anger as " 'the desire to return pain' or some such," while the latter would define it as the boiling of the blood around the heart (403a30–b1). Neither definition is satisfactory by itself:

The one gives the matter, the other the form and the account; for he gives the account of the thing, though for its actual existence it is necessary for this to be in that matter. . . . Which of these, then, is the [real] physicist? The one who talks about the matter and is ignorant of the account, or the one who talks only of the account? Is it not rather the one who combines both? (403b1–2; 7–9)

Not only, then, will the proper physicist – and a fortiori the proper psychologist – define his subject matter by reference to its form; he will also need to make reference to its matter.

What, then, of the distinction between form and matter? One way to achieve consistency would be to construe that distinction as holding between the form and particular pieces or collections of matter, rather than between the form and material types. When, for instance (in *Met* VII.8), Aristotle says that Socrates and Callias have the same form, but differ in virtue of their matter, his point is that the composite substance is "such and such a form in *this* flesh and *these* bones" (1034a5–6). This is quite consistent with his making reference to flesh and bones generally in the specification of the human form.[19] In the case of the eye, what is necessary is that it contain water and not that it contain the particular water it does.

19 Cf. VII.10, 1035b29–30, for the matter of a human body taken generally.

Taking this way out, Aristotle could have allowed that what *sort* of matter something is made of can be partially constitutive of its being the kind of thing it is.

This is not the line he takes. At *Met* VII.11, he addresses precisely this question. Noting that, when a particular form is instantiated only in a particular material type, it is difficult to effect even a conceptual separation of the form and the matter, he goes on to affirm that they are nevertheless distinct:

> The form of man is always found in flesh and bones and parts of this kind; are these then also parts of the form and the account [*logos*]? No, they are matter; but because man is not found also in other materials we are unable to effect the severance.   (1036b3–7)[20]

He is right to maintain this line. For just as material explanation is made a prerequisite of a satisfactory psychology by the need to show why a substance's material constitution is necessitated by its form, so this makes it explanatorily essential that the substance's form should be specifiable independently of its matter.

For a material explanation to be informative, the formal and material levels of description must be conceptually independent of each other. It would be true but entirely uninformative to be told that for there to be a human being, there needs to be a collection of matter of the sort to instantiate the human form – just as it is true, but uninformative, to say that a drug puts people to sleep because it has a virtus dormitiva. In *PA* I.1, Aristotle attributes the failure of his predecessors to come up with satisfactory explanations of this kind to their neglect of the notion of essence and the definition of substance (642a24–26). Rather than treating substances as conceptually autonomous, they thought they could be treated simply as functions of their constituent material components. Aristotle's claim is that it is only by treating the substance as conceptually prior to its matter that one will be able to achieve a properly integrated explanation of what the matter and its properties contribute to the substance it instantiates.

20 Indeed, even Aristotle finds himself saying at *Met* VII.8, 1033b23–25 that Callias and Socrates "are analogous to this bronze sphere, but man and animal to bronze sphere in general" – i.e., to something whose *logos* makes reference to matter.

FORM AND MATTER

Aristotle's method, then, requires that the formal and material descriptions of living things be conceptually independent of each other. It is not obvious, however, that his notion of matter achieves this independence. The living body is constituted by its organic parts (heart, eyes, ears, fingers, etc.): it is "divided into these parts as its matter" (*Met* VII.10, 1035b20–21; cf. *GA* 715a10). As Aristotle emphasizes many times, a dead organ is not an organ at all. Not only are organs ontologically dependent on the bodies of which they are parts – sever an organ from the body and it loses its capacity (*Met* VII.10, 1035b23–24) – but the very notion of an organ is dependent on that of the living body. One could not understand what it is for something to be a finger or an eye without knowing that it is a part of a living body.[21]

It is important to see quite where this objection bites, if it bites at all. For it is certainly not uninformative to be told that a particular *type* of living body – that of a chimpanzee, say – has eyes or fingers or legs. The notion of a living body is not such that anything which is a living body must possess these organic parts; plants possess none of them. We have already seen that Aristotle maintains that one cannot investigate the *psuchê* before giving an account of its capacities – precisely because *psuchai* are not uniform. Different species of living things have different combinations of psychic capacities. Any particular species will be defined (at least in part) by reference to the combination of capacities it enjoys. This means that the psychic capacities themselves are not conceptually dependent on their being possessed by any particular species, even in the case of capacities which are in fact possessed by only one species.

This is all to the good, since one has to be able to treat the organic parts as constitutive of the living body if one is to provide proper persistence conditions for living material substances. In contemporary debates about personal identity, for instance, it is sometimes thought that if one takes the condition for a person's existence over time to be the continuity of, say, his brain (and perhaps nervous system), one is

21 For a full statement of this line of objection, see J.L. Ackrill, "Aristotle's Definitions of *psuchê*," in Barnes, Schofield, and Sorabji, *Articles* 4, 65–75, especially pp. 70ff.

thereby providing a materialist account of what it is to be a person over time. This is true in a sense, since the brain and nervous system are, like Aristotelian organs, material substances – but this does not mean that they can be *identified* with their matter. Brains, no less than eyes in Aristotle, are functional entities. Outside thought-experiments, people maintain the same body throughout their lives, but the stuff of which it is constituted changes regularly. One does not give someone a new brain by performing a lobotomy on them, but one certainly produces a mass of connected brain cells which is not identical with (because smaller than) the mass of connected brain cells which was there before. Even in the case of trees and plants, what gives identity over time is the continuity of a functioning organism and not the persistence of a certain mass of cells. The matter which a tree or an animal or a human is constituted by at one time need not be the same matter as that which constitutes it at another time, and an organism can change its matter without ceasing to exist.

So, it is neither unmotivated nor unsound for Aristotle to take the living body to be constituted by its organic parts. What this does not offer, of course, is an explanation of the animate in terms of the inanimate. Unless Aristotle can move to a level of material description which is not itself conceptually dependent upon the notion of a living substance, he will not be able to explain how some material substances are capable of life without begging the question. Since – the objection goes – his account does not have conceptual room for this level of material description, he is forced, willingly or unwillingly, to leave the psychological unexplained and hence mysterious.

It will already be seen that this objection fails. The overall structure of his analysis of the living body is made clear at the beginning of the *GA*. While it is certainly true that "the non-uniform parts [i.e., the organs] are the matter of the animal as a whole," the analysis does not stop there: "the uniform parts are the matter of the non-uniform, and the corporeal elements, as they are called, are the matter of these" (I.1, 715a10–12).[22] Where Aristotle needs to introduce

22 Translation adapted from A.L. Peck, *Aristotle: Generation of Animals* (London/Cambridge, Mass., 1953). Examples of uniform parts are blood, marrow, semen, bile, milk, flesh, bone, and sinew: cf. *PA* II.2. For a useful discussion of their composition, see J. Whiting, "Living Bodies," in M.C. Nussbaum and A.O. Rorty, eds., *Essays on Aristotle's De Anima* (Oxford: Clarendon Press, 1992), 75–92.

reference to matter under non-psychological descriptions is not in describing the constitution of the body, but rather in explicating that of the organs themselves. So, to possess the capacity for sight, the eye has to contain water – and to describe matter as water is not to use a description which is conceptually dependent on the *psuchê*.

That Aristotle's account allows an autonomous level of material description is emphasized by those cases in which the explanatory relation between the formal or psychological and the material levels is reversed. Centrally, the psychologist will start from an understanding of a psychic capacity and move to show how this necessitates that its organ have a particular material constitution. He will also need, however, to show the psychological consequences of the organ's having that constitution. Although these will standardly be that the organ is capable of exercising its capacity, they are by no means so restricted.

So, the claim that the affections of the *psuchê* are "enmattered accounts" is taken by Aristotle to have consequences for their definition. His argument for that claim relies on deviant cases of psychological states:

Sometimes when there are violent and striking occurrences, one is neither excited nor afraid, whilst at other times one is affected by slight and feeble things – when the body is angry, that is when it is in the same condition as when one is angry. Here is a still clearer case: in the absence of any external cause of fear, we find ourselves in the state of someone frightened. If this is so, it is obvious that the affections of the *psuchê* are enmattered accounts.

(*An* I.1, 403a19–25)

This is rather quick, but the argument clearly relies on the claim that when there is a particular affection of the *psuchê*, there is a material state which is sufficient for its occurrence. No doubt, in standard conditions, that material state will occur only when one perceives something which is frightening, but it can occur at other times, and the result is that the subject will be frightened. Similarly, one will feel angry if the blood boils round one's heart, even if there is no external cause of this. The argument here assumes that there is a description of the condition of the body when one is angry which is independent of the psychological level, and shows that Aristotle accepts that particular material conditions are sufficient as well as necessary for particular affections of the *psuchê*.

This might seem puzzling if, as I have claimed, the sense organs undergo alterations which are of the same type as those undergone by inanimate substances. That this is so is confirmed by *Physics* VII.2, whose argument that all alteration requires contact between the agent and patient (possibly via a medium) relies on the claim that the perceptual and non-perceptual alterations are the same.[23] The only difference is that the subject is aware of perceptual alterations: "the inanimate is not capable of alteration in respect of the senses – i.e., the inanimate is not aware [*lanthanei*] of the alteration, whilst the animate is aware of it" (244b15–245a1). Both the water in my glass and the water in my eye take on the colour of the carpet, but only in the second case is there awareness of the resulting affection. The apparent problem is that if the alteration were sufficient for perception, the glass would perceive the carpet. Since the glass is insensate, the eye's taking on the carpet's colour is not sufficient for it to perceive the carpet.

The mistake here is to forget that, for Aristotle, the senses constitute a complete physiological system. In the *De Somno*, he gives the reason for the insensitivity of animals while asleep as the incapacity of the master or primary sense organ: "whenever this has become incapacitated, all the other sense organs are necessarily incapable of perception" (2, 455b10–11). This central sense organ is the heart, which is connected to the individual sense organs. When these are affected by their objects, the affections pass through the blood stream to the heart.[24] Although each sense is defined by reference to its specific activity, "there is a common capacity which accompanies them all, by which one perceives that one sees and hears (for it is not by sight that one sees that one sees . . . but by a part which is common to all the organs – for there is one sense and one master (*kurios*) sense organ)" (455a15–21). This common

23 Scholars have been suspicious of VII's claim to its place in the *Physics* (cf. W.D. Ross, *Aristotle's Physics* [Oxford: Clarendon Press, 1936], 11–19). For a defence of the book, see Robert Wardy, *The Chain of Change* (Cambridge: Cambridge University Press, 1990), especially pp. 85ff.

24 Aristotle makes the claim with reference to touch in the *De Insomniis*: "That part which has become heated by something hot, heats the part next to it, and this propagates the affection on to the origin. This must therefore happen in perception, since actual perceiving is an alteration. This explains why the affection continues in the sense organs, both in their deeper and in their more superficial parts" (*Insomn* 2, 459b2–7).

capacity of perceptual awareness is something which each sense possesses – but not *as that sense:* it is a capacity it has in virtue of being part of the perceptual capacity as a whole and not of being that particular sense.

That similarity of the material affections of the perceptual system is sufficient for similarity of perceptual state is clear from *De Insomniis* 2, where Aristotle explains faul:y perceptual judgments by reference to the fact that the controlling part and the part by which perceptual, or quasi-perceptual, images (*phantasmata*) are formed are not the same (460b16–18):[25] "The cause of our being mistaken is that any appearances whatever present themselves, not only when its object affects a sense, but also when the sense by itself alone is changed, provided it is changed in the same way as it is by the object" (460b22–25). What accounts for the way things appear to the subject is the material nature of the affection: again, there must be a non-psychological description of the affection such that any affection which satisfies this will produce an appearance of the same sort.

The heart is not only the central sense organ, it is the locus of all the psychic capacities: "the capacities of perception, nutrition and that for moving the animal are all in the same part of the body" (*PA* II.1, 647a25–26; cf. also *Somn* 2, 455b34).[26] This is necessary if the animal's perceptions are to give rise to action: "if the region of the origin [i.e., the heart] is altered through perception and thus changes, the adjacent parts change with it and they too are extended or contracted, and in this way the movement of the animal necessarily

25 For the pictorial nature of the affections of the sense organs, see *De Memoria* 450b20–27.

26 At times, indeed, Aristotle seems to talk as if the heart is the location of the *psuchê* itself. In *An* I.4, he says that in the case of memory, change "starts from the *psuchê* and terminates in the changes or states of rest in the sense organs" (I.4, 408b14–18), apparently contrasting changes in the sense organs with changes in the *psuchê*. In *Met.* VII.10, he says that the heart (or possibly the brain) is neither prior nor posterior to the living body of which it is a part, "since it is this which is controlling [*kurios*] and which primarily has the account and the substance" (1035b25–27). At the end of *MA* 10, he actually goes so far as to deny that there is *psuchê* in all parts of the body: "it is in some governing origin of the body, and the other parts have life because they are naturally connected to this" (703a37–b1).

follows" (*MA* 9, 702b21–25). This material explanation of animal movement underlies the explanation given two chapters earlier in the *MA* according to which such movements are caused by beliefs and desires:

"I want to drink," says appetite. "That's drink," says perception or *phantasia* or thought: immediately he drinks. In this way animals are impelled to move and to act, and desire is the last cause of movement.

(*MA* 7, 701a32–35)

Again, although the material changes will standardly be such as to produce movements which are rationally explicable in terms of the agent's beliefs and desires, this can be disrupted. So, when in *NE* VII, Aristotle explains *akrasia* by saying that the agent is ignorant of the conclusion of the relevant practical syllogism, he says that the akratic is in the same state as people who are angry or mad – states which "alter the body" (*NE* VII.3, 1147a16). Explaining how the akratic leaves that state (and so, presumably, what caused it) is the business of the physiologist (1147b8–9). If one is ignorant of the physiology, one can say what happens in the case of akratic action, but one will not be able to explain why it happens.

COMMON AFFECTIONS

Aristotle says in *Sens* 1 that such affections as perception and desire are "common" to the *psuchê* and the body (436a7–8). He used this formulation earlier in *An* I.1 when he raised the question whether all the affections of the *psuchê* are common to the *psuchê* and the body, or whether any is specific (*idion*) to the *psuchê* (403a3–5). With the possible exception of abstract thought (*nous*), all are common: "It is apparent that all the affections of the *psuchê* are with body . . . in all these the body undergoes some affection" (403a15–19). Now, Aristotle's talk of common affections should seem strange at first. Given his general account of the *psuchê* as the form of living things, "the body" and "the *psuchê*" here do not denote two different substances: there is only one substance which can be affected, and that is the living body. So, in saying that perception is common to the *psuchê* and the body, Aristotle cannot be joining Descartes in thinking of it as an activity which essentially involves two different substances working as a system.

One way to make sense of this would be to identify the alteration in the organ with the actualization of its capacity. There would then be one event, describable in two different ways: both as a change to a living substance and as a change in a certain material structure. Aristotle's talk of an affection which is common to the *psuchê* and the body would, in effect, be shorthand for an affection which is common to the body, in virtue of having a *psuchê*, and the body, in virtue of its material constitution.

This is not Aristotle's position, however. In *An* II.5, he says that the change in respect of the capacity is not, strictly, an alteration at all. He distinguishes between straightforward qualitative change – alteration – and the change from the mere possession of a capacity to its exercise. The first is "the change to conditions of privation," whilst the second is "the change to a thing's dispositions and to its nature," – i.e., the move from first to second actuality (417b14–16). The latter, he says, is either not properly called an "alteration" or is an alteration in some special sense. Some commentators have taken *An* II.5 to deny that, in perception, the organ undergoes any alteration at all.[27] This is too hasty. Although the actualization of the capacity is not an alteration proper, this does not mean that the change in the organ, described materially, is not one either. What it does mean is that one cannot identify the actualization of the capacity with the alteration of the organ. If the latter is an alteration and the former is not, then the two cannot be identical.[28]

Aristotle's position is not, then, that we have one event which is describable either as a seeing or as a colouring: rather, we have two events – a seeing and a colouring – both of which involve the same substance, the eye (remembering that to be an eye at all, it has to be connected to the heart). That the same substance is involved in both must be what encourages Aristotle to talk of perception as a common affection, but this is incautious, suggesting as it does that there

27 See, for instance, Myles Burnyeat, "Is an Aristotelian Philosophy of Mind Still Credible: A Draft," in Nussbaum and Rorty, *Essays on De Anima*, 19ff.

28 This blocks any interpretation of Aristotle according to which he comes out as a precursor of functionalism: the point of that doctrine is that non-mental states or events can satisfy mental descriptions in virtue of playing a particular causal role. On Aristotle's account, the alteration in the eye satisfies no proper psychological description.

is only one event. His formulation a few lines later in *An* I.1 – that all the affections of the *psuchê* are "with body," that "the body undergoes some affection at the same time" (403a16–19) – is more considered. Of course, it is not merely that the body is affected at the same time as the actualization, but that the activity of the capacity occurs in virtue of the bodily alteration.

Aristotle is not driven into a substantial dualism by the need to explain mental events. He countenances only individual living substances which are material.[29] He is not, however, a physicalist, if we take that to require the acceptance of the thesis that every psychological event also satisfies some more basic description – i.e., a description which can be satisfied by events involving inanimate things. It is not merely that Aristotle denies that what it is to see something blue is to have one's pupil turned blue by an object; he also denies that any token perception of something blue is identical with any token alteration of the pupil (or set of alterations to the perceptual system). His denial of this sort of physicalism does not, however, commit him to the idea that psychological events somehow float free of the physical: the psychological states and changes of an organism are determined by its physical states and changes.[30] Aristotle does not allow that a living creature could have had the same history, physically described, but a different psychological history (except, perhaps, in respect of its poetic activity – its thoughts about universals).[31] Moreover, the determinism which obtains at the physical level ensures determinism at the psychological level as well.

29 Actually, it would be better to say that for present purposes he is not a substantial dualist. The claim needs to be restricted to the sublunary realm: he *does* seem to allow that the divine mind, whose only activity is abstract thought, exists without matter. See *Met* XII.7–10.

30 Only the activities of *nous*, which has no organ (*An* III.4, 429a24–27), are physically undetermined and, for humans, even that requires the operation of *phantasia* (*An* I.1, 403a8–9; III.7, 431a16–17). The fact that Aristotle allows that there can be a capacity which lacks an organ shows that he is not committed on principle to the claim that every event must either be a physical event or state or be determined by a physical event or state. It must be said, though, that his discussion of *nous* in *An* III.4–5 is quite remarkably obscure.

31 I leave it open here whether its causal relations with other things should enter into its physical history.

The danger of this, however, is that it makes the events picked out by psychological descriptions causally irrelevant. In the *MA*, as we have seen, there are two sets of descriptions of the events which give rise to action. At one level, when the organs are altered, the resulting *phantasmata* affect the heart, which is thereby caused to move the parts around it, and this gives rise to the movement of the limbs. At the other level, the sight of the drink, together with the desire for drink, causes the animal to pick up the glass in front of it. The problem here is to see what can justify Aristotle's claim that the desire is the cause of the action (*MA* 7, 701a35). Since the movement of the limbs materially determines the action, it is legitimate for him to claim that the movement of the parts around the heart causes the action – but this is not sufficient to make the desire causally efficacious, since the desire is not to be identified with those movements. That the agent has the desire for drink now seems causally irrelevant to his drinking.

This raises some subtle and difficult issues, but it is at least possible to sketch an Aristotelian response. The first point to note is that, for Aristotle, psychological states and events are necessarily enmattered. Just as living bodies cannot be identified with their matter, so psychological events cannot be identified with theirs. The action is not identical with the set of limb movements, and seeing the drink is not identical with the set of alterations to the sense organs. Nevertheless, for the action to occur, there must be a series of bodily movements, and if there is such a series, this is sufficient for the action to occur. That he recommends that the psychologist produce definitions of psychological processes which make reference to matter – even if these would not count as definitions in the strict sense articulated in *Metaphysics* VII – demonstrates the tightness of the relation between physical and psychological events within his system.[32] Psychological events, then, stand to certain physical events as form to matter: the bodily movements are the matter of the action, and some

32 For the issue of how to square Arisotle's claim that natural bodies will be defined (at least by the physicist) by reference to their matter as well as to their form with his apparent commitment in *Met* VII to the principle that things are to be defined by reference to their form alone, see M. Frede, "The Definition of Sensible Substances in Met. Z," in D. Devereux and P. Pellegrin, eds., *Biologie, Logique et Métaphysique chez Aristote* (Paris: Editions du CNRS, 1990), 113–29.

states of the heart are the matter of the desire. If Aristotle is to justify treating psychological events as causally relevant, he must show why they should bring about their effects in virtue of their form rather than just in virtue of their matter.

At least two responses are, it seems, open to Aristotle. The first is that something will not be an action at all unless it is causally explicable by reference to the agent's psychological states. He would thus deny that for an action to occur, it is sufficient that there is a series of bodily movements: such a series would have to be caused by some physical event (or events) which instantiates a desire. This is plausible in the case of actions, but is not obviously generalizable to all cases of psychological causation. A (compatible) alternative is for him to emphasize his general principle that one cannot understand the behaviour of a substance merely as a system of matter. The natural scientist has to show how such a system is necessitated by the nature of the substance of which it is the matter. The movements around the heart bring about the movement of the limbs – but there is a material system capable of acting and being acted on in this way only because this is required for the animal to be able to act on the world around it. It is because the relevant physical events instantiate psychological events that they occur at all. Since the relation between the physical events and the psychological events they instantiate is thus not an accidental one, this is sufficient to allow the latter the causal efficacy which Aristotle attributes to them.[33]

Although Aristotle does not think that all events are physical events, he is not encouraged into this position by any reflection on the difficulty of placing consciousness within the natural order. There is nothing at all Cartesian in the motivation for his pluralism about events. A plant's taking nourishment is no more a physical event than is my feeling frightened or wanting a cigarette. What motivates him is not the recognition of a distinction between mental events and physical events, but of one between those events which are actualizations of the capacities of living things and those which are alterations in a stricter sense. Aristotle is not vulnerable to the charge that his theory of the *psuchê* rests on an understanding

33 This clearly requires more substantial consideration than it receives here. For a sophisticated discussion of these issues, see Chapter 5 of D. Charles, *Aristotle's Philosophy of Action* (London: Duckworth, 1984).

of matter which is incredibly vitalistic. He simply accepts that certain systems of matter, suitably disposed, are capable of awareness. He does not explain why those systems have consciousness whilst others do not – but then, neither has anyone else. Unless we are dualists, we accept that certain material substances enjoy consciousness and that whether a substance is conscious depends on its material constitution. We can no more say *why* certain systems of matter are such as to be conscious than Aristotle could. In recognizing that one does not have to attempt an identification of mental events with physical events in order to integrate the psychological within the physical world, Aristotle at least shows a greater sophistication than is perhaps common even now.

7 Ethics

INTRODUCTION

a. Aristotle's will

When Aristotle died in 322 B.C. he left a will, which gives us a valuable insight into his personal affairs and private moral opinions. He had a fairly large estate, two teenage children, a common-law wife (the mother of his children had died), and a trusted circle of friends. The provisions for Herpyllis, his common-law wife, are very generous, "for she was good to me"; she was to have her choice of Aristotle's houses, various servants, a large quantity of silver in addition to what she had already been given, and a handsome dowry if she wanted to get married. He left instructions for the dedication of various statues: one of his mother, one of his sister, and one of his brother, which was to be set up as a memorial to him "since he died childless." He also left instructions for a pair of life-size statues to be erected in Stagira, the city of his birth: one of Zeus Saviour, the other of Athena Saviouress. Aristotle leaves a great deal of discretion to his executors. Herpyllis is to have the house of her choice furnished "with whatever seems both proper to them and satisfactory to her." "Let Nicanor take care of both my daughter and my son Nicomachus in whatever way he judges appropriate to their affairs, as though he were both father and brother to them".[1] Many of the themes that he discussed with his students also play a prominent role in his will – the importance of friends and family and successful children, the social roles proper to gentlemen of property,

---

1 Aristotle's will is transmitted in Diogenes Laertius, *Lives of the Philosophers*, V.11–16. (See above, pp. 2–3.)

generosity and dignity in the service of others, and the good judgment of trustworthy men. Aristotle reveals himself in this testament as having the virtues you would expect of a gentleman of ample property, who recognizes the responsibilities that come with wealth.

b. Aristotle's Exhortation to Philosophy

So much for Aristotle as an old man, but what was he like as a young man? We have no private documents from that period, but we do know about a fine essay, the Exhortation to Philosophy, which he published in his early thirties. This essay reveals a quite different strand in the fabric of Aristotle's thinking, and supplements what we can learn about him from his will.

The good things that we enjoy, says Aristotle, like wealth and health, have no value if our soul is not good. Just as the soul is superior to the body, so is the rational part of the soul superior to the irrational part. The best thing we can do is to bring out the best in the best part of us, which is to be as rational as possible, and to come to know the most important things. This state of knowing is a virtue in itself and brings its own rewards, since we naturally enjoy understanding things. It is natural and right for us to develop into rational animals, and if we do not, then we might be living men, but we are not living *as men*; we might enjoy ourselves while living, without *enjoying living*. The only way for us to realize our human nature is to realize our divine nature, and the mind is the divine element in us; by virtue of possessing reason, we can approach the happy state of the gods. "Man deprived of perception and mind is reduced to the condition of a plant; deprived of mind alone he is turned into a brute; deprived of irrationality but retaining mind, he becomes like God."

What is the use of philosophy? one might ask. Some things, replies Aristotle, are good for what they can bring us, but others are good in themselves; philosophy is good in itself, and the fact that it is worthwhile without bringing us anything extra means that it is one of the very highest goods, not that it is useless. Suppose we lived in Paradise and were freed from our bodily needs; what would we do but contemplate and admire the universe? We travel to see the Olympic Games, and we don't ask what good that brings us; we pay money to go to the theatre and look at men dressed up as other people; how much more satisfying and worthwhile it would be to have a vision of the universe itself, with all its wonders revealed! When Anaxagoras was asked, "What is the meaning of life? Why would somebody choose to come into the world and live?" he is said to have answered, "To observe the heavens, and the stars and moon and sun in them," everything else being unimportant. A successful life is either a life of understanding, or a life of pleasure, or a life of moral virtue; whichever it is, the most important contribution we can make to it is to take up the study of philosophy.[2] Clearly, the *Exhortation to Philosophy* was a passionate argument for dedicating one's life to philosophy; it expresses the intellectual strand in the fabric of Aristotle's thinking, which contrasts with and complements the social strand expressed in his will.

c. Aristotle's ethical works

Aristotle published many other books which earned him a reputation for brilliance and elegant expression. All of these are lost to us (except for fragments quoted by other authors), and what we have instead are unpolished and inelegant, but brilliant, collections of notes. In ethics, there are two closely related collections, the *Nicomachean Ethics* and the *Eudemian Ethics*.[3] These notes are associated with lectures and discussions that took place in Aristotle's Lyceum (at one point Aristotle refers to a blackboard for illustration), but it is not clear whether they were his lecture-notes, written before he delivered his lectures, or his research-notes, written down after his lectures and discussions; perhaps they served both purposes.

The *Nicomachean Ethics* consists of ten "books" of roughly equal

2 *Exhortation to Philosophy* (= '*Protrepticus*'), ed. I. Düring (available in English on pp. 2403–2416 of *The Complete Works of Aristotle*), fragments B2–4, B11–17, B19, B21, B23–24, B28–29, B42–44, B54–57, B59–67, B70–77, B79–96, B108–110.

3 It is not known why these collections have the titles they have. The *Eudemian Ethics* was either dedicated to Eudemus of Cyprus (who died young and was a close friend of Aristotle) or else edited by Eudemus of Rhodes; and the *Nicomachean Ethics* was either dedicated to Nicomachus, Aristotle's father (who also died young), or else dedicated to or edited by Nicomachus, Aristotle's son.

size, transmitted to us by ancient manuscripts from a time when its standard editions occupied ten papyrus rolls, or "books". The *Eudemian Ethics* consists of seven "books", of which the last is sometimes divided into two. Three of these books are exactly the same as three books of the *Nicomachean Ethics*. Why? Either because Aristotle himself used them in both lecture courses, or, more likely, because some ancient editor copied them from one work to another to fill a gap. From which work to which would they have been copied? Most recent scholars incline to believe that these "common books" were originally part of the *Eudemian Ethics*. Why would there have been a gap in the *Nicomachean Ethics*? Either because it was left unfinished when Aristotle died, or, more likely, because some of its books went missing. When I refer to a passage in the common books, I use an asterisk: for example, *NE* 1173a29–b20 is a passage in the *Nicomachean Ethics; EE* 1230b9–20 is a passage in the *Eudemian Ethics;* and **NE* 1154a22–b20 is a passage in the common books, hence probably from the *Eudemian Ethics*. (It is confusing that these common books are included in modern editions of the *Nicomachean Ethics*, but not of the *Eudemian Ethics*.) The *Eudemian Ethics* (including the common books) is the earlier work, according to most recent scholars, and the *Nicomachean Ethics* (excluding the common books) transmits a later version of Aristotle's ethical thinking; but the differences between the two are usually relatively minor.

It is useful to keep in mind whom Aristotle was addressing in these lecture courses. In the first place, they were all men; women had a distinct social position in the ancient Greek world, and were governed by different expectations and obligations. For this reason, when I report Aristotle's views I speak of "man" (not "person") and "his" (not "his or hers") and so on; but this is not to say that there is no relevance at all in Aristotle's thought for modern women (nor can modern men simply assume that what Aristotle said applied to them). In the second place, they were young (older men for the most part did not attend educational institutions), which explains Aristotle's starting point, that one must be mature and plan one's life intelligently. Aristotle is not reluctant to say things that would be obvious to older, more experienced, men, and he conceives his task to be making clear the general outline of the good life, not pausing to discuss the difficulties of detail that often concern older men. In the third place, they were usually young gentlemen of property, whose family estate (usually managed by a steward) provided sufficient income that they did not need to work for a living. This makes some of Aristotle's discussion quite irrelevant to modern young men who are not in such favourable circumstances. But there remains an enormous amount of abiding good sense and hard-earned wisdom in what Aristotle says, which can be appreciated by modern people, of both sexes, all ages, and various social positions.

The main difficulty that modern students have in understanding Aristotle's thought is that they easily lose the thread of it among his numerous digressions. What I have concentrated on, therefore, is arranging a clear presentation of what I take to be the central elements of Aristotle's moral view. This means that I have had to change the order of Aristotle's exposition very substantially, and sometimes in the course of a single paragraph I refer to several different passages scattered across the two works; but the references at the end of each paragraph will enable readers to know where they are in Aristotle's text. In what follows I will simply report Aristotle's main ideas in as lucid an arrangement as I can; readers should assume that what is being said is Aristotle's opinion, not mine, unless otherwise indicated.

LIVING SUCCESSFULLY

The main question a young man has to face is this: "How can I make my life a success?" Obviously a sensible young man will plan his life with *some* objective in mind, and being successful is the finest, the best, and the most satisfying possible achievement. But don't confuse being successful with having what is necessary for being successful. Some men, for example, confuse being successful with being powerful or wealthy; but such things are valuable only for what they enable us to do, and to succeed in life is to make good use of them while living. Other men (especially moral philosophers) confuse being successful with simply being a virtuous sort of man. Virtue is indeed a fine and necessary thing, but only those who make active use of their virtues can be said to be living successfully – just as only those who actually compete in the Olympics can win. Making your life a success is making sure that your life as a whole consists of successful activities[4] (*EE* 1214a1–8, 1214b6–27, 1215a20–25; *NE* 1098b29–99a7, 1099a22–31).

What kinds of life are successful – what kinds of life are worth living? This is a surprisingly difficult question. Is it obvious that life *is* worth living? Life involves many circumstances that make death preferable; and nobody in his right mind would choose to live in order to sleep (like plants), or to eat and have sex (like animals), or to have immature fun (like children), or to go about the drudgery of one's daily business (like most adults). There are actually only three reputable reasons to prefer living to not living: enjoying the more refined pleasures; earning a good name for yourself in your own eyes and in the eyes of others in your community; and appreciating an understanding of the universe in which we find ourselves. These correspond to the three career choices open to young gentlemen of property: a life of pleasant amusement; a career of public service; and a life devoted to philosophy. (Nobody who has to earn his own living, no matter in what fashion, can make a real success of his life, because he does not enjoy personal independence.) Everyone whose circumstances permit him to choose how to live will choose one of these three ways of life (*EE* 1215a25–16a10; *NE* 1095b14–96a10).

Two of these three ways of life will turn out to be successful ways of living, according to Aristotle, but before he announces which they are, he undertakes a deeper analysis of the concept of success. It is the greatest and best thing that we human beings can attain – animals, who have no share of the divine, cannot hope to live successfully, and the gods enjoy a different sort of ideal existence. There is no point considering what cannot be changed, or what only the gods can bring about. What we can bring about is either a particular achievement, like running a mile, or the objective for the sake of which we attempt that achievement, like being physically fit. All the skills and kinds of knowledge that we use in our lives pursue certain objectives for the sake of higher objectives, and the higher

---

4 What I speak of as "success" (*eudaimonia*) is usually translated "happiness," and what I render as "happy" (*makarios*) is usually translated "blessed" (in other words, "enjoying something like the felicity of the gods"). I regret that this might cause some temporary confusion for readers of the usual translations, but I believe that these terms make much clearer sense of Aristotle's train of thought, and hope my readers will come to agree.

objectives are therefore better than the lower objectives. If there is a single highest objective of all that we do, it would be good to understand it well, for that would be the best thing in life – the target, as it were, at which all our decisions ought to be aimed. And there does seem to be this single highest objective – everybody calls it success, in other words, living well and faring well (EE 1217a18–40; NE 1094a1–24, 1095a14–20, 1099b32–1100a1).

Everybody agrees that the highest objective for men is to live their lives successfully, but Aristotle offers a more rigorous demonstration of the point. An objective A is more perfect than another objective B when A is worth pursuing for its own sake and B is not, or, if both are worth pursuing for their own sakes, when A is not pursued for the sake of something else, and B is. An objective is perfect in the highest degree, therefore, if it is always worth pursuing for itself, and never for the sake of something else. Succeeding in life fits this description, because it is always worth pursuing in its own right; and whereas we choose pleasure, honour, having a virtuous character, and other good things for what they contribute to living successfully, we choose succeeding in life for nothing beyond itself. Now, imagine a perfect objective that offers us everything that we might want out of life; that good would be "self-sufficient," something that "when taken by itself, makes life desirable and lacking in nothing." Obviously there can be only one such objective, for if there were a second objective, then the second one would also be worth having, and the first objective would not be sufficient to make life lacking in nothing. Succeeding in life fits this second description, too, and by this pair of arguments Aristotle shows that success in life is the one and only perfect objective for men (NE 1097a15–b21).

Plato had held that the Idea of the Good was the best thing in the world, and so Aristotle reluctantly turns aside from his exposition to criticize this doctrine. Many of these arguments are technical, even quite obscure, and Aristotle refers his readers to his other works for a fuller criticism of Plato's Idealism. For the purpose of discussing ethics, however, Aristotle focuses on what men are able to achieve, and such an abstract thing as the Idea of the Good is not something that we can achieve. But wouldn't a knowledge of the Idea of the Good help us to understand which goods are worth achieving? This seems like a reasonable suggestion, but in fact the various skills and kinds of knowledge that explain which goods to pursue and how to pursue them manage to do so without reference to anything like an Idea of the Good. The goods which are relevant for Aristotle's investigation are the objectives pursued by "politics," "economics," and "wisdom," the deliberative skills required by a man who is to be responsible for a political community, a household, or himself. Aristotle refers to the combination of these practical skills as the "master skill," the main sort of knowledge a sensible young man needs to acquire.⁵ It is neither possible nor desirable, concludes Aristotle, to search for any profound metaphysical doctrine of "goodness," if we are to achieve clarity about the best way for men to live their lives (EE 1217b1–18b24; NE 1096a11–97a14).

What then is the most successful way for us to live? Like every other creature in the world, man has a particular nature, and the best way for a man to live is to live up to his nature, which is to be a creature directed by a rational soul. The proper function of rational human souls is to make men live well – in other words, in a rational way. Living a well-lived life is the best possible good for man, and this is what it is to succeed as a human being. Living well means living one's life under the guidance of the virtues of the soul. Since success is a perfect and self-sufficient objective, it must include the whole of life and all the most important virtues. Success in life, the best possible good for man, is therefore living one's whole life in a rational way, under the guidance of the best virtues of the rational soul (EE 1218b31–19a39; NE 1097b22–98a20).

Here then is Aristotle's provisional definition of success: living a life of entirely virtuous activity throughout an entire lifetime. He derives confirmation of his definition from several further considerations. It is very fitting that success is to be acquired by the discipline and education which foster virtuous activity; if success was a natural endowment or a matter of luck, then nobody would deserve it, and it would not be the splendid and quasi-divine prize that it is. We praise men for their virtues, but we congratulate them for being

5 Aristotle changed his mind in the Nicomachean Ethics and chose to regard only political wisdom as the "master skill," a change consonant with the more prominent role played by politics in the later work – it begins by arguing that politics is the master skill, and it ends with a transition to a course of lectures on politics much like the Politics that has been transmitted to us (NE 1094a25–b12, 1102a5–26, 1179a32–81b23).

successful; this means that success is the higher good, because we praise men for the qualities that help them achieve the prizes of life, and the achievements are higher goods than the qualities. Aristotle's understanding of success is consonant with all the reputable opinions on the subject: it involves having wisdom; it involves having the virtues; it involves living well and doing things well; it even involves pleasure, for the man of virtue finds it satisfying to live up to his ideals (*EE* 1214a30–b6, 1215a8–19, 1219a39–b4, 1219b8–16; *NE* 1098b9–99a21, 1099b9–25, 1101b10–02a4).

A successful life also needs some degree of good fortune. It is hard to be happy if you are ugly, born to a humble position, or disappointed with your children. It is impossible to serve the public well without the help of friends, wealth, and political influence. This does not mean, however, that success is the same as good fortune, nor that it needs a great deal of it – indeed, too much good fortune can actually be harmful to some men. The best amount of such things is that which fosters our authentic rational self, as much as possible, the amount that "will most produce the contemplation of god" and make us "take notice of the irrational part of the soul, as such, as little as possible" (see below, p. 205). Such a man will be what Aristotle calls a "gentleman" ("noble-and-good" is how the Greek is literally translated), a man who makes proper use of the goods fortune brings his way, and who deserves to enjoy the advantages he enjoys. Only a gentleman can be "magnanimous" (Aristotle's highest term of moral praise), a man who is confident in his possession of all the moral virtues, and confident of deserving what he deserves (see below, pp. 226–228) (*EE* 1248b8–49b25; *NE* 1099a31–b9, 1124a1–4).

Here then is Aristotle's final definition: success is entirely excellent activity, together with moderate good fortune, throughout an entire lifetime. This explains why we never call a boy successful (except in anticipation of future success), and why we cannot have temporarily successful lives. Indeed, a famous proverb advises, "Never call a man successful before his life is over"; only the grave is security against misfortune. Aristotle approves this proverb in the *Eudemian Ethics*, but later he gave it deeper thought. Whether a man's life is successful depends on what he makes of it, which depends on the calibre of his activities, which cannot easily be taken away from a virtuous man; so virtue is the real security against failure. Not even misfortunes on a very large scale can turn our lives into failures, if we have the virtues with which to rise above them and make the best of them (although Aristotle admits that an otherwise successful man will not actually be *happy* when utter disaster strikes). The grave is not the only security against misfortune; nor is it a complete security, for it is widely believed that what happens to our descendents and our reputations can affect whether our life is to be counted a success. Aristotle agrees that such things have *some* effect on the welfare of the dead, although he holds that the effect cannot be significant enough to turn a happy or successful life into an unhappy or failed life. A man will be a happy man if he lives his life virtuously, and enjoys moderate good fortune, and is destined to do so until the end of his days (*EE* 1219b4–8; *NE* 1100a1–01b9).

THE BEST WAYS OF LIFE

Which of the three career alternatives is best – the life of pleasant amusement, the life of virtuous public service, or the life of philosophy? One mistaken argument in favour of pleasant amusement is that those who have absolute power to choose (kings and tyrants and others in high places) often lead lives entirely abandoned to it. But this preference is shared with slaves and animals, who know no other sort of pleasure; and Aristotle refuses to accept the verdict of these powerful men, who have probably never known the satisfactions of higher activities. It would be far better to consult thinking men, like Anaxagoras, men who have known the rewards of intellectual activity as well as the pleasures of the flesh and other unworthy amusements. It would be silly and childish to exert oneself so as to be able to amuse oneself; the proper thing is to treat amusement as relaxation, amusing oneself in order to be better able to work at the serious business of life (*EE* 1216a10–19; *NE* 1095b14–22, 1176b9–77a11).

While the life of pleasure is suitable only for children, slaves, and animals, the political life of virtue is suitable for men. Man is the sort of animal whose nature it is to live in a political community, says Aristotle in the *Politics*, and in his lecture courses on politics his main audience consisted of young men whose future involved returning to their home cities to take up a prominent role in public affairs. This is a fine and proper way of life, and Aristotle never says anything against it. But he does stress that it is fine and proper only if one has the virtues and is prepared to serve the public; the sort of political life that is aimed at lining one's pocket or becoming famous is not to be recommended (*EE* 1216a19–27; *NE* 1095b22–96a4, 1178a9–b7; *Pol* 1253a1–18).

But the highest possible way of life is that which expresses the highest element in us, the divine element of reason. This is the life devoted to the appreciation of truth, the activity that Aristotle calls intellectual contemplation. "If intellect is divine, then, in comparison with man, the life according to it is divine in comparison with human life. But we must not follow those who advise us, being men, to think of human things, and, being mortal, of mortal things, but must, so far as we can, make ourselves immortal, and strain every nerve to live in accordance with the best thing in us; for even if it be small in bulk, much more does it in power and worth surpass everything." "Whether it [the best thing in us] be itself also divine or only the most divine element in us, the activity of this in accordance with its proper virtue will be perfect success." This element is what we really are, since it is the highest and most authoritative element in us; it would be absurd to favour any other element in us, because that would be to prefer to live outside ourselves (*NE* 1177a12–18, 1177b26–1178a8).

Much else can be said in favour of the intellectual life. It is more self-sufficient than the political life, requiring less of what is in the control of fortune – wealth, power, and the support of other men. Contemplating the truth is the least wearying of the serious activities, and we can contemplate the truth more continuously than we can do anything else. The pleasures of truth are particularly pure and long-lasting. Contemplation is an activity especially suitable for leisure and aims at nothing beyond itself. The gods themselves cannot be supposed to have the moral virtues – what would they need them for? Their only activity is contemplation, and so the intellectual life is the life that is closest to the way the gods live, the life most favoured by the gods (*NE* 1177a18–78a8, 1178a21–79a32).

REASON AND THE VIRTUES OF THE MIND

Man is a rational animal, and he is at his best when he uses his reason in the best way. The correct and best use of reason is to know the truth. The dispositions of the mind which enable us to know the truth are called "intellectual virtues," to distinguish them from moral virtues, the dispositions of our emotions which help us respond correctly to practical situations. The rational side and the emotional side are different aspects of our nature, and their virtues do not overlap, with one important exception: the intellectual virtue called practical wisdom, whose function is to enable us to know the correct way to behave. While practical wisdom is not itself a moral virtue, it is closely associated with the moral virtues, as the discussion below will make clear.

The best place to start is with the intellectual virtue called "knowledge" or "scientific knowledge." Aristotle speaks of this virtue in terms of his discussion of scientific knowledge in the *Prior Analytics* and *Posterior Analytics*. According to those books, scientific knowledge consists of deductions from more basic principles of nature. In order to make the right deductions, we have to be able to hit upon the correct basic principles of nature – not an easy business.[6] This ability is the second intellectual virtue, which is called "comprehension" or "intuition." The third intellectual virtue is called "wisdom" or "scientific wisdom" and consists of the combination of the first two; it is the ability to have a complete and profound understanding of nature. The activity of this combined virtue is what Aristotle calls "contemplation," appreciating the truths that organize the universe in which we find ourselves. This activity of contemplation is the finest activity available to us, as we have seen above (*NE 1139b18–36, 1140b31–41b8).

These three intellectual virtues concern the facts about the universe that cannot be altered. The two other virtues of the mind, practical wisdom and skill, concern the things that we can bring about or change. A skill (or "art") enables us to know what steps to take to bring something into being; examples of skill include shoemaking, which brings into being something material (a shoe), and medicine, which brings into being something immaterial (health). Aristotle says little about skills, because the young gentlemen whom he is addressing have no need of them, being members of the landholding class, and because Aristotle generally disdains men of the working class. Some philosophers had argued that practical wisdom was a

6 Which Aristotle describes in a very sketchy way in the last chapter of the *Posterior Analytics*.

sort of skill, because it brought about correct conduct. But Aristotle strictly separates conduct from other kinds of product ("making and acting are different") and he treats practical wisdom quite separately (*NE 1140a1–23, 1140b21–30; Pol 1319a19–32).

Practical wisdom is the intellectual virtue which mainly interests Aristotle. He distinguishes it from the knowledge of lower goods (e.g., health, wealth, and strength, which are good only when they lead to a higher human good); it is an awareness of the highest goods, what is good for men as human beings. He defines it as "a true and reasoned state of capacity to act with regard to the things that are good or bad for man" (*NE 1140a24–b21).

He also distinguishes it from all the other intellectual virtues and from related intellectual qualities. Practical wisdom includes excellent deliberation, and excellent deliberation is correct practical thinking, which can quickly reach the correct conclusion from the correct premises by means of the correct inference. Practical wisdom is not the same as the associated state called "understanding," because understanding is good judgment of what others do or say, and is not itself practically oriented (*NE 1142a23–43a24).

Practical wisdom has various forms: one relating to the individual man, another relating to the household, and another relating to the political community. Political wisdom itself has two aspects: a general one, which is called legislative wisdom, and one that makes particular decrees and decisions, which is known by the overall term "political wisdom." In the same way, while part of practical wisdom involves a general appreciation of the human good as such, another part tells us what to do in particular cases and therefore involves an appreciation of particular facts. This explains why older men, who have much experience of particular facts, tend to have more practical wisdom (*NE 1141b8–42a23).

All in all, practical wisdom is an appreciation of what is good and bad for us at the highest level, together with a correct apprehension of the facts of experience, together with the skill to make the correct inferences about how to apply our general moral knowledge to our particular situation, and to do so quickly and reliably. It is used in our own cases when we are obliged to commit ourselves to some course of action. Obviously it is a very important asset; if we had it, we would always act in the right ways and our lives would be successful and happy.

But this seems to raise a problem. Since the moral virtues make us do what is right (see below, pp. 213–214), why should we need to have practical wisdom to perform the same function? But a closer analysis reveals that their functions are not quite the same. If we have a virtue, then we will have the right objective, e.g., to be gracious to our guest. But it requires an intellectual ability to know the right steps to take in order that our guest be treated graciously. A proper function of practical wisdom is to put into practice the correct orientation of values, which the moral virtues provide. It is possible to have the right values without knowing how to achieve them in practice – a sort of moral clumsiness. Likewise it is possible to know how to execute objectives without having the right values, in which case we are perhaps clever, but not wise. It's better to have sensible virtue than naive virtue, and better to have virtuous good sense than amoral cleverness (*NE 1143b18–33, 1144a11–b17).

Indeed, real wisdom involves knowing the right values, "the things that are good or bad for man," as well as being able to put them into practice; so it is not possible to be really wise without having the moral virtues as well. Likewise, it is not possible to have a fully developed moral virtue without having practical wisdom as well. Socrates had argued that all the virtues are the same because they are all forms of knowledge. Aristotle disagreed; he thought that the virtues differ from each other because they involve different emotions. But Aristotle also holds that if a man has one virtue, he must have them all, because if he has one fully developed virtue, he has practical wisdom, and if he has practical wisdom, then he has all the virtues. And Aristotle recognizes that his view has turned out to be very similar to the Socratic one. "Socrates, then, thought the virtues were forms of reason (for he thought they were, all of them, forms of knowledge), while we think they involve reason." Still, Aristotle insists that Socrates' view is not quite right; every kind of knowledge can be misused for bad purposes, but practical wisdom cannot be misused; so practical wisdom is akin to virtue, "not a species of knowledge, but another kind of cognition" (*NE 1144b17–45a6, EE 1246a26–b36).

RESPONSIBILITY FOR ACTIONS AND DECISIONS

A man reveals himself by what he voluntarily does. Acting voluntarily is not to be defined as "acting on one's desires," because it cannot be defined as acting on any of the three kinds of desire that Plato elucidated[7] – sensual appetite, moral passion, and rational will. Nor is acting voluntarily to be defined as "acting on one's decisions," because one may act voluntarily on the spur of the moment, without having made any decision, or even against the decision one has already made. On the other hand, what makes an action *in*voluntary is being unaware of something important about it. If I am mistaken about who I am dealing with, or what I am using, or what is likely to result, then I am not voluntarily poisoning my long-lost father, for example, although I am voluntarily offering this gray-bearded stranger a refreshing drink. If the excuse of ignorance is to be a valid excuse, my ignorance must be reasonable and not my fault, as when I am drunk or careless. Nor is ignorance of my legal or moral duties a valid excuse. (Nor can I offer the excuse of ignorance unless I regret the outcome.) If this is what makes an action *in*voluntary, then acting voluntarily is to be defined as "acting with reasonable knowledge of the circumstances" (*EE* 1223a21–24a7, 1225a36–b16; *NE* 1110b18–11b3).

But this definition is not yet adequate, because sometimes men are compelled to do things for which we are reluctant to hold them responsible. If I was pushed into you, then although I did knowingly strike you, I couldn't help it. If my ship runs into a storm I may have to throw your cargo overboard. Perhaps acting voluntarily is to be defined as this: "acting with reasonable knowledge of the circumstances, provided one could have acted otherwise." But this proviso can be abused, and the excuse is not always valid. If I have to kill you to win a parlour game, does that excuse the murder? People often say that they "had to" do something, when what they really mean is that they thought it was better than the alternatives. Strictly speaking, then, acting voluntarily is "acting with reasonable knowledge of the circumstances, unless it was literally impossible to do otherwise." Even in cases where our range of choice is restricted by unfavourable circumstances, we remain responsible for what we choose to do; but any assessment of our behaviour must take into account the alternatives we faced, and Aristotle calls these "mixed" actions (*EE* 1224a7–25a36; *NE* 1109b35–10b17).

A decision (or "choice") is neither an intention nor a desire nor an

7 In the *Republic* 435d–444a.

opinion about what is best. A decision is defined as "a deliberate desire to do something within the agent's immediate range of alternatives." Aristotle calls it a "deliberate desire" because it is a desire formed after a process of deliberation, in which the agent considers how to put his objectives into practice. In the process of deliberating, one starts from some objective (e.g., health) and considers how to achieve it (e.g., better nutrition), and then how to achieve that (e.g., become a better cook), and then how to achieve that (e.g., enroll in a cooking school), reasoning backwards, so to speak, until one reaches something that one can actually do. Decisions reveal the man, because his decisions indicate his values and the quality of his practical thinking. His character determines his basic values, and his practical intellect determines how to put them into effect (see above pp. 205–208). Everybody pursues what he regards as good, although men with the wrong values are mistaken about what actually *is* good (*EE* 1225b18–28a19; *NE* 1111b4–13b2).

It is right to praise and blame us for our decisions and for our voluntary actions, because they accurately reveal the sort of men we are. If this needs further proof, consider the practice of rewarding and punishing: if men weren't in control of their behaviour, there would be no point in rewarding and punishing them. But here's a possible objection: if I'm a thoughtless or careless sort of man, then I can't effectively control my behaviour. That is no excuse, says Aristotle, because you are responsible for having turned into that sort of man. Indeed, we influence the development of *all* aspects of our personalities by how we choose to spend our time and what we choose to do; it is obvious that gambling produces gamblers and military exercises produce bravery. Although I cannot be a different sort of man just by deciding to, I remain responsible for having encouraged myself to become the sort of man I have become, just as I cannot stop the stone that I threw at you, although I remain responsible for having thrown it. Aristotle is confident in holding bad men responsible for their wickedness, and believes that any argument that could absolve them of their badness would also deprive good men of their goodness (*NE* 1113b3–15a3).

UNDERSTANDING PLEASURE

Although Aristotle takes a dim view of what he calls the life of pleasure, he is not opposed to pleasure itself. To have an opinion about whether pleasure is good or bad, one needs to know what pleasure actually is – not an easy question, and one on which Aristotle's fellow philosophers had widely varying opinions. Plato thought that the paradigm case of pleasure is eating and drinking; the pleasure comes from noticing that we are being restored to our natural state of fullness. On this view, what is good is the state of fullness, and it is a confusion to regard the pleasure as good, because it is only a process toward something good.

For Aristotle, on the contrary, the paradigm case of pleasure is being aware of something that holds our attention, e.g., listening to good music or understanding an elegant mathematical theorem. When our awareness is unimpeded and when what we are aware of is really interesting, then pleasure will perfect the experience, "as an end which supervenes, as the bloom of youth does on those in the flower of their age." The attractiveness of a pleasant activity is not something extra, beyond the activity's being a good one of its kind; the pleasure is like the beauty of a young person in the prime of life. Likewise for other activities that may not involve awareness – Aristotle's general view is that pleasure is involved in any unfrustrated activity that exercises our natural capacities (*NE* 1174b14–75a3).

On Aristotle's analysis, whether a pleasure is good depends entirely on whether the associated activity is good. In general he holds that knowledge and other kinds of awareness are good, although he ranks intellectual knowledge above sense perception, and seeing and hearing above tasting and touching (see below pp. 219–220). Different species have different pleasures, and so do different men. How do we decide which pleasures are the proper pleasures for us? We should regard as a standard the man who is in a normal condition, the man who has the virtues of the human condition. If others enjoy different things, that is because their natures have been corrupted, and what they enjoy cannot be said to be proper pleasures for men. Since a successful and happy life is a life of activities well performed, it will also be a life full of pleasures, and it is right, as Aristotle says, to weave pleasure into our ideal of the happy life. But the pleasures of the ideal life will come directly from its serious and worthy activities, not from the frivolous amusements of the so-called life of pleasure (*NE* 1152b25–33; *NE* 1175b24–76a29).

Aristotle rejects Plato's analysis of pleasure for various reasons. On Plato's view, pleasure presupposes a previous deprivation, but Aristotle points out that some pleasures, notably the pleasures of mental and perceptual awareness, do not. On Plato's view, since pleasure is a process of restoration, then it must be incomplete and unfinished until it reaches its goal; but this is not true of pleasure, says Aristotle, because whenever we are enjoying ourselves we can also say that we have enjoyed ourselves. On Plato's view, since pleasure is a process to a goal, it must have a velocity; but we cannot be pleased quickly or slowly, says Aristotle. Plato was wrong to base his understanding of pleasure on bodily pleasures, although this was understandable, says Aristotle, because they are the most intense of pleasures – some unrefined men are actually unaware of any other sort. Plato's definition of pleasure was "perceptible process to a natural condition," but Aristotle's alternative definition is "unimpeded activity of a natural condition" (*NE 1152b33–53a17, 1154a22–b20; NE 1173a29–b20).

Apart from Plato's argument, there were others that implied that pleasure was not good, all of which Aristotle rejects. "Pleasure is bad because wicked pleasure-seekers pursue it." Answer: what is bad is only the wrong pleasures or the excess of bodily pleasure, not pleasure itself. "Pleasure is bad because many pleasures are unhealthy." Answer: all good things are bad in some respect or other, in some circumstances at least. There are no valid arguments to show that pleasure is generally a bad thing (*NE 1153a17–35; NE 1173b20–31, 1174a13–b14).

On the contrary, pleasure must be generally a good thing, because its opposite, pain, is bad. Moreover, every living creature, both rational and irrational, aims at pleasure and chooses to have it, and unless nature is thoroughly mistaken, that must indicate that pleasure is good. Furthermore, something is particularly worth choosing and good if it is chosen for its own sake, not for the sake of something else, and this is true of pleasure – we enjoy ourselves for the sake of the enjoyment, not for any further purpose. Pleasure is indeed a good thing, in Aristotle's view, when it arises from the proper activities of men in proper moral condition, and our highest good, a successfully lived life, will include pleasure as one of its blessings (*NE 1153b1–54a21; NE 1172b9–73a13, 1175a10–21).

EMOTIONS AND THE MORAL VIRTUES

A man who wants to have a successful and happy life must become an excellent man. We are composed of a rational part and an irrational part, and proper moral character consists in having the irrational elements controlled by the rational elements. The irrational elements are the emotions: for example, anger, fear, love, lust, thirst, hunger, envy, hatred, ambition, resentment, pity, elation, and in general the mental events and conditions that are accompanied by pleasure and pain. The moral virtues are settled habits of character which express themselves in the correct emotional response. What is the correct emotional response? It is what reason says it should be (*EE* 1219b26–20a13, 1220b7–20; *NE* 1102a26–03a10, 1105b19–06a12).

The problem with emotions is that they are not easily controlled by reasoning; it is usually quite pointless to try to reason yourself out of a feeling of hatred or anger or lust. Emotions need to be controlled in a different way, by being trained over a long period of time, preferably from early youth. Aristotle's moral philosophy is remarkable for the stress it places on the efficacy of moral training and the inefficacy of moral argument. "If arguments were in themselves enough to make men good, they would justly, as Theognis said, have won very great rewards, and such rewards would have been provided; but as things are . . . they are not able to encourage many men to become gentlemen." Men must rather be well trained and habituated, under the guidance of the community's laws, customs, and education, and the discipline of the family. Of course, it is possible for young men to receive *bad* training: "it makes no small difference, then, whether we form habits of one kind or another from our very youth; it makes a very great difference, or rather *all* the difference" (*EE* 1220a22–b7; *NE* 1103a14–04b3, 1179b4–10).

Since the emotions are bound up with pleasure and pain, the moral virtues and vices, which are dispositions of emotions, will also be bound up with pleasure and pain. Our moral characters are formed by the judicious application of pleasure and pain, when we are punished and rewarded for our youthful behavior. Most men evaluate their own conduct in terms of pleasure and pain, and there is a certain pleasure in doing what you know to be right, even when it is contrary to your inclinations. Indeed, if you didn't enjoy doing what was right, that would be a sign that you didn't have the relevant virtue. For example, if you restrained yourself from indulging in some tasty delicacy, but did so with difficulty and resentment, that would indicate that you were not self-controlled; only if you cheerfully declined the excessive indulgence could you be said to have the virtue of self-control (EE 1220a34–39, 1221b27–22a5; NE 1099a7–21, 1104b3–05a16).

But there seems to be a paradox. The moral virtues are said to be developed by training in the appropriate behaviour, but how can we develop them? To become brave, for example, we need to do brave things; but to do brave things don't we already need to be brave? Aristotle offers two solutions: 1) in the case of technical skills, like handwriting, we first practise under the guidance of another person, which enables us to do the appropriate thing without yet having the skill, and the same is true of moral qualities; 2) moral virtues are different from technical skills in that the goodness of the performance resides mainly in expressing the character of the man. If an action is really to have the goodness that an act of bravery has, it must be done by a man whose character is firmly and permanently brave, and it must be done by him for its own sake, because he knows it is the right thing to do. If this is what virtuous conduct is, then youthful training in bravery does not require that the boy already be brave. He is only practising what will make him brave, and only after much practice will he turn into a brave man (NE 1105a17–b18; *NE 1144a11–20).

MORAL WEAKNESS

Human nature admits of many sorts of good and bad conditions. The worst depravities of human nature are rare and to be found "chiefly among foreigners," says Aristotle (with a frank xenophobia common to many ancient Greeks); but they can also result from disease, madness, or extremely bad habits. In this category are cannibalism, ritual murder, outrageous cruelty, chewing one's nails (or coal or dirt or raw meat), and effeminate homosexuality. Any extremely developed vice is also a depravity; extreme cowardice, like being afraid of weasels or mice, is depraved, as is the extreme foolishness of those "distant foreigners" who live by their senses alone, like animals (*NE 1145a27–33, 1148b15–49a20).

Although such depravities of human nature are rare, ordinary human vice is all too common. A vice is a condition of the soul in which an emotion is incorrectly adjusted, and the rational part of us does not realize that anything is wrong; the emotion is felt either too much or too little, but to the man himself it seems about right. Moral weakness ("incontinence") is similar to vice in that our emotions are out of adjustment and cause us to do the wrong thing; it is also dissimilar to vice in that our rational part is aware that what we do is wrong. Yet we still do it, because the moral and rational side of us is weaker than the emotional side. Vice and moral weakness are different conditions, although they sometimes lead to the same results. Moral weakness is aware of itself, but vice is not; it involves regret, but vice does not. Moral weakness is easier to cure because the man with vice has got his priorities so thoroughly wrong that he cannot be persuaded out of his false opinions. Vice is thorough badness, but moral weakness is only partial badness (*NE 1146a31–b2, 1150b29–51a20).

Moral strength is partial goodness because morally strong men manage to do the right thing, despite the fact that their emotions are incorrectly adjusted and they must struggle with bad impulses. It is the same state as moral weakness, except that the rational side retains the upper hand. Virtue is a quite different state, in which the emotions are correctly adjusted as well; there is no need for the moral personality to be strong because there is no struggle with incorrect impulses. Virtue is thorough goodness, but there is also a still higher state, a state of "godlike" virtue, which rises above human virtue much as the state of depravity (literally "animality") falls below human vice. Aristotle says very little about godlike virtue here, but in the *Politics* he recognizes the possibility of such a man, and says that this sort of man would have the moral authority to rule over entire societies with absolute and legitimate power (*NE 1145a15–b20, 1151a20–28; Pol 1284a3–17, 1284b22–34, 1288a15–b29).

The virtues and vices are admirably discussed elsewhere in Aristotle's ethical works, and since Aristotle treats moral strength entirely in terms of moral weakness, the important condition to understand is moral weakness. Aristotle discusses only three major kinds of moral weakness, the ones which have to do with pleasure, pain, and anger, and he considers all other kinds of moral weakness to be extensions of these central cases. Further, these three major kinds effectively boil down to one, because although he gives a different name to the moral weakness involved with pain ("softness"), he assimilates the desire to avoid pain to the desire to enjoy pleasure, and he argues, in a series of unusually unconvincing arguments, that moral weakness in respect of anger is not as disreputable as moral weakness in respect of pleasure, and therefore reserves the name "moral weakness" for the variety which has to do with pleasure (*NE 1147b20–48b14, 1149a24–b23, 1150a9–b19).

Moral weakness is thus reduced to an excessive enthusiasm for the pleasures of food, drink, and sex, the same as are relevant to "temperance" (see below, pp. 219–220), except that the morally weak man has the correct opinion about which pleasures not to enjoy. Some men get so excited by the presence of wrong pleasures that it doesn't occur to them that they shouldn't enjoy them until afterward, when it is too late. Others realize that they shouldn't enjoy a certain pleasure, but fail to act in the light of their moral understanding. The latter are in a worse and less curable state than the former, and Aristotle concentrates on trying to understand their condition (*NE 1148a4–17, 1150b19–28, 1152a27–33).

Socrates had denied that it was possible to realize what it was right to do and yet not do it, and Aristotle fundamentally agrees with him in holding that practical wisdom is the highest authority in the soul. Yet it's a plain fact of experience that men do behave in this puzzling way. How can this be explained? Practical thinking involves two kinds of realization: a general view that things of a certain type would be bad (or good) for certain people, in situations of a certain type, to do; and the perception that this would be a thing of the relevant type, and that I am in a situation of the relevant type. The combination of the two realizations results in the appropriate action. But the presence of strong passions, like anger and sexual desire, can disconnect a man's thinking, much as drunkenness does; and even if men in these conditions might say, "No, you're a married woman" or "No, not here," they don't fully grasp what they are saying – they have the awareness and yet, in a sense, they don't have it. This is Aristotle's general explanation for moral weakness: we fully realize the general truth that certain sorts of things are right and wrong, but we don't quite realize that our own immediate situation is one of

them, because the passion which affects us disconnects our appreciation of our situation. Because we don't quite have this realization to
combine with the general principle, our rational self cannot apply
the principle, and the way is clear for passion to be temporary cham-
pion of the field. Aristotle manages to find an explanation of moral
weakness that disturbs the Socratic position as little as possible[8]
(*NE 1145b21–47b19).

MORAL VIRTUES AS MIDDLE STATES

What is the opposite of bravery? Cowardice, right? Not quite. According to Aristotle, there are *two* opposites of bravery – cowardice and
rashness. Cowardice is having too much fear, and rashness is having
too little. The same is true of every other virtue. Every virtue lies in
the middle between two associated vices, one in the direction of too
much emotion, the other in the direction of too little emotion. This
is one of Aristotle's most famous doctrines, the "doctrine of the
mean."

To say that the right amount of emotion is in between two wrong
amounts is not to say that it is the average of those two amounts.
Sometimes the right amount is much closer to one than to the other.
In fact, the right amount varies very much according to the individual circumstances of the case. For example, you ought to feel different degrees of generosity for different people, depending on their
relationship to you and on their needs. Aristotle expresses this fact,
that the correct amount is variable, by referring to it as "the intermediate relatively to us ... which is neither too much nor too little –
and this is not one, nor the same for all" (NE 1106a26–b7).

Every virtue is in the middle between two vices. This does not
mean that every vice is a matter of degree. For example, all adultery
and all assault are wrong, even once in a while. Envy and spite are
wrong emotions to feel, whenever you feel them. The very words
"adultery" and "spite" indicate that they are wrong, unlike "sex"
and "anger", which are in many circumstances perfectly acceptable
(EE 1221b18–26; NE 1107a8–27).

---

8 It should be noted that this passage has several obscurities and has given
   rise to numerous discussions, including entire books, so there is no
   doubt more that could be said.

A man with a virtue will always have the right response, but not vice versa; a man with a vice will not always have the wrong response. For example, a man who is good-tempered will never have too much anger; but there are many ways of being bad-tempered (indeed we have a whole vocabulary to describe them), and a bad-tempered man will not be bad-tempered on every occasion. A quick-tempered man becomes angry too quickly, a grumpy man gets angry at too many provocations, and a bitter man stays angry too long. These are all "bad-tempered" men, but a grumpy man is not usually quick-tempered, nor is a quick-tempered man usually bitter. There is one way of being right, but there are many different ways of being wrong (EE 1221b9–17; NE 1106b8–35).

Every virtue is in between two vices; but this does not mean that each of the vices is equally close to the virtue. Indeed, the virtue is normally closer to one of the vices than to the other. For example, many men tend to be excessively enthusiastic about pleasure, and "intemperance" is naturally supposed to be the opposite of "temperance." But there is another opposite, more unusual and more similar to temperance, the disposition to desire pleasures insufficiently. This is such an unusual state that it does not have a name of its own in common currency, and Aristotle coins the term "insensibility." Human nature is more or less constant and tends toward one vice rather than the other; it is the vice to which we tend (e.g., intemperance) that we refer to as "the opposite" of the virtue. This usage is strictly speaking incorrect because there are *two* opposites of every virtue, but it is nevertheless a comprehensible usage, which expresses a truth of human nature (EE 1222a22–b4, 1234a34–b13; NE 1108b11–09a19).

All this explains why it is no easy matter to be virtuous. To have a particular virtue we need to cultivate a disposition which always involves us in the correct degree of emotional response. One can go wrong in many ways, and, as Aristotle says, it takes skill to find the exact middle of a circle. One thing that helps is to know your own weaknesses, to know the directions in which you tend to make mistakes, and in those cases "we must drag ourselves away to the contrary extreme; for we shall get into the intermediate state by drawing well away from error, as men do in straightening sticks that are bent." The doctrine of the mean is useful as well as true, and if it seems very abstract as I have just described it, it will

become clearer below when I discuss the various individual virtues
(*NE* 1109a20–b7).

MORAL VIRTUES AND VICES

a. Anger

Men feel angry toward other men when they resent being insulted
or frustrated by them. Feeling angry too much is obviously not
desirable, and Aristotle calls such men irascible or bad-tempered.
He also thinks it a fault to feel anger insufficiently; he calls such
men slavish and stupid, and in the *Eudemian Ethics* this appears
to be as serious a fault as its opposite. But he modified his position, and in the *Nicomachean Ethics* he says that excessive anger
is the worse fault, and the more common one. Bad temper comes
in a variety of forms: hot-tempered men get angry too quickly;
choleric men get angry too often; "bad-tempered" men get too
angry when they get angry; violent men express their anger physically; and sulky or bitter men stay angry too long. Fortunately,
nobody can be irascible in all these ways. It is not easy to know
exactly how much anger is appropriate, and there is nothing wrong
in deviating slightly from the mean (*EE* 1221b9–15, 1231b5–26;
NE 1125b26–26b10).

b. Sensual pleasure

The symposium, or drinking-party, was an evening of dining, heavy
drinking, and amusement, usually with paid entertainers and prosti-
tutes. Obviously this could be taken too far, and Aristotle criticizes
the excessive desire for food, drink, and sex as the serious vice he
calls dissoluteness (or intemperance or profligacy). Aristotle thinks
that we should have only a little desire for such pleasures, that our
desires should be only moderately strong, that they should be only
for the pleasures that are strictly necessary for our health, that they
should be entirely under the control of reason, and that we shouldn't
mind if we can't satisfy them. This is "temperance," the virtuous
middle, in Aristotle's rather puritan view. The opposite flaw, having
an insufficient enthusiasm for pleasure, is very rare, and there is no

established term for it (*EE* 1230b9–20, 1231a26–b2; *NE* 1109b7–13, 1118b8–19a33).

What Aristotle criticizes in dissolute men is a quite specific flaw. He criticizes the desire for pleasures of the body, not the desire for pleasure in general, since there are excellent pleasures in thinking and in virtuous activity. Among the pleasures of the body's senses, Aristotle has no objection to the pleasures of the visual or musical arts or sweet smells. But the only smells that dissolute men enjoy are sexy perfumes and savoury dinners, because they remind them of what they want, the pleasures of touching and tasting, the two senses that operate by contact in a rather crude animal way. In fact, they don't even really discriminate between different flavours; they enjoy their food and drink in the backs of their throats rather than on the tips of their tongues – Philoxenus, a notorious gourmand who prayed to have his throat as long as a crane's, is cited as evidence. Nor do they enjoy being touched in every part of their body (there is nothing wrong with enjoying respectable rub-downs after exercise). The specific flaw that Aristotle criticizes is excessive desire for oral and genital stimulation, a sort of basic immaturity which Aristotle despises. Such men knowingly risk death with their excesses – they would even be happy to die if dying felt good – but that doesn't make them courageous, says Aristotle snidely (*EE* 1230a37–b8, 1230b21–31a26; *NE* 1117b23–18b8, 1119a33–b18).

c. Fear

Men feel frightened in the face of many threats, most obviously when other men are threatening them with death. This is actually the only fear that Aristotle thinks is relevant to the virtue of courage, for if one fears that one will suffer from envy or insult or shame or poverty or discomfort or disease, then that is not real fear, and being able to put up with these things is not real courage. The threat of death which a courageous man succeeds in facing is immediate (not distant or hypothetical) but within the power of man to resist (not supernatural or inevitable). Courage is expressed in battle, for this is man's finest hour (*EE* 1229a32–b25; *NE* 1115a6–b6).

The opposite of fear is confidence, and Aristotle says that the coward has too much fear and too little confidence, and the fool-hardy man has too much confidence and too little fear, with the courageous man in the middle. The brave man endures frightening things more than cowards do, not because he has more fears to endure, but because fewer frightening situations are frightening *to him*. The foolhardy man goes too far in this direction, and not enough situations are frightening to him (*EE* 1228a26–b38; *NE* 1115b24–16a9).

But it also matters *why* a man faces up to frightening situations, as can be seen by looking at what Aristotle calls "false courage." Some men have a special fund of confidence, like seasoned merce-naries who know the enemy's real strength, or men who have been lucky in the past or are drunk. Other men have no fear because they would welcome death anyway. Other people are fearless be-cause they don't know what to be afraid of, like children and mad-men who pick up snakes and face moving vehicles. Still other creatures (especially "foreigners" and animals) have what looks like courage because they are overcome with anger or other strong emotion, and many citizen-soldiers face the enemy only because they have a stronger fear of disgrace (*EE* 1229a11–31, 1229b25–30a21; *NE* 1116a10–17a27).

Real courage is different, says Aristotle, because the courageous man's reason for facing the enemy is that it is the right and proper thing to do. If the situation is desperate, then he is afraid he might be killed, but he faces the enemy all the same, because that is what is right. Clearly, having moderate fear and confidence is only part of what courage is; the more important part is having the will to overcome one's fears in the service of what is right. This can be a struggle, and no doubt this is why Aristotle admits that courage is an exception to his view that men enjoy acting virtuously. This also means that courage turns out to be a sort of moral strength, not at all the same thing as virtue. Perhaps courage is actually two things, not one – a proper adjustment of the emotions of fear and confidence, and a moral strength to do the right thing, against the promptings of the emotions if necessary. Aristotle seems to ac-knowledge that there is more to say on the subject, concluding that "we have now spoken tolerably adequately for our present pur-pose" (*EE* 1228b38–29a11, 1230a21–36; *NE* 1104b3–8, 1115b7–24, 1117a29–b22).

d. Social justice

The justice system of any society will prohibit wrong actions and permit good ones, so justice and injustice in the broadest sense is what is legal and illegal. But Aristotle focuses on a narrower sense, in which we blame a man for injustice when he does something wrong *for his own advantage*. Justice is a kind of equality; therefore injustice is a kind of inequality, and the unjust man aims at an unequal share of something good. In fact, there are two different kinds of justice, for which Aristotle offers two different mathematical analyses (*NE 1129a17–31a9).

The first kind of justice regulates the distribution of what is produced in a common enterprise, for example, in a commercial partnership. Here is Aristotle's mathematical analysis of distributive justice:

$$\frac{\text{man A}}{\text{man B}} = \frac{\text{benefit A}}{\text{benefit B}} \quad or \quad \frac{\text{man A}}{\text{benefit A}} = \frac{\text{man B}}{\text{benefit B}}$$

In other words, take the value of what one man contributes to a common enterprise and the value of the benefit that he derives from it; if this ratio is the same as the ratio for other contributors, then he has an equal share. The most important case of a common enterprise is society itself, and a merit of Aristotle's analysis is that it explains the struggle between democrats and oligarchs as a dispute about justice; democrats claim that all freely born citizens are equal partners in society, and oligarchs claim that the rich contribute more. Aristotle himself holds that virtuous citizens (not necessarily the rich) do make greater contributions to their societies, and that they should expect greater rewards in honour and respect (*NE 1131a9–b24, 1134a23–b18).

The second kind of justice ensures that transactions between two individuals do not introduce new inequalities. When I buy a pair of shoes from you at a fair price, we exchange things of equal value. Money is a conventional representative of demand, which makes it possible for any commodity to be exchanged with any other, in proportions which depend on the relative demand for them. Three pairs of shoes, for example, may be exchanged for the price of a bed. On the assumption that we were on an equal footing before, the fair exchange preserves the equality between us.⁹ Buying and selling are voluntary transactions, and a similar analysis governs what Aristotle calls "involuntary transactions," illegal actions in which one man profits at another's expense. For example, if you have stolen from me, you have more and I have less, and, on the law's assumption that we were equal before, we are now unequal. Justice requires me to be compensated and you to be punished, so that our equality is restored (*NE 1131b25–33b28).

In both kinds of justice, the just outcome is a mean between unfair gain and unfair loss. If you have less than is fair of what is good (or more of what is bad), then you have been unjustly treated. If you have more than is fair of what is good, then you have benefited from injustice. If you have caused yourself to benefit in this way, then you have committed an act of injustice. If you deliberately chose to benefit from injustice, then you are an unjust and wicked man. You are a just man if your will is always to ensure that everybody gets a fair share, others as well as yourself. Being just is more difficult than simply knowing the provisions of the law; you need to know how to apply them in particular cases, which is the difficult part that requires practical wisdom (*NE 1129a6–17, 1133b30–34a23, 1135a15–36a9, 1137a4–26).

Who commits the injustice, the man who receives the unfairly large share or the man who distributes it to him? When these are different men, it is the distributor who commits the injustice, either accidentally or else deliberately (when bribed, for example). When they are the same man, he is obviously committing an injustice. But what if he knowingly assigns to himself an unfairly *small* share? Is he treating himself unjustly? No, because treating someone unjustly requires that somebody be treated unjustly. Is he treated unjustly? No, because it is not against his will that he has the share he has. The only sense in which a man could be said to treat himself

9 Aristotle thinks it illuminating to represent the equality before the exchange as a proportionate equality:

$$\frac{\text{the carpenter}}{\text{the shoemaker}} = \frac{\text{a bed}}{\text{a pair of shoes,}}$$

the same sort of proportion as in distributive justice. But I can't see how this illuminates the situation, nor can other scholars, whose interpretations of this passage differ widely.

unjustly is metaphorical, when he favours the inferior parts of his nature at the expense of the superior parts (*NE 1136a10–37a4, 1138a4–b13).

Justice is a difficult virtue to master because it requires the interpretation of universal principles in particular situations. These universal principles are of two sorts, unwritten principles of justice, which are generally valid and have the force of "natural" justice, and written laws, which decree standards, prohibitions, and injunctions in particular jurisdictions. Some philosophers had argued that there was no natural justice because there were no laws common to all jurisdictions; but it is quite possible for some or all jurisdictions to be mistaken, argues Aristotle, and every well-legislated society will use both kinds of legal principle. Applying a legal principle to a particular case will inevitably involve awkwardness from time to time; "the reason is that all law is universal, but about some things it is not possible to make a universal statement which shall be correct." This calls for "equity" (or fair-mindedness, an aspect of the virtue of justice) to apply the principles of law in a flexible way to the complexities of life (*NE 1134b18–35a13, 1137a31–38a3).

e. Social graces

We appreciate certain qualities in the men we socialize with, such as friendliness, unpretentiousness, and wittiness; but does that make them moral virtues? No, according to Aristotle in the *Eudemian Ethics*; he thought they were unreflective qualities that did not express themselves in conscious choices – "that's just the way he is," one often says of friendly or witty men. But in the *Nicomachean Ethics*, he apparently recognized that one can cultivate these qualities and deliberately decide to live up to them, which makes them virtues like all the others (EE 1234a23–34).

It is good to be friendly and obliging, but one can take that too far by never causing disappointment and always gratifying the wishes of others. To do so is to be obsequious, unless you have an ulterior motive, in which case you are a sycophant. The opposite sort of man, who makes no effort to avoid causing offence, is churlish and obviously bad. The virtue in the middle is something like friendliness and is characterized by the desire to please others whenever that is compatible with what is right and expedient. The friendly man will refuse a request when it would be improper or harmful to him or the other man. He will adjust his response according to whether the other man is of high or low social station, or of close or distant acquaintance (*EE* 1233b29–38; *NE* 1126b11–27a12).

Pretentious men claim more reputable qualities than they actually have, because they are pathetically mistaken, or else foolishly vain, or else downright charlatans (if their purpose is to profit from the deceit). Unpretentious men take care not to overstate their merits, since they respect truth in all things. Actually they tend to slightly understate their merits, which puts them closer to the other extreme. This extreme is the self-deprecation we notice in men like Socrates, who disclaim qualities they obviously have. This can actually be a sort of inverse pretentiousness, and the best policy is to be straightforward in all such matters, using only a little bit of subtle understatement (*EE* 1233b38–34a3; *NE* 1127a13–b32).

Witty men are good company, both because they can make good jokes and pleasantries and because they can be amused by the ones we make. This can be taken too far, of course, if you make jokes that break the bounds of good taste, as buffoons do. Aristotle is quite careful to respect the limits of good taste, preferring innuendo to indecency in his entertainments, and suggesting that there should perhaps be laws prohibiting jokes on certain topics. Most men are overinclined to amusement, and "the ridiculous side of things is not far to seek"; but on the other hand there are some unpolished and uncivilized men who contribute nothing to the pleasure of social life and cannot be amused (*EE* 1234a4–23; *NE* 1127b33–28b4).

f. Money and wealth

If you spend much more than you receive, you will soon be in financial trouble. If you spend much less than you receive, you are probably making the mistake of caring too much for wealth. Most men are too reluctant to spend and too eager to receive, although many are too eager to receive precisely because they are too eager to spend, and need to fuel their spending habits. The right attitude to wealth is not easy to arrive at, but the first step is to cultivate the right attitude to income. Know what you can reasonably expect from your situation, and don't abandon your principles in order to get more, as do gamblers, usurers, pimps, and thieves. The next step is to adjust your expenditure proportionately to your income, and to discriminate between the necessary expenses and the discretionary expenses. With the latter you should be as free as your circumstances permit, gladly spending on such things and for the benefit of such people as is appropriate. Aristotle calls this sort of man "liberal," a word derived from the word meaning "free"; this is how a man of independent dignity is expected to behave (EE 1231b27–32a18; NE 1119b22–22a17).

If you happen to be a rich man, you have the opportunity to display a somewhat different virtue. In Greek states, rich men were required to provide direct funding for expensive public services, such as putting on the year's dramatic or athletic festival, or sending a sacred mission to a distant temple or festival. They were also expected to be lavish in the private sphere, paying for marriage feasts, building and equipping their villas to the appropriate standard, receiving foreign dignitaries, and erecting statues to the gods and funerary monuments to their ancestors (all of which Aristotle himself did). The virtue in this area is a sort of aesthetic taste, which avoids vulgar and showy excess as well as a penny-pinching tightness of fist. This virtue, which Aristotle calls "magnificence," can be enjoyed only by liberal men who are blessed with wealth. Magnificent men will correctly judge the relative dignity of their own station as well as the relative scale of the enterprise they are engaged in; a beautifully made ball can be a magnificent gift for a child (EE 1233a31–b14; NE 1122a18–23a33).

g. Respect and honour

In ancient Greek society there were large differences of social status. Men who were descended from superior families or enjoyed superior power or wealth respected themselves on that account, and expected others to show them respect. Aristotle opposed this social differentiation, not because of the modern dogma that all human beings deserve equal respect, but because men based their claims to respect on the wrong grounds, on what came to them by fortune, not on their own moral qualities. Men whose real merits are great should recognize that fact and should expect others to recognize it, too. Aristotle believed in aristocracy, the rule of the best; but he insisted that those who rule should really *be* best, in other words, be morally superior (NE 1124a20–b6).

Men whose moral merits are moderate or low should expect to be respected accordingly. It is wrong to be ambitious and seek to be respected too much and by the wrong men, although the love of honour is a fine thing, and sometimes "ambitious" is used as a term of praise. Likewise, it is wrong and unmanly to be unambitious and refuse to be honoured even when one deserves it, although modesty is pleasing to others and sometimes we call someone "unambitious" in order to praise his self-restraint. The virtue is in the middle, but is obscured by the two extremes, and there is no satisfactory name for it (EE 1233a16–30; NE 1125b1–25).

Aristotle's main interest is the man whose moral merits are great. Like the rich man who is "magnificent," the morally good man who is "magnanimous" (sometimes translated "proud") is able to display a virtue on a grand scale. He will behave in a dignified way that expresses his awareness of his own superiority to others. He will expect them to respect him and obey him, because he deserves the greatest things, namely respect and political authority. The only way to deserve such things is to have the other virtues as well, so this virtue is "a sort of crown of the virtues." Like other virtues, magnanimity lies in the mean between two vices, vanity and humility. The problem with the vain man is not that he claims too much respect, but that he does not deserve it enough, and he tends to confuse the outward marks of dignity with dignity itself. The humble man thinks he deserves less than he does, a trait which Aristotle disdains; he would prefer us to be vain than humble, because humility "is both commoner and worse" (EE 1232a19–38, 1232b31–33a16; NE 1123a34–24a4, 1125a16–34).

In modern times it has become difficult to appreciate Aristotle's portrait of the "magnanimous" man, but it was an attractive ideal to many men for many centuries. The magnanimous man knows that he possesses what it is important for a man to possess, and he places little value on anything else. He is pleased when gentlemen of taste recognize his merits, but he disdains praise from the wrong men or for the wrong reasons. He is only moderately pleased by power and wealth and other goods of fortune, and makes the best of bad fortune. Only a few things are important enough to make him take risks; but he will be supremely courageous when necessary, because not even his own life is important to him, if preserved at the expense of his values. He is pleased to confer benefits on others, but never asks for them in return and is reluctant to receive them. He will not wrong other people, but if they wrong him he is quick to forget it. His manner is dignified to those in positions of power and influence, but unassuming to those of middle station, and self-deprecating to those of lower rank. He is open in his loyalties and animosities and speaks his mind plainly, for scheming is foreign to his nature. He will not allow his life to revolve around anybody else, except a true friend. He will not gossip, for neither the good nor the bad qualities of others are his concern. He will not raise his voice or rush about in excitement, for that would indicate that the details of life matter more than they do. He is dignified, because he enjoys the dignity of a man who deserves respect (*EE* 1232a38–b31; *NE* 1100b30–33, 1124a4–20, 1124b6–25a16).

FRIENDS

The last topic that Aristotle discusses, friendship, is one of the most important, for friends contribute a great deal of what makes life worth living, and nobody would choose to live without friends. Friendship is a relationship between two men who have affection for each other and who recognize each other's affection. It is possible for there to be affection between people who are on different social levels, but in this case they are not really friends in the sense that interests Aristotle. For example, a man cannot be a friend with his wife, because he is ruler and she is ruled, nor with his son, because the father is the benefactor (he gives him life and sustenance and education) and the son is the beneficiary. Likewise, a person can be superior to another in moral virtue, or in the dignity of his family, or in age, but "it would be absurd for a man to be the friend of a child." In these cases, while there could be a mutual affection, it could not be equally reciprocated, and while one could call it a "friendship," one couldn't call them real friends. What Aristotle's friendship turns out to be is the mutually affectionate relationship voluntarily entered into for various purposes between adult men of comparable social status. If this seems like a narrow definition, it is worth remembering that in a political and economic system like that of Athens, the state played little role in alleviating hardship, regulating business, and encouraging prosperity, and it was an economic necessity for households to enter into relationships of mutual confidence;

in poverty and in other misfortunes, says Aristotle, friends are thought to be our only refuge (*EE* 1235b13–36a15; *NE* 1155a5–12, 1155b17–56a5, 1158b11–28, 1161b11–62a33).

Indeed, the most important kind of friendship, if we are to judge by the numbers, is that in which the friends find each other useful. The affection that exists between friends can vary in strength from the extra courtesy one offers to a business partner to the passionate feeling experienced by lovers, but what matters is not the intensity of the feeling but the reciprocity of it. The main difference between kinds of friendships, according to Aristotle, is whether they are based on mutual utility, or the mutual expectation of pleasant company, or mutual respect for each other's character. The one based on mutual utility is the friendship of the majority; the one based on the mutual expectation of pleasure is especially prevalent among the young; but the friendship of the best men is the friendship of mutual respect and virtue. It is the best kind of friendship, and therefore the "primary" example of friendship, although the others are friendships too (*EE* 1236a15–b26; *NE* 1156a6–57b5, 1158b1–11).

Problems arise when the two parties have conflicting conceptions of what sort of friendship they are having (or had). One party may be attracted to the other as a pleasant man, while the other is attracted to the first as a useful man. When the parties to a friendship bring two different things to it, it can be difficult to measure their value. Aristotle refers to various kinds of quarrels to illustrate his point, but goes on to say, quite implausibly, that the solution is simple: if, for example, a student complains about the fee that his teacher charges, one should decide the case by the proportionate value of wisdom and money, just as the farmer trades with the cobbler by assessing the proportionate value of their work. Here he is applying the mathematical approach he used in the discussion of fair exchange (see above, pp. 222–223), with no better success (*EE* 1243b14–38; *NE* 1162b21–63a23).

Justice is very close to Aristotle's mind throughout his treatment of friendship. For example, problems can arise when men enter into a financial relationship that is also a personal relationship. When the partnership is of a kind governed by the law, then it is clear what terms will govern it, but when it is left to each party to fix the return for the other's services, as in ordinary friendships, then recriminations can arise. The problem is that friendships which exist for the sake of mutual utility and friendships which express mutual respect are different sorts of thing, and should not be confused. When recriminations do arise, they tend to be insoluble because it cannot be decided whether to assess the service by what it cost its giver or by its value to the recipient, although Aristotle offers a few suggestions.[10] Moral: try to keep business partnerships separate from personal friendships, and if you do run into trouble of this sort, the honourable course is to settle up as if the arrangement had been clear from the start (*EE* 1241b12–40, 1242b31–43b14; *NE* 1158b29–33, 1159b25–61b10, 1162a34–64b21).

Aristotle has other sensible things to say about friendship. What do we enjoy about having a friend – having affection felt toward us, or feeling affection toward others? The latter, for two reasons: 1) even inanimate objects are the object of affection, and of course they don't enjoy it; and 2) feeling affection is the activity of friendship, and according to Aristotle's doctrine of pleasure (see above pp. 210–212) the activity of our powers, when all goes well, is pleasant. Friendship takes a long time to come into being because it requires mutual confidence, which needs to be fostered by experience. A man cannot be healthy just by deciding to be healthy, and men cannot be friends just by deciding to be friends. It is impossible to have the best kind of friendship with more than a few men, partly because one cannot feel that way toward many men and partly because friends need to be tested by experience. Don't throw away old friends like old clothes in favour of the newest style, because the new ones may not really suit you after all, and you can know that only with time. On the other hand, men do change with time, and if one's friend turns to the bad, there is nothing wrong in abandoning him; and if one outgrows one's friends in maturity and judgment, then one cannot remain friends with them, although it is decent to maintain *some* affection for them (*EE* 1237a18–38a10, 1239a27–b2; *NE* 1156b25–32, 1158a10–18, 1159a25–b1, 1165b13–36, 1170b29–71a20).

When we have a deep friendship of the best kind, we wish for the

10 Aristotle seems to be addressing his own students when he says that one should make payment to those with whom one has studied philosophy by reciprocating their good will, "for their worth cannot be measured against money, and they can get no honour which will balance their services, but still it is perhaps enough, as it is with the gods, to give them what one can" (*NE* 1164b2–6).

friend what we wish for ourselves – life, health, happiness, and the fulfillment of his desires. Does this indicate that the best friendship is the friendship of a man with himself? Obviously a man is not literally his own best friend, says Aristotle, for friendship requires two men; and bad men, who are in a state of conflict with themselves, are not their own friends at all. Yet good men, whose reason and emotions are in friendly harmony, are much like a loving couple who feel the same way as each other, and a true friend is like a second self (EE 1240a8–b37; NE 1166a1–b29).

Do good men act for the benefit of others or for the benefit of themselves? Surely selfishness is a very great fault, which all right-thinking men should avoid. But since one should act for the benefit of one's friends, and since one is, in a way, one's own best friend, then surely one should act for one's own benefit. Aristotle resolves this paradox in the following admirable way: men are said to be selfish because they take more than their share of the external goods which people compete for – wealth, honour, and pleasure; but men are right to act for their own benefit if they act for their real benefit, which is to act in accordance with the virtues. This latter course is really self-regarding, because one secures for oneself the best things in the world, and because it gratifies the intellectual element in us, which is our true self (see above p. 205). This higher selfishness is in the common interest, and if everybody acted that way, all would be for the best. The man with higher selfishness will sometimes sacrifice honour, wealth, and even life itself for the sake of friends and country, but he gains moral nobility in return, which is a higher good. He may even sacrifice, for the sake of his friend, the opportunity to distinguish himself, and this can also be a fine thing – a subtle truth which is easy to overlook (NE 1168a28–69b2).

Perhaps the most interesting question Aristotle raises is whether a good and happy man needs friends. Why should he? The best and most successful man is almost as happy as the gods and has the fewest needs; and the gods look for nothing from mortals, who can offer them nothing except respect; so a perfectly happy and self-sufficient man will not need friends as well. But this cannot be right, because our very picture of a happy man includes a circle of friends. Aristotle's solution to this paradox depends mostly on applying ideas which were already prominent in the Exhortation. The finest activity of human life is perception and knowledge, and since a good friend is like a second self, when one is with one's friend one is, in a way, perceiving oneself. When one is thus aware of oneself being active in the best sorts of ways, then one has the pleasure of awareness to add to the pleasure of the activity. And the better the activity, the more valuable is the society of our friends; "men should contemplate in common and feast in common, only not on the pleasures of food" but on the pleasures of discussion and thought. The best kind of man will indeed have friends, and the best kind of friendship will be the comradeship of fellow-philosophers (*EE* 1244b1–45b19; *NE* 1169b3–70b19, 1171b29–72a15).

Even while discussing the social meaning of friendship, Aristotle remained true to the inspiration of the *Exhortation* and the appeal of the intellectual life. To judge from his will, he ought to have died a happy man, because among his closest friends were several fellow-philosophers, including Theophrastus, his close colleague and his successor as head of the Lyceum, the institution of higher learning where he spent most of the last decade of his life. Unfortunately, he had a stroke of bad luck in the end; after the death of Alexander the Great there were anti-Macedonian disturbances in Athens, and Aristotle found it necessary to leave the Lyceum and go to his family estate at Chalcis, where he died soon afterwards, far away from his colleagues and friends.

8 Politics

One of the superficially most surprising features of Aristotle's practical philosophy is his application of the name *politikê* (sc. *methodos* or *epistêmê*, i.e., political enquiry or science) not to an enquiry into the nature of the state, or into the foundations of political authority, but to moral theory itself. The kind of enquiry exemplified by Aristotle's ethical treatises is regularly designated by that term (e.g., *NE* 1095a2, a15–17), and the treatise in the Aristotelian corpus which bears the title *Politics* is represented by Aristotle as a continuation of the *NE*, required to complete the programme of the latter work (*NE* 1181b12–23). The reason is that the ethical treatises are practical enquiries directed toward the achievement of the good life, an aim which, given the social nature of human beings, cannot be achieved except in the context of a political society. Political theory, then, is for Aristotle neither a distinct subject from moral theory nor the application of moral theory to the political sphere; rather, it is a discipline ancillary to moral theory. Given the identification of human good achieved by the latter, political theory narrowly conceived seeks to identify which forms of society are more and which less conducive to the achievement of that good, to explain the defects of the imperfect forms, and to suggest how those defects might be remedied. The question of political authority, central to most modern political philosophy, is, then, absent from Aristotle's agenda. That question, which may be phrased as "What are the grounds, and what are the limits, of the individual's obligation to obey the state?," presupposes a background of thought in which the central concept is that of obligation and in which the state is seen as something external to the individual, a coercive agency whose power to interfere and to limit stands in need of justification. Aristotle's presuppositions are quite different. His fundamental concept is not that of obligation, but of human good; while in his view the role of the state, so far from limiting the individual's freedom of action with the aim of securing a common good, is precisely that of enabling the individual to realize his or her potential to achieve his or her individual good, an achievement impossible unless in the context of the state. From either perspective, questions about the relation of the state to the individual are central, but the questions are different. For the modern theorist the central problem is why the individual should accept the authority of the state; Aristotle has rather to make good the claim that individual good is unattainable except to an active participant in a political community.

The *Politics* explicitly assumes the account of human good arrived at in the *Ethics*, viz., "activity of the soul in accordance with excellence," that is to say, the excellent realization of those capacities which are distinctive of human life, specifically the capacities for practical and theoretical rationality.[1] The perfection of practical rationality is the life of complete virtue of character, guided by practical wisdom (*phronêsis*), while the perfection of theoretical rationality is the life of theoretical contemplation (*theôria*). Why does either kind of perfection require participation in political life?

We must emphasise the word "political" if the question is to be properly understood. The *NE* advances a number of plausible arguments for the thesis that a good human life must be a communal life. No one, Aristotle reasonably asserts, would wish to live in isolation, without friends. Quite apart from whatever extrinsic benefits we may derive from others, such as help in time of trouble, we find the sharing of a life with like-minded friends an intrinsic good, in that such a life is more enjoyable and more worthwhile to us than a life without friends (1169b16–22). (Some of Aristotle's arguments for this conclusion may be dubious, e.g., that we value friends partly because we value our own fine actions, and we can more easily appreciate actions of those kinds done by our friend, who is "another self," than by our own self (1169b30–1170b10). Irrespective of this, the conclusion is certainly true.) Again, most of the virtues of

---

1 For the account of the good in the *NE*, see 1098a16–18; in the *Politics*, see 1295a35–37, 1328a37–8, and 1332a7–9. On the vexed question of the relation of practical to theoretical excellence in the good life, see this chapter, section III.

character, in whose performance the excellence of the practical life consists, require interaction with others; e.g., generosity and justice require people to be generous and just to others, temperance involves refraining from wanton insolence to others (1178a28–b3). But these arguments show merely that in order to live well we must live in some kind of community, not that we must live in a political community, still less that we must take an active part in political life. As Aristotle recognizes (*Pol* I) other forms of community than the political, he cannot be assumed to have overlooked the distinction. Rather, he thinks that considerations of the relations between the political and other forms of community provide grounds to accept the thesis that a good human life must be a political life.

In fact Aristotle's claim is the more specific one that a good human life must be a life of participation in a specific form of political organisation, viz., the city-state (*polis*). He was of course aware of other types of state, such as the Persian kingdom, but is unwilling to count them as *poleis*, apparently on the ground that they are too big (1326b2–7). (He seems confused on this point, since he says that a nation is hardly capable of having a form of government [*politeia*], yet he counts monarchy as a form of government and knew that some nations (and indeed groups of nations) were governed by monarchs.) We must start, then, by examining his account of the *polis* and its relation to other forms of community, to see whether he can make good his claim that participation in the life of the *polis* is essential for a good human life.

I

Aristotle's account of the *polis* is firmly rooted in his philosophy of nature. The connection is expressed in two fundamental theses, 1) that the *polis* exists by nature, and 2) that a human being is a being of a kind naturally adapted to live in a *polis* (1253a1–3). While his enunciation of both theses in a single sentence indicates their intimate interconnection, the precise nature of his view of the logical relation between the two is not entirely clear. The same evidence, he says (ibid.) is sufficient to establish both, which is compatible with material or formal equivalence, or with entailment in either direction. In outline, his train of argument is as follows. The continuation of the human species requires two primitive forms of interpersonal

relation, that between male and female for the purpose of reproduction and that between master and slave for survival. Hence the most
primitive social unit is that constituted by individuals bearing those
relations to one another, viz., the household (oikia), while the village
(kômê) is a further natural development, a permanent association of
households existing for the fulfilment of needs (presumably both
economic needs and the need for protection against animals and
other human groups).[2]

Households and villages are thus natural forms of association in
that they develop in response to certain natural human needs. We
might note in passing that the notion of "natural" in play here is not
entirely unproblematic. If "natural" is understood as "such as will
inevitably come about unless prevented by external interference,"
then Aristotle is surely unjustified in claiming that the household
and the village, as he understands them, are natural in that sense.
Plainly, the basic human needs of reproduction and survival may be
satisfied in numerous kinds of organization (e.g. the nomadic tribe)
other than those which he has identified. Again, it is unclear to what
extent "natural" (or, equivalently, "by nature") is opposed to "conventional" or "artificial." The master–slave relation, even if natural
in some sense (see below, section V), is conventional to the extent
that a slave is by definition the property of the master, so that the
existence of the relation presupposes the conventions constitutive
of the institution of private property. Even at this most basic stage,
Aristotle has built into his account of what is natural a considerable
element of description of the fundamentals of ancient Greek society.

He now (1252b27–31) argues that since the polis is the complete
or perfect type of community, it must be a natural form of community if, as has already been shown, the more primitive forms are
natural. The argument is an application of a principle of his biology,
that the nature of a kind is realized when the instances of that kind
achieve their complete development, i.e. their mature or adult
form.[3] The development from household via village to polis is thus
presented as analogous to that e.g. from acorn via sapling to mature
oak. But what reason does he give us to accept that analogy? His

2 Cf. Plato, Protagoras 322b.
3 See Phys 193b3–12. For a valuable discussion of Aristotle's use of this
   principle here, see Stephen Everson, "Aristotle on the Foundations of
   the State," Political Studies 36 (1988): 89–101.

argument is that the process of development from the household is a purposive one, in which people who as individuals lack self-sufficiency (*autarkeia*) combine to form communities of increasing complexity, until the aim of producing a self-sufficient community is achieved by (and only by) the development of the *polis*. If self-sufficiency is understood, as the discussion of the primitive forms of community has suggested, simply as the ability to sustain and reproduce individual life, then the claim that the development of the *polis* is not only sufficient but also necessary for that end must be rejected. But there is a suggestion in the text that that conception of self-sufficiency is inadequate, in Aristotle's remark (1252b29–30) that the *polis* comes into being for the sake of life, but exists for the sake of the good life. If we accept that the good life is correctly specified in his ethical writings as the life shaped by exercise of the virtues of intellect and character, the previous objection – that mere sustenance and reproduction does not require the *polis* – lapses. But our problems are not over. For even if we allow Aristotle the highly controversial claim that the life of virtue is impossible except within the specific form of the *polis*, we still may question whether that way of life is the goal or completion toward which the primitive forms of organization are to be seen as tending. Aristotle's description of the *polis* as coming into existence for the sake of life, but existing for the sake of the good life, suggests that simple survival and subsistence was the goal which explains the original development of the *polis*, and that the conception of it as existing to promote the good life is a subsequent development, which presupposes the general adoption of a system of values itself made possible by the conditions of life in the *polis*. If so, then in what sense is it true that the primitive forms of organization are natural stages in a process of development which is complete when and only when that conception of the good is realized? Primitive communities may evolve, and no doubt have actually evolved, into a variety of types of political organization; what entitles one such form to be identified as *the* goal toward which the process of evolution tends?

Aristotle's first argument for his thesis that the *polis* exists by nature is as follows: the *polis* is the goal of the primitive communities; nature is a goal; therefore, the *polis* exists by nature (1252b30–32). We have seen that he has not established the first premiss. Further, the conclusion does not follow; even granted that the *polis* is the goal of the primitive communities, and that nature is a goal, it need not be the case that the *polis* is a natural entity. For it could be the case that the kind of goal which the development of the primitive communities has is such that it requires a non-natural means of achievement, as the goal of flying is for humans. To meet that objection the first premiss would have to be formulated as "The *polis* is the natural goal of the primitive communities." But then the desired conclusion would already be assumed, and the argument therefore otiose. Aristotle further argues (1252b34–1253a1) that that for the sake of which something is, i.e., its goal, is the best thing, and self-suffiency is a goal and the best thing. Assuming that there is precisely one best thing, it follows that self-sufficiency is that for the sake of which (sc. the primitive communities evolve into more developed ones), but it still does not follow that the kind of self-sufficiency which is achieved by the development of the *polis* is natural.[4]

As we have seen, Aristotle asserts that the grounds for the thesis that the *polis* exists by nature are also grounds for the thesis that "Man is by nature a political animal". Like most slogans, this, perhaps the most famous of Aristotle's political pronouncements, is susceptible of various interpretations. He clearly intends to assert that, in the way outlined in the previous discussion, human beings are adapted by nature for life in the *polis*, in that life in that context is necessary and sufficient for the attainment of individual human good. He supports this claim by an interesting application (1253a7–18) of his principle that "Nature does nothing in vain" (a9). While animals are generally able to express pleasure and pain by their cries, humans and only humans possess speech, which enables them to make judgments of what is beneficial and harmful, right and wrong. That is to say, the human capacity for practical judgment marks the species out for life in the *polis*, since (it is implied) it is in that context, and only in that context, that that capacity is properly exercised. This claim is a powerful one; it implies, for example, that modern political institutions systematically deprive

4 For a fuller discussion see David Keyt, "Three Fundamental Theorems in Aristotle's *Politics*," *Phronesis* 32 (1987): 54–79. A revised version, entitled "Three Basic Theorems in Aristotle's *Politics*," appears in David Keyt and Fred D. Miller, Jr., eds., *A Companion to Aristotle's* Politics, (Oxford and Cambridge, Mass.: Basil Blackwell 1991), 118–41.

their participants of the full exercise of one of their most fundamentally human capacities.

Some of these points will be discussed further below. For the moment I turn to a yet more disturbing aspect of Aristotle's slogan. This is the claim that the *polis* is prior to the individual, since the whole must be prior to the part and the individual is a part of the *polis* (1253a18–29). The sense of "prior" in question is that of priority in essence or being (*ousia*), in which A is prior to B if and only if A can exist without B, but not vice versa.[5] That this is the kind of priority at issue is made clear by Aristotle's use of the analogy of bodily parts; a hand or a foot cannot exist in isolation from the body as a whole, for a detached part is not a part properly so called, but is so-called only homonymously, as the hand of a statue is not strictly speaking a hand (or, as we might more naturally say, not a real hand).[6] The point is that bodily parts are functionally identified, via their relation to other parts and to the functioning of the whole system into which they fit; physically isolated from that context they are at best potential parts (if they retain the possibility of being reintegrated into a functioning system), at worst dead, i.e., former, parts. Aristotle makes analogous claims about the relation between individual and *polis*; an individual *incapable* of membership of a *polis* is not, strictly speaking, a human being, but rather a (non-human) animal, while one who is self-sufficient apart from the *polis* is superhuman, or, as Aristotle puts it, a god (a25–9). His point is not the uncontentious one that one cannot be a *citizen* except in the context of a *polis*, as one cannot be a wicket-keeper (as opposed to a former, or a potential, wicket-keeper) except as a member of a cricket team. It is the stronger point that one cannot be a human being except in the context of a *polis*. The context need not be actual; so Robinson Crusoe does not cease to be human during the period of his total isolation. But nevertheless the analogy commits Aristotle to holding that what makes any of us human is our capacity for *polis* membership, just as what makes this quantity of organic matter a hand is its capacity to play a particular role in a functioning human body. The political implications of this analogy are momentous, since the parts

5 See, e.g., *Met* 1019a2–4: "[Prior] by nature and essence are such things as can exist without others, whereas the latter cannot exist without them." Cf. *Phys* 260b18–19.
6 Cf. *An* 412b18–22.

of an organism have no interests independent of the interests of the organism as a whole. Rather, the good of the part is its being such as to make its proper contribution to the good of the organism. That is the sense in which "the same thing is good for the part and for the whole" (1255b9–10).[7] If this analogy is taken seriously, Aristotle must be committed to an extreme form of totalitarianism: not merely the doctrine that the independent good of the individual must be subordinated to the greater good of the state, but the yet more extreme doctrine that the individual has no independent good, his or her good being identified with his or her contribution to the good of the state.[8] The relation of slave to master appears to give the nearest analogy to the relation of the individual to the state: as individuals we are living parts of the state, as the slave is a living part of the master (1255b11–12); and like the slave we find our good not in the realization of any aims of our own, but in the fulfilment of the aims of that of which we are a part.

In fact Aristotle's predominant view of the individual–state relation is the antithesis of this. He expressly distinguishes political rule from the rule of master over slave (I.7) on the ground that, whereas the latter is, properly, exercised over those who are incapable of exercising rational control over their own lives (1254b16–23, 1260a12), the former is exercised over those who are "free and equal" and must consequently have as its aim the promotion of the good of those who are freely to accept it (1279a28–32). The good of the individual is not, therefore, merely independent of the good of the *polis;* in two of the many ways in which one thing can be prior to another it is prior to it, in that (a) the aim of political organization is to promote the good life for the citizens, and therefore (b) the good of the state is defined via that of the individual, in that the state is well organized when it is so organised as to fulfil its aim, which is as specified in (a).[9] Further, that aim is not such as could be imposed on the individual for his or her own good. For the good of the individual is to live the life of moral and

7 On the application of that doctrine to the master–slave relation, see below, section V.
8 I distinguish various kinds of totalitarianism (including those just mentioned) in "Plato's Totalitarianism," *Polis* 5.2 (1986): 4–29.
9 A is prior to B *logôi* (= in definition) if and only if the definition of A is included in the definition of B, but not vice versa (*Met* 1028a32–36).

intellectual virtue, which requires that the individual directs his life by his autonomous practical reasoning. But at the same time the social requirements of human nature are such that the best exercise of autonomous practical reasoning is the promotion of the good life not for the individual in isolation, but for the whole community (*NE* 1094b7–10; *Pol* 1278a40–b5).

The thesis that the *polis* stands to the individual as whole to part is therefore an aberration on Aristotle's part; it commits him to denying two central theses of his ethico-political system, that the aim of the *polis* is the promotion of the good life for its citizens, and that the central activity of the good life is the exercise of autonomous practical rationality.[10] But we can see that Aristotle was led to that overstatement by another thesis equally central to that system, viz., the thesis that the good life is necessarily a social life. Nevertheless the fact that we cannot live a good life in isolation from others should no more lead us to conclude that we are essentially parts of a social whole than the fact that (for most people) we cannot lead a good life without some satisfactory sexual relations should lead us to conclude that we are essentially parts of some sexual whole. Aristotle ought to separate the claim that humans are creatures adapted for life in the *polis* from the claim that they are parts of the *polis* and, for the sake of consistency with his central doctrines, to repudiate the latter.

Why does the exercise of practical rationality require the *polis*, as distinct from other forms of (in the modern sense) political organization such as the nation state? Aristotle's answer is clear. The good life is the life directed by *phronêsis*, and the most perfect exercise of *phronêsis* is the application of that virtue to the common good of a community (see above). That is to say, the good life requires participation in the government of a self-governing community, i.e., a

10 Nevertheless, this claim is repeated at 1337a27–30; since the citizen is part of the state he belongs not to himself, but to the state. The assertion that the citizen does not belong to himself is identical with what is said of the natural slave, who does not belong to himself, but to someone else (1254a13–17). It is inconsistent with *Met* 982b25–26: "a free man is for his own sake and not for the sake of another," since what is for its own sake determines its activities for its own ends and so cannot be at the disposal of another. See T.H. Irwin, *Aristotle's First Principles* (Oxford: Clarendon Press, 1988), 411.

polis. Someone who has no share in the government of his or her community, say a subject of an absolute monarch, or someone who elects to play no part in political life, has, willingly or perforce, to surrender crucial aspects of his or her life to the direction of another, and thus abandons the task of *phronêsis,* "to deliberate well about what is good and advantageous for oneself, not in particular areas, such as what promotes health or strength, but with a view to living well overall" (*NE* 1140a25–28). While of course Aristotle had not envisaged modern representative democracy, we may surmise that he would have held that the same objection applied to it. Representative government removes the individual too far from day-to-day decision-making to allow it to count as giving the individual the degree of control over his or her life which the exercise of *phronêsis* requires. An objection to Aristotle's position (suggested, e.g., by *NE* X.7) is that the ideal life may be a life of total commitment to theoretical activity, requiring withdrawal from political activity altogether, the kind of life later undertaken by Epicurean communities. Aristotle's implied response is that such a life is possible only within a political framework on which the philosophical community must rely for its subsistence and protection, and that, once again, the imperative to perfect one's *phronêsis* requires that one participates in the government of the community which the philosophical life requires. That does not, it should be noticed, commit Aristotle to denying that theoretical activity is the most valuable human activity, and there is indeed more than a hint of that doctrine in *Pol* VII.3 (see below, section III). What it does commit him to denying is that the best possible human life is one devoted exclusively to theoretical activity. To repeat, the best form of human life is that directed by the agent's own *phronêsis,* and the best form of *phronêsis* is that directed toward the promotion of the good life for the whole community. In Aristotelian terms, the good human being must be *phronimos,* and the ideal *phronimos* is the *politikos* (1278b1–5).

It follows that the citizens of a *polis* must participate in its government; every *polis,* not merely the best, must be a participatory democracy. But Aristotle counts democracy as merely one form of the constitution of a *polis,* not in fact the best; he includes other forms, such as tyranny and monarchy, which allow little or no participation in government to their citizens, and he asserts in the *NE* that kingship (which is a form of monarchy) is the best form of constitution (1160a35–36). To confront these difficulties we must consider Aristotle's classification of types of political constitution.

II

A *polis* is a species of community, other species being the household, the village, and the nation. The various kinds are defined by the different forms of rule or subordination (*archê*) which govern the activities of their members. The rule of master over slave, of the patriarch over wife and children, and of monarch over subjects are different forms of rule from political rule, which we saw to be a) exercised over free and equal subjects (1255b20) and b) exercised with a view to promoting the common interest (1279a16–21). So a *polis* is by definition a community of individuals who participate in the government of the community. This is confirmed by Aristotle's account of the relation between the *polis* and the citizen (III.1); a *polis* is a community of citizens (*politai;* 1274b41), and a citizen is defined as one who is able to participate in the deliberative and judicial areas of government (1275b18–20). Yet this participatory account of the *polis* is, as we have seen, in tension with Aristotle's classification of kinds of constitution (*politeia*). First, he counts monarchy as a species of constitution (1279a32–34), containing two sub-species, kingship and tyranny (a32–b7). Then, despite the definition of political rule as directed to the common interest, he distinguishes (ibid.) various correct forms of constitution which satisfy that requirement from their corresponding deviant or perverted forms (*parekbaseis*), which aim, in contrast, at the promotion of various sectional interests instead of the common interest.

The tension is in fact generated by two aspects of Aristotle's enterprise, on the one hand the descriptive/classificatory, on the other the analytic/prescriptive. Under the former heading falls the activity of identifying and classifying the sorts of governmental systems actually to be found in those political communities which Aristotle and his contemporaries recognised as *poleis;* for this purpose a *polis* can simply be taken to be a more-or-less autonomous community, normally but not necessarily Greek (Aristotle counts Carthage as a *polis*), inhabiting a roughly continuous and fairly small tract of land, usually

244 THE CAMBRIDGE COMPANION TO ARISTOTLE

containing a single urban centre and a number of smaller settlements. *Poleis* thus conceived may be governed in a variety of ways: by monarchs of various kinds, by unconstitutional despots (tyrants), by various kinds of oligarchies, by varieties of democracies, or by systems combining elements of those diverse types. On the other hand the analytic programme rests on a number of principles, some of which we have already come across: a) we understand the nature of a natural entity when we see it fully developed; b) the *polis* is a specific form of community, and every community is a natural entity, developed in response to certain specific needs of its members; and c) the full development of the *polis* is the organizational state which enables it most fully to meet the specific needs which led to its institution. Given these principles, we can see that certain forms of actual political organization are best understood as deviations from the proper/ natural pattern of the development of a political community, deviations which arise from the substitution of sectional interest for the proper/natural goal of the community, viz., the common interest. We thus arrive at a simple and perspicuous classification of types of constitution: the common good may be sought by a) government by a single individual (kingship), b) by the few (aristocracy), and c) by the many (*politeia*), but each of those correct forms may be perverted into a form in which the ruling element seeks its own sectional interest instead of the common good, viz. a') tyranny, b') oligarchy, and c') democracy (Aristotle's own terms are used as labels). But while that will explain why the perverted forms of constitution are counted as political organizations at all, we need to look further for an explanation of why monarchy is so counted; if a *polis* is a community of citizens, and a citizen is one who has the opportunity to share in government, then surely a monarchy cannot be a *polis*.

This difficulty is alleviated, if not altogether eliminated, by Aristotle's distinction (1285b20–33) between various forms of kingship, some of which (e.g. the Spartan dual monarchy) were in fact forms of magistracy assigned specific roles (generalship in the Spartan case) within a system clearly political by Aristotle's criteria. In those cases the application of the name kingship (*basileia*) is presumably to be explained as a historical survival from a period in which a fuller range of powers had been concentrated in the hands of the king. But in that case we might expect Aristotle to say that kingship properly so called belongs to a prepolitical stage of social organization, and that only the restricted types of kingship can have a role in the *polis*. In fact, however, the type of kingship to which he devotes most attention is what he calls total kingship (*pambasileia*), in which the king has control of all matters (1285b29–31), a feature which is at odds with Aristotle's definition of citizenship (see above). This auto-cratic form of rule is that which the patriarch exerts over his house-hold, as he explicitly points out in his introduction of this kind of kingship (1285b31–33), describing it as "household management of a *polis* or of one or more nations." Strictly speaking, then, it ought to be classed rather as a special sort of *oikonomia* than as a kind of political rule. (The fact that the king rules with the consent of his subjects does not count against that, for so does the patriarch.) House-hold management involves the rule of the developed practical wis-dom of the patriarch over slaves, females, and children, all types of human being who, in Aristotle's view, lack that developed wisdom; "the slave does not have the faculty of deliberation, the female has it, but in a form lacking in authority [*akuron*], and the child has it, but in an incomplete form" (1260a12–14). Since that deficiency makes them unable to provide adequately for their own lives (and house-hold management is concerned at least primarily with the economic conditions of life), they must make good the deficiency by depen-dence on the wisdom of the patriarch.

The application of that model to a community of adult males suggests similarly that the subjects must be lacking the wisdom necessary for the proper organization of their own lives; otherwise why is it appropriate for them to be totally subject to the king? Aristotle seems to recognize this point; at 1287a10–12 he says that it seems to some that it is contrary to nature for one to be in control of everything (or "of all") when the community is composed of simi-lar people; and while he does not there explicitly endorse that view, he does so more unambiguously at 1287b41–1288a2: "From what has been said it is clear that among those who are alike and equal it is neither expedient nor just that one should be in control of all." Yet the endorsement is not unqualified, for he adds (a4–5) "not even if he is superior in excellence, unless in a certain way," a suggestion amplified at a15–19: "whenever it happens that a whole family or a single individual is so outstanding in excellence that it outstrips that of all the others, then it is just that that family should be royal and in control of all, and that one individual king." The reference in this passage is to 1284a3–14, where Aristotle states that if in a community there is an individual or group who so far surpasses the rest in virtue that the virtue of the others is not to be compared to his (or theirs), that individual or group cannot be counted as part of a *polis*; rather he is to be counted as a god among men and cannot be subject to law, for he is himself the law. Subjecting someone like that to control would be as absurd as presuming to control Zeus and share his rule; rather, everyone should gladly obey such a ruler, so that such people should be perpetual kings (b30–34).

It is clear first that Aristotle does not consider this a practicable ideal; such a king would have to be a person of literally superhuman excellence, a type whom Aristotle describes with surely intentional understatement as "not easy to find" (1332b23; cf. *NE* 1145a27–28). The requirement that there should literally be no comparison between the excellence of the ideal king and that of his subjects is so extreme that is hard to see how it could be fulfilled in any possible conditions. Moreover, as I have suggested, the fulfilment (per impossibile) of that requirement does not fit readily into Aristotle's developmental account of the *polis*. That account maintains that individuals need the *polis* in order to live the good life, i.e., the life shaped by the shared exercise of *phronêsis*. But under the rule of the godlike king, the only shared exercise of *phronêsis* would be acquiescence in the king's absolute rule; and even that acquiescence would hardly be a political act. The subjects of the ideal king are no more *politai* than are the children of an ideal patriarch. It is then unclear why the godlike king should rule over a *polis* rather than some other kind of community, whether smaller (a village) or larger (a nation).

Insofar as the *polis* is a human institution, developed by imperfect individuals to serve their need for a good form of communal life, monarchy does not provide a model for the ideal *polis*. The only form of monarchy suitable for imperfect individuals (including the monarch) is a monarchy limited by law (III.15–16), but in that form, as Aristotle recognizes, it is the law which has supreme authority, and the monarchy is in fact a form of magistracy (1287a3–6). Genuine, i.e. absolute, monarchy is in fact not a form of government of a human community, but is rather a sort of divine rule. Aristotle does not satisfactorily resolve the tension between the principles underlying his participatory conception of the *polis* and the principle that the best form of constitution is the rule of the best ruler (1288a33–34), since he does not insist on the restriction that the best ruler must be a human ruler. Once that restriction is granted, the equality between ruler and ruled which springs from their common human nature requires the participation of all in government (1332b25–29).[11]

A similar problem applies to oligarchy. Given the participatory account of citizenship, it is contradictory to define an oligarchy as a community in which participation in government is confined to a certain proportion *of the citizen body*, since those excluded from those functions are excluded by definition from the citizen body itself. One might of course identify an oligarchy by differentiating various aspects of citizenship, some of which, such as liability for military service or taxation, apply to all, whereas others, such as eligibility for various kinds of magistracies, are the prerogative of a minority, however defined, e.g. by a property qualification. Aristotle does not, however, attempt to define a minimum condition for citizenship purely in terms of obligations, such as those just mentioned, perhaps because such a criterion would not reliably distinguish from citizens such categories of resident non-citizens as resident aliens (*metoikoi*), who were subject to some such obligations. Rather he defines citizenship in terms of the right to participate in government in one way or another, and then faces the difficulty that in the typical oligarchy those rights are restricted to some of the citizens only. He makes the useful distinction (1275a23–26) between definite offices (i.e., those held for a fixed period) and indefinite (i.e., those without temporal restriction, such as eligibility for the assembly of the people), but recognizes that in some oligarchies not even the latter are available to all (b5–11). Aristotle accepts that his account of citizenship applies best to democratic states (b5–7) and that in practice the status of citizen is accorded on whatever grounds are found convenient in different states (b22–30). He offers his own account as an improvement (b30–32), yet has no answer to the difficulty we have just raised. His account is on the right lines, since he is right to think that the concept of citizenship cannot be defined purely in terms of residence or of subjection to authority, but implies

11 The question of the relation between monarchy and the ideal form of *polis* is ably discussed by P.A. Vander Waerdt in "Kingship and Philosophy in Aristotle's Best Regime," *Phronesis* 30 (1985): 249–73. He rejects the central claim urged here, viz., that the conception of the good life assumed in the *Pol* is a politically active life.

participation in the essential activity of a community, and also to see that participation is a matter of degree. A somewhat more liberal conception of participation, including such elements as the right to participate in ritual, or to identify oneself as a descendant of some mythical ancestor, might have helped him deal with the problem of non-participatory citizenship.

III

We have now to consider Aristotle's account of the best type of *polis*, or rather his accounts, for he distinguishes the ideally best type, discussed in Books VII–VIII, from the best type for most people (given their actual circumstances), discussed in IV–VI. We shall first consider the ideal type.

The character of the ideal state emerges directly from the account of the goal of the *polis* discussed earlier. Since a *polis* is a community existing not merely for the sake of subsistence and protection but for the sake of the good life, the best kind of community is that which makes the best life available to its citizens. Immediately this raises classical questions of distribution, familiar from consideration of utilitarianism. Is the best kind of community that in which each individual enjoys the best life available, given the restriction that every other must enjoy a life equally good? Or is it that in which the best life absolutely (assuming that conception to have a clear sense) is available to some, even if that requires that some have a life less good than the best life, or a life less good than the life that they could have had had others not enjoyed the best life, or even, perhaps, a life which is not good at all? Because Aristotle thinks that the constituents of the best life are not contested goods such as wealth or honours, which have to be distributed, but virtues of intellect and character, he does not confront these questions directly. Rather he assumes that the best state is that in which every citizen is given the opportunity to achieve complete excellence in these respects (1324a23–25: "it is clear that the best constitution is that organization by which everyone, whoever he is, would do the best things and live a blessed life"), and does not consider whether the conditions for the achievement of excellence by one might require the abridgement of the possibilities of excellence of another. But his theory does generate these problems, in various ways. Thus the cultivation of practical and theoretical

excellence requires leisure (VII.15), but leisure presupposes that the
necessities of life are already supplied by the labour of those whose
lack of leisure prevents their cultivating either kind of excellence. We
thus have a choice between an organization of the *polis* which requires everyone to divide their time between economic production
and cultivation of excellence, and one in which those distinct types
of activity are the province of different sections of the community.
Aristotle's preference for the latter then faces the objection that, like
Plato's *Republic*, his ideal state must contain a majority of non-ideal
citizens. Worse still, although the aim of the *polis* is to provide the
good life for its citizens, the best form of *polis* is one which frustrates
that aim in the case of the majority. Aristotle's response is that of
Plato in the *Laws:* the necessary economic functions are to be carried
out by non-citizens, slaves and resident aliens, who need not even be
Greeks (1329a24–26). But in that case the *polis* is no longer a community, i.e. an association of people self-sufficient for life, but a fraction
of such a community, dedicated to the pursuit of an aim, viz., the
pursuit of the good life, which is alien to the majority on whose
labours that fraction depends. Moreover, the unity of the larger unit,
comprised of citizens and non-citizens, is now problematic. What
explains the willingness of the latter to play their necessary role in
supporting the *polis* proper, under the government of the citizens?
Insofar as they are slaves, the question does not arise (although the
dependence on slavery challenges the claim to be a morally tolerable,
much less ideal community). But insofar as the producers are aliens,
there of their own choice, they must believe that they would be
better governed by Aristotle's moral elite than by themselves. But
Aristotle gives neither any explanation of why they would believe
that, nor any reason to think that it would be true. Of course, the
ideal citizens of Aristotle's ideal state are ex hypothesi possessed of
highly developed *phronêsis;* surely that guarantees that their subjects are better governed than by their own imperfect rationality. But
their perfect *phronêsis* guarantees that their political deliberation
produces the best possible organization. What is precisely at issue is
whether that organization is *best for* all those involved in it, or
merely best for the citizens for whom, and for whom alone, it provides the opportunity to live the best life. Granted Aristotle's emphasis on the centrality of the exercise of *phronêsis* in the good life,
one might have expected him to favour an arrangement in which

everyone had some share in the leisure necessary for the cultivation of excellence, whether by a system of part-time work throughout life, or by a system of recurrent "sabbaticals" devoted to participation in government. As it is, it is a cardinal feature of this ideal state that his citizens take turns to rule and be ruled (1332b26–29), the various governmental functions being shared out among the older, while the men of military age perform the function of defending the *polis* and are trained in the administration which they are to exercise later in life (VII.14). It would seem that the extension of that principle to the producers in his ideal state, i.e. their inclusion in the citizen body proper, would strengthen, not weaken, the consistency of his system. For that extension would allow the ideal *polis* to be a genuine community, unified by the common goal of enabling all citizens to share, to some extent or other, in the good life. As it stands, the so-called ideal *polis* is not a political community at all, since it is not self-sufficient for life, much less for the good life (1252b27–30). Rather, it is an exploiting elite, a community of free-riders whose ability to pursue the good life is made possible by the willingness of others to forgo that pursuit.[12] Even leaving aside the question of slavery, the "ideal" *polis* is thus characterized by systematic injustice.

Before leaving consideration of the ideal *polis* we should consider Aristotle's conception of the good life in a little more detail. Notoriously, in *NE* X.7–8 Aristotle praises the life of theoretical activity as the life of perfect well-being (*teleia eudaimonia*) and downgrades the life of practical excellence to a status of secondary value, thereby giving rise to a long-running debate as to whether the *NE* as a whole has a consistent position on the nature of the good life. Whatever the final verdict on that question, it may well appear that the *Politics* definitively rejects the "intellectualism" of *NE* X, since the good life which is shared by the citizens of the ideal *polis* is without doubt a practical life in which the citizens exercise their practical excellence to promote the common good. In fact, I doubt whether there is any major discrepancy between *NE* X and the *Politics*. (I also think that there is no discrepancy between *NE* X and the rest of that work, but that is not our present concern.)

Aristotle raises the question of the relative merits of the philosophic

12 Aristotle makes very much the same criticism of Plato's *Republic*, 1264a24–29.

and the practical life in VII.2. Having first said (1324a23–25) that it is clear that the best form of constitution is that in which each individual does best and lives "blessedly" (makariôs), i.e. achieves complete well-being, he continues that there is disagreement between those who think that the best life is the practical, political life and those who urge the claims of a purely theoretical life, completely divorced from external concerns (a25–29). Having devoted the rest of the chapter to rejection of the view that the life of domination over others is the best, he returns to the original dispute in the next chapter. Characteristically, he says that both parties are in a way right and in a way wrong. The supporters of the philosophic life are correct to think that the life of a free man (which is apparently how they describe the life of one free from practical concerns) is better than the life of a slave-master, but wrong to identify the latter with the political life (because of the earlier distinction between political and despotic rule). They are also wrong to rank inactivity above activity, since well-being consists in activity, and the acts of the virtuous are fine (1325a23–34). Aristotle does not state explicitly where the adherents of the practical life are either right or wrong. The point just mentioned, that virtuous activity is intrinsically fine, is presumably a point in their favour, while earlier they were said to share the view of their opponents that the theoretical life is inactive (1325a21–22), concluding, since well-being consists in activity, that that life cannot constitute well-being.

Aristotle now proceeds to identify that view as a crucial error. Well-being does indeed consist in activity, but pure thought is not inactivity. Rather, activities carried out for their own sake, of which pure thought is the prime example, are the best sort of activity, as is attested by the fact that that is the kind of activity proper to the gods, who enjoy supreme well-being (b16–30). The divine character of the theoretical life was, of course, one of the principal grounds of its elevation to supreme value in NE X (notably in 1178b8–28). Is Aristotle, then, simply endorsing that position in Pol VII, and with it accepting the claim of the theoretical life to supreme value? Here we have to distinguish the value of pure theoretical activity from the value of the theoretical life, i.e., the life devoted exclusively to theory. Aristotle, in my view, endorses in the Politics the position of the Ethics on the former question: theoretical activity is the best kind of activity that human beings can undertake, and the best form of political organization is that which makes that activity available to the best possible extent. (I adopt that deliberately vague formulation to avoid reopening the questions of distribution, discussed above, with respect to excellence generally.) On the latter question, he takes over the position of NE 1177b26–31 and 1178b5–7 that the exclusively theoretical life is not available to humans, whose nature demands that they live a social life. Given that requirement, the arguments reviewed earlier preclude a total withdrawal from political activity, for that would involve an abdication of *phronêsis*, and thus an abandonment of that total virtue which it is the aim of the good *polis* to promote.

We can now reconstruct Aristotle's position on the extent to which both parties to the dispute are partly right and partly wrong. The adherents of the theoretical life are right in thinking that pure thought is the most valuable activity, but wrong in drawing from that the conclusion that the best life for a human being is a life withdrawn from political activity. Their opponents, conversely, are right to think that the best life requires political activity, but wrong to think that that activity is the best thing in that life. I leave open a number of questions, some much discussed by commentators, about the relative contributions of theoretical and practical activity to the value of any individual life. I have sought merely to show that the discussion in the *Politics* does not require the hypothesis of a radical discontinuity between that work and *NE* X.

IV

As Aristotle insists on the practical value of his enquiry to would-be legislators, he has to investigate not merely what is the ideally best form of government but also what is the best available, given the limitations imposed by actual economic and other conditions. This requires comparison of the various types of actual constitution with a view to identifying their relative merits and defects, in order to guide the legislator in his task of either preserving an existing political order or improving it. This enterprise, to which books IV–VI are devoted, is illustrated by a wealth of empirical detail drawn from the comprehensive survey of the constitutions of Greek states (158 in all) which Aristotle organized, of which the sole survivor is the *Athenian Constitution*. I shall not attempt detailed discussion of this portion of the work, which is fully discussed by a number of able and acute commentators,[13] but shall confine myself to a few general remarks.

Broadly speaking, Aristotle regards wealth as the primary determinant of political organization.[14] Every community contains some who are rich, who tend to be in the minority, and the poor, who tend to be in the majority. Each class tends to favour a political organization which entrenches itself in power: where the rich minority are in power we have some type of oligarchy, and where the poor majority are in power we have some type of democracy (1290b17–20). Most actual regimes are one or the other (1296a22–23). The distinction between an oligarchic and a democratic regime is not sharp, but is rather a matter of degree; a regime is more or less democratic or oligarchic in virtue of being characterized by more or fewer of a cluster of features. Thus characteristically democratic features are payment for public service, including attendance at the legislative assembly and jury service, the selection of magistrates by lot, and the absence of a property qualification for office. Characteristically oligarchic features are a property qualification for office, election of magistrates, and financial penalties for non-attendance at deliberative or judicial bodies. Extreme instances of either kind will be characterized by all these features, less extreme by fewer, while some regimes are mixed, being characterized by both democratic and oligarchic features (1293a30–1294b13). Aristotle is unsympathetic to extremes of either type, which he sees as tending to promote the sectional interest of either rich or poor at the expense of the common interest. The common interest is best promoted in his view by a mixed regime, although, in line with his general principle that practical questions do not admit of exceptionless generalizations, he eschews any attempt to specify any particular mix as best in all cases. In line with his general position (see above), he assumes that a mixed constitution will also have an economic determinant, viz., the political predominance of those of

13 See, e.g., R.G. Mulgan, *Aristotle's Political Theory* (Oxford: Clarendon Press, 1977), with the bibliography contained therein.
14 For fuller discussion see T.H. Irwin, "Moral Science and Political Theory in Aristotle," in P. Cartledge and F. Harvey, eds., *Crux, Essays in Greek History presented to G.E.M. de Ste. Croix* (London: Duckworth, 1985), 150–67.

intermediate wealth (IV.11). Hence he tends to describe the best practically attainable type of constitution as an intermediate constitution (*mesê politeia*) indifferently in the sense of one characterized by a mix of democratic and oligarchic features, and in the sense of one in which the intermediate or middle class (*hoi mesoi*, lit. "the middle people") predominates (1295b34–1296b12). He does not explain why the predominance of the middle class is less likely to lead to the improper elevation of their sectional interest above the common interest than is the predominance of either rich or poor. Is it because they have no sectional interest of their own? But why should that be? Or is it because their sectional interest always coincides with the common interest? If so, what guarantees that fortunate coincidence?

V

Slavery is prominent in the introductory pages of Aristotle's discussion of the *polis*, since the master–slave relation is, as we have seen, an element in the most primitive form of community. Master and slave are described as types of human being who cannot do without each other (1252a26–27); just as male and female need one another for the perpetuation of the species, so master and slave need one another "for preservation" (a31). Preservation must mean not defence, but rather subsistence, since the role of the slave is elucidated by comparison not with a weapon, but with a tool (1253b32–33) and with a draught animal (1252b12). The master needs the slave, then, as the peasant needs a hoe or an ox; he uses the slave to perform a task which he could not do, or could do less easily, by himself. But why does the slave need the master, as the description "unable to do without one another" implies? Surely neither the ox nor the hoe needs the farmer. At this point another analogy surfaces, viz., that between soul and body. The body is naturally (and therefore properly) under the direction of the soul; without rational direction (provided by the soul) the body is unable to cope with the environment. So it is better *for the body* to be under the direction of the soul, not merely in the sense that is is better that the body should be under rational control than not, but in the sense that it benefits the body to be so controlled. Similarly, living beings which lack the capacity for rational self-direction are better off subject to the rational control of another than left to their own non-rational promptings (1254b2–23). Some humans are like that; they are natural slaves, who altogether lack the capacity for deliberation (1260a12). Hence, a) they find their natural role, and make their special contribution to the *polis*, as human draught animals, and b) they do what is best for themselves in so doing.

If we take the analogy with draught animals seriously, we must ask in what sense it is in the interest of the ox to be yoked to the plough. It can indeed be argued that domestication is in the interest a) of some species, in that it improves the survival chances of members of the species and b) of individual members of those species, in that e.g., this ox is looked after by the farmer but would soon be devoured by predators in the wild (1254b10–13). Here we apply the standard conception of interest, survival and health, to an animal species and to its members, and claim that there is a coincidence between that interest and the economic interest of the domesticator. Were Aristotle to apply that analogy to the case of slaves, he would have to argue that the enslavement of natural slaves benefits them by giving them a better life than they would have had had they been left at liberty (as some apologists for the modern slave trade argued that slavery benefited the slaves by giving them the opportunity to embrace Christianity). Perhaps that is implied by the description of natural slaves as lacking the capacity for deliberation; they might be thought of as mental defectives, who, left to themselves, would just blunder about helplessly until their (presumably speedy) extinction. But non-human animals get along all right without deliberation, guided as they are by instinct and perception; would it not be more plausible to think of natural slaves on those lines? If so, the claim that they would do worse left to themselves than enslaved looks shaky. Aristotle's other analogies, those of a tool and of a part of the body, tend if anything to confuse the issue. For here there is no coincidence of independent interest such as Aristotle appears to be claiming for master and slave; it may be good for a hoe to be kept clean and sharp, and for one's muscles to be given regular exercise, but what is good for these things is just whatever is conducive to their doing their job. So on those analogies the claim that the same thing is good for master and slave (1252a34) does not mean that the interests of master and slave coincide (as on the draught animals analogy), but that the interest of the latter is wholly determined by the interest of the former.

Aristotle's difficulties over natural slavery are revealed by his vacillation on the question of whether there can be friendship between master and slave. At 1255b4–15 he appeals to the principles that what is good for the whole is good for the part, and that the slave is a part of the master, to support the claims that there is identity of interest "and friendship towards one another" between those who stand in the natural master–slave relation. Friendship, according to the NE (1155b27–1156a5) requires mutual concern (antiphilêsis), the desire of each party for the good of the other. The master is certainly concerned for the good of his slave to the extent that the slave has to be in good condition in order to carry out his tasks; hence Aristotle says accurately that while in a way master and slave have the same interest, the relationship is concerned with the slave's good only incidentally, in that the subordination cannot be preserved (and the master's purposes thereby fulfilled) if the slave perishes (1278b32–37). But the converse relation is problematic. The problem is not primarily why the slave should be concerned for the welfare of the master; if, as Aristotle claims, the continuation of the relation were of mutual benefit to both, even to the limited extent suggested by the draught animal analogy, and if the slave were aware of that fact, the slave would have some reason to want the relation to continue and therefore to be concerned for the continued survival and prosperity of the master. Rather, the problem is to explain how a being supposedly totally lacking in deliberative capacity could have that concern for another. For such a being can have no conception of the long-term good of anything (including itself), or of the means by which that good might be fostered. Hence we find Aristotle saying with complete consistency (in NE 1161a33–b5) that where there is nothing in common between ruler and ruled there can be no friendship between them, giving as examples the impossibility of a friendship between a craftsman and his tools, a farmer and his animals, or a master and his slave "for the slave is a living tool, and the tool a lifeless slave."[15] He adds that while one cannot be a friend to a slave qua slave, one can be a friend to him or her qua human, "for in a certain way every human being can have a relation of justice with someone who can be a party to laws and agreements; and there can be friendship too, in so far as [the other party is] human" (b5–8). But the very features of humanity which make it

15 Cf. Pol 1253b30–1254a1.

possible to enter into relationships such as those of justice and friendship are incompatible with the status of a natural slave, since it is
insofar as one is a rational agent that one can be involved in these
relationships, whereas the natural slave is a natural slave precisely
because he or she lacks rationality.[16] The only sort of slave with whom
it is possible to be a friend is the sort who should not be a slave at all,
the rational agent who has been unjustly subjected to slavery through
the chance of war or similar circumstance (e.g. capture by pirates) (I.6).

Aristotle fails to provide a justification of slavery as actually
practised either in the Greek world or in any other known society.
The only form of slavery that his principles justify is that in
which the slave is a natural slave, but he gives no reason to
believe that there are any natural slaves. But could there even be
any such? On his account a natural slave would have to be a sort
of mental defective, lacking as he does the capacity for practical
reason; but such a being, to have survived to adulthood, must
have been taken care of by rational adults. The very idea of a
community of natural slaves is incoherent; yet the practice of
slavery as envisaged by Aristotle envisages that barbarian peoples
are just such communities, adapted by nature to serve as a contin-
ual source of slaves for the Greeks (1252b7–9). The only alternative would be to deny that non-Greek societies were communities
in Aristotle's sense, i.e., associations determined by shared purposes, and to attempt instead to explain their organization by
appeal to non-rational instinct, perhaps on the model of flocks of
birds. But since Aristotle uses the phenomenon of language precisely to differentiate human societies from associations of social
animals such as bees (1253a7–18), that would appear to commit
him to denying language to non-Greeks.[17]

16 Strictly speaking, the natural slave is not *totally* lacking in rationality;
   he "participates in reason so far as to perceive, but not to have it"
   (1254b22–23).
17 On Aristotle's treatment of slavery, see W.W. Fortenbaugh, "Aristotle on
   Slaves and Women," in Barnes, Schofield, and Sorabji, eds., *Articles on
   Aristotle Vol. 2: Ethics and Politics* (London, 1977); Nicholas D. Smith,
   "Aristotle's Theory of Natural Slavery," *Phoenix* 37 (1983): 109–22 (re-
   printed in Keyt and Miller, *op. cit.*, 142–55), and Bernard Williams,
   Shame and Necessity (Berkeley, Los Angeles, and Oxford: University of
   California Press, 1993), ch. 5.

VI

This brief study has necessarily been highly selective. In seeking to elucidate some central themes of Aristotle's political philosophy by exhibiting their connections with his ethical theory and his natural philosophy, I have been obliged by constraints of space to ignore not only the "empirical" books IV–VI (see above, pp. 252–253), but also much of philosophical interest, notably Aristotle's criticisms in Book II of various proposed ideal states (including Plato's) and his account in book VIII of the educational system of his own ideal state. I hope that this essay may stimulate the reader to independent exploration of these and other facets of this rich and complex work.

9 Rhetoric and poetics

I. AN ART OF RHETORIC?

Modern philosophy does not greatly occupy itself with rhetoric. Ancient philosophy did: philosophy was sometimes hostile and sometimes friendly, but it never ignored rhetoric. Indeed, one of the questions which preoccupied philosophers was precisely the question of what attitude philosophy should take to rhetoric.

The question standardly took this form: Is rhetoric an art, a *technê*? The task of oratory, it was universally supposed, is to persuade; and good orators have the capacity to persuade by their speeches. The object of rhetoric was to study and to teach this capacity, and rhetoric is an art only insofar as it can achieve its object by intellectually respectable means. In particular, an art is a body of knowledge, practical in aim but systematic in organization, in which particular theorems and precepts are shown to follow from a relatively small set of fundamental truths. (An art is to practice what a science is to theory; and the conception of an art which I have just sketched bears an evident relation to the concept of a demonstrative science.[1]) If rhetoric is an art, then it is in principle the sort of thing which a philosopher might study.

Plato, in the *Gorgias*, had argued that rhetoric was no art – it is a mere knack, like the skill shown by a good chef. (And what is more, it is a disreputable knack.) In his *Phaedrus* he modified his view: rhetoric, as it is commonly understood, is indeed pretty contemptible; but there is no reaon why there should not be developed a "philosophical" rhetoric. Plato's reflections formed the background against which philosophers and rhetoricians argued for centuries:

---

1 On which see pp. 109–113.

the debate eventually ossified, but at the start it was serious and lively enough. Aristotle joined in. We are told that in the *Grylos* – a lost work written while Aristotle was still a young man – he "produced for the sake of inquiry certain arguments of his usual subtlety" to show that rhetoric was not an art;[2] we may reasonably assume that similar arguments were used in the quarrels between the Academy and Isocrates' school, quarrels in which Aristotle participated; and no doubt the many books which Aristotle devoted to rhetoric[3] continued the debate.

Of these works only the *Rhetoric* has survived.[4] We might antecedently suppose that Aristotle would here have come to the view that rhetoric *was* an art, or at any rate that it had arty parts. For why else should a philosopher write at such length on the subject? And the opening of Book I proves the supposition true:

... everyone tries to discuss propositions and to maintain them, to defend themselves and to attack others. Laymen do this either at random or from practice and acquired habit. Since both these ways are possible, the subject can plainly be handled in a systematic way – for we can ask why some speakers succeed through practising and others spontaneously; and everyone will at once agree that such an inquiry is the function of an art.

(I 1, 1354a5–11)

Aristotle's argument is fragile, but his conclusion is plain: there is an art of rhetoric.

But Aristotle's art will not look like the standard treatises on the subject.[5] For their authors have missed the main point of the subject:

The modes of persuasion are the only true constituents of the art: everything else is accessory. But these writers say nothing about enthymemes, which are the substance of rhetorical persuasion, but deal largely with nonessentials. The arousing of prejudice, pity, anger, and similar emotions has nothing to do with the essential facts ...   (I 1, 1354a12–18)

2 Fragment 69 R[3] = Quintilian, II xvii 14.
3 See above, p. 8.
4 The so-called *Rhetoric to Alexander* is not by Aristotle: scholars generally ascribe it to Aristotle's contemporary, Anaximenes of Lampsacus.
5 Of which there were many; indeed, the word "art" or "*technê*" in one use simply meant "manual of rhetoric."

Aristotle, it appears, has a purified, a "philosophical", rhetoric in mind. The function of oratory is still, of course, public persuasion, so that rhetoric itself is an art aiming, at one remove, at persuasion. But the art is austere: although arousing the emotions may well be effective in getting an audience on your side, the study of the emotions is no part of Aristotle's rhetoric – it is not, strictly speaking, a mode of persuasion.

For the modes of persuasion are forms of argument – enthymemes are the substance of the subject. Aristotle is quite clear on the matter:

> It is plain, then, that the technical study of rhetoric is concerned with the modes of persuasion. Now persuasion is a sort of proof (since we are most persuaded when we consider a thing to have been proved); the orator's proofs are enthymemes,[6] and an enthymeme is a sort of deduction . . .
>
> (I 1, 1355a4–8)

Hence rhetoric, insofar as it is technical or an art, studies deductions, it studies logic.

This contention seems clear enough in itself – but it would surely have surprised Aristotle's contemporaries. Their surprise would quickly have turned to perplexity; for the contention of Chapter 1 seems to be rejected in Chapter 2. Here rhetoric is still concerned with "the modes of persuasion". But Aristotle now distinguishes among these modes. First, some modes are technical and others non-technical, the art of rhetoric restricting itself (of course) to the technical modes. But the "non-technical" modes of persuasion are not, as we might imagine, such operations as the arousing of pity; rather they are items "which are not supplied by the speaker" – written testimony, documents produced in evidence, and so on.[7] As for the technical modes,

> there are three kinds. The first kind depends on the personal character of the speaker; the second on putting the audience into a certain frame of mind; the third on the proof, or apparent proof, provided by the words of the speech itself.   (I 2, 1358a2–4)

The third of these items corresponds to the only item which Chapter 1 countenanced as a mode of persuasion; and the second item looks

---

6 On enthymemes see below, pp. 269–272.
7 These non-technical modes are nonetheless given a brief discussion in I 15.

suspiciously like the appeal to the emotions which Chapter 1 expressly banned, a suspicion which is confirmed a few lines later at 1358a13–14.

Something is awry. Perhaps a subtler scrutiny will show that the first two chapters of the work are after all consistent with one another? Perhaps we should rather suppose that the two chapters are "doublets," one of them originally written to supplant the other, which were unconvincingly published together by Andronicus?[8] Perhaps Aristotle was in a muddle himself? Most scholars now prefer the first of these suggestions. Myself, I opt for the second.

We might in any event wonder which of the two chapters is the more appropriate as an introduction to our *Rhetoric*. Chapter 1 is hardly appropriate at all. Logic, in a broad sense, is indeed the topic of Book I of the *Rhetoric* (except for I 15) and of the second part of Book II (II 20–26). But it is not the main subject of Book II, and it is not a subject at all for Book III. Chapter 2 seems more promising: after all, it distinguishes three "modes of persuasion," and our *Rhetoric* is divided into three books – one book for each mode? The third of the three modes is "proof"; and this corresponds well enough with Book I. The second mode, the exciting of the emotions, is explicitly introduced as the topic of Book II. But the first mode, character, is not the subject of Book III.

The mode of persuasion which "depends on the personal character of the speaker" is not a matter of being generally regarded as an honest broker. Rather,

this sort of persuasion, like the others, should be achieved by what a speaker says, not by what people think of his character before he speaks.

(I 2, 1356a9–11)

That is to say, the speaker, wishing to persuade his audience that P, must show, *by what he says*, that he is a credible character – and this will itself help to persuade the audience that P. At the beginning of Book II, Aristotle observes that three things will inspire confidence of this sort: good sense, goodness of character, goodwill. But these three items need no special discussion; for the first two have already been dealt with implicitly in Book I, and the third will be dealt with under the heading of the emotions (II 1, 1378a7–20).

8 See above, p. 11.

If the third part of the tripartite programme indicated in Chapter 2 dissolves into the other two parts, the third part of the *Rhetoric* emerges suddenly from the mists:

In making a speech you must study three items: first, the means of producing persuasion; secondly, the language; thirdly, the proper arrangement of the various parts of the speech. We have already distinguished the modes of persuasion, which we have shown to be three in number (III 1, 1403b5–10)

– it remains to discuss first language and then arrangement. Nothing in I 1 or in I 2 has hinted that this material will occupy one third of the whole *Rhetoric*; nor does III 1 explain or apologize for the new turn of events.

In sum, Chapter 1 and Chapter 2 do not seem to cohere with one another; and neither chapter serves as a particularly apposite introduction to our *Rhetoric*.

However that may be, the several parts of the *Rhetoric* are plainly written on the assumption that rhetoric is an art, or at least that there are technical aspects to rhetoric. The puzzles about Chapters 1 and 2 raise some questions as to what Aristotle took these aspects to be; but they do not suggest that he was in any doubt about the existence of an art. Was he right? It is tempting to think that he was not.

First, the three books of *Rhet* do not cohere into a *single* art. I do not mean that Aristotle – or his editor – has put together a broken-backed work; rather, whether *Rhet* has arranged its subject well or badly, that subject itself is intrinsically fragmented. As the previous paragraphs have indicated, substantial parts of *Rhet* deal with logic, substantial parts deal with what might be called moral psychology, and substantial parts deal with matters of language and composition. The three topics are quite different, and they are held together only by the fact that they all aim at the same goal, persuasion. There is nothing more to unify them – no common axioms, no common concepts, no common structures. (Why should there be? How could there be?) *Rhet* does not present an art inasmuch as it does not present *one* art: it presents three.

Or rather – and secondly – it presents fragments of three arts, and of three arts which exist quite independently of rhetoric. The sections on logic have the closest connections with dialectic and in part overlap with what Aristotle says in the *Topics*; the sections on the emotions[9] are linked both to the ethical and to the psychological writings; and Book III – as Aristotle himself indicates (III 1, 1404a37) – shares its subject matter with the *Poetics*. Rhetoric, as *Rhet* presents it, is not a constellation of three bright stars. A different metaphor is needed: rhetoric is a magpie, thieving a piece of one art and a piece of another, and then botching a nest of its own.[10]

It does not follow from this that rhetoric is not, after all, a technical subject. For we need to distinguish between two questions: Is rhetoric an art (like medicine, say, or navigation)? and: Is rhetoric a technical subject? The answer implicit in *Rhet* to the former question is NO; the answer explicit in *Rhet* to the latter is YES. Both answers seem to me to be right. (The ancient debate over the status of rhetoric was long and inconclusive in part because it never distinguished between the two questions.)

II. LANGUAGE, EMOTION AND LOGIC

Aristotle's own attitude to the content of Book III is curious.

In speaking we should properly be satisfied if we do not annoy our audience – we should not also try to please them; for we ought in justice to fight our case with no help beyond the facts, and nothing should matter except the proof of these facts. Nonetheless, as I have already said, other things have a considerable effect on the outcome because of the deficiencies of the audience. Hence the arts of language must have a small but genuine importance . . . But not as much importance as some people think.

(III 1, 1404a4–11)

Despite his apparent distaste for the subject, Aristotle has plenty to say. Much of it was no doubt inherited from the earlier writers of "Arts," which we know Aristotle to have read and in some cases summarized; but the introduction to the second half of the discussion – the account of arrangement – is polemical in tone:

A speech has two parts: you must state your case, and you must prove it. . . . The current divisions are absurd: narration is a part only of forensic

9 And also certain parts of the logical sections, namely those dealing with propositions about goodness and badness.
10 Note that Aristotle himself states that "rhetoric is a combination of the sciences of logic and of ethics" (I 4, 1359b8–9).

speeches – in a political speech or an epideictic speech how can there be a narration? . . .   (III 13, 1414a30–38)

Is Aristotle announcing a new rhetoric, a "philosophical" rhetoric, in which all the weight is on sober proof and such items as style and arrangement are assigned a low and ancillary role?

The bluff beginning to the discussion does not in fact preface any radically new set of prescriptions; indeed, the second part of Book III reads like a rehearsal of commonplaces, of views which either were already familiar or else would not cause any great consternation. Thus there are paragraphs on the right way to compose an Introduction, on how to calumniate your opponent and defend yourself from his calumnies, on Narration, on the role of arguments, and so forth. All this may be – may have been – sound and solid advice to a would-be orator; but it is, I fear, rather dutiful and dull.

The first part of Book III discusses language, but it is interested neither in syntax nor in semantics: the orator needs to be told, above all, about good style – that is to say, about effective style, about style which will serve the persuasive ends of the art. Thus there are remarks about frigidities of style and about appropriateness of vocabulary, remarks about the way in which a speech may be made impressive or grand or brilliant, remarks about prose rhythms and the balance of periods.

Syntax may seem to peep in at one point, in the discussion of "correctness of language" in III 5. Correctness of language is said – implausibly enough – to be contained under five heads. The last two heads are simple grammatical injunctions: get your genders right; and don't muddle singular and plural. But if there is elementary syntax here, we should not infer that correctness of language is a matter of syntax. For the second head urges us to avoid vague generality, and the third urges us to beware of homonymies.

Semantics might well be thought to make an appearance inasmuch as Aristotle spends some time on metaphor. Inappropriate metaphors will make a speech frigid (III 3, 1406b5–19), whereas appropriate metaphor will add brilliance and vivacity (III 10–11). In general it is clear that

metaphors must not be far-fetched, or they will not be understood; nor yet obvious, or they will have no effect.   (III 10, 1410b31–33)

Aristotle produces numerous illustrative examples. He explains why certain metaphors are likely to have the desired result, while others will seem pompous or absurd. He catalogues different kinds of metaphor.

None of this yet touches on the aspect of metaphor which most concerns modern philosophers. But semantic interests might be descried in at least one text. Aristotle distinguishes metaphors from similes, in the following way:

> Similes are also metaphors – the difference is slight. When Homer says "He leapt on his foe like a lion," it is a simile; when he says of him "The lion leapt," it is a metaphor – since both are brave, he has transferred[11] the word "lion" to Achilles.   (III 4, 1406b20–24)

The difference between a simile and a metaphor proper is simply this: a simile is introduced by some comparative particle such as "like" or "as." Aristotle thinks that this is a slight difference. It is tempting to suppose that he thinks that it makes no difference to the *sense* of what is said. Now if metaphors can be assimilated, semantically, to similes, and if similes are less problematical from a semantic point of view than metaphors, then Aristotle has indicated one way of dealing with the semantics of metaphor. But if this is the message implicit in the text I have just cited, it is not a message which Aristotle ever makes explicit; and it may be doubted whether, here or elsewhere in Book III, Aristotle had any interest in such semantic issues.

The emotions occupy the first eleven chapters of Book II, after which Aristotle turns to the related topic of traits of character. He deals with a number of particular emotions, one after the other, attempting in each case to explain three things: what it is to have the emotion in question; at what sort of people the emotion is typically directed; and on what sort of grounds it is typically directed against them. He begins by offering a brief general definition:

> The emotions are those feelings which change us in such a way as to effect our judgment and which are accompanied by pain or pleasure.
>   (II 1, 1378a21–22)

11 The Greek verb is *"metapherein"*, from which *"metaphora"* or "metaphor" derives.

The connection between the emotions and judgment has seemed striking: it is challenging to claim that it is an *essential* feature of, say, anger that it changes the judgments of those who are angry. Yet we should not read too much into the text. The reason why, in the *Rhetoric*, Aristotle refers to the effect of emotions on judgment is plain: the orator wants to persuade, or in other words to affect judgment – and stimulation of the emotions is therefore relevant to him only insofar as the emotions do affect judgment. It is hazardous to look for any profound philosophical reflection behind the sentence.

The descriptions of the individual emotions are also done with the orator's needs in mind, and we should be wary of seeing ethical or psychological theory in what is intended as practical help for public speakers. Nonetheless, readers of Aristotle's *Ethics* will find much of interest in these descriptions; and students of his psychology, who may be surprised to find that *On the Soul* pays next to no attention to the feelings, may usefully turn to these chapters of the *Rhetoric*.

Here, by way of illustration, is a summary of what Aristotle says about pity, in II 8.[12] The initial definition is this:

Pity may be defined as a feeling of pain at an apparent evil, destructive or painful, which befalls someone who does not deserve it and which we might expect to befall ourselves or some friend of ours – and to befall us soon.

(II 8, 1385b12–15)

When you lose all your money in the casino, then I will only feel pity for you if I think that I – or a friend of mine – might (soon) suffer the same misfortune. This seems a doubtful claim (at least a doubtful claim about what we normally call pity); but Aristotle infers from it that if you are completely destitute or utterly self-confident then you cannot feel pity at all. (In the latter case you will not, and in the former you cannot expect that anything bad will befall you.)[13] In fact it is the old and the weak and the educated who are most prone to pity – especially if they have living parents or children or spouses.

Aristotle also infers from the definition that if you feel pity then you believe that some people are good; for you must believe that the misfortune which arouses your pity is undeserved, and hence

12 My reason for choosing pity will emerge in the section on Tragedy.
13 Presumably your friends must also be destitute or conceited – or else you must be friendless.

(dubiously) that the sufferers are good. The characterization of pity as a state of mind ends with the claim that we feel pity if we "remember similar misfortunes happening to us or our friends or else expect them to happen in the future" (II 8, 1386a2–4). This appears to modify the definition, in which case Aristotle must retract his thesis that the destitute and the conceited cannot feel pity.

The paragraph on the grounds of pity is for most of its length a standard list of misfortunes. But it ends with two interesting contentions: we feel pity if we observe

the coming of good when the worst has happened (e.g. the arrival of the King of Persia's gifts for Diopeithes after his death); and also when nothing good has befallen a man at all, or when he has not been able to enjoy it when it has.
(II 8, 1386a14–16)

The complete absence of good fortune may perhaps count as misfortune; but the late arrival of the King's presents was surely neither destructive nor painful to Diopeithes – again, the initial definition appears to need modification.

Finally, for whom do we feel pity? Only for people who are rather like us – for otherwise we shall not suppose that what befell them may befall us. Aristotle also says that we must *know* the people we pity: does he mean that we cannot pity strangers? or is he perhaps only making the trivial point that in order to pity someone, we must know – or at least believe – that they have suffered some misfortune? However that may be, we do not feel pity for people who are very close to us:

Amasis did not weep, they say, when he saw his son being led to his death, but he wept when he saw a friend begging: the latter sight was pitiful, the former terrible.
(II 8, 1386a19–21)

The closeness is presumably closeness of affection, not of blood; you cannot pity someone whom you love.

I turn now to logic. In I 3 Aristotle distinguishes the three different types of rhetoric – deliberative or political, forensic, epideictic or show oratory – , and he remarks that orators of each type will need to have various "propositions" at their command. Hence the major part of Book I, chapters 4 to 14, is an assembly of relevant "propositions," or recipes for concocting "propositions," arranged under appropriate headings. The word "proposition" is *"protasis"*, a term often rendered by "premiss" rather than "proposition"; and in fact the "propositions" of I 4–14 are all to be thought of as potential premisses in rhetorical arguments or else as highly general truths the particular instances of which may serve as premisses in an orator's arguments. It is only insofar as I 4–14 are concerned with the provision of premisses that they can be regarded as contributions to logic.

There remain the general remarks on rhetorical argument in I 1–3, and the material in II 20–26. The latter chapters, and II 23 in particular, have close connections with the *Topics*, connections which Aristotle signals. In Book I Aristotle says that rhetoric is the "counterpart" of dialectic, which is the subject of the *Topics* (I 1, 1354a1); and he later remarks, with an explicit reference to this opening statement, that rhetoric is "a branch of dialectic and similar to it" (I 2, 1356a30–31). How, if at all, is rhetoric – or the logical part of rhetoric – distinguished from dialectic?

There is no general difference in principle between the types of argument used in rhetoric and elsewhere. For

anyone who persuades by proofs uses either enthymemes or inductions – there is no other way. And since anyone who proves anything at all is bound to use either deductions or inductions, ... it follows that each of the latter is the same as one of the former.   (I 2, 1356b6–10)

Deductions, when they occur in oratory, are called "enthymemes,"[14] inductions are called "examples."[15] What, then, marks off enthymemes in particular from deductions in general, examples in particular from inductions in general?

The distinction is made implicitly in the following two texts:

The task of rhetoric is to deal with those matters which we deliberate about without having arts or disciplines to guide us, and to deal with them in the hearing of people who cannot take in complicated arguments at a glance or follow a long chain of reasoning.   (I 2, 1357a2–4)

... we have also noted the difference between an enthymeme and a

14 In English logical textbooks the word "enthymeme" is sometimes used to mean a deduction with one or more suppressed premisses. Although Aristotle thinks that orators will and should suppress premisses in their arguments, the word "enthymeme", as he uses it, does not *mean* "argument with suppressed premisses."
15 On deduction and induction in Aristotle's logic see above, pp. 29–31.

dialectical deduction. Thus [in rhetorical speeches] we must not carry the
reasoning too far back, or the length of the argument will produce obscurity;
nor should we put in all the steps which lead to the conclusion, or else we
shall waste words in stating the obvious. . . . We must not start from any old
opinion but from those of definite groups of people, namely, the judges or
those whose authority they recognize . . . We must also base our arguments
on what happens for the most part as well as upon what necessarily happens.

(II 22, 1395b24–1396a3)

Thus the orator's subject matter and his audience each determine, to
some degree, the sort of argument he uses.

First, the audience. Speeches are heard, not read, and their audiences are not composed of subtle logicians. Hence an orator's arguments must be short and simple. (And they may properly omit material which the audience will readily supply.) Moreover, the orator
must persuade an actual audience. Hence his arguments must take
as premisses propositions which the audience is likely to believe or
to accept. Secondly, the subject matter. Orators do not argue about
technical issues: they will not attempt to prove geometrical theorems or to advance medical science. Hence they are not normally
concerned with what is fixed and certain knowledge. Again, their
concerns are with what men do – and in the world of action there are
no exceptionless rules, and things do not invariably turn out in the
same way. Hence the premisses of an orator's arguments will consist
mostly of propositions which hold "for the most part."

The most interesting point here – indeed the only point of strictly
logical interest – concerns these "for the most part" propositions
which form the components of typically rhetorical arguments.[16]

It is about actions that we deliberate and inquire, and all actions have a
contingent character – hardly any of them are determined by necessity.
Again, conclusions which state what holds for the most part must be drawn
from premisses which hold for the most part, just as necessary conclusions
must be drawn from necessary premisses. . . . It is thus evident that the
propositions on which enthymemes are based, though some of them may be
necessary, will in the main hold for the most part.   (I 2, 1357a25–32)

The objects of our deliberation hold for the most part; and "for the
most part" conclusions depend on "for the most part" premisses;

16 See also above, Chapter 4, pp. 113–115.

therefore the premisses in rhetorical arguments will in general hold
only for the most part.

What of the link between premisses and conclusions? Aristotle
says that

when it is shown that, certain propositions being true, a further and distinct
proposition must also be true in consequence, whether universally or for the
most part, this is called a deduction in dialectic and an enthymeme in
rhetoric.   (I 2, 1356b15–18)

In this sentence the qualifying phrase "whether universally or for
the most part" appears to refer not to the conclusion of an argument,
but rather to the link between premisses and conclusion. We might
then suppose that a characteristically rhetorical argument would
have the following form:

For the most part, P_1.
For the most part, P_2.
. . .
. . .
For the most part, P_n.
Hence for the most part: For the most part, Q.

And it is precisely the investigation of such argument-forms which
will give the logical part of rhetoric a character and an interest of
its own.

Alas, we look in vain in the *Rhetoric* for any such investigation.

There are the first steps towards an investigation in the *Analytics*[17] – whence it emerges that "for the most part" arguments are
not, in any event, the private property of rhetoric. (In ethics all
things and in physics many things hold only for the most part.) But
even in the *Analytics* things are disappointing, and for several reasons. First, the suggestion that the link between premisses and conclusion might hold only for the most part is never elaborated or even
suggested. (We might plausibly suspect that it makes only a phan-
tom appearance in the *Rhetoric*.) Secondly, it is not clear that for the
most part arguments contain propositions *of the form* "For the most
part, P": perhaps they are simply arguments of the form "P_1, P_2, . . . ,

17 See *An.Pr* I 13, 32b5–10; I 27, 43b32–36; *An. Post* I 30, 87b19–26; II 12,
    96a8–19. The explicit reference to *An.Pr* at *Rhet* I 2, 1357a30, is doubt-
    less a later addition: above, p. 19.

P_n; so Q," where as a matter of fact one or more of the component propositions holds for the most part. Thirdly, the few things which Aristotle says about for the most part deductions are unsystematic and of doubtful validity.[18]

Fourthly, and capitally, Aristotle does not explain how we are to understand the phrase "for the most part," and his actual use of the phrase suggests more interpretations than one. Sometimes it seems to express a statistical notion: "For the most part, P" means that most As are B. Sometimes it appears to be a modal operator, so that "For the most part, P" is rather like – perhaps indeed is a special case of – "Possibly P." Sometimes it looks like an independent operator with something like the sense of "By nature." These different interpretations are hardly consistent with one another, and each would validate a different set of rules and arguments.

Aristotle saw that "for the most part" propositions have a scientific importance and deserve logical investigation. But he did not himself pursue the subject very far – certainly not in the course of his rhetorical studies.

III. POETRY

Aristotle's *Poetics* are incomplete. Our text promises a discussion of all types of poetry and breaks off after discussing tragedy and epic. There is little doubt that Aristotle wrote a second Book for the *Poetics*, which contained his reflections on comedy. Some traces of these survive in later texts, most notably in a corrupt and jejune epitome known as the "Tractatus Coislinianus;" but it is not clear how accurately the traces mark the passage of Aristotle's own feet.[19]

The first Book of the *Poetics* – or the *Poetics*, as I shall call it for short – divides into three main parts. First, an introductory section presents the general notion of artistic "imitation" (*Poet* 1) and its different species (2), and charts the supposed development of poetry (4–5). The second and main part of the work is given to tragedy: after

18 *An.Pr* makes some advances. Thus whereas *Rhet* says, indeterminately, that for the most part conclusions depend on for the most part premisses, *An.Pr* I 27, 43b32–36 specifies that the premisses must "*all or some*" hold for the most part. Yet it remains unclear whether the determinate rule is true.

19 See Richard Janko, *Aristotle on Comedy* (London, 1984).

a definition and an anatomy of the subject (6), most of the discussion concerns the story or plot, which Aristotle takes to be the most important of the different "parts" or aspects of a tragedy (7–18). There are also chapters on character (15, inserted into the discussion of plot), on "thought" (19), and on diction (20–22).[20] The third part of the work discusses epic, briskly (23–24); it then raises a handful of questions about literary criticism (25); and it ends with a discussion of the relative merits of tragedy and epic (26).

The whole discussion is introduced, and united, by the notion of "imitation" or *mimêsis*. This notion defines the subject matter of the *Poetics*. For Aristotle takes poetry to be an "art" or *technê*[21] (alongside navigation and medicine and house-building and horse-breeding); and he distinguishes it from most other arts or *technai* inasmuch as it is "imitative." But it is not the only imitative art – a poet "is an imitator just like a painter or other maker of images" (25, 1460b7–8). Aristotle's imitative arts correspond, in a sense, to what we sometimes call the arts or the fine arts (literature and music and painting and sculpture and dancing and . . .); but the correspondence is rough and partial – and the differences between the Aristotelian concept and our own are perhaps more interesting than the similarities. However that may be, poetry is distinguished from the other imitative arts by its medium: poetry imitates *in language* (1, 1447a19–21).

Again, the concept of imitation explains the origin and the popularity of poetry.

Imitation is natural to men from childhood onward, one of the advantages of men over the other animals consisting precisely in this, that men are the most imitative of things and learn by imitation. In addition, it is natural for everyone to take pleasure in works of imitation.   (4, 1448b6–9)

Works of poetry will be in steady supply, since men are by nature prone to imitation and the poetic art is an imitative art. Works of poetry will meet a steady demand, since men by nature like to observe imitations. That is why poetry sells so much better than coca cola.

What is "imitation"? Aristotle offers no explanation. Presumably he supposed that his audience would be familiar with the term –

20 22 on style, 20–21 on grammar and related issues – some scholars suppose that 20–21 are out of place and perhaps not by Aristotle at all.
21 See above, p. 259.

perhaps from their reading of Plato. But in Plato, the word *"mimê-sis"* is used in at least two different senses. In the first sense, imitative poetry is contrasted with narrative poetry and illustrated by the speeches in Homer's poems (or, more generally, by dramatic poetry). Here it is the characters who speak rather than the author; and the author is said to be "imitating" inasmuch as he mimics or impersonates. "From nature's fairest . . . ": there is W.S. speaking to us in his own voice. "A horse, a horse . . . ": here is W.S. putting on the mask and impersonating – imitating – King Richard III. In the second sense, all poetry is imitative, and imitation is explained as the production of a likeness of something. Designers of mock Georgian mansions are imitators in this sense. According to Plato, painters too are imitators in this sense; for the painted bed which a painter produces is not a real bed but the likeness of a bed. And so too are poets imitators; for what do they do but produce copies and likenesses of things?[22]

When Aristotle remarks that we are natural imitators, he surely has the first sense of "imitate" in mind: we are natural mimics, not natural counterfeiters. But evidently not all poetry is imitative in this sense. Hence Aristotle must after all have the second sense in mind; and indeed, at 25, 1460b7–8, he classifies poets as "makers of likenesses."

Surely poets are not makers of likenesses.[23] Of what is "From nature's fairest . . . " a likeness? Perhaps, then, painters *make* likenesses whereas poets *describe* likenesses: a landscape artist imitates nature directly, producing a counterfeit nature on his canvas; a pastoral poet imitates nature indirectly, describing in his verse a fictional nature which his mind has contrived. But this suggestion is also, or so it must seem, open to devastating objection: it simply does not fit "From nature's fairest . . . " or any number of other poems. And it is tempting to suppose that Aristotle – and Plato before him – had observed that *pictures* are likenesses, and imprudently inferred that the same thing holds of poetry.

Not all paintings are likenesses. Portraits are, or perhaps ought to be. (But what exactly is it for a portrait of Nelson to be *like* Nelson –

22 Plato deploys the first sense in Books II and III of the *Republic*, the second in Book X.
23 Nor, evidently, are musicians. How could the Moonlight Sonata be a likeness of anything?

must it be short and have part of its frame missing?) Yet few pictures are portraits. On the other hand, very many pictures – and most ancient pictures – do *represent* things: *Déjeuner sur l'herbe* is not a likeness of a lunch party, but it surely represents a lunch party, it is a picture *of* a lunch party (though there is no lunch party of which it is a picture). And just as pictures are often representative, so poetry too may be said to represent things.[24] Perhaps, then, imitation is neither mimicry nor counterfeiting – rather, imitation is representation.

This is a happy suggestion, but it is not wholly adequate. Any writer may represent: indeed, a few odd forms of "experimental" writing apart all writers *do* represent. Thus Gibbon, in his *Decline and Fall*, certainly represented the degeneration of Rome; and we might say that Hume, in the *Treatise*, represented an atomistic empiricism. But historians and philosophers are not, in Aristotle's sense, imitative writers – history is sharply distinguished from poetry (9, 1451a38–b7), and Empedocles' philosophical verses are not poetry (1, 1447b15–19). For imitation differs from representation and is similar to counterfeiting, at least in this point: imitation connects with the untrue, the unreal, the fictional. In the *Centre Pompidou* in Paris you may look at an ordinary dining-chair which stands against the wall under the label "Chaise": it may be a work of art, it may represent a chair, but it is certainly not an Aristotelian imitation.

Imitation, then, is a special kind of representation: it is a matter of representing *a* so-and-so rather than of representing *the* so-and-so. It is sometimes true that you represent a so-and-so without there being any so-and-so which you represent. Gibbon represented a degenerate Empire – and there was a degenerate Empire which he represented. Manet represented a lunch, but there was no lunch which he represented. To imitate, let us say, is to represent not in the Gibbon fashion, but in the Manet manner.

This may be a useful way to put the matter. But I cannot see that it evades the dangers which the notion of "describing likenesses" supposedly runs. The Manet style of representation is a matter, so to speak, of producing a description where there is nothing in reality being described. In other words – more or less – poets imagine things

24 And music? It *can* be representative (the "Sea Interludes" from *Peter Grimes*); but most music is non-representational.

which are like reality and then describe them. The "more or less" glosses over some significant differences; but it is hard to think that the Manet version of imitation will find room for many items which the likeness interpretation excludes, or vice versa.

And we might reasonably conclude, not that Aristotle has made a hash of defining what we know as poetry, but rather that the notion of poetry which interests Aristotle – or at least, which interests him in the *Poetics* – is very different from ours. Certainly, Aristotelian poetry cannot be identified with verse and distinguished from prose: much verse is not Aristotelian poetry. Certainly, Aristotelian poetry is not to be identified with literature and contrasted with mere writing: Empedocles and Gibbon both wrote literature, yet neither wrote Aristotelian poetry. Rather, Aristotelian poetry comes close to our notion of fiction and is contrasted with non-fictional writing; for imitation is, roughly, fictional representation.

This is certainly not quite right, and it is certainly not perfectly clear.[25] But I am persuaded that it is roughly right. At any rate, it is interesting. And it also has some diverting consequences: perhaps the Trojan War really took place and the *Iliad* is not a poem after all.

IV. TRAGEDY

I shall limit my comments to the three most celebrated elements in Aristotle's account of tragedy: his definition of the genre, his account of the "tragic hero," and his theory of the "unity" of tragedy. Aristotle does not claim that these three things are the most important of his reflections; but their extraordinary influence on the later history of the subject – and on the later history of the theatre – warrants their selection here.

The definition of tragedy in Chapter 6 is presented as a summary of material already expounded.

A tragedy is the imitation of an action which is serious and, having grandeur, complete in itself, done in language seasoned with embellishments, each appearing separately in different parts of the work, in dramatic rather than narrative form, accomplishing by way of pity and fear the catharsis of such feelings.   (6, 1449b22–28)

25 Is "From nature's fairest . . ." fiction or non-fiction?

The serious nature of the action which it imitates marks tragedy off from comedy. The notion of "completeness" adverts to the unity of the piece, to which I shall return. In the next sentence Aristotle explains that by "embellishments" he means rhythm and harmony, and that the reference to "different parts of the work" indicates that some parts of the tragedy will be sung verse and others spoken verse. It is thus implicit in the definition that a tragedy is a *verse* drama.

The final clause of the definition has engaged the most critical attention. Later passages in the *Poetics* confirm a few points which we should otherwise take for granted. Thus tragedy operates "by way of pity and fear" inasmuch as it imitates incidents which arouse pity and fear (9, 1452a3–4); and the feelings may be aroused by the "spectacle," by what is actually *seen* on the stage, or else – and better – by the structure and nature of the plot (14, 1453b1–2). It is clear, too, that the pity and fear are aroused in *the audience* (or rather, in the spectators); for certain types of plot are dismissed as untragic on the grounds that they "do not appeal to our human feelings or to our pity or to our fear" (13, 1452b36–38).

When we go to the theatre and see Sophocles' *Oedipus Tyrannus*, certain incidents in the play arouse our pity, and certain incidents – perhaps the same incidents? – arouse our fear. (Perhaps other emotions are also aroused, pity and fear merely standing in as representatives of their kind?) Aristotle does not say that tragic authors write *in order* to produce this effect, nor does he say that we go to the theatre *in order to* experience it; but he does say that it happens – and he suggests that its happening constitutes the raison d'être of tragedy. For when it happens, it has an effect: it accomplishes a "catharsis."

The word "*katharsis*" is used in two relevant Greek contexts: in medical texts, it refers to purgation (to the effects of emetics and laxatives); in a religious context, it refers to purification. Does Aristotle mean that tragedy rids us of our emotions, or that it refines our emotions? No text gives us a clear answer to the question, and we may wonder whether either answer is particularly plausible as an account of the effect of tragedy on its audience.

Do the spectators feel pity and fear? Well, who do they pity? Oedipus, if anyone. But on Aristotle's own account of pity, this is impossible.²⁶ I can pity someone only if I know him or know that he has suffered some misfortune, and only if he is in some way close – but not too close – to me. I do not know Oedipus (there is no Oedipus to know), and I do not believe that he has suffered any misfortune. Even if I falsely took Sophocles to be reporting a story about a real king of Thebes, I cannot feel pity: Oedipus is nothing like me. Again, according to Aristotle I can pity someone only if I suppose that a similar misfortune is likely to befall me or one of my friends, and to do so soon. But I do not expect to marry my mother, or any close female relation; I do not expect to put out my own eyes, or to deprive myself of any other vital organ. Nor do I anticipate such a future for any of my friends.

What do I fear? – A fate like the fate of Oedipus, if anything. But I have never been afraid – not even in the theatre – of doing what Oedipus did; and I do not believe that many other members of an audience have done so either.

The *Oedipus* does not arouse pity for Oedipus, and it does not arouse fear of an Oedipodean fate. The theatre or the cinema may arouse genuine fear and genuine pity: a horror film may occasionally cause genuine fear (though it will usually cause rather a pleasurable frisson); and a romantic play, which half engages my attention, may lead me to dwell on the actual miseries of the middle-aged. But this is not the sort of thing which Aristotle has in mind. Indeed, he cannot have real pity and genuine fear in mind at all; for he refers to the *pleasure* which comes from the pity and the fear (14, 1453b12); and genuine pity and real fear do not cause pleasure.

He must mean that we feel a sort of quasi-pity for Oedipus, or perhaps that we quasi-feel pity for him: it is, somehow, *as though* we felt pity for him. Again, we do not fear an Oedipodean fate – but it is *as though* we had such a fear. There is no doubt that some emotions, or some quasi-emotions, are felt, or quasi-felt, in the theatre; and it seems plausible to think that tragic incidents are somehow connected to a special group of emotions, to which pity and fear belong. To this extent Aristotle is surely right. But if it is plain that we do not genuinely pity Oedipus, it is far from plain what is going on when we quasi-pity him.

However that may be, do these theatrical emotions, or quasi-

26 See above, p. 268.

emotions, have a purgative or a purificatory effect? After a performance of *Oedipus* do I perhaps cease to pity people like Oedipus, and do I cease to fear a fate like the fate of Oedipus? Or, more generally, do I cease, for a while at least, to feel any pity or any fear? Nothing like this happens to me, and I doubt if it happens to you: we are not purged by the theatre. Are we purified? Our emotions are "purified," let us suppose, if they come to be more appropriately felt – felt at more appropriate times, towards more appropriate people, for a more appropriate length, and so on. In other words, the purification of an emotion is a matter of bringing it closer to "the mean."[27] Well, are my feelings of pity and fear better balanced after a performance of *Oedipus*? Having seen a representation of great suffering, am I now, say, less inclined to fear a drop in my salary? Having seen a representation of an action which, had it been real, would have aroused intense pity, am I now, say, less inclined to feel sorry for old-age pensioners who cannot afford a second television set?

No doubt our emotions *may* be purified in this sort of way. But the suggestion that it is intrinsic to tragedy so to purify them incites three comments. First, I do not believe that tragedy *normally* has any such effect on me (or on my friends); so that the effect is at best occasional. Secondly, I doubt if tragedy is a peculiarly effective form of purification: history outpurifies fiction any day, and a five-minute film of Belsen will do more for your emotions than any number of *Oedipuses*. Thirdly, I cannot persuade myself that this is an important aspect of tragedy: to suppose that the primary reason, or even a main reason, for encouraging productions of *Oedipus* is that they clean up our feelings is to turn art into emotional therapy.

The fact that tragedies are to arouse pity and fear determines the nature of a tragic plot and hence the fate of a tragic hero. A bad man whose bad fortune turns to good will induce no pity at all: a bad man whose good fortune turns sour will arouse feelings – but not feelings of pity and fear. The fall of a good man will seem odious rather than pitiable.

There remains, then, the intermediate kind of person, a man not pre-eminently virtuous or just, but who enjoys a high reputation and prosperity, whose misfortune is brought upon him not by vice and depravity but by some fault.   (13, 1453a6–10)

27 On which see above, pp. 217–219.

Such a man was Oedipus.

Aristotle's analysis is not in all particulars convincing. We might suppose, for example, that the undeserved fall of a virtuous man could well, in suitable circumstances, be the sort of thing which, were it actual, would move us to pity; and, despite Aristotle's account of pity, we might imagine that the fall of a wicked man could itself properly excite pity. Again, why insist that a tragic hero be eminent and prosperous? Are there no tragedies of the little man? But the clause in the analysis which has occasioned most comment is the last clause: "by some fault."

The word for "fault" here is "*hamartia*". It is reasonably plain that a *hamartia* is not a defect of character – a *hamartia* is an event, an action, something that you do when you go wrong in some way. The misfortune of Aristotelian heroes depends on what they do.

Sins, or moral errors, are doubtless faults of a sort; and a tragic *hamartia* has sometimes been interpreted as a fault of this moral order. The fall of Adam was a tragic fall inasmuch as Adam disobeyed the commands of God and thus sinned. But the misfortune which follows the tragic fault must be an *undeserved* misfortune – otherwise it will not arouse pity. And although we may readily imagine cases in which a moral error leads to undeserved misfortune (perhaps because the misfortune is inappropriate or out of proportion to the sin), it seems clear that Aristotle does not think that his heroes will commit any moral crime. A tragic *hamartia* is simply a mistake.

Oedipus killed his father at the crossroads – hinc illae lacrimae. His *hamartia* was not the moral fault of patricide, nor even the moral fault of murder. His fault, his mistake, was his failure to realize that the man in the coach was his father.

Oedipus had no way of avoiding the mistake: he could not have found out that the man he met at the crossroads was his father. His fault was, practically speaking, unavoidable. (I do not mean that the whole thing was fated, or planned in advance by the gods – although this is a matter which properly exercises students of Sophocles' tragedy. I mean simply that, in the imagined circumstances, Oedipus had no chance to discover the truth.) Is this point a special feature of the case of Oedipus, or does Aristotle imply that the tragic fault is always and necessarily unavoidable? Some interpreters hold that he does – this is why the misfortune is undeserved: the hero's fault is not his fault. Then the pity which tragedy inspires will be the pity we feel when contemplating the victims of bad luck: we are always at the mercy of chance, and it is precisely this aspect of the human situation which is the stuff of tragedy.

This conclusion is not required by the text. And it is a conclusion which we might prefer to resist. Suppose that Oedipus could indeed have discovered, without extended researches, that the man at the crossroads was his father, but that he did not stop to ask the right questions: might he not thus be responsible for his fault and yet still a tragic hero? (We should not argue that his misfortune would then be deserved: when an avoidable error leads to disaster it does not follow that the disaster was deserved.) Moreover, might not the tragic error flow from and manifest a defect of character? Suppose that Oedipus was impetuous and that his impetuosity led him not to ask who the man at the crossroads was. There is still a fault, a *hamartia*; but it is caused by the character of the agent (who, we may recall, is supposed not to be "pre-eminently virtuous and just").

But there is no end to speculations of this sort: the text of the *Poetics* excites them.

Finally, a word on the unity of tragedy. Classical modern tragedy obeyed – or paid lip-service to – the theory of "the three unities": unity of time, unity of place, unity of action. Crudely speaking, the time which the play takes on stage should be the same as the time which the represented action would actually have taken; the place which the stage represents should be the same throughout the play; and there should be just one action which persists for that time in that place. Of these three unities, only the last, unity of action, is Aristotelian. If a tragedy exhibits, in addition, unity of time and of place, that will simply be the accidental consequence of the fact that it represents a single action.

But why should a tragedy observe any of the unities? By definition, a tragedy imitates a "complete" action. A complete action must have a beginning, a middle, and an end (7, 1450b26). The plot or story, therefore, must have a unity. But

the unity of a plot does not consist, as some suppose, in its having one man as its subject; for indefinitely many things may befall one man, not all of which it is possible to reduce to a unity.   (8, 1451a16–19)

No doubt – but might not the unity of the plot turn on the fact that it shows a coherent development of the *character* of a single man? (Perhaps the unity of *Hamlet* derives, in part, from something of this sort?) No, for

> tragedy is an imitation not of people but of action and of life. . . . In a play, then, people do not act in order to portray character: they include character for the sake of action.   (6, 1450a16–21)

The unity of plot must therefore derive from the fact that it represents a single action.

But what does all this all amount to – what, after all, is "one" action? How are actions to be individuated? The question is of some philosophical interest – and Aristotle offers implicit answers to it in his *Physics* and his *Ethics*. But he does not address it in the *Poetics*, and he has no reason to do so. For the *Poetics* is not concerned with the individuation of actions, and its point is unphilosophical: the insistence on "one action" serves to exclude two types of plot – first, the episodic plot, in which a sequence of unrelated incidents follow one another: secondly, a layered plot, in which plots and subplots intertwine.

And why exclude such things? Is Aristotle's insistence on "one action" anything more than a stipulative restriction, either trivial or pernicious? (Trivial if Aristotle simply refuses to apply the word "tragedy" to plays which do not limit themselves to a single action; pernicious if he hopes or intends to discourage playwrights from writing more complex plots.) For my part, I prefer complexity to simplicity, and I like character as well as plot; and I find nothing in the *Poetics* which makes me fear that my taste may be puerile or perverted.

v. the art of poetry

This last reflection leads to a final question: How valuable are Aristotle's reflections on tragedy? They had some little currency in antiquity; and, for a certain period, they gained an extraordinary hold over the modern stage. Why, and how justly?

Return to the definition of tragedy and consider the reference to "different parts of the work." No doubt every tragedy will have parts – what could be more innocuous? But a little later, Aristotle specifies what the parts must be, namely "prologue, episode, exode, and choral part, the last being divided into parode and stasimon" (12, 1452b17–18). He thus requires that every tragedy must have *these* parts – and, as it were incidentally, that every tragedy must have a chorus. In his comment on the definition in Chapter 6, he had already explained that the "different parts" will be some of them spoken verse and some of them sung. Thus a tragedy must be in verse; and parts of it must be set to music.

These claims seem curiously restrictive: must all tragedies really be in verse and have a chorus? We might perhaps admit that verse is a better medium than prose for tragedy, that a verse tragedy is likely to be aesthetically more satisfying and emotionally more powerful than a prose tragedy; but we shall surely not admit that it is actually *impossible* to write a tragedy in prose. (Still less that it is *impossible* for a tragedy to lack a chorus. – Why on earth *should* it be impossible?) What are we to do with a definition which implies that neither Shakespeare nor Ibsen wrote a tragedy?

It is no use to urge that Aristotle is defining not the English notion of a tragedy (not the English word "tragedy") but the Greek notion of a *tragôdia* (the Greek word "*tragôdia*"); and to remark that the English notion, though derived from the Greek notion, is largely different from it. That may be true enough; but it does not follow that Aristotle's account of tragedy is a decent analysis of the Greek concept. And it is hard to think that it is; for it is hard to believe that a Greek, faced with a prose *Oedipus* or an *Electra* without a chorus, would have said "But that's not a tragedy at all" rather than "What an interestingly avant garde (disgustingly novel) sort of tragedy."

Nonetheless, Aristotle's definition plainly does answer to the Greek facts rather than to the modern facts. His account of tragedy is based on a survey – or perhaps rather on an intimate knowledge – of the Greek theatre. He observed, or thought he observed, that tragedy had undergone a certain growth and development; and although he explicitly refrained from claiming that it had achieved its finished form (4, 1449a7–9), he plainly took it to be close to perfection. And he then set about describing, in general terms, the tragedies which he regarded as the best examples of the genre. The description is empirically based: it does not purport to be an account of the Greek use of the word "*tragôdia*" (let alone of the English word "tragedy"), and it does not imply that it is *conceptually* impossible for there to be, say, prose tragedies.

There cannot be prose tragedies in the way in which there cannot be black daffodils. A botanist, interested in the daffodil, observes the plant growing; he picks what he takes to be a number of mature and near-perfect specimens; and he offers a scientific description of "the daffodil." He does not thereby give an analysis of the *concept* of a daffodil; and if he states that all daffodils must have yellow or white flowers, he certainly does not mean that it is *conceptually* impossible for there to be black daffodils. Aristotle's student of poetry is supposed to act like a botanist. Aristotle does not say as much in the *Poetics,* but his procedure in the *Poetics* is comparable to his procedure in the *Politics:*

> As in other sciences, so in politics compounds should always be resolved into the simple elements or smallest parts of the whole. . . . And if you consider things in their first growth and origin, whether they are States or anything else, you will get the clearest view of them.   (*Pol* I 1, 1252a19–25)

Analyse a compound into its elements; and to do that, look at its origin and see how it grows. Aristotle supposes that States – and tragedy – are open to the same sort of scientific investigation as animals and plants. He does not suppose that tragedy – nor even that the State – is *simply* a product of nature; but he does suppose that it is sufficiently like a natural product to respond to the same method of inquiry. Hence the oddities of his definition, and of his subsequent discussions. For the supposition is false.

Aristotle's theory of poetry is defective in the way in which his theory of politics is defective: each is parochial. The reason is not that Aristotle lacked the imagination to picture different forms of social and cultural life: rather, it is that he followed, self-consciously, a certain method of study which is inappropriate to its objects.

Does this mean that the *Poetics* has, as they say, "no value for us today"? Not wholly. Aristotle's poetics had a solid basis in fact; and anyone interested in Greek tragedy will find his discussion of the phenomenon invaluable. Moreover, the *Poetics* was later used as a textbook for dramatists, and if you are interested in, say, the drama of Racine, then Aristotle will be indispensable. But unless you have these particular historical interests, the *Poetics* will be a disappointment. If you are a playwright, you should not look there for useful rules or helpful tips. If you are interested in the nature of tragedy in general, you will learn little from Aristotle, save incidentally. If you are concerned to understand the tragic power of Shakespeare or of Ibsen or of any contemporary author, the categories within which Aristotle discusses tragedy will seem irrelevant.

VI. ENVOI

Two of Aristotle's own poems have survived. This is a loose translation of his "hymn to virtue," written to commemorate the death of his uncle-in-law Hermias.[28]

> Virtue, whom men attain by constant struggle,
> our noblest aim in life, a goddess pure,
> in Greece we deem it sweet to die for you
> or anguish and unending toil endure.
> You fill our hearts with such immortal gifts –
> dearer than parents, gold, or sleep's soft rays –
> that Hercules, Zeus' son, and Leda's twins
> aspired through labours to bring home your bays.
> For love of you Achilles and Ajax both
> left the clear day of men for Hades' night.
> For your dear sake, Atarneus' noblest son
> forsook this upper world of sun and light.
> Therefore, immortal, famed for virtuous deeds,
> the Muses nine with honour him attend,
> daughters of Memory, who thus honour Zeus,
> the god of guests, and the firm love of friends.

28 See above, p. 5. The Greek text is in Diogenes Laertius, *Lives of the Philosophers*, V 7 = fragment 675 R³.

SUGGESTIONS FOR READING

Most readers of this *Companion* will be studying Aristotle in English translation. All the works included in Bekker's Aristotle (see "Aristotle's Writings" this volume, pp. xix) together with a generous selection of fragments can be found in

Jonathan Barnes (ed.): *The Complete Works of Aristotle – The Revised Oxford Translation* (Princeton, Princeton University Press, 1984).

Most of Aristotle's major works are also readily available in other editions: recent translations are, on the whole, reasonably reliable, and it is good practice to consult at least two different versions of a text.

The Loeb Classical Library includes most of Aristotle's writings. Loeb editions print English and Greek on facing pages. Even if you have only a smattering of Greek, you should be prepared to have go at a Loeb. You will be able, for example, to see that the word translated "virtue" in this passage is in fact the same in Greek as the word translated "excellence" in that passage. For readers with more Greek, the best editions of the texts of Aristotle's major works are these:

Cat and *Int*: Minio-Paluello, OCT (Oxford Classical Texts)
An.Pr and *An.Post*: Ross, OCT
Top and *SE*: Ross, OCT but Brunschwig, Budé, for *Top* I-IV)
Phys: Ross, OCT
Cael: Moraux, Budé
GC: Joachim (Oxford, 1922)
Meteor: Fobes (Cambridge, Mass., 1919)
An: Ross, OCT

287

Sens: Ross (Oxford, 1955)
HA: Balme, Loeb
PA: Peck, Loeb
MA: Nussbaum (Princeton, 1978)
GA: Drossaart Lulofs, OCT
Met: Ross (Oxford, 1923)
NE: Bywater, OCT
EE: Walzer/Mingay, OCT
Pol: Dreizehnter (Munich, 1970)
Rhet: Kassel (Berlin, 1976)
Poet: Kassel, OCT

*   *   *

Chapter I contains some remarks on the nature of Aristotle's surviving writings which have a moral for readers. The moral is simple: Read Aristotle Slowly. All decent philosophical writing is thick – you cannot read philosophy as you would a novel; but Aristotle, for the reasons given in Chapter I, is quite unusually thick. It is worth saying this to yourself three times before you start to read; otherwise you will get little profit, and you will probably be frustrated and bored. Aristotle is difficult, but he is not gruelling. If you read him slowly, very slowly, then he is inspiring and gripping.

Many students will start Aristotle in connexion with a course of lectures, and the lectures will suggest which texts to read. But if you are not so constrained, you will find yourself faced by nearly two thousand pages of tough philosophy, and you will reasonably ask: "Where should I begin? and what should I try to get through?"

It is easier to offer negative than positive advice. Thus, do not begin with *Met*, which is too difficult until you have read, say, *Cat* and *Phys*; do not start with *Pol*, which makes more sense after *NE* or *EE*; do not start with *Sens*, which presupposes *An*. Again, do not ignore the "scientific" works on the grounds that your interests in Aristotle are philosophical: thus, *PA* and *GA* include a vast amount of philosophical material, and *Cael* is more philosophical than astronomical.

As for positive suggestions, what I imagine to be the usual practice is not a bad practice. Most students, I imagine, begin with ethics, and usually with *NE* rather than *EE*. The subject matter makes the text accessible, and the similarities and the differences between Aristotle's ethics and modern moral philosophy provide an immediate excitement. An alternative starting point, to my mind equally to be recommended, is *Phys*, or rather the first four Books of *Phys*. The text is probably harder than *NE*, and not everything in it connects at once with modern philosophical concerns. But it is more centrally and more typically Aristotelian, and it shows Aristotle – or so I think – at his best.

Having started, it is easy to continue; for what you read in the first text will direct you to the second and third. You will properly claim a reasonable acquaintance with Aristotle when you have read something like the following items (not, of course, in this order): *Cat, Int, An.Pr* A 1–13, *An.Post* A, *Phys* A–Δ, *An, PA* A, *Met* A, Γ-Θ, *NE* (or *EE*), *Pol* A, *Poet*. Other scholars will offer you other lists.

* * *

The best aid to reading Aristotle is Aristotle himself. That is to say, if you want help in understanding Aristotle's observations in this passage about, as it might be, pleasure or chance, then see what he observes elsewhere on the same topic. Occasionally, Aristotle – or his ancient editor – will provide a cross-reference. Often, it is easy to guess what are the appropriate parallel texts. (In reading *NE* you should have *EE* to hand; in reading parts of *Met, Cat* will be a useful ally; for *Poet* there will be parallels in *Rhet*; and so on.) But many parallels are not obvious; and here you need to consult indexes. The *Complete Works* has a tolerable index; and there is also

T.W. Organ: *An Index to Aristotle in Translation* (Princeton: Princeton University Press, 1972).

Readers with Greek will find "Bonitz" indispensable:

H. Bonitz: *Index Aristotelicus* (Berlin, 1870).

Plato is also a help; for Plato's ideas are frequently in Aristotle's mind and underlie his thoughts and his arguments. Modern readers of Aristotle will lose much if they are not willing to turn up passages in Plato from time to time.

After that, there are commentaries. Readers of the *Companion* will find the commentaries in the Clarendon Aristotle series particularly congenial. They are done specifically for students of philosophy, and they presuppose no knowledge of Greek. In addition, many commentaries written for Greek speakers can be profitably pillaged by the Greekless; in particular, the commentaries by Sir David Ross on *Met, Phys, An.Pr* and *An.Post*, and *Sens* are stuffed with valuable observations (and the "analyses" or summaries which Ross includes are an invaluable guide to the general structure of the arguments). It is also worth mentioning the translations of the surviving ancient commentaries, edited by Richard Sorabji in the series *Ancient Commentators on Aristotle*: these works are sometimes longwinded and sometimes parochial in their concerns, but as a general rule they will be found more helpful than much of the modern literature.

*   *   *

Finally, some items from the modern secondary literature (which were selected by the authors of the chapters to which they pertain). For the reasons given in the Introduction, the list which follows is minimalist: readers who did not find those reasons compelling, or who have reached a level at which they no longer apply, should skip the next three pages and turn to the Bibliography.

Chapter 1. Life and Work

The texts relating to Aristotle's character and life are assembled and analysed in
  I. Düring: *Aristotle in the Ancient Biographical Tradition* (Göteborg, 1957).
(Düring does not translate the texts into English.) On Aristotle's works, the standard study is
  P. Moraux: *Les listes anciennes des ouvrages d'Aristote* (Louvain, 1948).
For the origins of our corpus, see
  P. Moraux: *Der Aristotelismus bei den Griechen* I (Berlin, 1973). All modern studies of Aristotle's intellectual development depend on
  W. Jaeger: *Aristotle: Fundamentals of His Development*, transl. Richard Robinson (Oxford, 1948) [first German edition, Berlin, 1923].
The conception of Aristotle as an aporetic thinker may be found deployed in several of the papers in
  S. Mansion (ed.): *Aristote et les problèmes de méthode* (Louvain, 1961).

Chapter 2. Logic

On *Cat* and *Int*, see

J.L. Ackrill: *Aristotle's* Categories *and* de Interpretatione (Oxford, 1962)

in the Clarendon Aristotle series. On *An.Pr*

R. Smith: *Aristotle's* Prior Analytics (Indianapolis, 1991);

and on *An.Post*

J. Barnes: *Aristotle's* Posterior Analytics (Oxford, 1994²),

again in the Clarendon Aristotle series, as is

R. Smith: *Aristotle's* Topics *Books I and VIII* (Oxford, 1994).

The general account of Aristotle's logic by Martha Kneale in

M. and W.C. Kneale: *The Development of Logic* (Oxford, 1962)

is still very much worth reading. Those wishing for more detail should turn to

G. Patzig: *Aristotle's Theory of the Syllogism* (Dordrecht, 1968).

In

R. McKirahan: *Principles and Proofs* (Princeton, 1992)

there is a detailed, but readable, study of *An.Post*.

Chapter 3. Metaphysics

Ross' commentary,

W.D. Ross: *Aristotle – Metaphysics* (Oxford, 1923),

is invaluable. And there are also two items in the Clarendon Aristotle series:

C.A. Kirwan: *Aristotle's* Metaphysics *Books ΓΔE* (Oxford, 1978),

and

J. Annas: *Aristotle's* Metaphysics *Books M and N* (Oxford, 1977).

The last few years have yielded a crop of books, some of them excellent, on Aristotle's metaphysical ideas; to choose among them would be invidious. Instead I recommend four classic papers by Gwil Owen – "Logic and Metaphysics in some earlier works of Aristotle", "The Platonism of Aristotle," "Aristotle in the Snares of Ontology", and "Particular and General in Aristotle". All are reprinted in

G.E.L. Owen: *Logic, Science and Dialectic* (London, 1985).

Chapter 4. Philosophy of Science

On *Phys* there are

W.D. Ross: *Aristotle's Physics* (Oxford, 1946),

and two Clarendon volumes:

W. Charlton: *Aristotle's Physics Books I–II* (Oxford, 1980),

E. Hussey: *Aristotle's Physics Books III–IV* (Oxford, 1983).

For a general description of Aristotle's picture of the world, see
  F. Solmsen: *Aristotle's System of the Physical World* (Ithaca, 1960).
Some of Aristotle's more particular ideas are discussed in the relevant chapters of Richard Sorabji's trilogy:
  R. Sorabji: *Necessity, Cause and Blame* (London, 1980),
  R. Sorabji: *Matter, Space and Motion* (London, 1988),
  R. Sorabji: *Time and the Continuum* (London, 1990).

Chapter 5. Science

There is a Clarendon Aristotle:
  D. Balme: *Aristotle's de Partibus Animalium I and de Generatione Animalium I* (Oxford, 1993²).
On the philosophical side of Aristotle's biology, see
  P. Pellegrin: *Aristotle's Classification of Animals* (Berkeley, 1986),
and the essays collected in
  A. Gotthelf and J.Lennox (edd.): *Philosophical Issues in Aristotle's Biology* (Cambridge, 1985).
On the mathematical sciences, see the paper on Aristotle's mechanics in
  G.E.L. Owen: *Logic, Science and Dialectic* (London, 1985).

Chapter 6. Psychology

Much of the best recent work has been published in the form of articles. There are two good anthologies:
  J. Barnes, M. Schofield, and R. Sorabji (edd.): *Articles on Aristotle: 4 – Psychology and Aesthetics* (London, 1979)
  M.C. Nussbaum and A.O. Rorty (edd.): *Essays on Aristotle's de Anima* (Oxford, 1992).
The closely related area of the philosophy of action is dealt with in:
  D. Charles: *Aristotle's Philosophy of Action* (London, 1984).

Chapter 7. Ethics

The most traditional secondary source for Aristotle's moral philosophy is the *Magna Moralia*, prepared in the centuries after Aristotle's death by a Peripatetic follower and transmitted to us under Aristotle's name. It is clear and remains quite helpful to a modern reader. English readers have a careful and comprehensive handbook in
  W.F.R.Hardie: *Aristotle's Ethical Theory* (Oxford, 1980²).
A stimulating book which concentrates on the central idea of *eudaimonia* is

J.M. Cooper: *Reason and Human Good in Aristotle* (Cambridge, Mass., 1975).
In
D.S. Hutchinson: *The Virtues of Aristotle* (London, 1986)
there is a short and clear account of the connections between Aristotle's conception of moral virtue and other themes in his philosophy. The political life and the intellectual life are discussed by
R. Kraut: *Aristotle on the Human Good* (Princeton, 1989).
For an example of how to apply Aristotelian ideas in a contemporary way, see
S. Broadie: *Ethics with Aristotle* (Oxford, 1991).

Chapter 8. Politics

In the Clarendon series there is
R. Robinson: *Aristotle's Politics Books III and IV* (Oxford, 1962).
There are also two useful translations of *Pol* in
T.A. Sinclair, rev. T.J. Saunders: *Aristotle: the Politics* (Harmondsworth, 1981)
S. Everson: *Aristotle: the Politics* (Cambridge, 1988)
For a general survey see
R.G. Mulgan: *Aristotle's Political Theory* (Oxford, 1977).
There are useful collections of articles in
J. Barnes, M. Schofield, and R. Sorabji (edd.): *Articles on Aristotle: 2 – Ethics and Politics* (London, 1977)
and in
D. Keyt and F.D. Miller (edd.): *A Companion to Aristotle's Politics* (Oxford, 1991).

Chapter 9. Rhetoric and Poetics

Philosophical literature on *Rhet* is relatively sparse. But there is a commentary
W.M.A. Grimaldi: *Aristotle's Rhetoric* (Amsterdam, 1990),
and some of the ideas in Book II are discussed in
W.W. Fortenbaugh: *Aristotle on the Emotions* (London, 1979).
In contrast, *Poet* has destroyed forests. Of numerous commentaries, the most thorough is perhaps
G. Else: *Aristotle's Poetics* (Cambridge, Mass., 1965).
J. Jones: *Aristotle on Tragedy* (London, 1980),
offers a lively study of the central themes of the work.

JONATHAN BARNES, MALCOLM SCHOFIELD,
RICHARD SORABJI

Bibliography

PREFACE

All bibliographies are tralaticious, this more than most. Its arche-
type was compiled in 1975 for an anthology of *Articles on Aristotle*.
In 1977 it was extensively revised and prepared for separate publication as an Oxford University Study Aid. The Study Aid received a
second edition in 1978 and a third in 1980; in 1988 a substantially
altered New Edition appeared. The present catalogue is a version,
thoroughly revised and considerably changed, of the New Edition.

The thing is meant for anglophone philosophers. Hence it this
bibliography lists relatively few studies which are exclusively historical or philological in character (and offers relatively thin cover-
age of Aristotle's own scientific and antiquarian researches); and it is
powerfully biassed in favour of books and articles written in English.
In addition, we have tended to favour more recent items (which are
generally more accessible), and we have concentrated on work done
in what is sometimes called the "analytical" tradition in philosophy.
Even within these limits the list is far from comprehensive. We hope
that we have missed little of the very first rank (and that we have
included little of the very last rank). But we have surely omitted, for
one reason or another, many worthy pieces; and other scholars
would doubtless have come forward with other selections.

The arrangement of the bibliography and its principles of division
ask for a word. Generally speaking, the chapters follow the order of
events in the standard editions of Aristotle: first logic, then physics
or philosophy of science, and so on. And generally speaking, within

each chapter the sections follow the order of events within Aristotle's works. (Within sections the material is usually subdivided along thematic lines. Within subdivisions items are ordered chronologically.) Thus topics will, as a rule, be found in their Aristotelian place rather than in the place to which modern philosophers might assign them. But there are several exceptions to this rule.

The first section of each chapter (after Chapter 11) contains material relevant to the whole chapter: if you are looking for reading on pleasure, you should scan not only section (N) of Chapter VIII but also section (A). Many of the books we cite contain chapters bearing on issues which fall outside the section in which they are listed; and in addition, it is often difficult to know whether to place an item in this section of the bibliography or in that: we have added cross-references (fewer, perhaps, than we might have done) to mitigate the effects of these indeterminacies. (Items are numbered consecutively within chapters, and they are referred to by chapter- and item-number. Thus "III.14" refers to item 14 in Chapter III.)

The bibliography will be out of date by the time you read it. It will be revised for each subsequent edition of the *Companion*. The editor will welcome any suggestions for its improvement.

ABBREVIATIONS

AGP	Archiv für Geschichte der Philosophie
AJP	American Journal of Philology
An	Analysis
APQ	American Philosophical Quarterly
AustJP	Australasian Journal of Philosophy
BACAP	Boston Area Colloquium in Ancient Philosophy
BICS	Bulletin of the Institute of Classical Studies
CJP	Canadian Journal of Philosophy
CP	Classical Philology
CQ	Classical Quarterly
CR	Classical Review
GRBS	Greek, Roman, and Byzantine Studies

H	Hermes
HPQ	History of Philosophy Quarterly
HSCP	Harvard Studies in Classical Philology
ICS	Illinois Classical Studies
JAAC	Journal of Art and Art Criticism
JHI	Journal for the History of Ideas
JHP	Journal of the History of Philosophy
JHPL	Journal for the History and Philosophy of Logic
JHS	Journal of Hellenic Studies
JP	Journal of Philosophy
JPh	Journal of Philology
M	Mind
MH	Museum Helveticum
Mn	Mnemosyne
OSAP	Oxford Studies in Ancient Philosophy
PAS	Proceedings of the Aristotelian Society
PASS	Proceedings of the Aristotelian Society, supplementary volume
PBA	Proceedings of the British Academy
PCPS	Proceedings of the Cambridge Philological Society
Phg	Philologus
Phil	Philosophy
Phron	Phronesis
PhSc	Philosophy of Science
PhSt	Philosophical Studies
PPR	Philosophy and Phenomenological Research
PQ	Philosophical Quarterly
PR	Philosophical Review
REG	Revue des études grecques
RhM	Rheinisches Museum
RIP	Revue internationale de philosophie
RM	Review of Metaphysics
RPA	Revue de la philosophie ancienne
RPL	Revue philosophique de Louvain
TAPA	Transactions of the American Philological Association

CONTENTS

INTRODUCTORY

(A) Texts

Greek texts of most of Aristotle's works can be found in the OCT, Teubner, Budé, and Loeb series: recommended editions are listed in the Suggestions for Further Reading.

The standard English version of Aristotle is the Oxford Translation, a revised version of which may be found in:

(1) J. BARNES (ed.): *The Complete Works of Aristotle* (Princeton, 1984)

There is a useful anthology in:

(2) J.L. ACKRILL (ed.): *A New Aristotle Reader* (Oxford, 1987)

The volumes in the Clarendon Aristotle series contain translations and notes tailored to the needs of the Greekless philosophical reader. The magisterial editions of Sir David Ross are invaluable, not least on account of the comprehensive and accurate English synopses which they contain. The ancient commentaries, many of which are now available in English translation, may still be profitably consulted. Individual references to these works are given in the appropriate chapters.

The concordance by:

(3) H. BONITZ: *Index Aristotelicus* (Berlin, 1870)

is indispensable; it can be used to advantage even by those with very little Greek. There is also an English concordance, based on the Oxford translation, by:

(4) T.W. ORGAN: *An Index to Aristotle in English Translation* (Princeton, 1949)

Comprehensive bibliographies of writings on Aristotle can be found in:

(5) M. SCHWAB: *Bibliographie d'Aristote* (Paris, 1896)

(6) H. FLASHAR: *Die Philosophie der Antike 3: Ältere Akademie, Aristoteles, Peripatos* (Basel/Stuttgart, 1983)

Many of the works mentioned in the following pages contain their own bibliographies; new publications are regularly posted in *The Philosopher's Index*, the *Répertoire bibliographique de la philosophie*, *L'année philologique*, and *Elenchos*.

(B) Biography

The surviving evidence for the life of Aristotle is collected and discussed in:

(7) I. DÜRING: *Aristotle in the Ancient Biographical Tradition* (Göteborg, 1957)

See also:

(8) A.H. CHROUST: *Aristotle* (London, 1973)

(9) H.B. GOTTSCHALK: 'Notes on the wills of the Peripatetic scholarchs,' *H* 100, 1972, 314–42

301

(10) D. Whitehead: 'Aristotle the metic', *PCPS* 21, 1975, 94–9
and:
(11) 'Aristote de Stagire', in R. Goulet (ed.), *Dictionnaire des philosophes antiques*, vol. 1 (Paris, 1989)
– an uneven article, by several hands, which contains a quantity of useful material.
There is a reconstruction of Aristotle's tutorial technique in:
(12) H. Jackson: 'Aristotle's lecture-room and lectures', *JPh* 35, 1920, 191–200
See also:
(13) C. Natali: 'Aristotele professore?', *Phron* 26, 1991, 61–74
The collection of texts and articles in:
(14) C. Natali (ed.): *La scuola dei filosofi* (L'Aquila, 1981)
includes Gottschalk I.9 and Jackson I.12.
Questions about the number and nature of Aristotle's writings are exhaustively discussed in:
(15) P. Moraux: *Les listes anciennes des ouvrages d'Aristote* (Louvain, 1951)
And problems of authenticity have been tackled with new weapons in:
(16) A.J.P.Kenny: 'A stylometric comparison between five disputed works and the remainder of the Aristotelian corpus', in Moraux and Wiesner I.47 and Kenny VIII.35.

(C) Aristotelianism
Theophrastus was Aristotle's immediate successor. Most of his works have failed to survive (apart from the *Characters* and a short essay on *Metaphysics*, there are two botanical writings: the *History of Plants* and the *Causes of Plants*). Fragments of the lost works are collected in:
(17) W.W. Fortenbaugh, P.M. huby, R.W.sharples, and D. Gutas (edd.): *Theophrastus of Eresus*, Philosophia Antiqua 54 (Leiden, 1992)
For the successors of Theophrastus nothing survives intact. Fragments and *testimonia* may be found in the several volumes of:
(18) F. Wehrli: *Die Schule des Aristoteles* (Basel, 1944–69)
For the history of the Peripatos see:
(19) K.O. Brink: 'Peripatos', *Pauly-Wissowas Realencyclopädie der klassischen Altertumswissenschaft*, suppt. 7, 1940, 899–949
(20) J.P. Lynch: *Aristotle's School* (Berkeley, 1972)
(21) P. Moraux: *Der Aristotelismus bei den Griechen* (Berlin, 1973, 1984)
(22) F.H. Sandbach: *Aristotle and the Stoics* (Cambridge, 1985)
(23) P. Moraux: 'Les débuts de la philologie aristotélicienne' in Cambiano I.80
(24) R. Sorabji (ed.): *Philoponus and the Rejection of Aristotelian Science* (London, 1987)
(25) R. Sorabji (ed.): *Aristotle Transformed* (London, 1990)
Aspects of the later history of Aristotelianism are examined in:

(26) L. MINIO-PALUELLO: *Opuscula: the Latin Aristotle* (Amsterdam, 1973)
(27) L. MINIO-PALUELLO: 'Aristotle: tradition and influence', in GILLISPIE I.71
(28) I. DÜRING: 'Von Aristoteles bis Leibniz', *Antike und Abendland* 4, 1954, 118–54 = MORAUX I.64

(D) General Studies
There is a masterly guide to all aspects of Aristotle's life and thought in:
(29) I. DÜRING: *Aristoteles* (Heidelberg, 1966)
A much abbreviated version in:
(30) I. DÜRING: *Aristoteles* (Stuttgart, 1968)
Of numerous shorter studies in English which give a general account of Aristotle's thought, the following may be mentioned:
(31) W.D. ROSS: *Aristotle* (London, 1923)
(32) D.J. ALLAN: *The Philosophy of Aristotle* (Oxford, 1952)
(33) G.E.R. LLOYD: *Aristotle* (Cambridge, 1968)
(34) J.L. ACKRILL: *Aristotle the Philosopher* (London, 1981)
(35) J. BARNES: *Aristotle* (London 1982)
(36) J. LEAR: *Aristotle: the Desire to Understand* (Cambridge, 1988)
It is still worth consulting:
(37) G. GROTE: *Aristotle* (London, 1883)
(38) F. BRENTANO: *Über Aristoteles – nachgelassene Aufsätze* (Hamburg, 1986)

(E) Collections
The proceedings of the triennial Symposia Aristotelica, which were inaugurated in 1957, provide excellent examples of modern Aristotelian scholarship. See:
(39) I. DÜRING and G.E.L. OWEN (edd.): *Aristotle and Plato in the mid-Fourth Century* (Göteborg, 1960)
(40) S. MANSION (ed.): *Aristote et les problèmes de méthode* (Louvain, 1961)
(41) G.E.L. OWEN (ed.): *Aristote on Dialectic* (Oxford, 1968)
(42) I. DÜRING (ed.): *Naturforschung bei Aristoteles und Theophrast* (Heidelberg, 1969)
(43) P. MORAUX (ed.): *Untersuchungen zur Eudemischen Ethik* (Berlin, 1970)
(44) P. AUBENQUE (ed.): *Etudes sur la Métaphysique d'Aristote* (Paris, 1979)
(45) G.E.R. LLOYD and G.E.L. OWEN (edd.): *Aristotle on Mind and the Senses* (Cambridge, 1978)
(46) E. BERTI (ed.): *Aristotle on Science* (Padua, 1981)
(47) P. MORAUX and J. WIESNER (edd.): *Zweifelhaftes im Corpus Aristotelicum* (Berlin, 1983)

(48) A. GRAESER (ed.): *Mathematics and Metaphysics in Aristotle* (Bern/ Stuttgart, 1987)

(49) G. PATZIG (ed.): *Aristoteles' 'Politik'* (Göttingen, 1990)

(50) D.J. FURLEY and A. NEHAMAS (edd.): *Philosophical Aspects of Aristotle's Rhetoric* (Princeton, 1994)

There are innumerable other collections of occasional papers; among them:

(51) A. MANSION: *Autour d'Aristote* (Louvain, 1955)

(52) D.O. MEARA (ed.): *Studies in Aristotle* (Washington, 1981)

(53) *Proceedings of the World Congress on Aristotle*, Thessaloniki, 1978 (Athens, 1981–84)

(54) J. IRMSCHER and R. MÜLLER (edd.): *Aristoteles als Wissenschaftstheoretiker* (Berlin, 1983)

(55) F.J. PELLETIER and J.A. KING-FARLOW (edd.): *New Essays on Aristotle, CJP* suppt. 10 (Edmonton, 1984)

(56) A. GOTTHELF (ed.): *Aristotle on Nature and Living Things* (Bristol, 1985)

(57) J. WIESNER (ed.): *Aristoteles – Werke and Wirkung* (Berlin, 1985 and 1987)

(58) M. MATTHEN (ed.): *Aristotle Today* (Edmonton, 1987)

(59) D.T. DEVEREUX and P. PELLEGRIN (edd.): *Biologie, logique et métaphysique chez Aristote* (Paris, 1990)

(60) M.A. SINACEUR (ed.): *Penser avec Aristote* (Toulouse, 1991)

There are many anthologies; among them:

(61) J.M.E. MORAVCSIK (ed.): *Aristotle* (Garden City, 1967)

(62) J. BARNES, M. SCHOFIELD, and R. SORABJI (edd.): *Articles on Aristotle* (London, 1975–79)

(63) A. PREUS and J.P. ANTON (edd.): *Aristotle's Ontology: Essays in Ancient Greek Philosophy* 5 (Albany, 1992)

and a group in the series *Wege der Forschung:*

(64) P. MORAUX (ed.): *Aristoteles in der neueren Forschung* (Darmstadt, 1968)

(65) F.-P. HAGER (ed.): *Metaphysik und Theologie des Aristoteles* (Darmstadt, 1968)

(66) F.-P. HAGER (ed.): *Logik und Erkenntnislehre des Aristoteles* (Darmstadt, 1972)

(67) F.-P. HAGER (ed.): *Ethik und Politik des Aristoteles* (Darmstadt, 1972)

(68) G.A. SEECK (ed.): *Die Naturphilosophie des Aristoteles* (Darmstadt, 1975)

Collections and anthologies given to specific aspects of Aristotle's thought will be listed in the appropriate chapters.

There will also be occasion to refer to a number of collections which are not devoted exclusively to Aristotle:

(69) H. FLASHAR and K. GAISER (edd.): *Synusia: Festgabe für W. Schadewaldt* (Pfullingen, 1965)

(70) R. BAMBROUGH (ed.): *New Essays on Plato and Aristotle* (London, 1965)
(71) C.C. GILLISPIE (ed.): *Dictionary of Scientific Biography* (New York, 1970)
(72) J.P. ANTON and G. KUSTAS (edd.): *Essays in Ancient Greek Philosophy* I (Albany, 1971)
(73) S. STERN, A. HOURANI, and V. BROWN (edd.): *Islamic Philosophy and the Classical Tradition* (Oxford, 1972)
(74) E.N. LEE, A.P.D. MOURELATOS, and R. RORTY (edd.): *Exegesis and Argument*, Phron suppt. I (Assen, 1973)
(75) M. SCHOFIELD and M.C. NUSSBAUM (edd.): *Language and Logos* (Cambridge, 1982)
(76) J. BOGEN and J. McQUIRE (edd.): *How Things Are* (Dordrecht, 1985)
(77) *Language and Reality in Greek Philosophy* (Athens, 1985)
(78) W.W. FORTENBAUGH (ed.): *Theophrastus of Eresus*, Rutgers University Studies in Classical Humanities 2 (New Brunswick, 1985)
(79) P. CARTLEDGE and F.D. HARVEY (edd.): *Crux* (Exeter, 1985)
(80) G. CAMBIANO (ed.): *Storiografia e dossografia nella filosofia antica* (Turin, 1986)
(81) S. KNUUTTILA and J. HINTIKKA (edd.): *The Logic of Being* (Dordrecht, 1986)
(82) W.W. FORTENBAUGH and R.W. SHARPLES (edd.): *Theophrastean Studies*, Rutgers University Studies in Classical Humanities 3 (New Brunswick, 1988)
Finally, some sets of collected papers:
(83) M. FREDE: *Essays on Ancient Philosophy* (Oxford, 1987)
(84) D.J. FURLEY: *Cosmic Problems* (Cambridge, 1989)
(85) K.J.J. HINTIKKA: *Time and Necessity* (Oxford, 1963)
(86) G.E.R. LLOYD: *Methods and Problems in Greek Science* (Cambridge, 1991)
(87) J. MANSFELD: *Studies in the Historiography of Greek Philosophy* (Assen, 1990)
(88) S. MANSION: *Etudes aristotéliciennes* (Louvain, 1984)
(89) K. OEHLER: *Antike Philosophie und byzantinisches Mittelalter* (Munich, 1969)
(90) G.E.L. OWEN: *Logic, Science, and Dialectic* (London, 1986)
(91) J. OWENS: *Collected Papers* (Albany, 1981)
(92) F. SOLMSEN: *Kleine Schriften* (Hildesheim, 1968)

II JUVENILIA

(A) Philosophical Development

A major part of the scholarly work done on Aristotle during the last seventy years has taken its start from the hypotheses on the development of Aristotle's thought advanced by:
(1) W.W. JAEGER: *Aristotle*, trans. R.Robinson (Oxford, 1948 [first published in German, 1923])

Two of the most ambitious contributions to this line of scholarship are:

(2) F. SOLMSEN: *Die Entwicklung der aristotelischen Logik und Rhetorik* (Berlin, 1929)

and:

(3) F.J. NUYENS: *L'évolution de la psychologie d'Aristote* (Louvain, 1948 [originally published in Flemish, 1939])

Solmsen's views are expounded in:

(4) J.L. STOCKS: 'The composition of Aristotle's logical works', *CQ* 27, 1933, 114–24 = HAGER I.66

and Nuyens' in the introduction to ROSS VI.3.

There are two classic papers on the subject:

(5) W.D. ROSS: 'The development of Aristotle's thought', *PBA* 43, 1957, 63-78 = DÜRING and OWEN I.39 = BARNES, SCHOFIELD, SORABJI I.62

(6) G.E.L. OWEN: 'The Platonism of Aristotle', *PBA* 50, 1965, 125–50 = BARNES, SCHOFIELD, SORABJI I.62 = OWEN I.90

See also:

(7) A. MANSION: 'La genèse de l'oeuvre d'Aristote d'après les travaux récents', in MORAUX I.64

(8) A.H. CHROUST: 'The first thirty years of modern Aristotelian scholarship', *Classica et Mediaevalia* 24, 1963/4, 27–57 = MORAUX I.64

A recent extended essay in the developmental tradition is:

(9) B. DUMOULIN: *Analyse génétique de la Métaphysique d'Aristote* (Paris, 1986)

Developmental studies of particular areas of Aristotle's thought are listed in the appropriate chapters.

(B) Aristotle on Plato

JAEGER II.1 argued that Aristotle began as a Platonist, broke with is master's principal doctrines, and gradually moved further and further away from Platonism. A crucial issue is that of Aristotle's attitude to lato's Theory of Forms. See, besides JAEGER II.1 and OWEN II.6:

(10) C.J. DE VOGEL: 'The legend of the Platonizing Aristotle', in DÜRING and OWEN I.39

(11) C.J. DE VOGEL: 'Did Aristotle ever accept Plato's theory of transcendent ideas?', *AGP* 47, 1965, 261–98

(12) I. DÜRING: 'Did Aristotle ever accept Plato's theory of transcendent Ideas?', *AGP* 48, 1966, 312–26

(13) C.H. CHEN: 'Aristotle's analysis of change and Plato's theory of transcendent Ideas', *Phron* 20, 1975, 129–45

(14) J. ANNAS: 'Forms and first principles,' *Phron* 19, 1974, 257–83

(15) J. ANNAS: 'Aristotle on substance, accident and Plato's Forms', *Phron* 22, 1977, 146–60

(16) G. FINE: 'Forms as causes: Plato and Aristotle', in GRAESER I.48

A central text for Aristotle's criticism of the theory is his *On Ideas*, fragments of which are edited by:

(17) W. LESZL: *Il "de Ideis" di Aristotele e la teoria platonica delle Idee* (Padua, 1975)
See especially:
(18) G. FINE: *On Ideas* (Oxford, 1993)
and also:
(19) S. MANSION: 'La critique de la théorie des Idées dans le *Peri Ideôn* d'Aristote', *RPL* 47, 1949, 169–202 = MANSION I.88
(20) P. WILPERT: *Zwei aristotelische Frühschriften über die Ideenlehre* (Regensburg, 1949)
(21) J.L. ACKRILL: review of WILPERT II.20, *M* 61, 1952, 102–13
(22) G.E.L. OWEN: 'A proof in the *Peri Ideôn*', *JHS* 77, 1957, 103–111 = OWEN I.90
(23) R. BARFORD: 'A proof from the *Peri Ideôn* | revisited', *Phron* 21, 1976, 198–218
(24) C.J. ROWE: 'The proof from relatives in the *Peri Ideôn:* further reconsideration', *Phron* 24, 1979, 270–81
(25) D.H. FRANK: *The Argument "From the Sciences" in Aristotle's* Peri Ideôn (New York, 1984)
On Aristotle's attitude to the "Third Man" argument see:
(26) G.E.L. OWEN: 'Dialectic and eristic in the treatment of the Forms', in OWEN I.41 = OWEN I.90
(27) J. KUNG: 'Aristotle on thises, suches and the Third Man argument', *Phron* 26, 1981, 207–47
(28) G. FINE: 'Owen, Aristotle and the Third Man', *Phron* 27, 1982, 13–33
(29) F.A. LEWIS: 'On Plato's Third Man argument and the "Platonism" of Aristotle', in BOGEN and McQUIRE I.76
Later sections contain items discussing Aristotle's criticism of particular aspects of Platonic philosophy.

(C) Early Philosophy

Aristotle's *juvenilia* survive only in fragments, the most important of which are translated in the Oxford Translation, I.1. There is an annotated edition:

(30) R. LAURENTI: *Aristotele: i frammenti dei dialoghi* (Naples, 1987)
For general accounts see:
(31) J. BERNAYS: *Die Dialoge des Aristoteles* (Berlin, 1863)
(32) E. BERTI: *La filosofia del primo Aristotele* (Padua, 1962)
In addition to *On Ideas*, the most important of these youthful works are the *Protrepticus* and the *de Philosophia*. The *Protrepticus* was discovered – or invented – by:
(33) I. BYWATER: 'On a lost dialogue of Aristotle', *JPh* 2, 1869, 55–69 = MORAUX I.64
For reconstructions, see:
(34) I. DÜRING: *Aristotle's* Protrepticus (Göteborg, 1961)
(35) A.H. CHROUST: *Aristotle's* Protrepticus (Notre Dame, 1964)
There is scepticism in:

(36) W.G. RABINOWITZ: *Aristotle's* Protrepticus (Berkeley, 1957)

(37) H. FLASHAR: 'Platon und Aristoteles im *Protreptikos* des Iamblichus', *AGP* 47, 1965, 53–79 = MORAUX I.64

See also:

(38) P. VON DER MÜHLL: 'Isocrates und der *Protreptikos* des Aristoteles', *Phg* 94, 1941, 259–65

(39) B. EINARSON: 'Aristotle's *Protrepticus* and the structure of the *Epinomis*', *TAPA* 67, 1963, 261–72

(40) D.J. ALLAN: 'Critical and explanatory notes on some passages assigned to Aristotle's *Protrepticus*', *Phron* 21, 1976, 219–40

and Chh. VII-X of vol.2 of CHROUST I.8.

The *de Philosophia* has been edited by:

(41) M. UNTERSTEINER: *Aristotele – della filosofia* (Padua, 1962)

Among studies of its contents see:

(42) H.D. SAFFREY: *Le* Peri philosophias *d'Aristote et la théorie platonicienne des idées nombres* (Leiden, 1955)

(43) H.F. CHERNISS: review of SAFFREY II.42, *Gnomon* 31, 1959, 36–51

(44) P. WILPERT: 'Die Stellung der Schrift "Über die Philosophie" in der Gedankenentwicklung des Aristoteles', *JHS* 77, 1957, 155–62 = MORAUX I.64

(45) J. PEPIN: 'L'interprétation du *de Philosophia* d'Aristote d'après quelques travaux recents', *REG* 77, 1964, 445–58

(46) W. HAASE: 'Ein vermeintliches Aristoteles-Fragment bei Johannes Philoponos', in FLASHAR and GAISER I.69

See also Chh. XII–XVI of vol.2 of CHROUST I.8.

Studies of other philosophically interesting works include:

(47) O. GIGON: 'Prolegomena to an edition of the *Eudemus*', in DÜRING and OWEN I.39

(48) P. MORAUX: *A la recherche de l'Aristote perdu: le dialogue 'Sur la justice'* (Louvain, 1957)

(49) A.H. CHROUST: 'Aristotle's *Politikos* – a lost dialogue', *RhM* 108, 1965, 346–53

(50) P.-M. SCHUHL: *Aristote – cinq oeuvres perdus* (Paris, 1968)

See also:

(51) H.F. CHERNISS: *The Riddle of the Early Academy* (Berkeley, 1945)

and the essays in DÜRING and OWEN I.39.

III LOGIC

(A) General

The standard edition of Aristotle's logical works, known collectively as the *Organon*, is:

(1) T. WAITZ: *Aristotelis Organon* (Leipzig, 1844–46)

The *Analytics* have been edited by:

(2) W.D. ROSS: *Aristotle's Prior and Posterior Analytics* (Oxford, 1955)

And note the ancient commentary:

(3) J. BARNES, S. BOBZIEN, K. FLANNERY, and K. IERODIAKONOU: *Alexander of Aphrodisias: On Aristotle, Prior Analytics 1.1–7* (London, 1991)
The Clarendon Aristotle includes:
(4) J.L. ACKRILL: *Aristotle's Categories and de Interpretatione* (Oxford, 1963)
(5) J. BARNES: *Aristotle's Posterior Analytics* (Oxford, 1994²)
(6) R. SMITH: *Aristotle's Topics, Books I and VIII* (Oxford, 1994)
There is an invaluable introduction to the Budé edition of *Top:*
(7) J. BRUNSCHWIG: *Aristote – Topiques, livres I–IV* (Paris, 1967)
See also:
(8) K. OEHLER: *Aristoteles: Kategorien* (Berlin, 1983)
(9) H. WEIDEMANN: *Aristoteles: de Interpretatione* (Berlin, 1994)
(10) R. SMITH: *Aristotle's Prior Analytics* (Indianapolis, 1989)
(11) W. DETEL: *Aristoteles: Analytica Posteriora* (Berlin, 1993)
There are general accounts of Aristotle's logic in:
(12) E. KAPP: *Greek Foundations of Traditional Logic* (New York, 1942)
(13) J.M. BOCHENSKI: *Ancient Formal Logic* (Amsterdam, 1951)
(14) W.C. and M. KNEALE: *The Development of Logic* (Oxford, 1962)
Some papers are collected in:
(15) A. MENNE and N. OFFENBERGER (edd.): *Zur modernen Deutung der aristotelischen Logik* (Hildesheim, 1982–90)
(16) J. CORCORAN (ed.): *Ancient Logic and its Modern Interpretations* (Dordrecht, 1974)
For the origins and development of the logic see SOLMSEN, II.2; TURNBULL, III.63; and items III.133–8. On the origins of the *Organon:*
(17) F. SOLMSEN: 'Boethius and the history of the *Organon*,' *AJP* 65, 1944, 69–74 = SOLMSEN I.92
(18) J. BRUNSCHWIG: 'Sur quelques malentendus concernant la logique d'Aristote', in SINACEUR I.60

(B) Language and Meaning
Reflexions on language can be found in various parts of Aristotle's works, notably in *Poet* and *Rhet* Γ. See, in general, the monumental work of:

(19) H. STEINTHAL: *Geschichte der Sprachwissenschaft bei den Griechen und Römern* (Berlin, 1890)
and also:
(20) R. BRANDT: *Die aristotelische Urteilslehre* (Marburg, 1965)
(21) R.H. ROBINS: *A Short History of Linguistics* (London, 1967), ch. 2
(22) M. LARKIN: *Language in the Philosophy of Aristotle* (The Hague, 1972)
(23) M. SORETH: 'Zum infiniten Prädikat im 10. Kapitel der aristotelischen Hermeneutik', in STERN, HOURANI, and BROWN I.73
(24) H. WEIDEMANN: 'Grundzüge der aristotelischen Sprachtheorie', in P. Schmitter (ed.), *Geschichte der Sprachtheorie*, vol. 2 (Tübingen, 1991)
For Aristotle's 'semantic theory' – which later scholars discovered in the first lines of *Int* – see

(25) G. NUCHELMANS: *Theories of the Proposition* (Amsterdam/London, 1973), ch. 3

(26) N. KRETZMANN: 'Aristotle on spoken sound significant by convention', in CORCORAN III.16

(27) J. PEPIN: '*Sumbola, sêmeia, homoiômata:* à propos de *de Interpretatione* 1, 16a3–8 et *Politique* VIII 5, 1340a6–39', in WIESNER I.57

(28) R. POLANSKI and M. KUCZIEWSKI: 'Speech and thought, symbol and likeness: Aristotle's *de Interpretatione* 16a3–9', *Apeiron* 23, 1990, 51–63

(29) J. BARNES: 'Meaning, saying and thinking', in K. DÖRING and T. EBERT (edd.), *Dialektiker und Stoiker* (Stuttgart, 1993)

On the history of the Aristotelian 'theory' see the texts assembled in:

(30) H. ARENS: *Aristotle's Theory of Language* (Amsterdam, 1984)

and the articles by:

(31) L.M. DE RIJK: 'Ancient and mediaeval semantics and metaphysics', *Vivarium* 16, 1978, 81–107; 18, 1980, 1–62; 19, 1981, 81–125

(32) L.M. DE RIJK: ' "Categorisation" as a key notion in ancient and mediaeval semantics', *Vivarium* 26, 1988, 1–23

Scholars have found semantic hints elsewhere in Aristotle's writings. See:

(33) R. BOLTON: 'Essentialism and semantic theory in Aristotle', *PR* 85, 1976, 514–45

(34) T.H. IRWIN: 'Aristotle's concept of signification', in SCHOFIELD and NUSSBAUM I.75

(35) R. BOLTON: 'Aristotle on the significance of names', in I.77

(36) P. TSELEMANIS: 'Theory of meaning and signification in Aristotle', in I.77

(37) D. CHARLES: 'Aristotle on meaning, natural kinds, and natural history', in DEVEREUX and PELLEGRIN I.59

(C) Homonymy

The notion of homonymy – or, roughly, multiplicity of sense – pervades Aristotle's thought. It is first developed in *Cat*,[1] on which see:

(38) J.P. ANTON: 'The Aristotelian doctrine of *homonyma* in the *Categories* and its Platonic antecedents', *JHP* 6, 1968, 315–26

(39) J.P. ANTON: 'Ancient interpretations of Aristotle's doctrine of *homonyma*', *JHP* 7, 1969, 1–18

(40) J.P. ANTON: 'The meaning of *logos tês ousias* in Aristotle's *Categories* 1a', *Monist* 52, 1968, 252–67

(41) J. BARNES: 'Homonymy in Aristotle and Speusippus' *CQ* 21, 1971, 65–80

(42) L. TARÁN: 'Speusippus and Aristotle on homonymy and synonymy', *H* 106, 1978, 73–99

The later ramifications of the notion are discussed by:

1. On the categories themselves see below, VIII (F).

(43) K.J.J. HINTIKKA: 'Aristotle and the ambiguity of ambiguity', *Inquiry* 2, 1959, 137–51 = HINTIKKA I. 85
and especially by:
(44) G.E.L. OWEN: 'Logic and metaphysics in some earlier works of Aristotle', in DÜRING and OWEN I.39 = HAGER I.65 = BARNES, SCHOFIELD, SORABJI I.62 = OWEN I.90
who anatomises the concept of 'focal meaning'. For further discussion see:
(45) H. WAGNER: 'Über das aristotelische *pollachôs legetai to on*', *Kant-studien* 53, 1961–2, 75–91
(46) W. LESZL: *Logic and Metaphysics in Aristotle* (Padua, 1970)
(47) E. BERTI: 'Multiplicité et unité du Bien selon *EE* I.8', in MORAUX I.43
(48) J. BARNES: review of MORAUX I.43, *AGP* 55, 1973, 335–36
(49) D.W. HAMLYN: 'Focal meaning', *PAS* 78, 1977/8, 1–18
(50) M.T. FEREJOHN: 'Aristotle on focal meaning and the unity of science', *Phron* 25, 1980, 117–28
(51) T. IRWIN: 'Homonymy in Aristotle', *RM* 34, 1981, 523–44
On the related notion of analogy see:
(52) M. HESSE: 'Aristotle's logic of analogy', *PQ* 15, 1965, 328–40
(53) E. DE STRYKER: 'Prédicats univoques et prédicats analogiques dans le *Protreptique* d'Aristote', *RPL* 66, 1968, 597–618
(54) E. BERTI: 'Logical and ontological priority among the genera of substance in Aristotle', in J. MANSFELD and L. M. DE RIJK (edd.), *Kephalaion* (Assen, 1975)
(55) C. RUTTEN: 'L'analogie chez Aristote', *RPA* 1, 1983, 31–48
On the homonymy of being see VII (E).

(D) Predication

In *Int*, Aristotle follows Plato and supposes that simple sentences are constructed from two heterogeneous items, a name and a verb. Elsewhere he prefers a subject/predicate analysis. See:

(56) P.T. GEACH: 'History of the corruptions of logic', in his *Logic Matters* (Oxford, 1972)
On the theory of predication see:
(57) J.M.E. MORAVCSIK: 'Aristotle on predication', *PR* 76, 1967, 80–97
(58) T. EBERT: 'Zur Formulierung prädikativer Aussagen in den logischen Schriften des Aristoteles', *Phron* 22, 1977, 123–45
(59) M.D. ROHR: 'Aristotle on the transitivity of *being said of*', *JHP* 16, 1978, 379–85
(60) H. WEIDEMANN: 'In defence of Aristotle's theory of predication', *Phron* 25, 1980, 76–87
(61) R. VAN BRENNEKOM: 'Aristotle and the copula', *JHP* 24, 1982, 1–18
For its relation to Plato:
(62) P. MERLAN: 'Zur Erklärung der dem Aristoteles zugeschriebenen Kategorienschrift', *Phg* 89, 1934, 35–53
(63) R.G. TURNBULL: 'Aristotle's debt to the "Natural Philosophy" of the *Phaedo*', *PQ* 8, 1958, 131–43

312   Bibliography

(64) A. Code: 'On the origin of Aristotle's theory of predication', in Bogen and McQuire I.76

(E) The Predicables

In *Top*, Aristotle develops a classification of types of predication known as the theory of predicables: every predicate is said to mean either a property or the definition or the genus or an accident of the subject:

(65) D. Hadgopoulos: 'The definition of the predicables in Aristotle', *Phron* 21, 1976, 266–76

(66) T. Ebert: 'Gattungen der Prädikate und Gattungen des Seienden bei Aristoteles', *AGP* 67, 1985, 113–38

Definitions and genera are dealt with elsewhere.[2] On properties and accidents see:

(67) G. Verbeke: 'La notion de propriété dans les *Topiques*', in Owen I.41

(68) J. Barnes: 'Property in Aristotle's *Topics*', *AGP* 52, 1970, 136–55

which has stimulated essays by:

(69) M.V. Wedin: 'A remark on *per se* accidents and properties', *AGP* 55, 1973, 30–35

(70) W. Graham: 'Counterpredicability and *per se* accidents', *AGP* 57, 1975, 182–87

(71) H. Granger: 'The *differentia* and the *per se* accident in Aristotle', *AGP* 63, 1981, 118–29

(72) H. Granger: 'Aristotle on *genus* and *differentiae*', *JHP* 22, 1984, 1–23

See also:

(73) T. Ebert: 'Aristotelischer und traditioneller Akzidenzbegriff', in G. Patzig, E. Scheibe, W. Wieland (edd.), *XI deutscher Kongress für Philosophie* (Hamburg, 1977)

(74) J. Barnes, J. Brunschwig, and M. Frede: 'Le propre de la prudence', in R. Brague and J.-F. Courtine (edd.), *Herméneutique et ontologie: hommage à Pierre Aubenque* (Paris, 1991)

(F) Future Contingents

Chapter 9 of *Int* is devoted to a celebrated argument about fatalism. The Chapter has caused a scholarly buzz. See Łukasiewicz's papers of 1920, 1922 and 1930 in:

(75) S. McCall (ed.): *Polish Logic 1920–39* (Oxford, 1967)

and then:

(76) A.N. Prior: 'Three-valued logic and future contingents', *PQ* 3, 1953, 317–26

(77) R.J. Butler: 'Aristotle's sea-fight and three-valued logic', *PR* 64, 1955, 264–74

(78) G.E.M. Anscombe: 'Aristotle and the sea-battle', *M* 65, 1956, 1–15 = Moravcsik I.61 = Hager I.66

(79) K.J.J. Hintikka: 'The once and future sea-fight', *PR* 73, 1964, 461–92 = Hintikka I.85 = Hager I.66

2. See III (N) – and, for accidents, note also IV (F).

(80) D. Frede: *Aristoteles und die 'Seeschlacht'* (Göttingen, 1970)

(81) D. Frede: *'omne quod est quando est necesse est esse'*, AGP 54, 1972, 153–67

(82) G. Fine: 'Truth and necessity in *de Interpretatione* 9', HPQ 1, 1984, 23–48

(83) D. Frede: 'The sea-battle reconsidered: a defence of the traditional interpretation', OSAP 3, 1985, 31–87

(84) S. Broadie: 'Necessity and deliberation: an argument from *de Interpretatione* 9', CJP 17, 1987, 289–306

(85) L. Judson: 'La bataille navale d'aujourd'hui: *de Interpretatione* 9', RPA 6, 1988, 5–38

(86) A. Bäck: 'Sailing through the sea-battle', AP 12, 1992, 133–51

A useful survey:

(87) V. Celluprica: *Il capitolo 9 del 'De Interpretatione' di Aristotele* (n.p., 1977)

Information about the mediaeval discussions of the problem may be found in:

(8) L. Baudry: *La querelle des futurs contingents* (Paris, 1950)

On the related issue of the Master Argument, see:

(89) N. Rescher: 'A version of the "Master Argument" of Diodorus', JP 63, 1966, 438–45

(90) K.J.J. Hintikka: 'Aristotle and the "Master Argument" of Diodorus', in Hintikka I.85

See also:

(91) R.W. Sharples: 'Aristotelian and Stoic conceptions of necessity in the *de Fato* of Alexander of Aphrodisias', Phron 20, 1975, 247–74

(92) C.A. Kirwan: 'Aristotle on the necessity of the present', OSAP 4, 1986, 167–88

Note in addition the items in IV (F) on determinism and in VIII (I) on free will.

(G) Modality

Aristotle initiated the logical study of the anankastic modalities. The pioneering work on his modal logic is:

(93) A. Becker: *Die aristotelische Theorie der Möglichkeitsschlüsse* (Berlin, 1933)

More recently see:

(94) G. Seel: *Die aristotelische Modaltheorie* (Berlin, 1982)

(95) S. Waterlow: *Passage and Possibility* (Oxford, 1982)

(96) J. van Rijen: *Aspects of Aristotle's Logic of Modalities* (Dordrecht, 1989)

On the treatment of modality in *Int*, see:

(97) J.M. Bochenski: 'Notes historiques sur les propositions modales', Revue des sciences philosophiques et théologiques 31, 1937, 673–92

(98) K.J.J. Hintikka: 'Aristotle's different possibilities', Inquiry 3, 1960, 17–28 = Hintikka I.85 = Moravcsik I.61

(99) K.J.J. Hintikka: 'On the interpretation of *de Interpretatione* 12–3', Acta Philosophica Fennica 14, 1962, 5–22 = Hintikka I.85

(100) R. BLUCK: 'On the interpretation of Aristotle, *de Interpretatione* 12–13', *CQ* 2, 1963, 214–23

(101) E.P. BRANDON: 'Hintikka on *akolouthein*', *Phron* 23, 1978, 173–78
In some Aristotelian texts, modality and time are linked; and some have ascribed to Aristotle a version of the 'principle of plenitude' ('everything possible is at some time actual'). See:

(102) K.J.J. HINTIKKA: 'Aristotle on the realization of possibilities in time', in HINTIKKA I.85 = BARNES, SCHOFIELD, SORABJI I.62

(103) K.J.J. HINTIKKA: *Aristotle on Modality and Determinism*, Acta Philosophica Fennica 29 (Helsinki, 1977)
Hintikka's ideas are investigated by:

(104) C.J.F. WILLIAMS: 'Aristotle and corruptibility', *Religious Studies* 1, 1965, 95–107, 203–15

(105) J. BARNES: review of HINTIKKA I.85, *JHS* 97, 1977, 183–86

(106) M.J. WHITE: 'Aristotle and temporally relative modalities', *An* 39, 1979, 88–93

(107) L. JUDSON: 'Eternity and necessity in *de caelo* I. 12', *OSAP* 1, 1983, 217–55

(108) J. VAN RIJEN: 'The principle of plenitude, the *de omni/per se* distinction, and the development of modal thinking', *AGP* 66, 1984, 61–88

(109) M. MIGNUCCI: 'Aristotle's *de caelo* I.13 and his notion of possibility', in DEVEREUX and PELLEGRIN I.59
Note also:

(110) C. FREELAND: 'Aristotle on possibilities and capabilities', *AP* 6, 1986, 69–90

(111) W. CHARLTON: 'Aristotelian powers', *Phron* 32, 1987, 277–89
and SORABJI IV.72, part II.
On the quasi-modal notion of what holds 'for the most part' see:

(112) J. BARNES: ' "Sheep have four legs" ', in I.53

(113) M. MIGNUCCI: '*Hôs epi to polu* et nécessaire dans la conception aristotélicienne de la science', in BERTI I.46

(114) G. STRIKER: 'Notwendigkeit mit Lücke: Aristoteles über die Kontingenz der Naturvorgänge', *Neue Hefte für Philosophie* 24/5, 1985, 146–64

(115) L. JUDSON: 'Chance and "always or for the most part" in Aristotle', in JUDSON IV.15

(116) D. FREDE: 'Necessity, chance, and "what happens for the most part" in Aristotle's *Poetics*', in RORTY X.45
On 'hypothetical' necessity see V (E); on modal syllogistic see III (I).

(H) Syllogistic

Aristotle's syllogistic is expounded and discussed in *An. Pr.* There is an informal exposé of the theory in:

(117) E. KAPP: 'Syllogistic', in BARNES, SCHOFIELD, SORABJI I.62 [first published in German in 1931]'
The classic modern interpretation is:

Bibliography 315

(118) J. ŁUKASIEWICZ: *Aristotle's Syllogistic* (Oxford, 1957²)
reviewed by:
(119) J.L. AUSTIN: review of ŁUKASIEWICZ III.118, M 61, 1952, 395–404
Łukasiewicz' account was developed and modified by:
(120) G. PATZIG: *Aristotle's Theory of the Syllogism* (Dordrecht, 1969)
[first published in German in 1959]
reviewed by:
(121) J.L. ACKRILL: review of PATZIG III.120, M 71, 1962, 107–17
ŁUKASIEWICZ and PATZIG remain indispensable, but better interpretations
of the syllogistic have been advanced. See:
(122) J.C. SHEPHERDSON: 'On the interpretation of Aristotelian syllogistic', *Journal of Symbolic Logic* 21, 1956, 137–47
(123) K. EBBINGHAUS: *Ein Formales Modell der Syllogistik des Aristoteles* (Göttingen, 1964)
(124) W. WIELAND: 'Zur Deutung der aristotelischen Logik', *Philosophische Rundschau* 14, 1966, 1–27
(125) T. SMILEY: 'What is a syllogism?', *Journal of Philosophical Logic* 2,
1973, 136–54
(126) J. CORCORAN: 'A mathematical model of Aristotle's syllogistic',
AGP 55, 1973, 191–219
(127) J. CORCORAN: 'Aristotelian syllogisms: valid arguments or true univer-
salised conditionals?', M 83, 1974, 278–81 = MENNE and OFFENBERGER III.15
(128) J. CORCORAN: 'Aristotle's natural deduction system', in CORCORAN
III.16
(129) P. THOM: *The Syllogism* (Munich, 1981)
The question of the origin of Aristotle's syllogistic has aroused contro-
very. In addition to SOLMSEN, II.2, and the introduction to ROSS, III.2, see:
(130) P. SHOREY: 'The origins of the syllogism', *CP* 19, 1924, 1–19
(131) W.D. ROSS: 'The discovery of the syllogism', *PR* 48, 1939, 251–72
(132) F. SOLMSEN: 'The discovery of the syllogism', *PR* 50, 1941, 410–21
(133) F. SOLMSEN: 'Aristotle's syllogism and its Platonic background', *PR*
60, 1951, 563–71 = HAGER, I.66
(134) J. LOHMANN: 'Vom ursprunglichen Sinn der aristotelischen Syllogistik', *Lexis* 2, 1951, 205–36 = HAGER I.66
(135) A. MANSION: 'L'origine du syllogisme et la théorie de la science
chez Aristote', in MANSION I.40 = HAGER I.66
The 'square of opposition' underlies the syllogistic. See:
(136) H.L.A. HART: 'A logicians's fairy tale', *PR* 60, 1951, 198–212
(137) M. THOMPSON: 'On Aristotle's square of opposition', *PR* 62, 1953,
251–62 = MORAVCSIK I.61
And on a closely related matter:
(138) M.V. WEDIN: 'Aristotle on the existential import of singular sentences', *Phron* 23, 1978, 179–96
(139) W. JACOBS: 'Aristotle and non-referring subjects', *Phron* 24, 1979,
282–300

(140) M.V. WEDIN: 'Negation and quantification in Aristotle', *JHPL* 11, 1990, 131–50
For other aspects of Aristotle's 'metalogical' ideas, see:
(141) J. BRUNSCHWIG: 'La proposition particulière et les preuves de non-concluance chez Aristote', *Cahiers pour l'analyse* 10, 1969, 3–26 = MENNE and OFFENBERGER III.15
(142) J. LEAR: 'Aristotle's compactness proof', *JP* 76, 1979, 198–215
(143) J. LEAR: *Aristotle and Logical Theory* (Cambridge, 1980)
(144) T. EBERT: 'Warum fehlt die 4. Figur bei Aristoteles?', *AGP* 62, 1980, 13–31 = MENNE and OFFENBERGER III.15
(145) M. SCANLAN: 'On finding compactness in Aristotle', *JHPL* 4, 1982, 1–8
(146) R. SMITH: 'Aristotle as a proof theorist', *Philosophia Naturalis* 21, 1984, 590–97
(147) R. SMITH: 'Immediate propositions and Aristotle's proof theory', *AP* 6, 1986, 47–68
(148) M. MIGNUCCI: 'Expository proofs in Aristotle's syllogistic', *OSAP* suppt 1991, 9–28
See also:
(149) M. FREDE: 'Stoic vs. Aristotelian syllogistic', *AGP* 56, 1974, 1–32 = FREDE I.83

(I) Modal Syllogistic
Aristotle's modal syllogistic disappointed his successors and perplexes modern interpreters. For Theophrastus' reaction see:

(150) J.M. BOCHENSKI: *La logique de Théophraste* (Fribourg, 1947)
The fundamental modern work is BECKER III.93. Among the many items devoted to the topic since Becker, it is enough to mention:
(151) S. McCALL: *Aristotle's Modal Syllogisms* (Amsterdam, 1963)
(152) W. WIELAND: 'Die aristotelische Theorie der Notwendig-keitsschlüsse,' *Phron* 11, 1966, 35–60 = HAGER I.66
(153) W. WIELAND: 'Die aristotelische Theorie der Möglichkeitsschlüsse', *Phron* 17, 1972, 124–52 = MENNE and OFFENBERGER III.15
(154) W. WIELAND: 'Die aristotelische Theorie der Syllogismen mit modal gemischten Prämissen', *Phron* 20, 1975, 77–92
(155) W. WIELAND: 'Die aristotelische Theorie der Konversion von Modalaussagen', *Phron* 25, 1980, 109–16 = MENNE and OFFENBERGER III.15
(156) K.J.J. HINTIKKA: 'On Aristotle's modal syllogistic', in HINTIKKA I.85
(157) R. PATTERSON: 'The case of the two Barbaras', *OSAP* 7, 1989, 1–40
(158) K.J. SCHMIDT: 'Ein modal prädikatenlogische Interpretation der modalen Syllogistik des Aristoteles', *Phron* 34, 1989, 80–106
(159) D. JOHNSTON: 'Aristotle's apodeictic syllogism', *Dialogue* 29, 1990, 111–21
(160) R. PATTERSON: 'Conversion principles and the base of Aristotle's modal logic', *JHPL* 11, 1990, 151–72

(J) Non-syllogistic Logic

If syllogistic forms the crowning achievement of Aristotle's logical studies, non-syllogistic inferences are also discussed – or at least alluded to – in *An.Pr* B, in *Top* and in *Rhet*. On propositional inferences, or 'hypothetical syllogisms' as the later tradition called them, see:

(161) J.M. BOCHENSKI: 'Non-analytical laws and rules in Aristotle', *Methodos* 3, 1951, 70–80

(162) W. and M. KNEALE: 'Prosleptic propositions and arguments', in STERN, HOURANI, and BROWN I.73

(163) B.H. SLATER: 'Aristotle's propositional logic', *PhSt* 36, 1979, 35–49

(164) G. STRIKER: 'Aristoteles über Syllogismen "Aufgrund einer Hypothese" ', *H* 107, 1979, 34–50

and, for the later history:

(165) J. BARNES: 'Theophrastus and hypothetical syllogistic', in WIESNER I.57 = FORTENBAUGH I.78

(166) J. BARNES: 'Terms and sentences', *PBA* 69, 279–326

On induction:[3]

(167) K. VON FRITZ: '*Epagôgê* bei Aristoteles', *Sitzungsberichte der bayerischen Akademie der Wissenschaften*, phil.-hist.Kl. (Munich, 1964)

(168) D.W. HAMLYN: 'Aristotelian *epagôgê*', *Phron* 21, 1976, 167–84

(169) T. ENGBERG-PEDERSEN: 'More on Aristotelian *epagôgê*', *Phron* 24, 1979, 301–19

(170) K.J.J. HINTIKKA: 'Aristotelian induction', *RIP* 34, 1980, 422–40

(171) R. MCKIRAHAN: 'Aristotelian *epagôgê* in *Prior Analytics* II.21 and *Posterior Analytics* I.1', *JHP* 21, 1983, 1–13

(172) S. KNUUTTILA: 'Remarks on induction in Aristotle's dialectic and rhetoric', *RIP* 47, 1993, 78–88

On the related topic of inferences from 'signs':

(173) E.H. MADDEN: 'Aristotle's treatment of probability and signs', *PhSc* 24, 1957, 167–72

(174) M.F. BURNYEAT: 'The origins of non-deductive inference', in J. BARNES, J. BRUNSCHWIG, M.F. BURNYEAT, M. SCHOFIELD (edd.), *Science and Speculation* (Cambridge, 1982)

(175) H. WEIDEMANN: 'Aristotle on inferences from signs', *Phron* 34, 1989, 342–51

Arguments based on *topoi* – 'commonplaces' or, roughly speaking, general logical principles – are discussed in *Top* and *Rhet*. See the introduction to BRUNSCHWIG III.7, and:

(176) E. HAMBRUCH: *Logische Regeln der platonischen Schule in der aristotelischen Topik* (Berlin, 1904)

(177) E.H. MADDEN: 'The enthymeme: crossroads of logic, rhetoric and metaphysics', *PR* 61, 1952, 368–76

---

3. Aristotle's '*epagôgê*' is usually translated as "induction", but the word is often used in ways which have little enough to do with what we think of as inductive inference. See ROSS III.2, pp. 47–51.

(178) S. RAPHAEL: 'Rhetoric, dialectic, and syllogistic argument: Aristotle's position in *Rhetoric* I–II', *Phron* 19, 1974, 153–67

(179) D.J. HADGOPOULOS: '*Protasis* and *problêma* in the *Topics*', *Phron* 21, 1976, 266–76

(180) S. VAN NOORDEN: 'Rhetorical arguments in Aristotle and Perelman', *RIP* 127/8, 1979, 178–87

(181) M.F. BURNYEAT: 'Enthymeme: Aristotle on the logic of persuasion', in FURLEY and NEHAMAS I.50

On fallacies, which are the subject of *SE*, see:

(182) C.L. HAMBLIN: *Fallacies* (London, 1970)

(183) J.D.G. EVANS: 'The codification of false refutations in Aristotle's *de sophisticis elenchis*', *PCPS* 21, 1975, 42–52

(184) C.A. KIRWAN: 'Aristotle and the so-called fallacy of equivocation', *PQ* 29, 1979, 35–46

And there is a mass of fascinating material in:

(185) S. EBBESEN: *Commentators and Commentaries on Aristotle's Sophistici Elenchi*, Corpus latinum commentariorum in Aristotelem graecorum 7 (Leiden, 1981)

(K) Dialectic

Aristotle distinguishes 'dialectical' from 'demonstrative' arguments. On the art of 'dialectic', which forms the subject of *Top*, see the introduction to BRUNSCHWIG III.7, and:

(186) E. WEIL: 'La place de la logique dans la pensée aristotélicienne', *Revue de métaphysique et de morale* 56, 1951, 283–315 = HAGER I.66 = BARNES, SCHOFIELD, SORABJI I.62

(187) W.A. DE PATER: *Les Topiques d'Aristote et la dialectique platonicienne* (Fribourg, 1965)

(188) G. RYLE: 'Dialectic in the Academy', in OWEN I.41

(189) P. MORAUX: 'La joute dialectique d'après le huitième livre des *Topiques*', in OWEN I.41

(190) J.D.G. EVANS: *Aristotle's Concept of Dialectic* (Cambridge, 1977)

(191) J. CROISSANT: 'La dialectique chez Aristote', in her *Etudes de philosophie ancienne* (Brussels, 1986)

(192) A. BERIGER: *Die aristotelische Dialektik* (Heidelberg, 1989)

Dialectic has an important part to play in Aristotle's general philosophical and scientific studies. On this, see especially:

(193) G.E.L. OWEN: '*Tithenai ta phainomena*', in MANSION, I.40 = BARNES, SCHOFIELD, SORABJI I.62 = OWEN I.90

with:

(194) G.E.L. OWEN: 'Aristotle', in GILLISPIE I.71 = OWEN I.90

(195) M. NUSSBAUM: 'Saving Aristotle's appearances', in SCHOFIELD and NUSSBAUM I.75

(196) W. WIANS: 'Saving Aristotle from Nussbaum's *phainomena*', in PREUS and ANTON I.63

Note also the supposed distinction between a 'weak' and a 'strong' form of dialectical argument made by:
(197) T.H. IRWIN: *Aristotle's First Principles* (Oxford, 1988), chh.2–3
– discussion in:
(198) J. BARNES: 'Philosophie et dialectique', in SINACEUR I.60
(199) D.W. HAMLYN: 'Aristotle on dialectic', *Phil* 65, 1990, 465–76
(200) R. WARDY: 'Transcendental dialectic', *Phron* 26, 1991, 86–106
See also:
(201) W. WIELAND: 'Das Problem der Prinzipienforschung und die aris-totelische Physik', *Kantstudien* 52, 1960/1, 206–19 [English translation in BARNES, SCHOFIELD, SORABJI I.62]
(202) J. BRUNSCHWIG: 'Dialectique et ontologie chez Aristote', *Revue Philosophique* 89, 1964, 179–200
(203) E. BERTI: 'Aristote et la méthode du *Parménide* de Platon', *RIP* 34, 1980, 341–58
(204) D. L. BLANK: 'Dialectical method in the Aristotelian *Athenaiôn Politeia*', *GRBS* 25, 1984, 275–84
(205) R. BOLTON: 'The epistemological basis of Aristotle's dialectic', in DEVEREUX and PELLEGRIN I.59
(206) J. BRUNSCHWIG: 'Remarques sur la communication de R. Bolton', in DEVEREUX and PELLEGRIN I.59
(207) H. BALTUSSEN: 'Peripatetic dialectic in the *de sensibus* of Theophrastus', in FORTENBAUGH and SHARPLES I.82

(L) Philosophical Method
Dialectical arguments deal with *endoxa* or reputable propositions. The assembly of such items typically gives rise to puzzles or *aporiai*, on which see:
(208) S. MANSION: 'Les apories de la métaphysique aristotélicienne', in MANSION I.51 = HAGER I.65 = MANSION I.88
(209) P. AUBENQUE: 'Sur la notion aristotélicienne d'aporie', in MANSION I.40
(210) E. HALPER: 'The origin of the *aporiai* in Aristotle's *Metaphysics* B', *Apeiron* 21, 1988, 1–27
Nonetheless, philosophical and scientific advance require a critical understanding of past and current ideas. Thus quasi-historical expositions of the pertinent *endoxa* regularly preface Aristotle's treatises. See:
(211) S. MANSION: 'Le rôle de l'exposé et de la critique des philosophies antérieures chez Aristote', in MANSION I.40
(212) K. OEHLER: 'Der Consensus Omnium als Kriterium der Wahrheit in der antiken Philosophie und der Patristik', in OEHLER I.89
Aristotle's reputation as a historian of ideas was vigorously attacked by:
(213) H.F. CHERNISS: *Aristotle's Criticism of Presocratic Philosophy* (Baltimore, 1935)
(214) H.F. CHERNISS: *Aristotle's Criticism of Plato and the Academy* (Baltimore, 1944)

and Cherniss II.51. There has been no general rehabilitation. But see:

(215) O. GIGON: 'Die Geschichtlichkeit der Philosophie bei Aristoteles', *Archivio di Filosofia* 1, 1954, 129–50

(216) W.K.C. GUTHRIE: 'Aristotle as a historian of philosophy', *JHS* 77, 1957, 35–41 = MORAUX I.64

(217) W. BURKERT: *Lore and Science in Early Pythagoreanism* (Cambridge Mass., 1972), ch. 1

(218) J.G. STEVENSON: 'Aristotle as a historian of philosophy', *JHS* 94, 1974, 138–43

(219) J. MANSFELD: 'Aristotle and others on Thales', *Mn* 38, 1985, 109–29 = MANSFELD I.87

(220) J. MANSFELD: 'Aristotle, Plato, and the Peripatetic doxography and chronography', in CAMBIANO I.80 = MANSFELD I.87

(221) E. BERTI: 'Sul carratere "dialettico" della storiografia di Aristotele', in CAMBIANO I.80

On Aristotle's scientific and philosophical method in general, and the links between his theoretical and his practical interests see:

(222) R. EUCKEN: *Die Methode der aristotelischen Forschung* (Berlin, 1872)

(223) J.M. LE BLOND: *Eulogos et l'argument de convenance chez Aristote* (Paris, 1938)

(224) J.M. LE BLOND: *Logique et méthode chez Aristote* (Paris, 1939)

(225) L. BOURGEY: *Observation et expérience chez Aristote* (Paris, 1955) [excerpts translated in BARNES, SCHOFIELD, SORABJI I.62]

(226) I. DÜRING: 'Aristotle's method in biology – a note on *PA* I, 639b30–640a2', in MANSION I.40 = SEECK I.68

(227) P. MORAUX: 'La méthode d'Aristote dans l'étude du ciel', in MANSION I.40

(228) W. KULLMANN: 'Zur wissenschaftlichen Methode des Aristoteles', in FLASHAR and GAISER I.69 = SEECK I.68

(229) D.M. BALME: 'Aristotle, *PA* I.2–3, argument and text', *PCPS* 196, 1970, 12–21

(230) A. PREUS: 'Science and philosophy in Aristotle's *Generation of Animals*', *Journal of the History of Biology* 3, 1970, 1–52

(231) W. KULLMANN: 'Der platonische *Timaios* und der Methode der aristotelischen Biologie', in *Studia Platonica – Festschrift für Hermann Gundert* (Amsterdam, 1974)

(232) G.E.R. LLOYD: 'Empirical research in Aristotle's biology', in GOTTHELF and LENNOX V.72 = LLOYD I.86

(233) W. KULLMANN: *Wissenschaft und Methode* (Berlin, 1974)

See further the items on ethical method in VIII (B).

(M) Demonstration

Demonstrative arguments, or proofs, are discussed in *An. Post* A, where Aristotle develops his theory of demonstrative science. On the aim of the theory see:

(234) J. BARNES: 'Aristotle's Theory of Demonstration', *Phron* 14, 1969, 123–52 = BARNES, SCHOFIELD, SORABJI I.62

(235) R. BOLTON: 'Definition and scientific method in Aristotle's *Posterior Analytics* and *Generation of Animals*', in GOTTHELF and LENNOX V.72

(236) A. GOTTHELF: 'First principles in Aristotle's *Parts of Animals*', in GOTTHELF and LENNOX V.72

(237) J.G. LENNOX: 'Divide and explain: the *Posterior Analytics* in practice', in GOTTHELF and LENNOX V.72

(238) W. WIANS: 'Aristotle, demonstration, and teaching', *Apeiron* 9, 1989, 254–53

On the elements of the theory, see BARNES III.5, and:

(239) H. SCHOLZ: 'The ancient axiomatic theory', in BARNES, SCHOFIELD, SORABJI I.62

(240) K.J.J. HINTIKKA: 'On the ingredients of an Aristotelian science', *Nous* 6, 1972, 55–69

(241) D. FREDE: 'Comment on Hintikka's paper', *Synthèse* 28, 1974, 79–89

(242) G.G. GRANGER: *La théorie aristotélicienne de la science* (Paris, 1976)

(243) G. PATZIG: 'Erkenntnisgründe, Realgründe, und Erklärungen (zu *Anal.Post.* A 13)', in BERTI I.46 = MENNE and OFFENBERGER III.15

(244) J.E. TILES: 'Why the triangle has two right angles *kath' hauto*', *Phron* 27, 1983, 1–16

(245) G.B. MATTHEWS: 'Aristotelian explanation', *ICS* 11, 1986, 173–9

(246) A. KOSMAN: 'Necessity and explanation in Aristotle's *Analytics*', in DEVEREUX and PELLEGRIN I.59

(247) M. FEREJOHN: *The Origins of Aristotelian Science* (New Haven, 1991)

(248) R.D. McKIRAHAN: *Principles and Proofs* (Princeton, 1992)

For an appreciation of the theory by a modern logician see:

(249) E.W. BETH: *The Foundations of Mathematics* (Amsterdam, 1964)

And note:

(250) B.C. VAN FRAASSEN: 'A re-examination of Aristotle's philosophy of science', *Dialogue* 19, 1980, 20–45

On the question of the connexion between syllogistic and the theory of demonstration, see:

(251) J. BARNES: 'Proof and the syllogism', in BERTI I.46

(252) J. BRUNSCHWIG: 'L'objet et la structure des *Secondes Analytiques*', in BERTI I.46

(253) R. SMITH: 'The relationship between Aristotle's two *Analytics*', *CQ* 32, 1982, 327–35

(254) R. SMITH: 'The syllogism in *Posterior Analytics* I', *AGP* 64, 1982, 113–35

On the connection between Aristotle's theory of demonstration and the Greek achievements in axiomatised mathematics, see:

(255) T.L. HEATH: *The Thirteen Books of Euclid's Elements* (Cambridge, 1925)

(256) B. EINARSON: 'On certain mathematical terms in Aristotle's logic', *AJP* 57, 1936, 33–54, 151–72

(257) I. MUELLER: 'Greek mathematics and logic', in CORCORAN III.16

The nature of the first principles or *archai* on which every demonstrative science is based is discussed in IRWIN III.197, ch.1, and:

(258) H.D.P. LEE: 'Geometrical method and Aristotle's account of first principles', *CQ* 29, 1935, 113–24

(259) K. VON FRITZ: 'Die APXAI in der griechischen Mathematik', *Archiv für Begriffsgeschichte* 1, 1955, 13–103

(260) A. GOMEZ-LOBO: 'Aristotle's hypotheses and the Euclidean postulates', *RM* 30, 1977, 430–39

(261) T.H. IRWIN: 'Aristotle's discovery of metaphysics', *RM* 31, 1977/8, 210–29

(262) B. INWOOD: 'A note on commensurate universals in the *Posterior Analytics*', *Phron* 24, 1979, 320–29

(263) A. GOMEZ-LOBO: 'The so-called question of existence in Aristotle, *An.Post.* 2.1–2', *RM* 34, 1980, 71–89

(264) A. GOMEZ-LOBO: 'Definitions in Aristotle's *Posterior Analytics*', in O'MEARA I.52

(265) B. LANDOR: 'Definitions and hypotheses in *Posterior Analytics* 72a19–25 and 76b35–77a4', *Phron* 26, 1981, 308–18

(N) Definition

Definitions are among the first principles of demonstrative sciences and the relation between definition and demonstration is a central problem of *An.Post* B. On this see:

(266) J.L. ACKRILL: 'Aristotle's theory of definition: some questions on *Posterior Analytics* II 8–10', in BERTI I.46

(267) M. FEREJOHN: 'Definition and the two stages of Aristotle's demonstration', *RM* 36, 1982, 375–95

(268) J. CROISSANT: 'Sur la théorie de la définition dans les *Secondes Analytiques* d'Aristote', in her *Etudes de philosophie ancienne* (Brussels, 1986)

(269) D. DEMOSS and D.T. DEVEREUX: 'Essence, existence, and nominal definition in Aristotle's *Posterior Analytics* II 8–10', *Phron* 32, 1988, 133–54

(270) M. DESLAURIERS: 'Aristotle's four types of definition', *Apeiron* 23, 1990, 1–26

(271) M. DESLAURIERS: 'Plato and Aristotle on division and definition', *AP* 10, 1990, 203–19

The main Aristotelian texts on definition itself (in *Top* Z, *An.Post* B, *PA* A, *Met* Z and H) are surveyed by:

(272) J.M. LE BLOND: 'La définition chez Aristote', *Gregorianum* 20, 1939, 351–80 [English translation in BARNES, SCHOFIELD, SORABJI I.62]

See also:

(273) M.S. ROLAND-GOSSELIN: 'Les méthodes de définition d'Aristote', Revue des sciences philosophiques et théologiques 6, 1912, 236–52, 661–75

(274) A.J. FESTUGIERE: 'Les méthodes de la définition de l'âme', Revue des sciences philosophiques et théologiques 20, 1931, 83–90

(275) R. SORABJI: 'Aristotle and Oxford philosophy', APQ 6, 1969, 127–35

(276) S. MANSION: 'To simon et la définition physique', in AUBENQUE I.44 = MANSION I.88

(277) J.E. HARE: 'Aristotle and the definition of natural things', Phron 24, 1979, 168–79

(278) R. SORABJI: 'Definitions: why necessary and in what way?', in BERTI I.46

(279) D. MORRISON: 'Some remarks on definition in Metaphysics Z', in DEVEREUX and PELLEGRIN I.59

According to Met Z 12, definition is to be given by genus and difference⁴: on the way this requirement is worked out see:

(280) D.M. BALME: 'Aristotle's use of division and differentiae', in GOTTHELF and LENNOX V.72

And compare the essay on definition by a notable student of Aristotle:

(281) R. ROBINSON: Definition (Oxford, 1950)

(O) Epistemology

Aristotle nowhere considers epistemological issues at any great length. For a survey of what he does say, see:

(282) C.C.W. TAYLOR: 'Aristotle's epistemology', in S. EVERSON (ed.), Companions to Ancient Thought: 1 Epistemology (Cambridge, 1990)

For Aristotle's conception of epistêmê – scientific knowledge or understanding – see IRWIN III.197, chh.6–7, and:

(283) W. LESZL: 'Knowledge of the universal and knowledge of the particular in Aristotle', RM 26, 1972–73, 278–313

(284) S. MANSION: Le jugement d'existence chez Aristote (Louvain, 1976²)

(285) M.F. BURNYEAT: 'Aristotle on understanding knowledge', in BERTI I.46

(286) S. MANSION: 'La signification de l'universel d'après APst 1.1', in BERTI I.46 = MANSION I.88

On the sciences, epistêmai, and the relations among them, see:

(287) J. KUNG: 'Aristotle's de Motu Animalium and the separability of the sciences', JHP 20, 1982, 65–76

(288) J. BARNES: 'Aristotle's philosophy of the sciences', OSAP 11, 1993, 225–41

4. Note here the readings on biological taxonomy in V (F).

And on *nous*,⁵ which is sometimes taken to be 'intuition' and by which we grasp the first principles of the sciences (*An.Post* B 19), see:

(289) J.H. LESHER: 'The meaning of *nous* in the *Posterior Analytics*', *Phron* 18, 1973, 44–68

(290) L.A. KOSMAN: 'Understanding, explanation and insight in the *Posterior Analytics*', in LEE, MOURELATOS and RORTY I.74

For Aristotle's attitude to scepticism:

(291) J. BARNES: 'Aristotle, Menaechmus, and circular proof', *CQ* 26, 1976, 78–92

(292) A.A. LONG: 'Aristotle and the history of Greek scepticism', in O'MEARA I.52

(293) J. BARNES: 'An Aristotelian way with scepticism', in MATTHEN I.52

Note also:

(294) A. GOMEZ-LOBO: 'Aristotle's first philosophy and the principles of particular disciplines', *Zeitschrift für Philosophische Forschung* 32, 1978, 183–94

(295) M.T. FEREJOHN: 'Meno's paradox and *de re* knowledge in Aristotle's theory of demonstration', *HPQ* 5, 1988, 99–117 = PREUS and ANTON I.63

IV PHILOSOPHY OF SCIENCE

(A) General

This Chapter deals primarily with the subject matter of Aristotle's *Physics*. Here, again, Ross' edition is indispensable:

(1) W.D. ROSS: *Aristotle's Physics* (Oxford, 1936)

The ancient commentaries on *Phys* are particularly rich. See:

(2) A.R. LACEY: *Philoponus: On Aristotle, Physics 2* (London, 1993)

(3) J.O. URMSON: *Simplicius: On Aristotle, Physics 4.1–5, 10–14* (London, 1992)

(4) D. KONSTAN: *Simplicius: On Aristotle, Physics 6* (London, 1989)

and, in addition to URMSON IV.121, and FURLEY and WILDBERG IV.125:

(5) R.W. SHARPLES: *Alexander of Aphrodisias: Quaestiones 1.1–2.15* (London, 1992)

There is a German edition, which includes an extensive bibliography:

(6) H. WAGNER: *Aristoteles: Physikvorlesung* (Berlin, 1967)

The Clarendon series contains:

(7) W. CHARLTON: *Aristotle's Physics I–II* (Oxford, 1992²)

(8) E. HUSSEY: *Aristotle's Physics III–IV* (Oxford, 1983)

and, for the *GC:*

(9) C.J.F. WILLIAMS: *Aristotle's de Generatione et Corruptione* (Oxford, 1982)

for which see also:

(10) H.H. JOACHIM: *Aristotle on coming-to-be and passing-away* (Oxford, 1922)

5. See further below, VI (G).

General surveys of Aristotle's 'physics' or philosophy of science may be found in:

(11) A. MANSION: *Introduction à la physique aristotélicienne* (Louvain, 1945)

(12) F. SOLMSEN: *Aristotle's System of the Physical World* (Ithaca, 1960)

(13) W. WIELAND: *Die aristotelische Physik* (Göttingen, 1970²)

There are collections of papers in DÜRING I.42, SEECK I.68, and:

(14) P.K. MACHAMER and R.J. TURNBULL (edd.): *Motion and Time, Space and Matter* (Ohio, 1976)

(15) L. JUDSON: *Aristotle's Physics* (Oxford, 1991)

(B) Nature

The term 'physics' derives from the Greek *'phusis'* or 'nature'. On Aristotle's conception of nature, see:

(16) S. WATERLOW: *Nature, Change, and Agency in Aristotle's Physics* (Oxford, 1982)

and also:

(17) A. MANSION: 'La notion de nature dans la physique aristotélicienne', *Université de Louvain: annales de l'institut supérieur de philosophie* 1, 1912, 471–567

(18) A.P.D. MOURELATOS: 'Aristotle's "powers" and modern empiricism', *Ratio* 9, 1967, 97–104

(19) H.S. THAYER: 'Aristotle on nature', *RM* 28, 1975, 725–44

(20) R. SMITH: 'Filling in nature's deficiencies', in PREUS and ANTON I.63

General discussions of the relation of physics to metaphysics in Aristotle are given by:

(21) A. MANSION: 'La physique aristotélicienne et la philosophie', *Revue néoscolastique de philosophie* 39, 1936, 5–26

(22) E. BERTI: 'Physique et métaphysique selon Aristote', in AUBENQUE I.44

(C) Change

Nature is a principle of change, and Aristotle confronts the puzzles of change in *Phys* A. See chh.4–9 of WIELAND V.13, and:

(23) G. BOAS: 'Aristotle's presuppositions about change', *AJP* 68, 1947, 404–13

(24) B. JONES: 'Aristotle's introduction of matter', *PR* 83, 1974, 474–500

(25) G. MORROW: 'Qualitative change in Aristotle's *Physics*', in DÜRING I.42

(26) R. DANCY: 'On some of Aristotle's second thoughts about substances: matter', *PR* 87, 1978, 372–413

(27) D. BOSTOCK: 'The principles of change in *Physics* I', in SCHOFIELD and NUSSBAUM I.75

(28) M.L. GILL: 'Aristotle on the individuation of changes', *AP* 4, 1984, 122–33

(29) A.P.D. MOURELATOS: 'Aristotle's rationalist account of qualitative interaction', *Phron* 29, 1984, 1–16.

(30) J. KOSTMAN: 'Aristotle's definition of change', *HPQ* 4, 1987, 3–16

(31) C.J.F. WILLIAMS: 'Aristotle on Cambridge change', *OSAP* 7, 1989, 41–57

(32) J. BOGEN: 'Change and contrariety in Aristotle', *Phron* 37, 1992, 1–21

(33) R. BOLTON: 'Aristotle's method in natural science: *Physics* 1', in JUDSON IV.15

See also:

(34) S. MANSION: 'Sur la composition ontologique des substances sensibles chez Aristote', in R. B. PALMER, R. HAMERTON-KELLY (edd.), *Philomathes* (The Hague, 1971) = BARNES, SCHOFIELD, SORABJI I.62 = MANSION I.88

(35) K. OEHLER: 'Das aristotelische Argument: Ein mensch zeugt einen Menschen', in OEHLER I.89

The concept of change involves the notions of matter and form, which will be treated in a later chapter (see VII (I) and (J)). The concept also involves the notion of agency, for which see:

(36) M.L. GILL: 'Aristotle's theory of causal action in *Physics* III.3', *Phron* 25, 1980, 129–47

(D) Explanation

Agents are causes – according to Aristotle's celebrated doctrine of the 'four causes' or modes of explanation, agents are 'efficient' causes. On the 'four causes' (*Phys* B), see:

(37) M. HOCUTT: 'Aristotle's four becauses', *Phil* 49, 1974, 385–99

(38) G.R.G. MURE: 'Cause and because in Aristotle', *Phil* 50, 1975, 356–57

Aristotle's conception of causality has been analysed by:

(39) L. ROBIN: 'La conception aristotélicienne de la causalité', *AGP* 23, 1909/10, 1–28, 184–210

(40) D.J. ALLAN: 'Causality ancient and modern', *PASS* 39, 1965, 1–18

(41) W. WIELAND: 'Zeitliche Kausalstrukturen in der aristotelischen Logik', *AGP* 54, 1972, 229–37

(42) J.M.E. MORAVCSIK: '*Aitia* as generative factor in Aristotle's philosophy', *Dialogue* 14, 1975, 622–38

See also:

(43) M. FREDE: 'The original notion of cause', in M. SCHOFIELD, M.F. BURNYEAT, J. BARNES (edd.), *Doubt and Dogmatism* (Oxford, 1980) = FREDE I.83

(44) J. ANNAS: 'Inefficient causes', *PQ* 32, 1982, 311–26

(45) M.J. WHITE: 'Causes as necessary conditions: Aristotle, Alexander of Aphrodisias, and J. L. Mackie', in PELLETIER and KING-FARLOW I.55

And on the closely connected notion of scientific explanation see:

(46) B.A. BRODY: 'Towards an Aristotelian theory of scientific explanation', *PhSc* 39, 1972, 20–31

(47) T. McCarthy: 'On an Aristotelian model of scientific explanation', *PhSc* 44, 1977, 159–66

(48) J.M.E. Moravcsik: 'Aristotle on adequate explanations', *Synthèse* 28, 1974, 3–17

(49) M. Schofield: 'Explanatory projects in *Physics* 2.3 and 7', *OSAP* suppt 1991, 29–40

(50) J.M.E. Moravcsik: 'What makes reality intelligible? Reflections on Aristotle's theory of *aitia*', in Judson IV.15

(51) C. Freeland: 'Accidental causes and real explanations', in Judson IV.15

See also Irwin III.197, ch.5, and the readings on demonstration in III (M). On a particular point:

(52) A.C. Lloyd: 'The principle that the cause is greater than its effect', *Phron* 21, 1976, 146–56

(53) S. Makin: 'An ancient principle about causation', *PAS* 91, 1990/1, 135–52

(E) Teleology

Of the four causes, the 'final' cause has perhaps occasioned most debate.[1] The main texts on teleology – or the thesis that 'Nature does nothing in vain' – are in *Phys* B and *PA* A. See ch.3 of Wieland IV.13 [English version in Barnes, Schofield, Sorabji I.62], part 3 of Sorabji IV.43, and the inaugural lecture by:

(54) D.M. Balme: *Aristotle's Use of Teleological Explanation* (London, 1965)

The source materials on ancient teleological theory are gathered in:

(55) A.S. Pease: 'Caeli enarrant', *Harvard Theological Review* 34, 1941, 163–200

See also:

(56) D.M. Balme: 'Greek science and mechanism', *CQ* 33, 1939, 129–38; 35, 1941, 23–8

(57) J.M. Rist: 'Some aspects of Aristotelian teleology', *TAPA* 96, 1965, 337–49

(58) K. Gaiser: 'Das zweifache Telos bei Aristoteles', in Düring I.42

(59) J. Owens: 'The teleology of nature in Aristotle', *Monist* 52, 1968, 159–73 = Owens I.91

(60) W. Kullmann: 'Different concepts of the final cause in Aristotle', in Gotthelf I.56

(61) D.J. Furley: 'The rainfall example in *Physics* ii 8', in Gotthelf I.56

(62) C.H. Kahn: 'The place of the prime mover in Aristotle's teleology', in Gotthelf I.56

(63) A. Gotthelf: 'Aristotle's conception of final causality', *RM* 30, 1976/7, 226–54 = in Gotthelf and Lennox V.72

1. On material and formal causes see VII (I) and (J).

(64) A. Gotthelf: 'The place of the good in Aristotle's natural teleology', *BACAP* 4, 1988, 113–39

(65) S. Broadie: 'Nature and art in Aristotelian teleology', in Devereux and Pellegrin I.59

(66) D.N. Sedley: 'Is Aristotle's teleology anthropocentric?', *Phron* 36, 1991, 179–96

(67) S. Sauve Meyer: 'Aristotle, teleology, and reduction', *PR* 101, 1992, 791–825

(68) R. Wardy: 'Aristotelian rainfall or the lore of averages', *Phron* 38, 1993, 18–30

(69) D. Charles: 'Teleological causation in the *Physics*', in Judson IV.15

See also:

(70) R.J. Hankinson: 'Galen on the best of all possible worlds', *CQ* 39, 1989, 206–27

(71) J. Lennox: 'Theophrastus on the limits of teleology', in Fortenbaugh and Sharples I.82

Teleology is connected with a form of necessity, namely hypothetical necessity:

(72) R. Sorabji: *Necessity, Cause and Blame* (London, 1980), part III

(73) M. Bradie and F. D. Miller: 'Teleology and natural necessity in Aristotle', *HPQ* 1, 1984, 133–46

(74) W. Kullmann: 'Notwendigkeit in der Natur bei Aristoteles', in Wiesner I.57

(75) D.M. Balme: 'Teleology and necessity', in Gotthelf and Lennox V.72

(76) J. Cooper: 'Hypothetical necessity and natural teleology', in Gotthelf and Lennox V.72

(77) D. Charles: 'Aristotle on hypothetical necessity and irreducibility', *Pacific Philosophical Quarterly* 69, 1988, 1–53

(F) Chance and Determinism

On Aristotle's account of chance in *Phys* B 4–5, see Sorabji IV.72, part I, and:

(78) H. Weiss: *Kausalität und Zufall bei Aristoteles* (Basel, 1942)

(79) D.M. Balme: 'Development of biology in Aristotle and Theophrastus – theory of spontaneous generation', *Phron* 7, 1962, 91–104

(80) J. Lennox: 'Teleology, chance, and Aristotle's theory of spontaneous generation', *JHP* 20, 1982, 219–38

(81) J. Lennox: 'Aristotle on chance', *AGP* 66, 1984, 52–60

(82) R. Heinaman: 'Aristotle on accidents', *JHP* 23, 1985, 311–24

(83) S. Everson: 'L'explication aristotélicienne du hazard', *RPA* 6, 1988, 39–76

(84) A. Gotthelf: 'Teleology and spontaneous generation in Aristotle', *Apeiron* 22, 1989, 181–93

(85) D. Frede: 'Accidental causes in Aristotle', *Synthèse* 92, 1992, 39–62

And on the issue of causal determinism see, apart from Hintikka III.103:

(86) M.J. White: 'Fatalism and causal determination: an Aristotelian essay', *PQ* 31, 1981, 231–41

(87) G. Fine: 'Aristotle on determinism', *PR* 90, 1981, 61–79

(88) A. Madigan: '*Metaphysics* E 3: a modest proposal', *Phron* 29, 1984, 123–36

(89) D. Frede: 'Aristotle on the limits of determination: accidental causes in *Metaphysics* E 3', in Gotthelf I.56

(90) H. Weidemann: 'Aristoteles und das Problem des kausalen Determinismus', *Phron* 31, 1986, 27–50

(91) M.J. White: *Agency and Integrality* (Dordrecht, 1986)

(92) P.L. Donini: *Ethos: Aristotele e il determinismo* (Turin, 1989)

See also the items on fatalism in III (F), and those on free will in VIII (I).

(G) Motion

The concept of *phusis* includes the concept of motion, and a major part of *Phys* is devoted to an analysis of *kinêsis*, or motion in the broadest sense, and of the associated concepts of space and time. Motion itself is discussed in *Phys* Γ, and again in E, Z and H.[2] On Aristotle's difficult account of *kinêsis* see:

(93) L.A. Kosman: 'Aristotle's definition of motion', *Phron* 14, 1969, 40–62

(94) A.L. Peck: 'Aristotle on *kinêsis*', in Anton and Kustas I.72

(95) T. Penner: 'Verbs and the identity of actions', in G. Pitcher and O. P. Wood (edd.), *Ryle* (New York, 1970)

(96) P. Machamer: 'Aristotle on natural place and natural motion', *Isis* 69, 1978, 377–87

(97) S. Waterlow: 'Instants of motion in Aristotle's *Physics* VI', *AGP* 65, 1983, 128–46

(98) R. Heinaman: 'Aristotle on housebuilding', *HPQ* 2, 1985, 145–62

(99) D. Graham: 'Aristotle's definition of motion', *AP* 8, 1988, 209–15

There are two monographs devoted to Book H:

(100) B. Manuwald: *Das Buch H der aristotelischen Physik* (Meisenheim, 1971)

(101) R. Wardy: *The Chain of Change* (Cambridge, 1990)

See also:

(102) G. Verbeke: 'L'argument de livre VII de la *Physique*', in Düring I.42

On the Aristotelian 'laws of motion':

(103) I. Drabkin: 'Notes on the laws of motion in Aristotle', *AJP* 59, 1938, 60–84

(104) H. Carteron: 'Does Aristotle have a mechanics?', in Barnes, Schofield, Sorabji I.62

(105) G.E.L. Owen: 'Aristotelian mechanics', in Gotthelf I.56 = Owen I.90

(106) E. Hussey: 'Aristotle's mathematical physics: a reconstruction', in Judson IV.15

And note:

2. On the Unmoved Movers, discussed in *Phys* H and Θ, see VII (M).

(107) O. BECKER: 'Eudoxos-Studien III: Spuren eines Stetigkeitsaxioms in der Art des Dedekind'schen zur Zeit des Eudoxos', *Quellen und Studien zur Geschichte der Mathematik, Astronomie und Physik* B3, 1936, 236–44

(H) Infinity
According to Aristotle, space, time and matter are continuous or infinitely divisible; Aristotle's account of the continuum and his rejection of atomism are among the topics of:
(108) A. VAN MELSEN: *From Atomos to Atom* (Pittsburgh, 1952)
(109) D.J. FURLEY: *Two Studies in the Greek Atomists* (Princeton, 1967)
(110) R. SORABJI: *Time, Creation, and the Continuum* (London, 1983), part V
(111) M.J. WHITE: 'On continuity: Aristotle versus topology?', *JHPL* 9, 1988, 1–12
(112) M.J. WHITE: *The Continuous and the Discrete* (Oxford, 1992)
(113) D. BOSTOCK: 'Aristotle on continuity in *Physics* VI', in JUDSON IV.125
The special problems raised by the Aristotelian notion of infinity and the discussion in *Phys* Γ 4–8 are dealt with by:
(114) K.J.J. HINTIKKA: 'Aristotelian infinity', *PR* 75, 1966, 197–212 = BARNES, SCHOFIELD, SORABJI I.62 = HINTIKKA I.85
(115) K. VON FRITZ: 'Das *apeiron* bei Aristoeles', in DÜRING I.42
(116) D.J. FURLEY: 'Aristotle and the atomists on infinity', in DÜRING I.42
(117) J. LEAR: 'Aristotelian infinity', *PAS* 80, 1980, 187–210
(118) D. KONSTAN: 'Points, lines, and infinity: Aristotle's *Physics* Z and Hellenistic philosophy', *BACAP* 3, 1987, 1–32
(119) W. CHARLTON: 'Aristotle's potential infinites', in JUDSON IV.15

(I) Place
Place, *topos*, occupies *Phys* Δ 1–5; see:
(120) J.O. URMSON: *Simplicius: Corollaries on Place and Time* (London, 1992)
(121) M. DEHN: 'Raum, Zeit, Zahl bei Aristoteles vom mathematischen Standpunkt aus', *Scientia* (Bologna) 60, 1936, 12–21; 69–74 = SEECK I.68
(122) H.R. KING: 'Aristotle's theory of *topos*', *CQ* 44, 1950, 76–96
(123) R. SORABJI: 'Theophrastus on place', in FORTENBAUGH and SHARPLES I.82

(J) Space and Void
Space and the void are discussed in Δ 6–9. On these topics see, once again, the ancient commentaries:
(124) D.J. FURLEY and C. WILDBERG: *Philoponus: Corollaries on Space and Void, and Simplicius: against Philoponus on the Eternity of the World* (London, 1991)
and also:
(125) M. JAMMER: *Concepts of Space* (Cambridge, Mass., 1954)
(126) J. MOREAU: *L'espace et le temps selon Aristote* (Padua, 1965)

(127) H. BARREAU: 'L'espace et le temps chez Aristote', *Revue de métaph·sique et de morale* 80, 1975, 417–38

(128) R. SORABJI: *Matter, Space, and Motion* (London, 1988), part II

(129) H. MENDELL: '*Topoi* on *topos:* the development of Aristotle's concept of space', *Phron* 32, 1987, 206–31

On empty space, or 'void', see:

(130) D.J. FURLEY: 'Aristotle and the atomists on motion in a void', in MACHAMER and TURNBULL IV.14

(131) B. INWOOD: 'The origins of Epicurus' concept of void', *CP* 76, 1981, 273–85

(132) D.N. SEDLEY: 'Two conceptions of vacuum', *Phron* 27, 1982, 175–93

(133) J. THORP: 'Aristotle's *horror vacui*', *CJP* 20, 1990, 149–66

(K) Time

On time, which is the subject of *Phys* Δ 10–14, see in addition to SORABJI IV.110, DEHN IV.122, and MOREAU IV.127:

(134) J.F. CALLAHAN: *Four Views of Time in Ancient Philosophy* (Cambridge, Mass., 1948)

(135) P.F. CONEN: *Die Zeittheorie des Aristoteles* (Munich, 1964)

(136) W. VON LEYDEN: 'Time, number, and eternity in Plato and Aristotle', *PQ* 14, 1964, 35–52

(137) J. MOREAU: 'Le temps de l'instant selon Aristote', in DÜRING I.42

(138) G.E.L. OWEN: 'Aristotle on time', BARNES, SCHOFIELD, SORABJI I.62 = OWEN I.90

(139) F.D. MILLER: 'Aristotle on the reality of time', *AGP* 56, 1974, 132–55

(140) J. ANNAS: 'Aristotle, number and time', *PQ* 25, 1975, 97–113

(141) D. CORISH: 'Aristotle's attempted derivation of temporal order from that of movement and space', *Phron* 1976, 241–51

(142) D. BOSTOCK: 'Aristotle's account of time', *Phron* 25, 1980, 148–69

(143) S. WATERLOW: 'The Aristotelian "now" ', *PQ* 34, 1984, 104–28

(144) G. VERBEKE: 'Les apories aristotéliciennces sur le temps', in WIESNER I.57

(145) D. BOSTOCK: 'Time and the continuum', *OSAP* 6, 1988, 255–70

(146) M.J. WHITE: 'Aristotle on "time" and "a time" ', *Apeiron* 22, 1989, 207–24

(147) M. INWOOD: 'Aristotle on the reality of time', in JUDSON IV.15

(148) T. MAUDLIN: 'Substance and space-time: what Aristotle would have said to Einstein', in DEVEREUX and PELLEGRIN I.59

(L) Zeno

Aristotle's views of motion lead him in *Phys* Z to discuss Zeno's notorious paradoxes. The paradoxes have collected a vast modern literature. Some excellent pieces are collected in:

(149) W.C. SALMON (ed.): *Zeno's Paradoxes* (Indianapolis, 1969)

See also:

(150) J. BARNES: *The Presocratic Philosophers* (London, 1982²), chh.12–13
On Aristotle's reply to Zeno, see especially:
(151) G.E.L. OWEN: 'Zeno and the mathematicians', *PAS* 58, 1957/8, 199–222 = SALMON IV.149 = OWEN I.90
(152) D. BOSTOCK: 'Aristotle, Zeno, and the potential infinite', *PAS* 73, 1972–3, 37–51
(153) P. SCHOEDEL: *Aristoteles' Widerlegungen der zenonischen Bewegungsparadoxien* (Göttingen, 1975)
(154) F.R. PICKERING: 'Aristotle on Zeno and the now', *Phron* 23, 1978, 253–57
(155) J. LEAR: 'A note on Zeno's arrow', *Phron* 26, 1981, 91–104
and SORABJI IV.110, ch.21.
The related puzzles about the instant of change are discussed by:
(156) R. SORABJI and N. KRETZMANN: 'Aristotle on the instant of change', *PASS* 50, 1976, 69–115 = BARNES, SCHOFIELD, SORABJI I.62
and SORABJI IV.110, ch.26. Mediaeval continuations of Aristotle's discussion are treated by:
(157) A.C. WILSON: *William Heytesbury* (Madison, Wis., 1956)
(158) N. KRETZMANN: 'Incipit/desinit', in MACHAMER and TURNBULL IV.14
(159) N. KRETZMANN: 'Socrates is whiter than Plato begins to be white', *Nous* 11, 1977, 3–15

V SCIENCE

(A) General

There are discussions of Aristotle's scientific achievements in SOLMSEN IV.12, and in:

(1) G.M. LEWES: *Aristotle: a Chapter from the History of Science* (London, 1864)
(2) J.R. PARTINGTON: *A History of Chemistry* (London, 1970)

and, on a smaller scale, in the introduction to:

(3) J.M. LE BLOND: *Aristote: traité sur les parties des animaux I* (Paris, 1945)

See also:

(4) T.E. LONES: *Aristotle's Researches into Natural Science* (London, 1912)
(5) W.A. HEIDEL: *The Heroic Age of Greek Science* (Baltimore, 1933)

Some of the spurious works included in the Aristotelian corpus give an idea of the scientific or quasi-scientific tradition among the later Peripatetics. See:

(6) G. MARENGHI (ed.): *Aristotele: Problemi di Medicina* (Milan, n.d.)
(7) H. FLASHAR (ed.): *Aristoteles: Mirabilia* (Berlin, 1981)
(8) M.E. BOTTECCHIA (ed.): *Aristotele: MHXANIKA* (Padua, 1982)
(9) H. FLASHAR (ed.): *Aristoteles: Problemata Physica* (Berlin, 1983)

Readings on scientific method have been given in III (L).

(B) Mathematics
It has seemed to many scholars that Aristotle's science is characteristically inferior to modern science in virtue of two pervasive features: its non-mathematical approach and its penchant for teleological explanation. For Aristotle's teleology see IV (E). It used to be a platitude that Aristotle himself was no mathematician. The classic paper on this is:

(10) G. MILHAUD: 'Aristote et les mathématiciens', *AGP* 16, 1902/3, 367–92
The mathematical material in the Aristotelian *corpus* has been collected, translated and expounded by:

(11) T.L. HEATH: *Mathematics in Aristotle* (Oxford, 1949)
The platitude about Aristotle's incompetence is questioned by OWEN, III.194, and by:

(12) R. SORABJI: 'Aristotle, mathematics, and colour', *CQ* 22, 1972, 293–308
See also:

(13) S. BOCHNER: *The Role of Mathematics in the Rise of Science* (Princeton, 1966)

(14) J. KLEIN: *Greek Mathematical Thought and the Origins of Algebra*, trans. E. BRAUN (Cambridge, Mass., 1968)
And compare, on Aristotle's dynamics, CARTERON IV.104, OWEN IV.105, and:

(15) T.S. KUHN: 'A function for thought-experiments', in *Mélanges Alexandre Koyré* (Paris, 1964)
and the relevant chapters of:

(16) M. HESSE: *Forces and Fields* (London, 1961)

(17) M. JAMMER: *Concepts of Force* (Cambridge, Mass., 1957)

(18) M. JAMMER: *Concepts of Mass* (Cambridge, Mass., 1961)

(C) Astronomy
Cosmological and astronomical issues are discussed in *Cael* (and also in *Met* Λ¹). There are editions of *Cael* by:

(19) W.K.C. GUTHRIE: *Aristotle: On the Heavens*, Loeb Classical Library (London, 1939)

(20) P. MORAUX: *Aristote: du Ciel* (Paris, 1965)

(21) L. ELDERS: *Aristotle's Cosmology* (Assen, 1966)
There is some discussion in:

(22) S. TOULMIN and J. GOODFIELD: *The Fabric of the Heavens* (London, 1963)
and a characteristically amusing argument in:

(23) N.R. HANSON: 'On counting Aristotle's spheres', *Scientia* 98, 1963, 223–32
answered by:

(24) D.R. DICKS: *Greek Astronomy from Thales to Aristotle* (London, 1970)
See also MORAUX III.227, and

(25) N.R. HANSON: *Constellations and Conjectures* (Dordrecht, 1974)

1. For which see VII (M).

The eternity of the universe is the subject of:

(26) E. ZELLER: 'Über die Lehre des Aristoteles von der Ewigkeit der Welt', *Abh. Berlin Ak. Wiss.*, phil. hist. Kl. (Berlin, 1878 [= his *Vorträge und Abhandlungen* III (Leipzig, 1884)])

(27) J. BERNADETE: 'Aristotle's argument from time', *JP* 54, 1957, 151–52

(28) W. WIELAND: 'Die Ewigkeit der Welt', in D. HENRICH, W. SCHULZ, and K.-H. VOLKMANN-SCHLUCK (edd.), *Die Gegenwart der Griechen in neuerer Denken: Festschrift für H. G. Gadamer* (Tübingen, 1960) and WILLIAMS III.104, SORABJI IV.110, part III. See also:

(29) C. WILDBERG: *Philoponus: against Aristotle on the Eternity of the World* (London, 1987)

(D) Chemistry

Aristotle's chemistry – if we may call it such – is to be found primarily in *Meteor* Δ. There is an edition by:

(30) I. DÜRING: *Aristotle's Chemical Treatise* (Göteborg, 1944)

For the debate about the authenticity of the work, see:

(31) H. GOTTSCHALK: 'The authorship of *Meteorologica* book IV', *CQ* 11, 1961, 67–79

(32) H. STROHM: 'Beobachtungen zum vierten Buch der aristotelischen *Meteorologie*', in MORAUX and WIESNER I.47

(33) D. J. FURLEY: 'The mechanics of *Meteorologica* IV', in MORAUX and WIESNER I.47

(34) C. BAFFIONE: *Il IV libro dei 'Meteorologica' di Aristotele* (Naples, 1981)

For the ideas expounded in the work, see:

(35) H.H. JOACHIM: 'Aristotle's conception of chemical combination', *JPh* 29, 1904, 72–86

(36) H. KAPP: 'Der chemische Traktat des Aristoteles', in FLASHAR and GAISER I.69

(37) R.A. HORNE: 'Aristotelian chemistry', *Chymia* 11, 1966, 21–7 = SEECK I.68

(38) R. SHARVY: 'Aristotle on mixtures', *JP* 80, 1983, 439–57

(39) J. MANSFELD: 'Zeno and Aristotle on mixture', *Mn* 36, 1984, 306–12 = MANSFELD I.87

(40) R. SORABJI: 'The Greek origin of the idea of chemical combination: can two bodies be in the same place?', *BACAP* 4, 1988, 35–63

Some related topics – mineralogy:

(41) D.E. EICHHOLZ: 'Aristotle's theory of the formation of metals and minerals', *CQ* 43, 1949, 141–46

colour: SORABJI V.11 and:

(42) P. KUCHARSKI: 'Sur la théorie des couleurs et des saveurs dans le *de Sensu* aristotélicien', *REG* 67, 1954, 355–90

(43) B.E. HARRY: 'A defence of Aristotle, *Meteorologica* III 375ab', *CQ* 21, 1971, 397–401

light:

(44) S. SAMBURSKY: 'Philoponus' interpretation of Aristotle's theory of light', *Osiris* 13, 1958, 114–26
weight:
(45) D. O'BRIEN: 'Heavy and light in Democritus and Aristotle', *JHS* 97, 1977, 64–74
Aristotle's theories of colour and of sound are compared to the theories of his successors by:
(46) H.B. GOTTSCHALK: 'The *de Coloribus* and its author', *H* 92, 1964, 59–85
(47) H.B. GOTTSCHALK: 'The *de Audibilibus* and Peripatetic acoustics', *H* 96, 1968, 435–60
and in several of the studies in FORTENBAUGH and SHARPLES I.82.

(E) Biology
Aristotle's biological works, though by no means devoid of theory, are at least more empirical than his treatises on physical science. JAEGER II.1, detected an evolution in his thought from the theoretical to the empirical approach to science; but against this see:
(48) H.D.P. LEE: 'Place-names and the date of Aristotle's biological works', *CQ* 42, 1948, 61–67 = SEECK I.68
(49) G.E.R. LLOYD: 'The development of Aristotle's theory of the classification of animals', *Phron* 6, 1961, 59–81 = LLOYD I.86
(50) F. SOLMSEN: 'The fishes of Lesbos and their alleged significance for the development of Aristotle', *H* 106, 1978, 467–84 = SOLMSEN I.92
(51) H.D.P. LEE: 'The fishes of Lesbos again', in GOTTHELF I.56
(52) J.S. ROHM: 'Aristotle's elephant and the myth of Alexander's scientific patronage', *AJP* 110, 1989, 566–75
For the biological writings there is a volume in the Clarendon series:
(53) D.M. BALME: *Aristotle's de Partibus Animalium I and de Generatione Animalium I* (Oxford, 1992²)
and there are editions in the Loeb Classical Library:
(54) A.L. PECK: *Aristotle: Parts of Animals* (London, 1937)
(55) A.L. PECK: *Aristotle: Generation of Animals* (London, 1953)
(56) A.L. PECK: *Aristotle: Historia Animalium I–VI* (London, 1965 and 1970)
(57) D.M. BALME: *Aristotle: History of Animals VII–X* (London, 1991)
Note also:
(58) J.B. MEYER: *Aristoteles' Thierkunde* (Berlin, 1855)
(59) W. OGLE: *Aristotle's Parts of Animals* (London, 1882)
(60) P. LOUIS: *Aristote: Histoire das animaux* (Paris, 1964–69)
and see:
(61) D.M. BALME: 'Aristotle *Historia Animalium* Book Ten', in WIESNER I.57
There are several good appreciations of Aristotle as a biologist:
(62) W. D'A. THOMPSON: *On Aristotle as a Biologist* (Oxford, 1912)
(63) M. MANQUAT: *Aristote naturaliste* (Paris, 1932)

(64) D.M. BALME: 'Aristotle: natural history and zoology', in GILLISPIE I.71

(65) L.G. WILSON: 'Aristotle: anatomy and physiology', in GILLISPIE I.71

(66) D.M. BALME: 'The place of biology in Aristotle's philosophy', in GOTTHELF and LENNOX V.72

See also:

(67) C. SINGER: 'Greek biology and its relation to the rise of modern biology', in C. SINGER (ed.), Studies in the History and Method of Science II (Oxford, 1921)

(68) W. D'A. THOMPSON: 'Aristotle the naturalist', in his Science and the Classics (Oxford, 1940)

(69) D.M. BALME: 'Aristotle and the beginnings of zoology', Journal of the Society for the Bibliography of Natural History 5, 1970, 272–85

(70) S. BYL: Recherches sur les grandes traités biologiques d'Aristote (Brussels, 1980)

(71) M. FURTH: 'Aristotle's biological universe: an overview', in GOTTHELF and LENNOX V.72

There is a collection of papers:

(72) A. GOTTHELF and J. LENNOX (edd.): Philosophical Issues in Aristotle's Biology (Cambridge, 1987)

Items on Aristotle's method in biology are given in III (L).

(F) Taxonomy

Aristotle's attempts to organise and classify the material in his biological writings have been particularly studied. See:

(73) P. LOUIS: 'Remarques sur la classification des animaux chez Aristote', in MANSION I.51

(74) D.M. BALME: 'Aristotle's use of differentiae in zoology', in MANSION I.40 = BARNES, SCHOFIELD, SORABJI I.62

(75) D.M. BALME: 'Genos and eidos in Aristotle's biology', CQ 12, 1962, 81–98 = SEECK I.68

(76) A.C. LLOYD: 'Genus, species, and ordered series in Aristotle', Phron 7, 1962, 67–90

(77) J. LENNOX: 'Aristotle on genera, species and "the more and the less" ', Journal of the History of Biology 13, 1980, 321–46

(78) P. PELLEGRIN: Aristotle's Classification of Animals (Berkeley, 1986 [first published in French, 1982])

(79) P. PELLEGRIN: 'Aristotle: a zoology without species', in GOTTHELF I.56

(80) P. PELLEGRIN: 'Les fonctions explicatives de l'Histoire des Animaux d'Aristote', Phron 31, 1986, 148–66

(81) G.E.R. LLOYD: 'Aristotle's zoology and his metaphysics', in DEVEREUX and PELLEGRIN I.59 = LLOYD I.86

(82) P. PELLEGRIN: 'Taxinomie, moriologie, division: réponses à G.E.R. Lloyd', in DEVEREUX and PELLEGRIN I.59

On a related issue:

(83) H.B. TORREY and F. FELIN: 'Was Aristotle an evolutionist?', *Quarterly Review of Biology* 12, 1937, 1–18

(84) L. EDELSTEIN: 'Aristotle and the concept of evolution', *Classical Weekly* 37, 1943/4, 148–50

See also:

(85) W. JACOBS: 'Art and Biology in Aristotle', *Paideia* 7, 1978, 16–29

(86) J. LENNOX: 'Are Aristotelian species eternal?', in GOTTHELF I.56

And a final curio:

(87) J.B.S. HALDANE: 'Aristotle's account of bees' dances', *JHS* 75, 1955, 24–25

VI PSYCHOLOGY

(A) General

Aristotle's psychology and philosophy of mind are closely connected to his biology, his ethics, and his metaphysics. The main body of his thought on the subject is contained in the *de Anima* and the collection of short treatises known as the *Parva Naturalia*. On *An* the two best commentaries are:

(1) G. RODIER: *Aristote: Traité de l'âme* (Paris, 1900)

(2) R.D. HICKS: *Aristotle: de Anima* (Cambridge, 1907)

See also:

(3) W.D. ROSS: *Aristotle's de Anima* (Oxford, 1956)

and in the Clarendon Aristotle series:

(4) D.W. HAMLYN: *Aristotle's de Anima Books II and III* (Oxford, 1993²)

Note also the introduction to:

(5) H. LAWSON-TANCRED: *Aristotle: de Anima* (Harmondsworth, 1986)

and:

(6) D.S. HUTCHINSON: 'Restoring the order of Aristotle's *de Anima*', *CQ* 37, 1987, 373–81

On the *Parva Naturalia*, see:

(7) W.D. ROSS: *Aristotle's Parva Naturalia* (Oxford, 1955)

(8) P. SIWEK: *Aristotelis Parva Naturalia graece et latine* (Rome, 1963)

For the *de Sensu* and *de Memoria*, there is a commentary by:

(9) G.R.T. ROSS: *Aristotle: De Sensu et De Memoria* (Cambridge, 1906)

On the *de Memoria* see also:

(10) R. SORABJI: *Aristotle on Memory* (London, 1972)

On the *de Somno* and *de Insomniis*:

(11) H.J. DROSSAART LULOFS: *De Insomniis et De Divinatione per Somnum* (Leyden, 1947)

(12) D. GALLOP: *Aristotle on Sleep and Dreams* (Peterborough Ont., 1990)

For general accounts of Aristotle's views in this area see:

(13) F. BRENTANO: *The Psychology of Aristotle*, trans. R. GEORGE (Berkeley, 1977)

(14) P. SIWEK: *La psychophysique humaine d'après Aristote* (Paris, 1930)

(15) E. HARTMAN: *Substance, Body, and Soul* (Princeton, 1977)

(16) M. FURTH: *Substance, Form, and Psyche* (Cambridge, 1988)
(17) D.N. ROBINSON: *Aristotle's Psychology* (New York, 1989)
(18) T.H. IRWIN: 'Aristotle's philosophy of mind', in S. EVERSON (ed.), *Companions to Ancient Thought: 2 Psychology* (Cambridge, 1991)
In addition to LLOYD and OWEN I.42 there are two collections of essays:
(19) M.C. NUSSBAUM and A.O. RORTY (edd.): *Essays on Aristotle's* de Anima (Oxford, 1992)
(20) M. DURRANT (ed.): *Aristotle's* de Anima *in Focus* (London, 1993)

(B) The Soul

The soul or *psuchê* is the central concept. On Aristotle's definitions of the soul in *An* B 1–3, see:

(21) J.L. ACKRILL: 'Aristotle's definitions of *psuchê*', *PAS* 76, 1972/3, 119–33 = BARNES, SCHOFIELD, SORABJI I.62
(22) S. MANSION: 'Soul and life in the *de Anima*', in LLOYD and OWEN I.45
(23) S. MANSION: 'Deux définitions différentes de la vie chez Aristote', *RPL* 71, 1973, 425–50 = MANSION I.88
(24) R. BOLTON: 'Aristotle's definitions of the soul: *de Anima* II 1–3', *Phron* 23, 1978, 258–78
(25) W. CHARLTON: 'Aristotle's definition of soul', *Phron* 25, 1980, 170–86 = DURRANT VI 20
(26) D. WIGGINS: *Sameness and Substance* (Oxford, 1980)
(27) G.B. MATTHEWS: '*De anima* 2.2–4 and the meaning of *life*', in NUSSBAUM and RORTY VI.19
(28) A. CODE and J.M.E. MORAVCSIK: 'Explaining various forms of living', in NUSSBAUM and RORTY VI.19

Note also:

(29) R.K. SPRAGUE: 'Aristotle, *de Anima* 414a4–14', *Phoenix* 21, 1967, 102–7
(30) R. SHINER: 'More on Aristotle, *de Anima* 414a4–14', *Phoenix* 24, 1970

On the soul as a cause see:

(31) H.J. EASTERLING: 'A note on *de Anima* 413a8–9', *Phron* 11, 1966, 159–62
(32) D. J. FURLEY: 'Self movers', in LLOYD and OWEN I.45
(33) A. CODE: 'Soul as efficient cause in Aristotle's embryology', *Philosophical Topics* 15, 1987, 51–60

For some historical background bearing upon Aristotle's concerns in *An* A see:

(34) G.M. STRATTON: *Theophrastus and the Greek Physiological Psychology before Aristotle* (London, 1917)
(35) F. SOLMSEN: 'Antecedents of Aristotle's psychology and scale of beings', *AJP* 76, 1955, 148–64 = SOLMSEN I.92
(36) F. SOLMSEN: 'Greek philosophy and the discovery of the nerves', *MH* 18, 1961, 150–97 = SOLMSEN I.92

(37) T.M. OLSHEWSKY: 'On the relations of soul to body in Plato and Aristotle', *JHP* 14, 1976, 391–404

(38) D.B. CLAUS: *Toward the Soul* (New Haven, 1981)

(39) B.A.O. WILLIAMS: *Shame and Necessity* (Berkeley, 1993), ch.2

and for Aristotle's views of his predecessors:

(40) H.B. GOTTSCHALK: 'Soul as *harmonia*', *Phron* 16, 1971, 179–98

(41) W. CHARLTON: 'Aristotle and the *harmonia* theory', in GOTTHELF I.56

(42) C. WITT: 'Dialectic, motion, and perception: *de Anima* book I', in NUSSBAUM and RORTY VI 19

Aristotle does not distinguish sharply between what we would call philosophical questions and what we would call scientific questions; and his psychology is continuous with his biology. On the 'physiological' side of his work in this area see:

(43) J. NEUHAUSER: *Aristoteles' Lehre von dem sinnlichen Erkenntnisvermögen und seinen Organen* (Leipzig, 1878)

(44) F. SOLMSEN: 'Tissues and the soul', *PR* 59, 1950, 435–68 = SOLMSEN I.92

(45) A.L. PECK: 'The connate *pneuma*: an essential factor in Aristotle's solutions to the problems of reproduction and sensation', in E.A. UNDERWOOD (ed.), *Science, Medicine and History* (Oxford, 1953)

(46) T. TRACY: *Physiological Theory and the Doctrine of the Mean in Plato and Aristotle* (The Hague, 1969)

(47) G.E.R. LLOYD: 'The empirical basis of the physiology of *Parva Naturalia*', in LLOYD and OWEN I.45 = LLOYD I.86

(48) G. VERBEKE: 'Doctrine du *pneuma* et entéléchie chez Aristote', in LLOYD and OWEN I.45

(49) J. WIESNER: 'The unity of the *de Somno* and the physiological explanation of sleep in Aristotle', in LLOYD and OWEN I.45

(50) J. THORP: 'Le mécanisme de la perception chez Aristote', *Dialogue* 19, 1980, 575–98.

(51) P. WEBB: 'Bodily structure and psychic faculties in Aristotle's theory of perception', *H* 110, 1982, 25–50

(52) G.E.R. LLOYD: 'Aspects of the relationship between Aristotle's psychology and his zoology', in NUSSBAUM and RORTY VI.19

See also:

(53) P.M. HUBY: 'The paranormal in the works of Aristotle and his circle', *Apeiron* 13, 1979, 53–62

(C) Body and Soul

The soul, according to *An* B, is the form of the living body: what sort of psychological ism does this commit Aristotle to? and did his view develop from some less sophisticated theory? On the latter question NUYENS II.3 provides the starting-point, and the discussion is continued in:

(54) D.A. REES: 'Bipartition of the soul in the early Academy', *JHS* 77, 1957, 112–8

(55) D.A. REES: 'Theories of the soul in the early Aristotle', in DÜRING and OWEN, I.39

(56) I. BLOCK: 'The order of Aristotle's psychological writings', *AJP* 82, 1961, 50–77

(57) W.F.R. HARDIE: 'Aristotle's treatment of the relation between the soul and the body', *PQ* 14, 1964, 53–72

See also chapter 5 of HARDIE VIII.17, and:

(58) C. LEFEVRE: 'Sur le statut de l'âme dans le *de Anima* et les *Parva Naturalia*', in LLOYD and OWEN I.45

(59) C. LEFEVRE: *Sur l'évolution d'Aristote en psychologie* (Louvain, 1972)

(60) W.W. FORTENBAUGH: 'Zur Zweiteilung der Seele in EN I 7 und I 13', *Phg* 120, 1976, 299–302

Was Aristotle perhaps a dualist? On this suggestion see:

(61) D.W. HAMLYN: 'Aristotle's Cartesianism', *Paideia* 7, 1978, 8–15

(62) H.M. ROBINSON: 'Mind and body in Aristotle', *CQ* 28, 1978, 107–24

(63) H.M. ROBINSON: 'Aristotelian dualism', OSAP 1, 1983, 123–44

(64) M.C. NUSSBAUM: 'Aristotelian dualism: reply to Howard Robinson', *OSAP* 2, 1984, 197–207

Or did he anticipate Brentano? See BRENTANO VI.13, and:

(65) J. BARNES: 'Aristotle's concept of mind', *PAS* 75, 1971/2, 101–14 = BARNES, SCHOFIELD, SORABJI I.62

(66) R. SORABJI: 'From Aristotle to Brentano: the development of the concept of intentionality', *OSAP* suppt. 1991, 227–60

Or was he – as many recent scholars have urged – some sort of functionalist? See:

(67) R. SORABJI: 'Body and soul in Aristotle', *Phil* 49, 1974, 63–89 = BARNES, SCHOFIELD, SORABJI I.62 = DURRANT VI.20

(68) A. KOSMAN: 'Animals and other beings in Aristotle', in GOTTHELF and LENNOX V.72

(69) C. SHIELDS: 'Body and soul in Aristotle', *OSAP* 6, 1988, 103–38

(70) H. GRANGER: 'Aristotle and the functionalist debate', *Apeiron* 23, 1990, 27–49

(71) M.F. BURNYEAT: 'Is an Aristotelian philosophy of mind still credible?', in NUSSBAUM and RORTY VI.19

(72) M.C. NUSSBAUM and H. PUTNAM: 'Changing Aristotle's mind', in NUSSBAUM and RORTY VI.19

(73) S.M. COHEN: 'Hylomorphism and functionalism', in NUSSBAUM and RORTY VI.19

(74) J. WHITING: 'Living bodies', in NUSSBAUM and RORTY VI.19

See also:

(75) P. AUBENQUE: 'La définition aristotélicienne de la colère', *Revue philosophique* 147, 1957, 300–17

(76) M. MANNING: 'Materialism, dualism, and functionalism in Aristotle's philosophy of mind', *Apeiron* 19, 1985, 11–23

(77) B. WILLIAMS: 'Hylomorphism', *OSAP* 4 1986, 186–99

(78) W. CHARLTON: 'Aristotle on the place of mind in nature', in GOTTHELF and LENNOX V.72

(79) C. SHIELDS: 'Soul as subject in Aristotle', *CQ* 38, 1988, 140–40 = PREUS and ANTON I.63

(80) R. HEINAMAN: 'Aristotle and the mind-body problem', *Phron* 35, 1990, 83–102

(81) M. FREDE: 'On Aristotle's conception of the soul', in R. W. SHARPLES (ed.), *Ancient Thinkers and Modern Thinkers* (London, 1993) = NUSSBAUM and RORTY VI.19

(82) C. SHIELDS: 'The homonymy of the body in Aristotle', *AGP* 75, 1993, 1–30

(D) Perception

Aristotle's account of perception is found in *An* B and *Sens.* For general analyses see:

(83) J. BEARE: *Greek Theories of Elementary Cognition* (Oxford, 1906)

(84) D.W. HAMLYN: 'Aristotle's account of *aisthêsis* in the *de Anima*', *CQ* 9, 1959, 6–16

(85) F. SOLMSEN: *Aisthêsis in Aristotle and Epicurus* (Amsterdam, 1961) = SOLMSEN I.92

(86) T. SLAKEY: 'Aristotle on sense perception', *PR* 70, 1961, 470–84 = DURRANT VI.20

(87) T. EBERT: 'Aristotle on what is done in perceiving', *Zeitschrift für Philosophische Forschung* 37, 1983, 181–98

(88) D. MODRAK: *Aristotle – the power of perception* (Chicago, 1987)

(89) T.W. BYNUM: 'A new look at Aristotle's theory of perception', *HPQ* 4, 1987, 163–78 = DURRANT VI.20

(90) R. SORABJI: 'Intentionality and physiological process: Aristotle's theory of sense-perception', in NUSSBAUM and RORTY VI.19

For the theory that perceiving involves receiving form without matter, see, besides BRENTANO VI.13:

(91) G. VAN REIT: 'La théorie thomiste de la sensation externe', *RPL* 51, 1953, 374–408

(92) C.J.F. WILLIAMS and R. J. HIRST: 'Form and sensation', *PASS* 39, 1965, 139–72

(93) O. ANDERSEN: 'Aristotle on sense-perception in plants', *Symbolae Osloenses* 51, 1976, 81–5

For the idea that perception involves a 'mean':

(94) A. BARKER: 'Aristotle on perception and ratios', *Phron* 25, 1981, 248–66

(95) J.K. WARD: 'Perception and *logos* in *de Anima* II.12', *Apeiron* 8, 1988, 217–33

On the objects of perception, and the distinction among the different senses, see:

(96) I. BLOCK: 'Aristotle and the physical object', *PPR* 21, 1960, 93–101

(97) R. SORABJI: 'Aristotle on demarcating the five senses', *PR* 80, 1971, 55–79 = BARNES, SCHOFIELD, SORABJI I.62

(98) S. CASHDOLLAR: 'Aristotle's account of incidental perception', *Phron* 18, 1973, 156–75

(99) A. GRAESER: 'On Aristotle's framework of sensibilia', in LLOYD and OWEN I.45

(100) T. MAUDLIN: '*De Anima* III.1: is any sense missing?', *Phron* 31, 1986, 51–67

(101) A. SILVERMAN: 'Colour and colour-perception in Aristotle's *de Anima*', *AP* 9, 1989, 271–92

(102) C. FREELAND: 'Aristotle on the sense of touch', in NUSSBAUM and RORTY VI.19

And on the connection between perception and truth:

(103) I. BLOCK: 'Truth and error in Aristotle's theory of sense perception', *PQ* 11, 1961, 1–9

(104) R.G. TURNBULL: 'The role of the "special sensibles" in the perception theories of Plato and Aristotle', in P.K. MACHAMER and R.G. TURNBULL (edd.), *Studies in Perception* (Columbus, Ohio, 1978)

and KENNY VII.37, SCHOLAR VII.38.

(E) Common Sense

The idea of a 'common sense' is expounded in *An* Γ and in parts of the *Parva Naturalia*. For some discussion see:

(105) M. DE CORTE: 'Notes exégétiques sur la théorie aristotélicienne du *sensus communis*', *New Scholasticism* 6, 1932, 187–214

(106) I. BLOCK: 'Three German commentators on the individual senses and the common sense in Aristotle', *Phron* 9, 1964, 58–63

(107) I. BLOCK: 'On the commonness of the common sensibles', *Aust/P* 43, 1965, 189–95

(108) D.W. HAMLYN: '*Koinê aisthêsis*', *Monist* 52, 1968, 195–209

(109) A.C. LLOYD: 'Was Aristotle's theory of perception Lockean?', *Ratio* 21, 1979, 135–48

(110) D. MODRAK: '*Koinê aisthêsis* and the discrimination of sensible difference in *de Anima* III.2', *CJP* 11, 1981, 404–23

On consciousness:

(111) A.C. LLOYD: '*Nosce teipsum* and *conscientia*', *AGP* 46, 1964, 188–200

(112) C.H. KAHN: 'Sensation and consciousness in Aristotle's psychology', *AGP* 48, 1966, 43–81 = BARNES, SCHOFIELD, SORABJI II.62

(113) J. SCHILLER: 'Aristotle and the concept of awareness in sense-perception', *JHP* 13, 1975, 283–96

(114) A. KOSMAN: 'Perceiving that we perceive: "On the soul", III.2', *PR* 84, 1975, 499–519

(115) W.F.R. HARDIE: 'Concepts of consciousness in Aristotle', *M* 85, 1976, 388–411

(116) G.B. MATTHEWS: 'Consciousness and life', *Phil* 52, 1977, 13–26

(117) D. MODRAK: 'An Aristotelian theory of consciousness?', *AP* 1, 1981, 160–70

(118) C. Osborne: 'Aristotle, *de Anima* 3.2: how do we perceive that we perceive?', *CQ* 33, 1983, 401–11

(119) I. Block: 'Aristotle on common sense: a reply to Kahn and others', *AP* 8, 1988, 235–49

(120) J. Brunschwig: 'Les multiples chemins aristotéliciens de la sensation commune', *Revue de métaphysique et de morale* 96, 1991, 455–74

(F) Imagination

For Aristotle's views on *phantasia* or imagination, which are found primarily in *An* Γ 3, see:

(121) K. Lycos: 'Aristotle and Plato on appearing', *M* 73, 1964, 496–514

(122) D.A. Rees: 'Aristotle's treatment of *phantasia*', in Anton and Kustas I.72

(123) M. Schofield: 'Aristotle on the imagination', in Lloyd and Owen I.45 = Barnes, Schofield, Sorabji I.62 = Nussbaum and Rorty VI.19

(124) J. Engmann: 'Imagination and truth in Aristotle', *JHP* 14, 1976, 259–66

(125) H.J. Blumenthal: 'Neoplatonic interpretations of Aristotle on *phantasia*', *RM* 31, 1977, 242–57

(126) G. Watson: '*Phantasia* in Aristotle *de Anima* 3.3', *CQ* 32, 1982, 100–13

(127) J.-L. Labarrière: 'Imagination humaine et imagination animale chez Aristote', *Phron* 29, 1984, 17–49

(128) D. Modrak: '*Phantasia* reconsidered', *AGP* 68, 1986, 47–96

(129) G. Watson: Phantasia *in Classical Thought* (Galway, 1988)

(130) M. Wedin: *Mind and Imagination in Aristotle* (New Haven, 1988)

(131) D. Modrak: 'Aristotle the first cognitivist?', *Apeiron* 23, 1990, 65–75

(132) D. Frede: 'The cognitive side of *phantasia* in Aristotle', in Nussbaum and Rorty VI.19

and Essay 5 in:

(133) M.C. Nussbaum: *Aristotle's de Motu Animalium* (Princeton, 1985²)

On memory, see Sorabji VI.10, and:

(134) H.S. Lang: 'On memory: Aristotle's corrections of Plato', *JHP* 18, 1980, 379–93

(135) J. Annas: 'Aristotle on memory and the self', *OSAP* 4, 1986, 99–118 = Nussbaum and Rorty VI.19

and on dreams, Drossaart Lulofs VI.11, Gallop VI.12, and:

(136) A. Preus: 'On Dreams 2, 459b24–460a33, and Aristotle's *opsis*', *Phron* 13, 1968, 175–82

(137) R.K. Sprague: 'Aristotle and the metaphysics of sleep', *RM* 31, 1977/8, 230–41

(138) H. Wijsenbeek-Wijler: *Aristotle's Concept of Soul, Sleep, and Dreams* (Amsterdam, 1978)

(139) M. Lowe: 'Aristotle's *de Somno* and his theory of causes', *Phron* 23, 1978, 279–91

(140) D. GALLOP: 'Aristotle on sleep, dreams, and final causes', *BACAP* 4, 1988, 257–90
There is background material in chapter 4 of
(141) E.R. DODDS: *The Greeks and the Irrational* (Berkeley and Los Angeles, 1963)

(G) Thought
On Aristotle's obscure account of the nature of thinking (*An* Γ 4–6), see:
(142) O. HAMELIN: *La théorie de l'intellect d'après Aristote et ses commentateurs* (Paris, 1953)
(143) K. OEHLER: *Die Lehre vom noetischen und dianoetischen Denken bei Platon und Aristoteles* (Munich, 1962)
(144) R. NORMAN: 'Aristotle's philosopher-god', *Phron* 14, 1969, 63–74 = BARNES, SCHOFIELD, SORABJI I.62
(145) J. OWENS: 'A note on Aristotle's *de Anima*, III.4, 429b9', *Phoenix* 30, 1976, 107–18
(146) T. LOWE: 'Aristotle on kinds of thinking', *Phron* 28, 1983, 17–30 = DURRANT VI.20
(147) D. MODRAK: 'Aristotle on thinking', *BACAP* 2, 1987, 209–36
(148) M.V. WEDIN: 'Aristotle on the mechanics of thought', *AP* 9, 1989, 67–86 = PREUS and ANTON I. 63
and also HINTIKKA IV.115, SORABJI IV.110, ch.10.
For non-discursive thought, consult:
(149) S.H. ROSEN: 'Thought and touch: a note on Aristotle's *de Anima*', *Phron* 6, 1961, 127–37
(150) A.C. LLOYD: 'Non-discursive thought – an enigma of Greek philosophy', *PAS* 70, 1969/70, 261–74
(151) E. BERTI: 'The intellection of "indivisibles" according to Aristotle *de Anima* III.6', in LLOYD and OWEN I.45
(152) P. AUBENQUE: 'La pensée du simple dans la *Métaphysique* (Z 17 et Θ 10)', in AUBENQUE I.44
(153) P. HARVEY: 'Aristotle on truth and falsity in *de Anima* 3.6', *JHP* 16, 1978, 219–20
(154) R. SORABJI: 'Myths about non-propositional thought', in SCHOFIELD and NUSSBAUM I.75
And see the items under on *nous* in III (O).
Aristotle's distinction between 'active' and 'passive' intellect in *An* Γ 5 puzzled his immediate successors:
(155) E. BARBOTIN: *La théorie aristotélicienne de l'intellect d'après Théophraste* (Paris, 1954)
and it has puzzled commentators ever since. See:
(156) W. CHARLTON: *Philoponus on Aristotle on the Intellect* (London, 1991)
(157) F. BRENTANO: *Aristoteles' Lehre vom Ursprung des menschlichen Geistes* (Leipzig, 1911) [partly translated in NUSSBAUM and RORTY VI.19]
(158) A. MANSION: 'L'immortalité de l'âme et de l'intellect d'après Aristote', *RPL* 51, 1953, 444–72

(159) P. MORAUX: 'A propos du *nous thurathen* chez Aristote', in MAN-SION I.53

(160) J. RIST: 'Notes on Aristotle, *de Anima* III.5', *CP* 61, 1966, 8–20

(161) S. BERNARDETE: 'Aristotle, *de Anima*, III.5', *RM* 28, 1975, 611–22

(162) J. LEAR: 'Active *epistêmê*', in GRAESER I.48

(163) A. KOSMAN: 'What does the maker mind make?', in NUSSBAUM and RORTY VI.19

(164) M.V. WEDIN: 'Tracking Aristotle's *nous*', in DURRANT VI.20 and ch.16 of HARDIE VIII.17.

VII METAPHYSICS

(A) General

For the *Metaphysics* there is Ross' commentary:

(1) W.D. ROSS: *Aristotle's Metaphysics* (Oxford, 1923)

In addition, it is worth consulting:

(2) H. BONITZ: *Aristotelis Metaphysica* (Bonn, 1848/9)

and perhaps the best of all ancient Greek commentaries on Aristotle:

(3) ALEXANDER of Aphrodisias: *In Aristotelis Metaphysica Commentaria*, ed. M. HAYDUCK (Berlin, 1891)

for which see:

(4) W.E. DOOLEY: *Alexander of Aphrodisias: On Aristotle, Metaphysics 1* (London, 1989)

(5) W.E. DOOLEY and A. MADIGAN: *Alexander of Aphrodisias: On Aristotle, Metaphysics 2 and 3* (London, 1992)

The Clarendon Aristotle series includes:

(6) C.A. KIRWAN: *Aristotle's Metaphysics, Books Gamma, Delta, Epsilon* (Oxford, 1971)

(7) J. ANNAS: *Aristotle's Metaphysics, Books Mu and Nu* (Oxford, 1976)

And note:

(8) M.F. BURNYEAT: *Notes on Zeta* (Oxford, 1979)

(9) M.F. BURNYEAT: *Notes on Eta and Theta* (Oxford, 1984)

(10) M. FREDE and G. PATZIG: *Aristoteles: Metaphysik Z* (Munich, 1988)

Jaeger's work on the development of Aristotle's thought began with a monograph on the *Metaphysics:*

(11) W.W. JAEGER: *Studien zur Entstehungsgeschichte der Metaphysik des Aristoteles* (Berlin, 1912)

Jaeger's investigations are taken up in many of the items included in this Chapter. They have been particularly influential in connexion with Aristotle's theology.[1] See:

(12) H. VON ARNIM: 'Die Entwicklung der aristotelischen Gotteslehre', in HAGER I.65

(13) W.K.C. GUTHRIE: 'The development of Aristotle's theology', *CQ* 27, 1933, 162–71; 28, 1934, 90–98 = HAGER I.65

---

1. For which see VII (M).

General works on the *Metaphysics* include:

[14] J. Owens: *The Doctrine of Being in the Aristotelian Metaphysics* (Toronto, 1978³)

[15] P. Aubenque: *Le problème de l'être chez Aristote* (Paris, 1966) and Anscombe's essay in:

[16] G.E.M. Anscombe and P.T. Geach: *Three Philosophers* (Oxford, 1961)

(B) The Nature of Metaphysics

'First Philosophy' is characterised by Aristotle both as the study of 'beings qua being' (*metaphysica generalis*) and as 'theology' (*metaphysica specialis*). The main texts are in Met A, Γ, and E, and they have been the object of much dispute. See especially Owen III.44, and:

[17] G. Patzig: 'Theologie und Ontologie in der *Metaphysik* des Aristoteles', *Kantstudien* 52, 1960/1, 185–205 [English translation in Barnes, Schofield, Sorabji I.62]

Also:

[18] P. Merlan: *From Platonism to Neoplatonism* (The Hague, 1960²)

[19] A. Mansion: 'Philosophie première, philosophie seconde et métaphysique chez Aristote', *RPL* 56, 1958, 165–221

[20] H. Wagner: 'Zum Problem des aristotelischen Metaphysiksbegriff', *Philosophische Rundschau* 7, 1959, 129–48

[21] P. Merlan: '*On hêi on* and *prôtê ousia:* Postskript zu einer Besprechung', *Philosophische Rundschau* 7, 1959, 148–53

[22] L. Routila: *Die aristotelische Idee der ersten Philosophie*, Acta Philosophica Fennica 23 (Amsterdam, 1969)

[23] V. Decarie: *L'objet de la métaphysique chez Aristote* (Montreal/ Paris, 1961)

[24] K. Oehler: 'Die systematische Integration der aristotelischen Metaphysik', in Aubenque I.44

[25] M. Frede: 'The unity of general and special metaphysics: Aristotle's conception of metaphysics', in Frede I.83

and also Irwin III.197, chh.8–9.

On the name 'metaphysics' in its application to Aristotle's treatise see:

[26] H. Reiner: 'Die Entstehung und ursprungliche Bedeutung des Namens Metaphysik', *Zeitschrift für Philosophische Forschung* 9, 1955, 77–99.

[27] P. Merlan: 'Metaphysik: Name und Gegenstand', *JHS* 77, 1957, 87–92 = Hager I.65

[28] P. Merlan: 'On the terms "metaphysics" and "being-qua-being" ', *Monist* 52, 1968, 174–94

(C) The Law of Contradiction

The study of beings in general includes the study of at least some logical laws. For Aristotle's discussion of the Principle of Non-contradiction in Met Γ² see, in addition to Anscombe VII.16 and Kirwan VII.6:

[29] J. Łukasiewicz: 'On the principle of contradiction in Aristotle', *RM*

---

2. For Book B, which is an assembly of *aporiai*, see III (L).

Bibliography

95, 1971, 485–509 = BARNES, SCHOFIELD, SORABJI I.62 = MENNE and OFFENBERGER III.15

(30) R. M. DANCY: *Sense and Contradiction* (Dordrecht, 1975)
(31) B. CASSIN and M. NARCY: *La décision du sens – le livre* Gamma *de la Métaphysique d'Aristote* (Paris, 1989)
See also:
(32) I. HUSIK: 'Aristotle on the law of contradiction and the basis of the syllogism', in his *Philosophical Essays* (Oxford, 1952)
(33) J. BARNES: 'The law of contradiction', *PQ* 19, 1969, 302–9
(34) J.G. STEVENSON: 'Aristotle and the principle of contradiction as a law of thought', *Personalist* 56, 1975, 403–13
(35) H.W. NOONAN: 'An argument of Aristotle on non-contradiction', *An* 37, 1977, 163–69
(36) A. CODE: 'Metaphysics and logic', in MATTHEN I.58
(37) D.S. HUTCHINSON: 'L'épistémologie du principe de contradiction chez Aristote', *RPA* 6, 1988, 213–28
Aristotle's arguments in this context against relativism are examined by:
(38) A.J.P. KENNY: 'The argument from illusion in Aristotle's *Metaphysics*', *M* 76, 1967, 184–97
(39) M.C. SCHOLAR: 'Aristotle *Metaphysics* IV 1010b1–3', *M* 80, 1971, 266–68
(40) J.D.G. EVANS: 'Aristotle on relativism', *PQ* 24, 1974, 193–203
(41) F.C.T. MOORE: 'Evans off target', *PQ* 25, 1975, 58–69

(D) Truth
Met E contains some remarks on truth (see also the last chapter of Θ). Aristotle's views on truth are expounded and discussed in:
(42) F. BRENTANO: *The True and the Evident*, trans. R.M. CHISHOLM (London, 1966)
(43) P. WILPERT: 'Zum aristotelischen Wahrheitsbegriff', in HAGER I.66
(44) J.G. DEHNINGER: *'Wahres sein' in der Philosophie des Aristoteles* (Meisenheim, 1961)
(45) K.J.J. HINTIKKA: 'Time, truth, and knowledge in ancient Greek philosophy', *APQ* 4, 1967, 1–4 = HINTIKKA I.85
(46) M. MATTHEN: 'Greek ontology and the *is* of truth', *Phron* 28, 1983, 113–35
(47) C. IMBERT: 'La vérité d'Aristote et la vérité de Tarski', in J. BRUNSCHWIG, C. IMBERT, and A. ROGER (edd.), *Histoire et Structure: à la mémoire de V. Goldschmidt* (Paris, 1985)
(48) C.J.F. WILLIAMS: 'Aristotle and Copernican revolutions', *Phron* 36, 1991, 305–12

(E) Being
'Being', the subject-matter of metaphysics, is analysed in Γ, Δ and E. Beings are homonymous or 'said in many ways';[3] for a full exposition of Aristotle's views see:

3. On homonymy in general see III (C).

348   Bibliography

(49) F. BRENTANO: *On the Several Senses of Being in Aristotle*, trans. R. GEORGE (Berkeley, 1975)
There is an essay by:
(50) G.E.L. OWEN: 'Aristotle on the snares of ontology', in BAMBROUGH I.70 = OWEN 1.90
and a series of studies by Charles Kahn:
(51) C.H. KAHN: 'The Greek verb "to be" and the concept of being', *Foundations of Language* 2, 1966, 245–65
(52) C.H. KAHN: 'On the terminology for *copula* and *existence*', in STERN, HOURANI, and BROWN I.73
(53) C.H. KAHN: *The Verb Be in Ancient Greek* (Dordrecht, 1973)
(54) C.H. KAHN: 'On the theory of the verb "to be" ', in M. MUNITZ (ed.), *Logic and Ontology* (New York, 1974)
(55) C.H. KAHN: 'Why existence does not emerge as a distinct concept in Greek philosophy', *AGP* 58, 1976, 323–34
(56) C.H. KAHN: 'Retrospect on the verb "to be" and the concept of being', in KNUUTILLA and HINTIKKA I.81
See also:
(57) R. DANCY: 'Aristotle on existence', in KNUUTILLA and HINTIKKA I.81
(58) K.J.J. HINTIKKA: 'The varieties of being in Aristotle', in KNUUTILLA and HINTIKKA I.81
On some particular issues raised by *Met* Δ see:
(59) R.A. COBB: 'The present progressive periphrasis and the *Metaphysics* of Aristotle', *Phron* 18, 1973, 80–90
(60) R.K. SPRAGUE: 'Aristotelian periphrasis: a reply to Mr. Cobb', *Phron* 20, 1975, 75–76
(61) J.W. THORP: 'Aristotle's use of categories', *Phron* 19, 1974, 238–56
(62) J. KUNG: 'Aristotle on "being is said in many ways" ', *HPQ* 3, 1986, 3–18
Aristotle's doctrine that being is not a genus, and its relation to his view that "be" is homonymous, are discussed by:
(63) J. COOK WILSON: *Statement and Inference* (Oxford, 1926), vol. 2, 696–706
(64) M.J. LOUX: 'Aristotle on the transcendentals', *Phron* 18, 1973, 225–39
See also on related matters:
(65) D. MORRISON: 'The evidence for degrees of being in Aristotle', *CQ* 37, 1987, 382–401
(66) J.J. CLEARY: *Aristotle on the Many Senses of Priority* (Carbondale, 1988)

(F) Categories

The homonymy of being is partly exhibited by the distinction Aristotle draws among the ten 'categories' of being. On *Cat* see ACKRILL III.4, and the ancient commentaries:

Bibliography

Bibliography 349

(67) J. DILLON: *Dexippus: On Aristotle, Categories* (London, 1990)
(68) S.M. COHEN and G. B. MATTHEWS: *Ammonius: On Aristotle, Categories* (London, 1991)
(69) S.K. STRANGE: *Porphyry: On Aristotle, Categories* (London, 1992)
The authenticity of the work has been debated – see:
(70) I. HUSIK: 'The *Categories* of Aristotle' in his *Philosophical Essays* (Oxford, 1952)
(71) L.M. DE RIJK: 'The authenticity of Aristotle's *Categories*', Mn 4, 1951, 129–59
(72) L.M. DE RIJK: *The Place of the Categories of Being in Aristotle's Philosophy* (Assen, 1952)
(73) M. FREDE: 'Titel, Einheit und Echtheit der aristotelishen Kategorienschrift', in MORAUX and WIESNER I.47
The origin and general character of Aristotle's doctrine of categories have been widely debated. Two notable contributors are:
(74) F.A. TRENDLENBURG: *Geschichte der Kategorienlehre* (Hildesheim, 1846)
(75) H. BONITZ: *Über die Kategorien des Aristoteles* (Vienna, 1853)
See also:
(76) C.M. GILLESPIE: 'The Aristotelian *Categories*', CQ 19, 1925, 75–84 = HAGER I.66 = BARNES, SCHOFIELD, SORABJI I.62
(77) K. VON FRITZ: 'Der Ursprung der aristotelischen Kategorienlehre', AGP 40, 1931, 449–96 = HAGER I.66
(78) C.H. KAHN: 'Questions and categories', in H. HIZ (ed.), *Questions* (Dordrecht, 1978)
and MERLAN III.62.
The theory of categories inspired the influential thesis of:
(79) G. RYLE: 'Categories', in his *Collected Papers*, vol.2 (London, 1971)
For some of the philosophical issues see:
(80) J.M.E. MORAVCSIK: 'Aristotle's theory of categories', in MORAVSCIK I.61
(81) A. EDEL: 'Aristotle's *Categories* and the nature of categorial theory', RM 29, 1975, 45–65
(82) M. FREDE: 'Categories in Aristotle', in O'MEARA I.52 = FREDE I.83
and the papers in:
(83) P. AUBENQUE (ed.): *Concepts et catégories dans la pensée antique* (Paris, 1980)
On particular categories see:[4]
(84) D. O'BRIEN: 'Aristote et la catégorie de quantité', *Les études philosophiques* 1, 1978, 25–40
(85) M. MIGNUCCI: 'Aristotle's definition of relatives in *Cat.* 7', Phron 31, 1986, 101–27
On the treatment of categories in the *Topics* see:
(86) S. MANSION: 'Notes sur la doctrine des catégories dans les *Topiques*', OWEN I.41 = MANSION I.88

4. For the category of substance see below VII (G).

The character of individuals in categories other than substance was explored in:

(87) G.E.L. OWEN: 'Inherence', *Phron* 10, 1965, 97–105 = HAGER I.66 = OWEN I.90

an essay which has provoked a good deal of discussion:

(88) G.B. MATTHEWS and S. M. COHEN: 'The one and the many', *RM* 21, 1967/8, 630–55

(89) R.E. ALLEN: 'Individual properties in Aristotle's *Categories*', *Phron* 14, 1969, 31–9

(90) B. JONES: 'Individuals in Aristotle's *Categories*', *Phron* 17, 1972, 104–23

(91) J. ANNAS: 'Individuals in Aristotle's *Categories:* two queries', *Phron* 19, 1974, 146–52

(92) R. HEINAMAN: 'Non-substantial individuals in the *Categories*', *Phron* 26, 1981, 295–307

(93) M. FREDE: 'Individuals in Aristotle', in FREDE I.83

(94) G.B. MATTHEWS: 'The enigma of *Cat* 1a20ff and why it matters', *Apeiron* 22, 1989, 91–104

(95) D.T. DEVEREUX: 'Inherence and primary substance in Aristotle's *Categories*', *AP* 12, 1992, 113–31

(96) M.V. WEDIN: 'Non-substantial individuals', *Phron* 38, 1993, 37–65

(G) Substance

The first category, and the primary mode of being, is substance, for which *Met* Z and H are central. See the commentaries by BURNYEAT VII.8 and VII.9, and by FREDE and PATZIG VII.10. There is a collection of essays:

(97) M.L. O'HARA (ed.): *Substances and Things: Aristotle's Doctrine of Physical Substance in Recent Essays* (Washington, 1982)

and a number of recent books:

(98) M. L. GILL: *Aristotle on Substance* (Princeton, 1989)

(99) C. WITT: *Substance and Essence in Aristotle* (Ithaca, 1989)

(100) F.A. LEWIS: *Substance and Predication in Aristotle* (Cambridge, 1991)

(101) M.J. LOUX: *Primary Ousia: an Essay on Aristotle's Metaphysics Z and H* (Ithaca, 1991)

On the treatment of the notion of substance in *Cat* see:

(102) C.L. STOUGH: 'Language and ontology in Aristotle's *Categories*', *JHP* 10, 1972, 261–72

(103) R.E. ALLEN: 'Substance and predication in Aristotle's *Categories*', in LEE, MOURELATOS and RORTY I.74

(104) R.M. DANCY: 'On some of Aristotle's first thoughts about substances', *PR* 84, 1975, 338–73

(105) B. JONES: 'An introduction to the first five chapters of Aristotle's *Categories*', *Phron* 20, 1975, 146–72

(106) J. DRISCOLL: 'The Platonic ancestry of primary substance', *Phron* 24, 1979, 253–69

It is a question whether the ontology of *Cat* is the same as, or even consistent with, that of *Met*. See:

(107) D.W. GRAHAM: *Aristotle's Two Systems* (Oxford, 1987)

On substance in *Met* see, besides many of the studies mentioned in the following three sections:

(108) E.D. HARTER: 'Aristotle on primary *ousia*', AGP 57, 1975, 1–20

(109) M. FURTH: 'Transtemporal stability in Aristotelian substances', *JP* 75, 1978, 624–46

(110) G.E.L. OWEN: 'Particular and general', PAS 99, 1978/9, 1–21 = OWEN I.90

(111) M. FREDE: 'Substance in Aristotle's *Metaphysics*', in GOTTHELF I.56 = FREDE I.83

(112) L.A. KOSMAN: 'Substance, being, and *energeia*', OSAP 2, 1984, 121–49

(113) M.L. GILL: 'Aristotle on matters of life and death', BACAP 4, 1988, 187–205

(114) M. FREDE: 'The definition of sensible substances in *Metaphysics* Z', in DEVEREUX and PELLEGRIN I.59

and IRWIN III.197, chh.4, 10.

(H) Essence

Substances can be defined, and definitions state their essences.[5] Aristotle elaborates his conception of essence in *Met* Z, 4–6 and 10–12. There is a useful philological monograph:

(115) C. ARPE: *Das ti ên einai bei Aristoteles* (Hamburg, 1938)

Among the numerous philosophical discussions see SORABJI IV.72, part IV, WITT VII.99, and:

(116) I.M. COPI: 'Essence and accident', *JP* 51, 1954, 706–19

(117) C.A. KIRWAN: 'How strong are the objections to essence?', PAS 71, 1970/1, 43–59

(118) M.J. CRESSWELL: 'Essence and existence in Plato and Aristotle', Theoria 37, 1971, 91–113

(119) N.P. WHITE: 'Origins of Aristotle's essentialism', RM 26, 1972/3, 57–85

(120) B. BRODY: 'Why settle for anything less than good, old-fashioned Aristotelian essentialism?', Nous 7, 1973, 351–65

(121) M.J. WOODS: 'Substance and essence in Aristotle', PAS 75, 1974/5, 167–80

(122) M. DURRANT: 'Essence and accident', M 84, 1975, 595–600

(123) J. KUNG: 'Aristotle on essence and explanation', PhSt 31, 1977, 361–83

(124) S.M. COHEN: 'Essentialism in Aristotle', RM 31, 1977/8, 387–405

(125) A.C. LLOYD: 'Necessity and essence in the *Posterior Analytics*', in BERTI I.46

5. On definition see III (N).

[126] C. Witt: 'Aristotelian essentialism revisited', *JHP* 27, 1989, 285–98
[127] G.B. Matthews: 'Aristotelian essentialism', *PPR* 51, 1990, 251–62
For essence in the biological works see:
[128] D.M. Balme: 'Aristotle's biology was not essentialist', *AGP* 62, 1980, 1–12 = Gotthelf and Lennox V.72
[129] A. Gotthelf: 'Notes towards a study of substance and essence in Aristotle's *Parts of Animals* ii–iv', in Gotthelf I.56

(I) Form
Substances are composed of matter and form, *hulê* and *eidos*.[6] On the notion of form see:
[130] G. Patzig: 'Bemerkungen über den Begriff der Form', *Archiv für Philosophie* 9, 1959, 93–111
[131] E.S. Haring: 'Substantial form in Aristotle's *Metaphysics* Z 1', *RM* 10, 1956–57, 308–32, 482–501, 698–713
[132] D.C. Williams: 'Form and matter', *PR* 67, 1958, 291–312, 499–521
[133] D.W. Hamlyn: 'Aristotle on form', in Gotthelf I.56
[134] C. Witt: 'Form, reproduction, and inherited characteristics in Aristotle's *de Generatione Animalium*', *Phron* 30, 1985, 46–57
[135] C. Witt: 'Hylomorphism in Aristotle', *JP* 84, 1987, 673–79
The following items concentrate on the relation of the ideas of form and substance to that of universal:
[136] J.A. Smith: '*Tode ti* in Aristotle', *CR* 35, 1921, 19
[137] A.R. Lacey: '*Ousia* and form in Aristotle', *Phron* 10, 1965, 54–69
[138] M.J. Woods: 'Problems in *Metaphysics* Z, chapter 13', in Moravcsik I.61
[139] J.H. Lesher: 'Aristotle on form, substance, and universals: a dilemma', *Phron* 16, 1971, 169–78
[140] R.D. Sykes: 'Form in Aristotle', *Phil* 50, 1975, 311–31
[141] A. Code: 'No universal is a substance: an interpretation of *Metaphysics* Z 13, 1038b8–15', *Paideia* 7, 1978, 65–74
[142] M.J. Loux: 'Form, species, and predication in *Metaphysics* Z, H, and Θ', *M* 88, 1979, 1–23
[143] A.C. Lloyd: *Form and Universal in Aristotle* (Liverpool, 1981)
[144] F. Lewis: 'Form and predication in Aristotle's *Metaphysics*', in Bogen and McQuire I.76
[145] M. Furth: 'Aristotle on the unity of form', *BACAP* 2, 1987, 209–36
[146] M.J. Woods: 'Form, species, and predication in Aristotle', *Synthèse* 96, 1993, 399–415
See also:
[147] G. Fine: 'Plato and Aristotle on form and substance', *PCPS* 29, 1983, 23–47
[148] C. Shields: 'The generation of form in Aristotle', *HPQ* 7, 1990, 367–90

6. Note also several of the items in VI (B) and (C).

(J) Matter

A massive discussion of Aristotle's concept of matter is offered by:

(149) H. HAPP: *Hyle: Studien zum aristotelischen Materie Begriff* (Berlin, 1971)

An older, classic discussion is by:

(150) C. BAEUMKER: *Das Problem der Materie in der griechischen Philosophie* (Munster, 1890)

On the word '*hulê*' see:

(151) F. SOLMSEN: 'Aristotle's word for "matter" ', in SOLMSEN I.92

There is a collection of essays:

(152) E. McMULLIN (ed.): *The Concept of Matter in Greek and Medieval Philosophy* (Notre Dame, 1963)

Various aspects of Aristotle's thoughts about matter are discussed by:[7]

(153) R. RORTY: 'Genus as matter', in LEE, MOURELATOS, and RORTY I.74

(154) V. CHAPPELL: 'Aristotle's conception of matter', *JP* 70, 1973, 679–96

(155) P. SUPPES: 'Aristotle's conception of matter and its relation to modern concepts of matter', *Synthèse* 28, 1974, 27–50

(156) M. GRENE: 'Is genus to species as matter to form?', *Synthèse* 28, 1974, 51–69

(157) M.J. WHITE: 'Genos as matter in Aristotle?', *International Studies in Philosophy* 7, 1975, 41–56

(158) F.D. MILLER: 'Aristotle's use of matter', *Paideia* 7, 1978, 105–19

(159) S. MANSION: 'La notion de la matière en *Métaphysique*, Z 10–11', in AUBENQUE I.44 = MANSION I.88

(160) J. BRUNSCHWIG: 'La forme, prédicat de la matière?', in AUBENQUE I.44

(161) J. KUNG: 'Can substance be predicted of matter?', *AGP* 60, 1978, 140–59

(162) S.M. COHEN: 'Aristotle's doctrine of material substrate', *PR* 93, 1984, 171–94

(163) D.W. GRAHAM: 'Aristotle's discovery of matter', *AGP* 66, 1984, 37–51

(164) C. PAGE: 'Predicating forms of matter in Aristotle's *Metaphysics*', *RM* 39, 1985, 57–82

(165) K.C. COOK: 'The underlying thing, the underlying nature, and matter', *Apeiron* 22, 1989, 105–19

The question whether Aristotle believed in 'prime matter', a single ultimate substratum of all change, has been much debated. The primary texts are *Met* Z 3 and *GC*. See:

(166) H.R. KING: 'Aristotle without *prima materia*', *JHI* 17, 1956, 370–89

(167) F. SOLMSEN: 'Aristotle and prime matter', *JHI* 19, 1958, 243–52 = SOLMSEN I.92

And then CHARLTON, in an appendix to IV.7 entitled 'Did Aristotle Believe in Prime Matter?', and:

7. See also IV (C), on change.

(168) H.M. Robinson: 'Prime matter in Aristotle', *Phron* 19, 1974, 168–88

(169) W. Charlton: 'Prime matter: a rejoinder', *Phron* 28, 1983, 197–211

(170) D. Graham: 'The paradox of prime matter', *JHP* 25, 1987, 475–90

See also:

(171) M. Schofield: '*Metaph*. Z 3: some suggestions', *Phron* 17, 1972, 97–101

(172) D. Stahl: 'Stripped away: some contemporary obscurities surrounding *Metaphysics* Z 3 (1029a10–26)', *Phron* 26, 1981, 177–80

Some philosophical assessments of the concept of matter may be found in:

(173) M. MacDonald: 'The philosopher's use of analogy', in A. Flew (ed.), *Logic and Language* (1st series) (Oxford, 1952)

(174) V. Chappell: 'Stuff and things', *PAS* 71, 1970–71, 61–76

(175) H.M. Cartwright: 'Chappell on stuff and things', *Nous* 6, 1972, 369–77

(176) K. Fine: 'Aristotle on matter', *M* 101, 1992, 35–57

(K) Individuation

The question whether it is matter or form which constitutes Aristotle's principle of individuation has been much discussed. See:

(177) J. Łukasiewicz, G. E. M. Anscombe, and K. Popper: 'The principle of individuation', *PASS* 27, 1953, 69–120 = Barnes, Schofield, Sorabji I.62

(178) A.C. Lloyd: 'Aristotle's principle of individuation', *M* 69, 1970, 519–29

(179) W. Charlton: 'Aristotle and the principle of individuation', *Phron* 17, 1972, 239–49

(180) E. Regis: 'Aristotle's principle of individuation', *Phron* 21, 1976, 157–66

The discussion has turned primarily around the problem of whether or not Aristotle countenances 'individual forms'. On this see Frede and Patzig VII.10, and:

(181) W. Sellars: 'Substance and form in Aristotle', *JP* 54, 1957, 688–99

(182) R. Albritton: 'Forms of particular substances in Aristotle's *Metaphysics*', *JP* 54, 1957, 699–708

(183) S.M. Cohen: 'Individual and essence in Aristotle's *Metaphysics*', *Paideia* 7, 1978, 75–85

(184) R. Burger: 'Is each thing the same as its essence?', *RM* 41, 1987/8, 53–76

(185) M. Furth: 'Specific and individual form in Aristotle', in Devereux and Pellegrin I.59

(186) M.J. Woods: 'Particular forms revisited', *Phron* 26, 1991, 75–87

(187) M.J. Woods: Universals and particular forms in Aristotle's *Metaphysics*', *OSAP* suppt. 1991, 41–56

(188) M.V. Wedin: 'Partisanship in *Metaphysics Z*', *AP* 11, 1991, 361–85

(L) Identity

Book Θ discusses actuality and potentiality: reading on these topics is given indirectly in III (G), VII (H), and VIII (N). Book I deals with 'oneness' – unity and identity. Aristotle's thoughts about identity have been examined by:

(189) N. WHITE: 'Aristotle on sameness and oneness', PR 80, 1971, 177–97

(190) F.D. MILLER: 'Did Aristotle have a concept of identity?', PR 82, 1973, 483–90

(191) J.M.E. MORAVCSIK: 'The discernibility of identicals', JP 73, 1976, 587–98

(192) F.J. PELLETIER: 'Sameness and referential opacity in Aristotle', Nous 13, 1979, 283–311

(193) G.B. MATTHEWS: 'Accidental unities', in SCHOFIELD and NUSSBAUM I.76

(194) F.A. LEWIS: 'Accidental sameness in Aristotle', PhSt 42, 1985, 1–36

(195) N. WHITE: 'Identity, modal individuation, and matter in Aristotle', Mid-West Studies in Philosophy 11, 1986, 475–94

(196) M. MIGNUCCI: 'Puzzles about identity', in WIESNER I.57

See also:

(197) C.J.F. WILLIAMS: 'Aristotle's theory of descriptions', PR 94, 1985, 63–80

(198) L. SPELLMAN: 'Referential opacity in Aristotle', HPQ 7, 1990, 17–31

(M) Theology

Just as substance is primary among the categories, so divine beings are primary among substances (see especially PATZIG IV.17). Book Λ contains Aristotle's theological reflexions. See:

(199) W.J. VERDENIUS: 'Traditional and personal elements in Aristotle's religion', Phron 5, 1960, 56–70

(200) H.J. KRÄMER: Der Ursprung der Geistmetaphysik (Amsterdam, 1967)

(201) H.J. KRÄMER: 'Grundfragen der aristotelischen Theologie', Theologie und Philosophie 44, 1969, 363–82, 481–505

(202) J. VUILLEMIN: De la logique à la théologie (Paris, 1967)

with the review by:

(203) J. BRUNSCHWIG: 'Le Dieu d'Aristote au tribunal de la logique', L'âge de la science 3, 1972, 323–43

The divine entities are 'unmoved movers'. Aristotle's arguments for unmoved movers, in Λ and also in the last books of Phys, have been examined by:

(204) P. MERLAN: 'Aristotle's unmoved movers', Traditio 4, 1946, 1–30

(205) P. MERLAN: Studies in Epicurus and Aristotle (Wiesbaden, 1960), ch. 3

(206) K. OEHLER: 'Der Beweis für den Unbewegten Beweger bei Aristoteles', Phg 99, 1955, 70–92

356   Bibliography

(207) H.J. EASTERLING: 'The unmoved mover in early Aristotle', *Phron* 16, 1970, 252–65
(208) H.S. LANG: 'God or soul: the problem of the first mover in *Physics* VII', *Paideia* 7, 1978, 86–104
(209) H.S. LANG: 'Aristotle's immaterial mover and the problem of location in *Physics* VIII', *RM* 35, 1981/2, 321–35
(210) A. KOSMAN: 'Divine being and divine thinking in *Metaphysics* Lambda', *BACAP* 3, 1987, 165–88
(211) J.L. ACKRILL: 'Change and Aristotle's theological argument', *OSAP* suppt. 1991, 57–66
(212) M.L. GILL: 'Aristotle on self-motion', in JUDSON IV.15
See also:
(213) D. FREDE: 'Theophrasts Kritik am unbewegten Beweger des Aristoteles', *Phron* 16, 1970, 65–79
(214) D.T. DEVEREUX: 'The relationship between Theophrastus' *Metaphysics* and Aristotle's *Metaphysics Lambda*', in FORTENBAUGH and SHARPLES I.82

(N) Philosophy of Mathematics
Aristotle's philosophy of mathematics is mostly contained in *Met* M and N, on which see ANNAS VII.7. On 'abstraction' see:
(215) M.D. PHILIPPE: 'Abstraction, addition, séparation chez Aristote', *Revue Thomiste* 48, 1948, 461–79
(216) J. CLEARY: 'On the terminology of abstraction in Aristotle', *Phron* 30, 1985, 13–45
More specifically on the nature of mathematical objects:
(217) I. MUELLER: 'Aristotle on geometrical objects', *AGP* 52, 1970, 156–71 = BARNES, SCHOFIELD, SORABJI I.62
(218) S. GAUKROGER: 'Aristotle on intelligible matter', *Phron* 25, 1980, 187–97
(219) J. ANNAS: 'Die Gegenstände der Mathematik bei Aristoteles', in GRAESER I.48
(220) I. MUELLER: 'Aristotle's approach to the problem of principles in *Met* M and N', in GRAESER I.48
(221) E. HUSSEY: 'Aristotle on mathematical objects', in I. MUELLER (ed.) *PERI TΩN MAΘHMATΩN* (Edmonton, 1991)
(222) M.J. WHITE: 'The metaphysical location of Aristotle's *mathêmatika*', *Phron* 38, 1993, 166–82
And on the philosophy of mathematics in general, as well as LEAR IV.118:
(223) J. LEAR: 'Aristotle's philosophy of mathematics', *PR* 91, 1982, 161–92
(224) J. BARNES: 'Aristotle's arithmetic', *RPA* 3, 1985, 97–133
(225) M. MIGNUCCI: 'Aristotelian arithmetic', in GRAESER I.48
On the Platonic background see ANNAS VII.7 and:
(226) J. COOK WILSON: 'On the Platonist doctrine of the *asumblêtoi arithmoi*', *CR* 18, 1904, 247–60

(227) M.F. BURNYEAT: 'Platonism and mathematics: a prelude to discussion', in GRAESER I.48

VIII ETHICS

(A) General
The fullest and in many respects the most helpful commentary on *NE* is in French:
(1) R.A. GAUTHIER and J.Y. JOLIF: *Aristote: l'Ethique à Nicomaque* (Louvain, 1970)
English readers will find much of value in three older commentaries:
(2) A. GRANT: *The Ethics of Aristotle* (London, 1885)
(3) J.A. STEWART: *Notes on the Nicomachean Ethics of Aristotle* (Oxford, 1892)
(4) J. BURNET: *The Ethics of Aristotle* (London, 1900)
See also:
(5) H.H. JOACHIM: *Aristotle: The Nicomachean Ethics* (Oxford, 1955)
and the notes to:
(6) J.L. ACKRILL: *Aristotle's Ethics* (London, 1973)
(7) T.H. IRWIN: *Aristotle's Ethica Nicomachea* (Indianapolis, 1986)
There is a German commentary by:
(8) F. DIRLMEIER: *Aristoteles: Nikomachische Ethik* (Berlin, 1966)
Four commentaries on individual books are: RODIER VIII.121; JACKSON, VIII.156; GREENWOOD VIII.240; FESTUGIERE VIII.270.
On *EE* see, in addition to BURNET VIII.4, the Clarendon volume:
(9) M.J. WOODS: *Aristotle's Eudemian Ethics Books I, II and VIII* (Oxford, 1992²)
and:
(10) F. DIRLMEIER: *Aristoteles: Eudemische Ethik* (Berlin, 1962)
Note also:
(11) D. HARLFINGER: 'Die Ueberlieferungsgeschichte der Eudemischen Ethik', in MORAUX I.43
On *MM* see:
(12) F. DIRLMEIER: *Aristoteles: Magna Moralia* (Berlin, 1968)
In his commentary, Dirlmeier defends the authenticity of the work, as does:
(13) J.M. COOPER: 'The *Magna Moralia* and Aristotle's moral philosophy', *AJP* 94, 1973, 327–49 = MÜLLER-GOLDINGEN VIII.39
The opposite view is argued for by:
(14) F. DIRLMEIER: 'Die Zeit der "Grossen Ethik" ', *RhM* 88, 1939, 214–43 = MÜLLER-GOLDINGEN VIII.39
(15) D.J. ALLAN: '*Magna Moralia* and *Nicomachean Ethics*', *JHS* 77, 1957, 7–11
(16) C.J. ROWE: 'Reply to John Cooper on the *Magna Moralia*', *AJP* 96, 1975, 160–72 = MÜLLER-GOLDINGEN VIII.39
A helpful companion to *NE* is provided by:
(17) W.F.R. HARDIE: *Aristotle's Ethical Theory* (Oxford, 1980²)

358   Bibliography

There are short introductions in:
(18) R.A. GAUTHIER: *La morale d'Aristote* (Paris, 1963)
(19) J.O. URMSON: *Aristotle's Ethics* (Oxford, 1987)
Among general studies of Aristotle's ethical theories, consult:
(20) R.W. SHARPLES: *Alexander of Aphrodisias: Ethical Problems* (London, 1990)
(21) M. WITTMANN: *Die Ethik des Aristoteles* (Regensburg, 1921)
(22) R. STARK: *Aristotelesstudien* (Munich, 1972²)
(23) J.M. COOPER: *Reason and Human Good in Aristotle* (Cambridge, Mass., 1975)
(24) T. ENGBERG-PEDERSEN: *Aristotle's Theory of Moral Insight* (Oxford, 1983)
(25) N. SHERMAN: *The Fabric of Character* (Oxford, 1988)
(26) R. KRAUT: *Aristotle on the Human Good* (Princeton, 1989)
(27) S. BROADIE: *Ethics with Aristotle* (New York, 1991)
See also:
(28) J. BARNES: introduction to *Aristotle: Nicomachean Ethics* (Harmondsworth, 1976)
(29) T.H. IRWIN: 'Aristotle's conception of morality', *BACAP* 1, 1985, 115–44
and the relevant sections of:
(30) J. ANNAS: *The Morality of Happiness* (New York, 1993)
For some historical background:
(31) K.J. DOVER: *Greek Popular Morality at the Time of Plato and Aristotle* (Oxford, 1974)
On the development of Aristotle's thought in ethics see:
(32) H. FLASHAR: 'The critique of Plato's theory of Ideas in Aristotle's *Ethics*', in BARNES, SCHOFIELD, SORABJI I.62 = MÜLLER-GOLDINGEN VIII.39
(33) C.J. ROWE: *The Eudemian and Nicomachean Ethics – a study in the development of Aristotle's thought* (Cambridge, 1971)
(34) A. VON FRAGSTEIN: *Studien zur Ethik des Aristoteles* (Amsterdam, 1974)
(35) A.J.P. KENNY: *The Aristotelian Ethics* (Oxford, 1978)
There are collections of papers in MORAUX I.43; vol.2 of BARNES, SCHOFIELD, SORABJI I.62; HAGER I.67; and:
(36) J.J. WALSH and H. L. SHAPIRO: *Aristotle's Ethics* (Belmont, Ca., 1967)
(37) A.O. RORTY (ed.): *Essays on Aristotle's Ethics* (Berkeley, 1980)
(38) S. PANAGIOTOU (ed.): *Justice, Law, and Method in Plato and Aristotle* (Edmonton, 1987)
(39) C. MÜLLER-GOLDINGEN: *Schriften zur aristotelischen Ethik* (Hildesheim, 1988)
(40) A. ALBERTI (ed.): *Studi sull'etica di Aristotele* (Naples, 1990)
(41) J.P. ANTON and A. PREUS (edd.): *Aristotle's Ethics: Essays in Ancient Greek Philosophy* 5 (Albany, 1991)

(B) Method in Ethics
There are scattered reflections on method in *NE* A and H and in *EE* A. On
Aristotle's method in ethics see OWEN III.193, and:
(42) W.W. JAEGER: 'Aristotle's use of medicine as a model of method in
his ethics', *JHS* 77, 1957, 54–61 = MÜLLER-GOLDINGEN VIII.39
(43) D.J. ALLAN: 'Quasi-mathematical method in the *Eudemian Ethics*',
in MANSION I.40 = MÜLLER-GOLDINGEN VIII.39
(44) G.E.R. LLOYD: 'The role of medical and biological analogies in Aristotle's ethics', *Phron* 13, 1968, 68–83 = MÜLLER-GOLDINGEN VIII.39
(45) J.D. MONAN: *Moral Knowledge and its Methodology in Aristotle*
(Oxford, 1968)
(46) T.H. IRWIN: 'Aristotle's method in ethics', in O'MEARA I.52
(47) T.H. IRWIN: 'First principles in Aristotle's *Ethics*', *Mid-West Studies
in Philosophy* 3, 1978, 252–72
(48) J. BARNES: 'Aristotle and the methods of ethics', *RIP* 34, 1980, 490–
511 = MÜLLER-GOLDINGEN VIII.39
(49) T.H. IRWIN: 'The metaphysical and psychological basis of Aristotle's
Ethics', in RORTY VIII.37
(50) T.D. ROCHE: 'On the alleged metaphysical foundation of Aristotle's
Ethics', *AP* 8, 1988, 49–62
(51) S. KLEIN: 'An analysis and defence of Aristotle's method in *Nicomachean Ethics* I and X', *AP* 8, 1988, 63–72
(52) E. BERTI: 'Il metodo della filosofia pratica secondo Aristotele', in
ALBERTI VIII.40
(53) R. BOLTON: 'The objectivity of ethics', in ANTON and PREUS VIII.41
(54) S. KLEIN: 'The value of *endoxa* in ethical argument', *HPQ* 9, 1992,
141–57
(55) T.D. ROCHE: 'In defence of an alternative view of the foundation of
Aristotle's moral theory', *Phron* 37, 1992, 46–84
(56) J.E. BARRETT: 'The moral status of "the many" in Aristotle', *JHP* 31,
1993, 171–90

(C) Moral Epistemology
Aristotle has no sustained discussion of the nature of moral knowledge,
but his works provide scattered evidence for a view, or a set of views. They
are discussed by ENGBERG-PEDERSON VIII.24, MONAN VIII.45, and:
(57) E.H. OLMSTED: 'The "moral sense" aspect of Aristotle's ethical
theory', *AJP* 69, 1948, 42–61 = MÜLLER-GOLDINGEN VIII.39
(58) W.W. FORTENBAUGH: 'Aristotle's conception of moral virtue and its
perceptive role', *TAPA* 95, 1964, 77–87
(59) M.J. WOODS: 'Intuition and perception in Aristotle's *Ethics*', *OSAP*
4, 1986, 145–66
(60) R.B. LOUDEN: 'Aristotle's practical particularism', *AP* 6, 1986, 123–
38 = ANTON and PREUS VIII.41
(61) R. HURSTHOUSE: 'Moral habituation', *OSAP* 6, 1988, 201–19

(62) C.D.C. REEVE: *Practices of Reason* (Oxford, 1992)

(63) R.J. HANKINSON: 'Perception and maturation: Aristotle on the moral imagination', *Dialogue* 29, 1990, 41–63

(D) Goodness

Aristotle's criticisms of Plato's Form of the Good and his own remarks about the different ways in which things are called good (*NE* A and *EE* A) have occasioned a quantity of comment. See FLASHAR VIII.32, and:

(64) D.J. ALLAN: 'Aristotle's criticism of Platonic doctrine concerning goodness and the good', *PAS* 64, 1963/4, 273–86

(65) W.W. FORTENBAUGH: '*Nicomachean Ethics* I, 1096b26–9', *Phron* 11, 1966, 185–94

(66) A. KOSMAN: 'Predicating the good', *Phron* 13, 1968, 171–74

(67) D. WIGGINS: 'Sentence-sense, word-sense, and difference of word-sense', in D.D. STEINBERG and L.A. JACOBOVITS (edd.), *Semantics* (Cambridge, 1971)

(68) J.L. ACKRILL: 'Aristotle on "good" and the categories', in STERN, HOURANI, and BROWN I.73 = BARNES, SCHOFIELD, SORABJI I.62

and OWEN III.44, BERTI III.47. Note also the items in II (B).

Aristotle's account of 'the good for man' is based upon his notion of man's *ergon* or 'function'. See:

(69) P. GLASSEN: 'A fallacy in Aristotle's argument about the good', *PQ* 7, 1957, 319–22

(70) R. SORABJI: 'Function', *PQ* 14, 1964, 289–302

(71) W.F.R. HARDIE: 'The final good in Aristotle's *Ethics*', *Phil* 40, 1965, 277–95

(72) J.M. RIST: 'Aristotle: the value of man and the origin of morality', *CJP* 4, 1974, 1–21

(73) B. SUITS: 'Aristotle on the function of man', *CJP* 4, 1974, 23–40

(74) W.F.R. HARDIE: 'Aristotle on the best life for man', *Phil* 54, 1979, 35–50

(75) K.V. WILKES: 'The good man and the good for man in Aristotle's *Ethics*', *M* 87, 1978, 553–71 = RORTY VIII.37

(76) R. KRAUT: 'The peculiar function of human beings', *CJP* 9, 1979, 53–62

(77) M. WEDIN: 'Aristotle on the good for man', *M* 90, 1981, 243–62

(78) C.M. KORSGAARD: 'Aristotle on function and virtue', *HPQ* 3, 1986, 259–79

(79) J.E. WHITING: 'Aristotle's function argument: a defence', *AP* 8, 1988, 33–48

(80) A. GOMEZ-LOBO: 'The *ergon* inference', *Phron* 34, 1989, 170–84 = ANTON and PREUS VIII.41

(81) D. ACHTENBERG: 'The rôle of the *ergon* argument in Aristotle's *Nicomachean Ethics*', *AP* 9, 1989, 37–47 = ANTON and PREUS VIII.41

There are analyses of Aristotle's conception of goodness by:

(82) B.A.O. WILLIAMS: 'Aristotle on the good – a formal sketch', *PQ* 12, 1962, 289–96

(83) C.A. KIRWAN: 'Logic and the good in Aristotle', *PQ* 17, 1967, 97–114
(84) S. MacDONALD: 'Aristotle and the homonymy of the good', *AGP* 71, 1989, 150–74
(85) H. RICHARDSON: 'Degrees of finality and the highest good in Aristotle', *JHP* 30, 1992, 327–52
(86) M. PAKULUK: 'Friendship and the comparison of goods', *Phron* 37, 1992, 111–30
See also:
(87) D.J. ALLAN: 'The fine and the good in the *Eudemian Ethics*', in MORAUX I.43
For some philosophical discussion of the issues behind Aristotle's position see:
(88) P.T. GEACH: 'Good and evil', *An* 17, 1956/7, 30–42
(89) R.M. HARE: 'Geach, good and evil', *An* 17, 1956/7, 101–11
(90) A.M. MacIVER: 'Good and evil and Mr Geach', *An* 18, 1957/8, 7–13
(91) S. HAMPSHIRE: 'Ethics – a defence of Aristotle', in his *Freedom of Mind* (Oxford, 1972)
(92) C.R. PIDGEN: 'Geach on "good" ', *PQ* 40, 1990, 129–54
and chapter 5 of:
(93) G.H. VON WRIGHT: *The Varieties of Goodness* (London, 1963)

(E) Happiness

Eudaimonia, or 'happiness',[1] is the good for man, and most of the items listed in the previous section perforce touch upon *eudaimonia*. See in general:

(94) J. LEONARD: *Le bonheur chez Aristote* (Brussels, 1948)
(95) A.J.P. KENNY: *Aristotle on the Perfect Life* (Oxford, 1992)
For the relation between happiness and goodness (*NE* A, *EE* A), see also:
(96) H.A. PRICHARD: 'The meaning of *agathon* in the *Ethics* of Aristotle', in MORAVCSIK I.61
(98) F.A. SIEGLER: 'Reason, happiness, and goodness', in WALSH and SHAPIRO VIII.36
(99) T. NAGEL: 'Aristotle on *eudaimonia*', *Phron* 17, 1972, 252–59 = RORTY VIII.37
(100) J. McDOWELL: 'The role of *eudaimonia* in Aristotle's *Ethics*', in RORTY VIII.37
Happiness is said to be complete or perfect, and self-sufficient. For reflection on this see:
(101) G. MÜLLER: 'Probleme der aristotelischen Eudaimonielehre', *MH* 17, 1960, 121–43
(102) A.J.P. KENNY: 'Happiness', *PAS* 66, 1965/6, 93–102 = BARNES, SCHOFIELD, SORABJI I.62

1. This is the standard translation, but it is in some ways misleading – some scholars prefer to speak of 'flourishing' or 'success'.

(103) R. HEINAMAN: 'Eudaimonia and self-sufficiency in the Nicomachean Ethics', Phron 33, 1988, 31–53
(104) G. SANTAS: 'Desire and perfection in Aristotle's theory of the good', Apeiron 22, 1989, 75–99
(105) H.J. CURZER: 'Criteria for happiness in Nicomachean Ethics I 7 and X 6–8', CQ 40, 1990, 421–32
(106) H.J. CURZER: 'The supremely happy life in Aristotle's Nicomachean Ethics', Apeiron 24, 1991, 47–69
(107) A.J.P. KENNY: 'The Nicomachean conception of happiness', OSAP suppt. 1991, 67–80
(108) P. STEMMER: 'Aristoteles' Glucksbegriff in der Nikomachischen Ethik: eine Interpretation von EN I 7, 1097b2–5', Phron 37, 1992, 85–110
(109) C.A. KIRWAN: 'Two Aristotelian theses about eudaimonia', in ALBERTI VIII.40
(110) R. HEINAMAN: 'Rationality, eudaimonia and kakodaimonia in Aristotle', Phron 38, 1993, 31–56
And on the related issue of 'moral luck':
(111) J.M. COOPER: 'Aristotle on the goods of fortune', PR 94, 1985, 173–96
(112) M. NUSSBAUM: The Fragility of Goodness (Cambridge, 1986)
(113) S. BOTROS: 'Precarious virtue', Phron 32, 1987, 101–31
(114) A.J.P. KENNY: The Heritage of Wisdom (Oxford, 1987), ch.1
(115) S.A. WHITE: Sovereign Virtue (Stanford, 1992)
Happiness is discussed both in NE A and in NE K.[2] The accounts in the two books have often been thought to be inconsistent with one another. See:
(116) J.L. ACKRILL: 'Aristotle on eudaimonia', PBA 60, 1974, 339–60 = RORTY VIII.37 = MÜLLER-GOLDINGEN I.39
(117) D. KEYT: 'Intellectualism in Aristotle', Paideia 7, 1978, 138–57
(118) R. KRAUT: 'Two conceptions of happiness', PR 88, 1979, 167–97
(119) J.E. WHITING: 'Human nature and intellectualism in Aristotle', AGP 68, 1986, 70–95
(120) D. KEYT: 'The meaning of BIOS in Aristotle's Ethics and Politics', AP 9, 1989, 15–21
On theôria or 'contemplation' and the substantive account of happiness in NE K and EE Θ, see:
(121) G. RODIER: Aristote: Ethique à Nicomaque, livre X (Paris, 1897)
(122) M. DEFOURNY: 'L'activité de contemplation dans les morales d'Aristote', in BARNES, SCHOFIELD, SORABJI I.62 = HAGER I.67
(123) P. MORAUX: 'Das fragment VIII.1 – Text und Interpretation', in MORAUX I.43
(124) W.J. VERDENIUS: 'Human reason and god in the Eudemian Ethics', in MORAUX I.43
(125) T.B. ERIKSEN: Bios Theôrêtikos (New York, 1977)

2. And also, of course, in EE A and Θ.

(126) A.O. RORTY: 'The place of contemplation in Aristotle's *Nicomachean Ethics'*, *M* 87, 1978, 343–58 = RORTY VIII.37 = MÜLLER-GOLDINGEN VIII.39

(127) A.W.H. ADKINS: *'Theôria* versus *praxis* in the Nicomachean Ethics and the Republic', *CP* 73, 1978, 297–313 = MÜLLER-GOLDINGEN VIII.39

(128) J.M. COOPER: 'Contemplation and happiness: a reconsideration', *Synthèse* 72, 1987, 187–216

(F) Moral Virtue
Virtue, *aretê*, enters into the account of what happiness is, and it is discussed in *NE* B and *EE* B. See generally:

(128) D.S. HUTCHINSON: *The Virtues of Aristotle* (London, 1986)

and IRWIN III.197, chh.17 and 21.

Aristotle's celebrated doctrine that moral virtue is a 'mean' is discussed in detail by:

(130) H.B.W. JOSEPH: *Essays in Ancient and Modern Philosophy* (Oxford, 1935)

(131) W.F.R. HARDIE: 'Aristotle's doctrine that virtue is a mean', *PAS* 66, 1964/5, 183–204 = BARNES, SCHOFIELD, and SORABJI I.62

(132) W.W. FORTENBAUGH: 'Aristotle and the questionable mean-dispositions', *TAPA* 99, 1968, 203–31

(133) J.O. URMSON: 'Aristotle's doctrine of the mean', *APQ* 10, 1973, 223–30 = RORTY VIII.37

(134) R. HURSTHOUSE: 'A false doctrine of the mean', *PAS* 81, 1981, 57–72

(135) S. PETERSON: ' "Horos" (limit) in Aristotle's *Nicomachean Ethics'*, *Phron* 33, 1988, 233–50

(136) U. WOLF: 'Über den Sinn der aristotelischen Mesonlehre', *Phron* 33, 1988, 54–75

On the 'unity' of the virtues see:

(137) T.H. IRWIN: 'Disunity in the Aristotelian virtues', *OSAP* suppt. 1988, 61–78

(138) E. TELFER: 'The unity of moral virtues in Aristotle's *Nicomachean Ethics'*, *PAS* 91, 1989/90, 35–48

On the historical background to the doctrine of the mean, see JAEGER, II.1, and:

(139) F. WEHRLI: 'Ethik und Medizin: zur Vorgeschichte der aristotelischen Mesonlehre', *MH* 8, 1951, 36–62

(140) H.J. KRÄMER: *Aretê bei Platon und Aristoteles* (Heidelberg, 1959), ch.6

(141) D.S. HUTCHINSON: 'Doctrines of the mean and the debate concerning skills in fourth-century medicine, rhetoric and ethics', in R.J. HANKINSON (ed.), *Medicine, Method, and Metaphysics* (Edmonton, 1988)

On the acquisition of moral virtue see HURSTHOUSE VIII.61, SORABJI VIII.223, and:

(142) W.K. FRANKENA: *Three Historic Philosophies of Education* (Glenview, Ill., 1965)

(143) M.F. BURNYEAT: 'Aristotle on learning to be good', in RORTY VIII.37

(G) Particular Virtues

NE Γ and Δ, and *EE* Γ, contain analyses of particular moral virtues. On the curious virtue of 'magnanimity' see:

(144) R.A. GAUTHIER: *Magnanimité* (Paris, 1961)

(145) D.A. REES: ' "Magnanimity" in the *Eudemian* and *Nicomachean Ethics*', in MORAUX I.43

(146) W.F.R. HARDIE: ' "Magnanimity" in Aristotle's *Ethics*', *Phron* 23, 1978, 63–79

(147) E. SCHÜTRUMPF: 'Magnanimity, *megalopsuchia* and the system of Aristotle's *Nicomachean Ethics*', *AGP* 71, 1989, 10–22

(148) H.J. CURZER: 'A great philosopher's not so great account of great virtue: Aristotle's treatment of "greatness of soul" ', *CJP* 20, 1990, 517–37

(149) H.J. CURZER: 'Aristotle's much-maligned *megalapsuchos*', *AustJP* 69, 1991, 131–51

On courage:

(150) D.F. PEARS: 'Aristotle's analysis of courage', *Mid-West Studies in Philosophy* 3, 1978, 273–85 = RORTY VIII.37

(151) M.J. MILLS: 'The discussions of *andreia* in the *Eudemian* and *Nicomachean Ethics*', *Phron* 25, 1980, 198–218

(152) S.R. LEIGHTON: 'Aristotle's courageous passions', *Phron* 33, 1988, 76–99

See also:

(153) M.J. MILLS: '*Phthonos* and its related *pathê* in Plato and Aristotle', *Phron* 30, 1985, 1–12

(154) J. HARE: '*Eleutheriotês* in Aristotle's *Ethics*', *AP* 8, 1988, 19–32

(155) C.M. YOUNG: 'Aristotle on temperance', *PR* 97, 1988, 521–42 = ANTON and PREUS VIII.41

(156) J.S. ZEMBATY: 'Aristotle on lying', *JHP* 31, 1993, 7–30

(H) Justice

The special virtue of justice is analysed in *NE* E. There are notes on this book in:

(157) H. JACKSON: Peri Dikaiosunês: *the Fifth Book of the Nicomachean Ethics of Aristotle* (London, 1879)

Aristotle's analysis is discussed by:

(158) R. BAMBROUGH: 'Aristotle on justice, a paradigm of philosophy', in BAMBROUGH I.70

(159) H. KELSEN: 'Aristotle's doctrine of justice', in WALSH and SHAPIRO VIII.36

(160) K. MARC-WOGAU: 'Aristotle's theory of corrective justice and reciprocity', in his *Philosophical Essays* (Lund, 1967)

(161) B.A.O. WILLIAMS: 'Justice as a virtue', in RORTY VIII.37

(162) W. VON LEYDEN: *Aristotle on Equality and Justice* (London, 1985)

(163) A. MacINTYRE: *Whose Justice? Which Rationality?* (London, 1988), ch.7

(164) E.J. WEINRIB: 'Aristotle's forms of justice', in PANAGIOTOU VIII.38

(165) D. KEYT: 'Aristotle's theory of distributive justice', in KEYT and MILLER IX.22

(166) P. KEYSER: 'A proposed diagram in Aristotle, *EN* V 3, 1131a24–b20 for distributive justice in proportion', *Apeiron* 25, 1992, 15–44

and IRWIN III.197, ch.20

On the connexions between Aristotle's conception of justice and the law see:

(167) M. HAMBURGER: *Morals and Law: the Growth of Aristotle's Legal Theory* (New Haven, Conn., 1951)

(168) A.R.W. HARRISON: 'Aristotle's *Nicomachean Ethics*, Book V, and the law of Athens', *JHS* 77, 1957, 42–47

(169) S. ROSEN: 'The political context of Aristotle's theories of justice', *Phron* 20, 1975, 228–40

(170) W. VON LEYDEN: 'Aristotle and the concept of law', *Phil* 42, 1967, 1–19

(171) J. RITTER: 'Le droit naturel chez Aristote – contribution au renouveau du droit naturel', *Archives de philosophie* 32, 1969, 416–57

(172) F.D. MILLER: 'Aristotle on natural law and justice', in KEYT and MILLER IX.22

On equity:

(173) M.S. MACRAKIS: '*Epieikeia* and satisficing', *AP* 5, 1985, 53–58

(174) C. GEORGIADIS: 'Equitable and equity in Aristotle', in PANAGIOTOU VIII.38

(175) R. SHINER: 'Aristotle's theory of equity', in PANAGIOTOU VIII.38

(I) Voluntary Actions

Virtuous and vicious action demand a certain state of mind in the agent. Aristotle's remarks on the mental preconditions of action are found in *EN* Γ, Z and H, and *EE* B. Modern discussions of this topic tend to circle about the problem of free will. For Aristotle's attitude to this issue see:

(176) P.M. HUBY: 'The first discovery of the free will problem', *Phil* 42, 1967, 353–62

(177) W.F.R. HARDIE: 'Aristotle and the free will problem', *Phil* 43, 1968, 274–78

(178) S. BROADIE: 'On what would have happened otherwise: a problem for determinism', *RM* 39, 1985/6, 433–54

(179) S. EVERSON: 'Aristotle's compatibilism in the *Nicomachean Ethics*', *RPA* 10, 1990, 81–99

And compare the items on fatalism in III (F) and on determinism in IV (F). On the connected issue of responsibility see SORABJI IV.72, part V; and:

366   Bibliography

(180) R. BONDESON: 'Aristotle on responsibility for one's character and the possibility of character change', *Phron* 19, 1974, 59–65
(181) T.H. IRWIN: 'Reason and responsibility in Aristotle', in RORTY VIII.37
(182) J. ROBERTS: 'Aristotle on responsibility for action and character', *AP* 9, 1989, 23–36
(183) R. CURREN: 'The contribution of *Nicomachean Ethics* III 5 to Aristotle's theory of responsibility', *HPQ* 6, 1989, 261–77
(184) J.N. MOLINE: 'Aristotle on praise and blame', *AGP* 71, 1989, 283–302
(185) S. SAUVE MEYER: *Aristotle on Moral Responsibility* (Oxford, 1993)
See also:
(186) V. HAKSAR: 'Aristotle and the punishment of psychopaths', *Phil* 39, 1964, 323–40
(187) J.C.B. GLOVER: *Responsibility* (London, 1970), ch.1
(188) R.W. SHARPLES: 'Responsibility and the possibility of more than one course of action: a note on Aristotle, *de Caelo* II 12', *BICS* 23, 1976, 69–72
Aristotle's account of *to hekousion*, or voluntariness, is examined by FURLEY IV.109. See also:
(189) R. LOENING: *Die Zurechnungslehre des Aristoteles* (Jena, 1903)
(190) F.A. SIEGLER: 'Voluntary and involuntary', *Monist* 52, 1968, 268–87
(191) J.L. ACKRILL: 'An Aristotelian argument about virtue', *Paideia* 7, 1978, 133–37
(192) A.J.P. KENNY: *Aristotle's Theory of the Will* (London, 1979)
(193) R. HURSTHOUSE: 'Acting and feeling in character: *Nicomachean Ethics* 3.1', *Phron* 29, 1984, 252–66
(194) A. MADIGAN: 'Dimensions of voluntariness in *EN* III.12, 1119a21–33', *AP* 6, 1986, 139–52
(195) R. HEINAMAN: 'The *Eudemian Ethics* on knowledge and voluntary action', *Phron* 31, 1986, 128–47
(196) R. HEINAMAN: 'Compulsion and voluntary action in the *Eudemian Ethics*', *Nous* 22, 1988, 253–81
The account is placed in its historical setting by:
(197) A.W.H. ADKINS: *Merit and Responsibility* (Oxford, 1960)
The legal background is discussed by:
(198) R. MASCHE: *Die Willenslehre im griechischen Recht* (Berlin, 1926)
(199) H.D.P. LEE: 'The legal background of two passages in the *Nicomachean Ethics*', *CQ* 31, 1937, 129–40
(200) R.R. DYER: 'Aristotle's categories of voluntary torts (*EN* 1135b8–25)', *CR* 25, 1965, 250–52
(201) D. DAUBE: *Roman Law: Linguistic, Social, and Philosophical Aspects* (Edinburgh, 1969), part III.1A
(202) M. SCHOFIELD: 'Aristotelian mistakes', *PCPS* 19, 1973, 66–70

Bibliography

On some of Aristotle's general views about the nature of human action
see PENNER IV.95, and:[3]

(203) J.L. ACKRILL: 'Aristotle on action', M 87, 1978, 595–601 = RORTY
VIII.37

(204) D. CHARLES: Aristotle's Philosophy of Action (London, 1984)

(205) C.A. FREELAND: 'Aristotelian actions', Nous 19, 1985, 397–414

(206) T.H. IRWIN: 'Aristotelian actions', Phron 31, 1986, 68–89

(207) D. CHARLES: 'Aristotle: ontology and moral reasoning', OSAP 4,
1986, 119–44

(J) Choice

Not all voluntary actions are intentional, or determined by choice or
prohairesis. On prohairesis see ch.7 of JOSEPH VIII.129; SORABJI VIII.223;
WIGGINS VIII.225; and:

(208) G.E.M. ANSCOMBE: Intention (Oxford, 1963)

(209) G.E.M. ANSCOMBE: 'Two kinds of error in action', JP 60, 1963, 393–401

(210) G.E.M. ANSCOMBE: 'Thought and action in Aristotle', in BAM-
BROUGH I.70 = BARNES, SCHOFIELD, SORABJI I.62

(211) A. MELE: 'Choice and virtue in the Nicomachean Ethics', JHP 19,
1981, 405–24

(212) M.C. NUSSBAUM: 'The "common explanation" of animal motion',
in MORAUX and WIESNER I.47

(213) N. SHERMAN: 'Character, planning, and choice,' RM 39, 1985/6, 83–
116

Prohairesis itself involves both desire, orexis, and deliberation. On the
notion of orexis, and the appetitive or emotional aspect of action, consult:

(214) W.W. FORTENBAUGH: 'Aristotle, emotion, and moral virtue', Are-
thusa 2, 1969, 163–85

(215) W.W. FORTENBAUGH: Aristotle on Emotion (London, 1975)

(216) N.J.H. DENT and J. BENSON: 'Varieties of desire', PASS 50, 1976,
153–92

(217) A. KOSMAN: 'On being properly affected: virtues and feelings in
Aristotle's ethics', in RORTY VIII.37

(218) S.R. LEIGHTON: 'Aristotle and the emotions', Phron 27, 1982, 144–74

(219) D.S. HUTCHINSON: 'Aristotle on the spheres of motivation: de
Anima III', Dialogue 29, 1990, 7–20

(220) H. RICHARDSON: 'Desire and the good in the de Anima', in NUSS-
BAUM and RORTY VI.19

(221) S. HALLIWELL: 'Pleasure, understanding, and emotion in Aristotle's
Poetics', in RORTY X.45

(K) Deliberation

Choice is not simply desire but rather deliberated desire. On deliberation
and the intellectual antecedents to action, see:

3. Note also the items at the end of VIII (N).

(222) T. ANDO: *Aristotle's Theory of Practical Cognition* (Kyoto, 1958)
(223) R. SORABJI: 'Aristotle on the role of intellect in virtue', *PAS* 74, 1973/4, 107–29 = RORTY VIII.37
(224) A. BROADIE: 'Aristotle on rational action', *Phron* 19, 1974, 70–80
(225) D. WIGGINS: 'Deliberation and practical reason', *PAS* 76, 1975/6, 29–51
(226) M.C. NUSSBAUM: 'The discernment of perception in Aristotle's conception of private and public morality', *BACAP* 1, 1985, 151–201
(227) S. BROADIE: 'The problem of practical intellect in Aristotle's *Ethics*', *BACAP* 3, 1987, 229–52

Aristotle compares deliberation to the process of 'geometrical analysis', on which see:
(228) K.J.J. HINTIKKA and U. REMES: *The Method of Analysis* (Dordrecht, 1974)
(229) J. BARNES: review of HINTIKKA and REMES VIII.228, *M* 86, 1977, 133–36

Deliberation involves reasoning or syllogizing. On the so-called 'practical syllogism', consult:
(230) D.J. ALLAN: 'The practical syllogism', in MANSION I.51
(231) W.W. FORTENBAUGH: '*Ta pros to telos* and syllogistic vocabulary in Aristotle's *Ethics*', *Phron* 10, 1965, 191–201
(232) S.J. ETHERIDGE: 'Aristotle's practical syllogism and necessity', *Phg* 112, 1968, 20–42
(233) D.K. MODRAK: '*Aisthêsis* in the practical syllogism', *PhSt* 30, 1976, 379–92
(234) J. BARNES: 'Aristote et la philosophie anglo-saxonne', *RPL* 75, 1977, 204–18·
(235) R.A. SHINER: '*Aisthêsis, nous,* and *phronêsis* in the practical syllogism', *PhSt* 36, 1979, 377–87
(236) M.T. THORNTON: 'Aristotelian practical reason', *M* 92, 1982, 57–76
(237) D.T. DEVEREUX: 'Particular and universal in Aristotle's conception of practical knowledge', *RM* 39, 1985/6, 483–504
(238) D. MCKERLIE: 'The practical syllogism and *akrasia*', *CJP* 21, 1991, 299–321

and Essay 4 in NUSSBAUM VI.133.
For the philosophical issues involved, see:
(239) M. MOTHERSILL: 'Anscombe's account of the practical syllogism', *PR* 70, 1962, 448–61
(240) A.J.P. KENNY: 'Practical inferences', *An* 26, 1965/6, 65–75
(241) R.M. HARE: 'Practical inferences', in his *Practical Inferences* (London, 1971)

(L) Intellectual Virtues
Some of the difficulties in *NE* Z are eased by:
(242) D.H.G. GREENWOOD: *Aristotle: Nicomachean Ethics Book Six* (Cambridge, 1909)

The 'intellectual virtues' which this book dissects have received scanty attention, with the exception of 'practical wisdom' or *phronêsis*. Some of the problems surrounding this notion are examined by LOENING VIII.189, and:

(243) J. WALTER: *Die Lehre von der praktischen Vernunft in der griechischen Philosophie* (Jena, 1874)

(244) D.J. ALLAN: 'Aristotle's account of moral principles', *Actes du XIe Congrès Internationale de Philosophie*, Vol. XII (Brussels, 1963) = BARNES, SCHOFIELD, SORABJI I.62 = HAGER I.67

(245) P. AUBENQUE: *La prudence chez Aristote* (Paris, 1963)

(246) P. AUBENQUE: 'La prudence aristotélicienne, porte-t-elle sur la fin ou sur les moyens?', *REG* 78, 1965, 40–51
See also:
(247) R. JACKSON: 'Rationalism and intellectualism in the *Ethics* of Aristotle', *M* 51, 1942, 343–60

(248) R. DEMOS: 'Some remarks on Aristotle's doctrine of practical reason', *PPR* 22, 1961/2, 153–62

(249) T.H. IRWIN: 'Aristotle on reason, desire and virtue', *JP* 72, 1975, 567–78

(250) C.J. ROWE: 'The meaning of "*phronêsis*" in the *Eudemian Ethics*', in MORAUX I.43 = MÜLLER-GOLDINGEN VIII.39

(251) A. MELE: 'Aristotle on the roles of reason in motivation and justification', *AGP* 66, 1984, 124–47

(252) D. DEMOSS: 'Acquiring ethical ends', *AP* 10, 1990, 63–79
On a related topic see:
(253) G. RYLE: 'On forgetting the difference between right and wrong', in A. I. MELDEN (ed.), *Essays in Moral Philosophy* (Seattle, 1958)

(M) Akrasia

On the puzzles surrounding Aristotle's discussion of moral weakness or *akrasia* in *NE* H, see:

(254) J. COOK WILSON: *On the Structure of Book Seven of the Nicomachean Ethics* (Oxford, 1912)

(255) R. ROBINSON: 'Aristotle on *akrasia*', in his *Essays on Greek Philosophy* (Oxford, 1969) = BARNES, SCHOFIELD, SORABJI I.62

(256) J. WALSH: *Aristotle's Conception of Moral Weakness* (New York, 1963)

(257) R.D. MILO: *Aristotle on Practical Knowledge and Weakness of Will* (The Hague, 1966)

(258) A.J.P. KENNY: 'The practical syllogism and incontinence', *Phron* 11, 1966, 162–89

(259) G. SANTAS: 'Aristotle on practical inference, the explanation of action, and *akrasia*', *Phron* 14, 1969, 162–89

(260) T.C. MCCONNELL: 'Is Aristotle's account of incontinence inconsistent?', *CJP* 4, 1975, 635–51

(261) A.W.H. ADKINS: 'Paralysis and *akrasia* in *Eth. Nic.* 1102b16ff', *AJP* 97, 1976, 62–64

(262) D. WIGGINS: 'Weakness of will, commensurability and the objects of deliberation and desire', PAS 79, 1978/9, 251–77 = RORTY VIII.37

(263) G. LAWRENCE: 'Akrasia and clear-eyed akrasia in Nicomachean Ethics 7', RPA 6, 1988, 77–106

(264) M.J. WOODS: 'Aristotle on akrasia', in ALBERTI VIII.40

(265) J.C.B. GOSLING: 'Mad, drunk, or asleep? – Aristotle's akratic', Phron 38, 1993, 98–104

See also CHARLES VIII.204, and:

(266) R.M. HARE: Freedom and Reason (Oxford, 1963), ch.5

(267) D. DAVIDSON: 'How is weakness of the will possible?', in J. FEINBERG (ed.), Moral Concepts (Oxford, 1969)

(268) J.C.B. GOSLING: 'The Stoics and akrasia', Apeiron 20, 1987, 179–202

(N) Pleasure

Various reasons make pleasure a central concern of the moral philosopher. There is a comprehensive study in:

(269) J.C.B. GOSLING and C.C.W. TAYLOR: The Greeks on Pleasure (Oxford, 1982)

Most of the problems raised by the dual accounts of pleasure in NE H and K are dealt with by:

(270) A.J. FESTUGIÈRE: Aristote: le plaisir (Paris, 1946)

(271) G. LIEBERG: Die Lehre von der Lust in den Ethiken des Aristoteles (Munich, 1958)

(272) J.M. RIST: 'Pleasure, 360–300BC', Phoenix 28, 1974, 167–79

(273) F. RICKEN: Der Lustbegriff in der Nikomachischen Ethik (Göttingen, 1976)

(274) P. WEBB: 'The relative dating of the accounts of pleasure in Aristotle's Ethics', Phron 22, 1977, 235–62 = MÜLLER-GOLDINGEN VIII.39

The challenging suggestions of:

(275) G.E.L. OWEN: 'Aristotelian pleasures', PAS 72, 1971/2, 135–52 = OWEN I.90 = MÜLLER-GOLDINGEN VIII.39

have been refuted by:

(276) J.C.B. GOSLING: 'More Aristotelian pleasures', PAS 1973/4, 15–34

See also:

(277) P. MERLAN: Studies in Aristotle and Epicurus (Wiesbaden, 1960)

For some analysis of Aristotle's different and perplexing remarks about the nature of pleasure and pleasures, see:

(278) J.O. URMSON: 'Aristotle on pleasure', in MORAVCSIK I.61

(279) A.O. RORTY: 'The place of pleasure in Aristotle's Ethics', M 83, 1974, 481–93

(280) J. ANNAS: 'Aristotle on pleasure and goodness', in RORTY VIII.37

(281) R. WEISS: 'Aristotle's criticism of Eudoxan hedonism', CP 74, 1979, 214–21

(282) C.C.W. TAYLOR: 'Urmson on Aristotle on pleasure', in R. DANCY, J.M.E. MORAVCSIK and C.C.W. TAYLOR (edd.), *Human Agency* (Stanford, 1988)

(283) P. GOTTLIEB: 'Aristotle's measure doctrine and pleasure', *AGP* 75, 1993, 31–46

A crucial feature of Aristotle's account is his claim that pleasure is not a change (*kinêsis*) but an activity (*energeia*). On this distinction see:

(284) J.L. ACKRILL: 'Aristotle's distinction between *energeia* and *kinêsis*', in BAMBROUGH I.70

(285) C.C.W. TAYLOR: 'States, activities, and performances', *PASS* 39, 1965, 85–102

(286) F.R. PICKERING: 'Aristotle on walking', *AGP* 59, 1977, 37–43

(287) D. GRAHAM: 'States and performances: Aristotle's test', *PQ* 30, 1980, 117–30

(288) M.J. WHITE: 'Aristotle's concept of *theôria* and the *energeia/kinêsis* distinction', *JHP* 18, 1980, 253–65

(289) C.T. HAGEN: 'The *energeia/kinêsis* distinction and Aristotle's theory of action', *JHP* 22, 1984, 263–80

(290) D. BOSTOCK: 'Pleasure and activity in Aristotle's *Ethics*', *Phron* 33, 1988, 251–72

(291) F.J. GONZALEZ: 'Aristotle on pleasure and perfection', *Phron* 36, 1991, 141–59

(292) M.T. LISKE: '*Kinêsis* und *energeia* bei Aristoteles', *Phron* 36, 1991, 161–78

and PENNER IV.95.

For the philosophical issues raised in all this the best text is still:

(293) A.J.P. KENNY: *Action, Emotion, and Will* (London, 1963)

(O) Friendship

There is a lengthy discussion of friendship or *philia* in *EN* Θ and I. On this see:

(294) E. HOFFMAN: 'Aristoteles' Philosophie der Freundschaft', in HAGER I.67

(295) A.W.H. ADKINS: 'Friendship and self-sufficiency in Homer and Aristotle', *CQ* 13, 1963, 30–45

(296) E. TELFER: 'Friendship', *PAS* 71, 1970/1, 223–41

(297) J.C. FRAISSE: '*Autarkeia* et *philia* en *EE* VII 12, 1244b1–1245b19', in MORAUX I.43

(298) W.W. FORTENBAUGH: 'Aristotle's analysis of friendship', *Phron* 20, 1975, 51–62

(299) J. ANNAS: 'Plato and Aristotle on friendship and altruism', *M* 86, 1977, 532–54

(300) J.M. COOPER: 'Aristotle on the forms of friendship', *RM* 30, 1977, 619–48

(301) J.M. COOPER: 'Friendship and the good in Aristotle', *PR* 86, 1977, 290–315 = RORTY VIII.37

(302) A.D.M. Walker: 'Aristotle's account of friendship in the *Nicomachean Ethics'*, *Phron* 24, 1979, 180–96

(303) C.H. Kahn: 'Aristotle and altruism', *M* 90, 1981, 20–40

(304) A.W. Price: *Love and Friendship in Plato and Aristotle* (Oxford, 1989)

(305) G.E.L. Owen: '*Philia* and *akrasia* in Aristotle', in Sinaceur I.60

(306) A. Alberti: '*Philia* e identità personale in Aristotele', in Alberti VIII.40

(307) D. McKerlie: 'Friendship, self-love, and concern for others in Aristotle's *Ethics'*, *AP* 11, 1991, 85–101

(308) J.E. Whiting: 'Impersonal friends', *Monist* 75, 1991, 3–29

Note also:

(309) G. Vlastos: 'The individual as object of love in Plato', in his *Platonic Studies* (Princeton, 1973)

IX POLITICS

(A) General

The classic commentary on the *Politics* is:

(1) W.L. Newman: *The Politics of Aristotle* (Oxford, 1887–1902)

This contains essays, copious notes, and learned appendices. The Budé:

(2) J. Aubonnet: *Aristote: Politique* (Paris, 1960–89)

is useful. For Books A–E there is:

(3) F. Susemihl and R.D. Hicks: *The Politics of Aristotle* (London, 1894)

For Books Γ and Δ in the Clarendon series:

(4) R. Robinson: *Aristotle's Politics Books III and IV* (Oxford, 1962)

For Book III see:

(5) E. Braun: *Das dritte Buch der aristotelischen Politik: Interpretation*, Sitzungberichte der österreichischen Akademie der Wissenschaften, Philos.-hist. Kl. 247.4 (Vienna, 1965)

Note also:

(6) E. Barker: *The Politics of Aristotle* (Oxford, 1946)

For the *Ath.Pol* see below, section (H); for the spurious work on 'economics' see:

(7) U. Victor: [*Aristoteles*]: *Oikonomikos* (Meisenheim, 1983)

There is background material in:

(8) W.W. Jaeger: *Paideia* (New York, 1943–44)

(9) T.A. Sinclair: *A History of Greek Political Thought* (London, 1951)

(10) M.I. Finley: *Democracy Ancient and Modern* (London, 1973)

For general accounts of Aristotle's political thought see:

(11) E. Barker: *The Political Thought of Plato and Aristotle* (London, 1906)

(12) M. Defourny: *Aristote: études sur la Politique* (Paris, 1932)

(13) K.R. Popper: *The Open Society and its Enemies*, vol.2 (London, 1945)

(14) G. Bien: *Die Grundlegung der politischen Philosophie bei Aristoteles* (Munich, 1973)

(15) R.G. MULGAN: *Aristotle's Political Theory* (Oxford, 1977)

(16) J.B. MORRALL: *Aristotle* (London, 1977)

(17) E. SCHÜTRUMPF: *Die Analyse der Polis durch Aristoteles* (Amsterdam, 1980)

(18) R. BODÉUS: *Le philosophe et la cité* (Paris, 1981)

(19) R. BODÉUS: *Philosophie et politique chez Aristote* (Namur, 1991)

and see also IRWIN III.197, ch.19.

There are collections of papers on Aristotle's political ideas in:

(20) *La politique d'Aristote*, Entretiens Hardt XI (Geneva, 1964)

(21) P. STEINMETZ (ed.): *Schriften zu den Politika des Aristoteles* (Hildesheim, 1973)

(22) D. KEYT and F.D. MILLER (edd.): *A Companion to Aristotle's* Politics (Oxford, 1991)

and PATZIG I.49

JAEGER's attempt in II.1 to establish a chronology for the political writings was opposed by the different scheme of:

(23) H. VON ARNIM: *Zur Entstehungsgeschichte der aristotelischen Politik*, Sitzungsberichte der österreichischen Akademie der Wissenschaft in Wien, Phil.-hist.Kl. 200.1 (Vienna, 1924)

See also:

(24) E. BARKER: 'The life of Aristotle and the composition and structure of the *Politics*', *CR* 45, 1931, 162–72

(25) J.L. STOCKS: 'The composition of Aristotle's *Politics*', *CQ* 31, 1937, 177–87

There is further controversy over the structure Pol: Bekker's edition, and the Oxford translation, print the books in the order found in all the MSS; but some scholars place H and Θ immediately after Γ. On this controversy, see ROSS II.5, and:

(26) W. THEILER: 'Bau und Zeit der aristotelischen *Politik*', *MH* 9, 1952, 65–78

(27) R. STARK: 'Der Gesamtaufbau der aristotelischen *Politik*', in IX.20

(28) J. MESK: 'Die Buchfolge der aristotelischen Politik', in STEINMETZ IX.21

See also:

(29) C.J. ROWE: 'Aims and methods in Aristotle's *Politics*', *CQ* 27, 1977, 159–72 = KEYT and MILLER IX.22

(30) P. PELLEGRIN: 'La *Politique* d'Aristote: unité et fractures', *Revue philosophique de la France et de l'Etranger* 110, 1987, 124–59

(31) C.H. KAHN: 'The normative character of Aristotle's *Politics*', in PATZIG I.49

(B) Ethics and Politics

The subject of *NE* is *political* science, and the end of the work turns to political questions and to the material discussed in *Pol*. On the connexions between ethics and politics see: NEWMAN IX.1 (vol.2, appx.A); VON FRITZ and KAPP IX.108; and:

(32) D.J. ALLAN: 'Individual and state in the *Ethics* and *Politics*', in IX.20 = HAGER I.67

(33) E. TREPANIER: 'La Politique comme philosophie morale chez Aristote', *Dialogue* 2, 1963/4, 251–79

(34) P. BETBEDER: 'Ethique et politique selon Aristote', *Revue des sciences philosophiques et théologiques* 20, 1970, 543–88

(35) H. FLASHAR: 'Ethik und Politik in der Philosophie des Aristoteles', *Gymnasium* 78, 1971, 278–93

(36) S. CASHDOLLAR: 'Aristotle's politics of morals', *JHP* 11, 1973, 145–60

(37) A.W.H. ADKINS: 'The connection between Aristotle's *Ethics* and *Politics*', *Political Theory* 12, 1984, 29–49 = KEYT and MILLER IX.22

(38) T.H. IRWIN: 'Moral science and political theory in Aristotle', in CARTLEDGE and HARVEY I.79

(39) J. ROBERTS: 'Political animals in the *Nicomachean Ethics*', *Phron* 34, 1989, 185–205

(40) C.J. ROWE: 'The good for man in Aristotle's *Ethics* and *Politics*', in ALBERTI VIII.40

(C) Nature and Society

Much of *Pol* A is concerned with *nature*.[1] For the state has a natural basis (and does not depend on agreement or contract). Aristotle's theory of the political nature of man is discussed by:

(41) E. WEIL: 'L'anthropologie d'Aristote', in his *Essais et conférences*, I (Paris, 1970)

(42) R.G. MULGAN: 'Aristotle's doctrine that man is a political animal', *H* 102, 1974, 438–45

(43) T.J. SAUNDERS: 'A note on Aristotle's *Politics* I 1', *CQ* 26, 1976, 316–17

(44) D. KEYT: 'Three fundamental principles in Aristotle's *Politics*', *Phron* 32, 1987, 54–79 = KEYT and MILLER IX.22

(45) W. KULLMANN: 'Man as a political animal', in KEYT and MILLER IX.22

(46) J. M. COOPER: 'Political animals and civic friendship', in PATZIG I.49

Aristotle's conception of the state as a natural growth is discussed by:

(47) A.C. BRADLEY: 'Aristotle's conception of the State', in E. ABBOTT (ed.), *Hellenica* (London, 1880) = KEYT and MILLER IX.22

(48) S. EVERSON: 'Aristotle on the foundations of the State', *Political Studies* 36, 1988, 89–101

(49) F.D. MILLER: 'Aristotle's political naturalism', *Apeiron* 22, 1989, 195–218

(D) Citizens

Citizenship is the central political concept. Aristotle's definition of citizenship in *Pol* Γ is discussed by:

(50) C. MOSSE: 'La conception du citoyen dans la *Politique* d'Aristote', *Eirene* 6, 1967, 17–21

1. For which see IV (B).

(51) J. PECIRKA: 'A note on Aristotle's definition of citizenship', *Eirene* 6, 1967, 23–26

(52) C. JOHNSON: 'Who is Aristotle's citizen?', *Phron* 29, 1984, 73–90

The nature of civic virtue in Γ 4 is discussed by:

(53) E. BRAUN: *Aristoteles über Bürger- und Menschentugend*, Sitzungsberichte der österreichischen Akademie der Wissenschaft in Wien, Philos.-hist.Kl. 236.2 (Vienna, 1961)

(54) R. DEVELIN: 'The good man and the good citizen in Aristotle's *Politics*', *Phron* 18, 1973, 71–79

(55) T.H. IRWIN: 'The good of political activity', in PATZIG IX.49

See also:

(56) J. BARNES: 'Aristotle and political liberty', in PATZIG I.49

(E) Slaves

Slavery is suited to the *nature* of certain men. For Aristotle's notorious views on slaves, see especially:

(57) P.A. BRUNT: 'Aristotle and slavery', in his *Studies in Greek History and Thought* (Oxford, 1993)

and also:

(58) O. GIGON: 'Die Sklaverei bei Aristoteles', in IX.20

(59) R.O. SCHLAIFER: 'Greek theories of slavery from Homer to Aristotle', *HSCP* 47, 1936, 165–204 = M.I. FINLEY (ed.), *Slavery in Classical Antiquity* (Cambridge, Mass., 1960)

(60) W.W. FORTENBAUGH: 'Aristotle on women and slaves', in BARNES, SCHOFIELD, SORABJI I.62

(61) A. BARUZZI: 'Der Freie und der Sklave in Ethik und Politik des Aristoteles', *Philosophisches Jahrbuch* 77, 1970, 15–28

(62) N.D. SMITH: 'Aristotle's theory of natural slavery', *Phoenix* 37, 1983, 109–22 = KEYT and MILLER IX.22

(63) T.J. SAUNDERS: 'The Controversy about slavery reported in Aristotle, *Politics* 1255a4 sqq', in A. MOFFATT (ed.), *Maistor: Studies for R. Browning* (Canberra, 1984)

(64) S.R.L. CLARK: 'Slaves and citizens', *Phil* 60, 1985, 27–46

(65) M. SCHOFIELD: 'Ideology and philosophy in Aristotle's theory of slavery', in PATZIG I.49

(F) Economics

Many of Aristotle's remarks on what we should call political economy occur in his discussions of justice,[2] but there are also some hints at economic analysis. On this see:

(66) J. SOUDEK: 'Aristotle's theory of exchange', *Proceedings of the American Philosophical Society* 96, 1952, 45–75

(67) K. POLANYI: 'Aristotle discovers the economy', in K. POLYANI, C.M. ARENSBERG, and H.W. PEARSON (edd.), *Trade and Market in the Early Empires* (Glencoe, Ill., 1957), 64–94

2. For which see VIII (H).

(68) M.I. Finley: 'Aristotle and economic analysis', *Past and Present* 47, 1970, 3–25 = Barnes, Schofield, Sorabji I.62

(69) S.T. Lowry: 'Aristotle's "natural limit", and the economics of price regulation', *GRBS* 15, 1974, 57–63

(70) T.J. Lewis: 'Acquisition and anxiety: Aristotle's case against the market', *Canadian Journal of Economics* 11, 1978, 69–90

(71) S. Meikle: 'Aristotle and the political economy of the *polis*', *JHS* 99, 1979, 57–73 = Keyt and Miller IX.22

(72) S. Meikle: 'Aristotle on equality and market exchange', *JHS* 111, 1991, 193–96

Karl Marx's views on Aristotle's economic theory are reported by:

(73) E.C. Weiskopf: *Die Produktionsverhältnisse im alten Orient und in der griechenrömischen Antike* (Berlin, 1957)

For Hobbes' attitude towards Aristotle on this and other matters see:

(74) J. Laird: 'Hobbes on Aristotle's *Politics*', *PAS* 43, 1942/3, 1–20

Aristotle offers no developed theory of property. His various remarks on the subject are analysed by:

(75) T.H. Irwin: 'Generosity and property in Aristotle's *Politics*', in E. F. Paul (ed.), *Beneficence, Philanthropy and the Public Good* (Oxford, 1987)

(76) F.D. Miller: 'Aristotle on property rights', in Anton and Preus VIII.41

(77) T.H. Irwin: 'Aristotle's defence of private property', in Keyt and Miller IX.22

(78) R. Mayhew: 'Aristotle on property', *RM* 46, 1992/3, 803–31

(G) Constitutions

In *Pol* B Aristotle discusses various constitutions, ideal and actual. For his criticism of the Spartan constitution, see:

(79) E. Braun: *Die Kritik der Lakedaimonischen Verfassung in den Politika des Aristoteles* (Klagenfurt, 1956)

(80) P. Cloche: 'Aristote et les institutions de Sparte', *Les études classiques* 11, 1942, 289–313 = Steinmetz IX.21

(81) R.A. de Laix: 'Aristotle's conception of the Spartan constitution', *JHP* 12, 1974, 21–30

For his criticisms of the Cretan constitution, see:

(82) G.L. Huxley: 'Crete in Aristotle's *Politics*', *GRBS* 12, 1971, 505–15

Aristotle's criticisms of Plato are discussed by:

(83) E. Bornemann: 'Aristoteles Urteil über Platons politische Theorie', *Phg* 79, 1923, 70–158, 234–57

(84) G.R. Morrow: 'Aristotle's comments on Plato's *Laws*', in Düring and Owen I.39

(85) M.C. Nussbaum: 'Shame, separateness, and political unity: Aristotle's criticism of Plato', in Rorty VIII.19

(86) P. Simpson: 'Aristotle's criticism of Socrates' communism of wives and children', *Apeiron* 24, 1991, 99–114

(87) R.F. STALLEY: 'Aristotle's criticism of Plato's *Republic*', in KEYT and MILLER IX.22

On Aristotle's theoretical classification of constitutions in *Pol* Γ and Δ, see:

(88) W.W. FORTENBAUGH: 'Aristotle on prior and posterior, correct and mistaken constitutions', *TAPA* 106, 1976, 125–37 = KEYT and MILLER IX.22

On monarchy, see:

(89) H. KELSEN: 'The philosophy of Aristotle and the Hellenic Macedonian policy', *Ethics* 48, 1937, 1–64 = BARNES, SCHOFIELD, SORABJI I.62

(90) V. EHRENBERG: *Alexander and the Greeks* (Oxford, 1938), ch.3

(91) R.G. MULGAN: 'Aristotle's sovereign', *Political Studies* 18, 1970, 518–19

(92) R. G. MULGAN: 'A note on Aristotle's absolute ruler', *Phron* 19, 1974, 66–69

Aristotle's views of democracy are discussed by:

(93) M. CHAMBERS: 'Aristotle's "forms of democracy" ', *TAPA* 92, 1961, 20–36

(94) M.C. NUSSBAUM: 'Aristotelian social democracy', in B. DOUGLASS, G. MARA, and H. RICHARDSON (edd.), *Liberalism and the Good* (New York, 1990)

(95) R. MULGAN: 'Aristotle's analysis of oligarchy and democracy', in KEYT and MILLER IX.22

(96) A. LINTOTT: 'Aristotle and democracy', *CQ* 42, 1992, 114–28

(97) C. EUCKEN: 'Die aristotelische Demokratiebegriff und sein historisches Umfeld', in PATZIG I.49

The democratic idea of 'pooled wisdom' is treated by:

(98) E. BRAUN: 'Die Summierungstheorie des Aristoteles', *Jahreshefte der österreichischen archäologischen Instituts, Wien* 44, 1959, 57–84 = STEINMETZ IX.21

Aristotle's own ideal state is discussed in *Pol* H and Θ (which together constitute a fragment of his Utopia). See:

(99) P.A. VANDER WAERDT: 'Kingship and philosophy in Aristotle's best régime', *Phron* 30, 1985, 249–73.

(100) G.L. HUXLEY: 'On Aristotle's best state', in CARTLEDGE and HARVEY I.79

On the goal of the ideal state, see DEFOURNY IX.12, and:

(101) J.L. STOCKS: '*Scholê*', *CQ* 30, 1936, 177–87

(102) F. SOLMSEN: 'Leisure and play in Aristotle's ideal state', *RhM* 107, 1964, 193–220 = SOLMSEN I.92

(103) F. SOLMSEN: 'Aristotle *EN* 10.7, 1177b6–15', *CP* 72, 1977, 42–43

Aristotle's city planning in *Pol* H and elsewhere is discussed by:

(104) G. DOWNEY: 'Aristotle as an expert on urban problems', *Talanta* 3, 1971, 56–73

Aristotle's treatment, in *Pol* Δ and E, of the prevention of revolution, is discussed by:

(105) M. WHEELER: 'Aristotle's analysis of the nature of political struggle', *AJP* 72, 1951, 145–61 = BARNES, SCHOFIELD, SORABJI I.62

(106) F. KORT: 'The quantification of Aristotle's theory of revolution', *American Political Science Review* 46, 1952, 486–93

(107) E. BRAUN: 'Ein Maxime der Staatkunst in den *Politika* des Aristoteles', *Jahreshefte der österreichischen archäologischen Instituts, Wien* 44, 1959, 386–98 = STEINMETZ IX.21

(H) History

The *Politics* is a work of theory, but it contains numerous historical asides. Aristotle's *Constitution of Athens* was discovered in Egypt in 1890. It is one of a set of 158 'constitutions' which he wrote – or at any rate oversaw. On this enterprise, see JAEGER II.1, ch.13. For the *Ath.Pol* see:

(108) K. VON FRITZ and E. KAPP: *Aristotle's Constitution of Athens and Related Texts* (New York, 1950)

(109) P.J. RHODES: *A Commentary on Aristotle's Athênaiôn Politeia* (Oxford, 1981)

The literature on this work is immense. Philosophical readers may find matter in:

(110) U. VON WILAMOWITZ-MOELLENDORF: *Aristoteles und Athen* (Berlin, 1893)

(111) H. BLOCH: 'Studies in the historical literature of the fourth century: Theophrastus' *Nomoi* and Aristotle', in *Athenian Studies presented to W. S. Ferguson, HSCP* suppt. 1, 1940

(112) H. BLOCH: 'Herakleides Lembos and his *Epitome* of Aristotle's *Politeiai*', *TAPA* 71, 1940, 29–39

(113) J. DAY and M. CHAMBERS: *Aristotle's History of Athenian Democracy* (Berkeley and Los Angeles, 1962)

(114) J.J. KEANEY: 'The structure of Aristotle's *Athênaiôn Politeia*', *HSCP* 67, 1963, 115–46

(115) J.J. KEANEY: 'The date of Aristotle's *Athênaiôn Politeia*', *Historia* 19, 1970, 326–36

(116) J.J. KEANEY: *The Composition of Aristotle's* Athênaiôn Politeia (New York, 1992)

For discussion of Aristotle as a historian, see:

(117) R. WEIL: *Aristote et l'histoire: essai sur la 'Politique'* (Paris, 1960)

(118) R. WEIL: 'Philosophie et histoire', in IX.20 = BARNES, SCHOFIELD, SORABJI I.62

(119) G.L. HUXLEY: 'On Aristotle's historical methods', *GRBS* 13, 1972, 157–59

(120) G.L. HUXLEY: 'Aristotle as antiquary', *GRBS* 14, 1973, 271–86

(121) K. VON FRITZ: 'Die Bedeutung des Aristoteles für die Geschichtsschreibung', in IX.20 = HAGER I.67

(122) G.E.M. DE STE.CROIX: 'Aristotle on history and poetry (Poetics 9, 1451a36–b11)', in *The Ancient Historian and his Materials: Essays in honour of C. E. Stevens* (Farnborough, 1975) = RORTY X.45
(123) G.L. HUXLEY: *On Aristotle and Greek Society* (Belfast, 1979)

X RHETORIC and POETICS

(A) Rhetoric

There are commentaries on *Rhet* by:

(1) L. SPENGEL: *Aristotelis ars Rhetorica* (Leipzig, 1867)
(2) E.M. COPE: *The Rhetoric of Aristotle with a Commentary* (Cambridge, 1877)
(3) W.M.A. GRIMALDI: *Aristotle's Rhetoric I* (New York, 1980)
(4) W.M.A. GRIMALDI: *Aristotle's Rhetoric II* (New York, 1988)

See also:

(5) E.M. COPE: *Introduction to Aristotle's Rhetoric* (London, 1867)
(6) M. DUFOUR: *Aristote: Rhétorique*, vol.1, (Paris, 1932)

and the translation, amplified for the benefit of students of composition and public speaking, by:

(7) L. COOPER: *The Rhetoric of Aristotle* (New York, 1932)

A curiosity from the sixteenth century:

(8) L.D. GREEN (ed.): *John Rainolds's Oxford Lectures on Aristotle's Rhetoric* (London, 1986)

There is a collection of papers in FURLEY and NEHAMAS I.50, and some of the older studies are reprinted in:

(9) R. STARK (ed.): *Rhetorika* (Hildesheim, 1968)

There has been much dispute about the date of *Rhet*, and about the unity of its three component books. See SOLMSEN II.2 and:

(10) P.D. BRANDES: 'The composition and preservation of Aristotle's Rhetoric', *Speech Monographs* 35, 1968, 482–91
(11) W.M.A. GRIMALDI: *Studies in the Philosophy of Aristotle's Rhetoric* (Wiesbaden, 1972)
(12) W.W. FORTENBAUGH: 'Persuasion through character and the composition of Aristotle's Rhetoric', *RhM* 84, 1991, 152–26

On the connection between Aristotle's *Rhetoric* and the 'exoteric' writings, see:

(13) W. WIELAND: 'Aristoteles als Rhetoriker und die exoterischen Schriften', *H* 86, 1958, 323–46

For the historical antecedents of Aristotle's *Rhetoric*, see:

(14) G. KENNEDY: *The Art of Persuasion in Greece* (London, 1963)
(15) V. BUCHHEIT: *Untersuchungen zur Theorie des Genos Epideiktikon von Gorgias bis Aristoteles* (Munich, 1960)

The texts are collected and annotated in:

(16) L. RADERMACHER: *Artium Scriptores*, Sitzungsberichte der österreichischen Akademie der Wissenschaft in Wien, 227.3 (Vienna, 1951)

For Aristotle's influence on the subsequent history of the subject, see:

(17) F. SOLMSEN: 'The Aristotelian tradition in ancient rhetoric', *AJP* 62, 1941, 35–50, 169–90
Aristotle's conception of rhetoric is discussed by:
(18) T.M. CREM: 'The definition of rhetoric according to Aristotle', *Laval théologique et philosophique* 12, 1956, 233–50
(19) K. BARWICK: 'Die Gliederung der rhetorischen *technê* und die horazische *Epistula ad Pisones*', *H* 57, 1922, 16–18
(20) W. RHYS ROBERTS: 'Notes on Aristotle's *Rhetoric*', *AJP* 45, 1924, 351–61
(21) A.O. RORTY: 'The direction of Aristotle's *Rhetoric*', *RM* 46, 1992, 63–95
For the logical parts of Aristotle's treatment of the subject – mostly in Book A – see the items in III (J), and also:
(22) J. BRUNSCHWIG: 'Rhétorique et dialectique: *Rhétorique* et *Topiques*', in FURLEY and NEHAMAS I.50
On the account of the emotions and their relation to rhetoric (Book B) see:[1]
(23) F. SOLMSEN: 'Aristotle and Cicero on the orator's playing upon the feelings', *CP* 33, 1938, 390–404
(24) W.W. FORTENBAUGH: 'Aristotle's *Rhetoric* on emotion', *AGP* 52, 1970, 45–53 = BARNES, SCHOFIELD, SORABJI I.62
(25) D. MIRHADY: 'Non-technical *pisteis* in Aristotle and Anaximenes', *AJP* 112, 1991, 5–28
For the relation of Aristotle's *Rhet* to his ethics, see:
(26) L.W. ROSENFIELD: 'The doctrine of the mean in Aristotle's *Rhetoric*', *Theoria* 31, 1965, 191–98
(27) E.E. RYAN: 'Aristotle's *Rhetoric* and *Ethics* and the ethos of society', *GRBS* 13, 1972, 291–308
(28) M. WÖRNER: *Das Ethische in der Rhetorik des Aristoteles* (Freiburg, 1990)
(29) S. HALLIWELL: 'Popular morality, philosophical ethics, and the *Rhetoric*', in FURLEY and NEHAMAS I.50
(30) J.M. COOPER: 'Ethico-political theory in the *Rhetoric*', in FURLEY and NEHAMAS I.50
For the topics of style and language which occupy much of *Rhet* Γ, see the items in III (B), and:
(31) S. HALLIWELL: 'Style and Sense in Aristotle's *Rhetoric* Book 3', *RIP* 47, 1993, 50–69

(B) Poetics

The *Poetics*, as we have it, is incomplete. Some fragments of an earlier work, *On Poets*, survive. There is a stimulating, but controversial, commentary by:

(32) G.F. ELSE: *Aristotle's Poetics: the Argument* (Cambridge, Mass., 1957)

1. On emotion, see also VIII (J).

The standard English commentary is probably still that of:
(33) S.H. BUTCHER: *Aristotle's Theory of Poetry and Fine Art* (London, 1932)
There are also commentaries by:
(34) I. BYWATER: *Aristotle on the Art of Poetry* (Oxford, 1909)
(35) A. GUDEMAN: *Aristoteles Poetik* (Berlin/Leipzig, 1934)
(36) G.M.A. GRUBE: *Aristotle on Poetry and Style* (New York, 1958)
(37) D.W. LUCAS: *Aristotle – Poetics* (Oxford, 1968)
(38) S. HALLIWELL: *The Poetics of Aristotle* (London, 1987)
(39) R. JANKO: *Aristotle – Poetics* (Indianapolis, 1987)
A major philological study, published as three articles in 1865, 1866, and 1867, has been collected into one book as:
(40) J. VAHLEN: *Beiträge zu Aristoteles Poetik* (Leipzig, 1914)
There are useful general studies by:
(41) H. HOUSE: *Aristotle's Poetics* (London, 1956)
(42) S. HALLIWELL: *Aristotle's Poetics* (Chapel Hill, 1986)
See also:
(43) F. SOLMSEN: 'The origins and methods of Aristotle's *Poetics*', *CQ* 29 1935, 192–201
(44) G.K. GRESSETH: 'The system of Aristotle's *Poetics*', *TAPA* 89, 1958, 312–35
A collection of essays:
(45) A.O. RORTY: *Essays on Aristotle's* Poetics (Princeton, 1992)
A concise account of the great influence of the *Poetics* on the Renaissance is supplied by:
(46) L. COOPER: *The Poetics of Aristotle, its Meaning and Influence* (New York, 1927)
See also:
(47) M.T. HERRICK: *The Poetics of Aristotle in England* (New Haven, 1930)
(48) K. EDEN: *Poetic and Legal Fiction in the Aristotelian Tradition* (Princeton, 1986)
(49) H. JOLY: 'Autour de l'Aristote de Brecht', in SINACEUR I.60
(50) S. HALLIWELL: 'The *Poetics* and its interpreters', in RORTY X.45

(C) Imitation
Aristotle defines poetry as a kind of *mimêsis* or 'imitation'. Imitation and the nature of poetry are discussed by:
(51) A.P. MCMAHON: 'Seven questions on Aristotelian definitions of tragedy and comedy', *HSCP* 28, 1917, 97–198
(52) F.L. LUCAS: *Tragedy* (London, 1957)
(53) A.W.H. ADKINS: 'Aristotle on the best kind of tragedy', *CQ* 16, 1966, 78–102
(54) N. GULLEY: *Aristotle on the Purposes of Literature* (Cardiff, 1971) = BARNES, SCHOFIELD, SORABJI I.62
(55) R. INGARDEN: 'A marginal commentary on Aristotle's *Poetics*', *JAAC* 20, 1971–72, 163–73, 273–85

(56) M.P. BATTIN: 'Aristotle's definition of tragedy in the *Poetics*', *JAAC* 33, 1974, 155–70; 34, 1975, 293–302

(57) S. HALLIWELL: 'Aristotelian *mimêsis* re-evaluated', *JHP* 29, 1991, 457–510

(58) A. KOSMAN: 'Acting: *drama* as *mimêsis* of *praxis*', in RORTY X.45

(59) P. WOODRUFF: 'Aristotle on *mimêsis*', in RORTY X.45

(60) M. HEATH: 'The universality of poetry in Aristotle's *Poetics*', *CQ* 41, 1991, 389–402

(D) Tragedy

Most of *Poet* is devoted to a consideration of tragedy – and many of the items listed in the previous section have discussed the nature of tragedy. See also:

(61) J. JONES: *Aristotle and Greek Tragedy* (London, 1962)

(62) E. BELFIORE: *Tragic Pleasures* (Princeton, 1992)

Character, plot, and their relative importance or unimportance are discussed by HOUSE X.41, ch. 5; and by:

(63) W.J. VERDENIUS: 'The meaning of *êthos* and *êthikos* in Aristotle's *Poetics*', *Mn* 12, 1945, 241–57

(64) C. LORD: 'Tragedy without character: *Poetics* 6, 1450a24', *JAAC* 28, 1969, 55–62

(65) E. BELFIORE: 'Pleasure, tragedy, and Aristotelian psychology', *CQ* 35, 1985, 349–61

(66) E. BELFIORE: 'Aristotle's concept of *praxis* in the *Poetics*', *Classical Journal* 79, 1983/4, 110–24

(67) A.O. RORTY: 'The psychology of Aristotelian tragedy', *Mid-West Studies in Philosophy* 16, 1991, 53–72 = RORTY X.45

(68) R. BITTNER: 'One action', in RORTY X.45

The plot requires an unexpected reversal (*peripeteia*). Is it the hero who fails to expect it, while the audience remains in the know? See VAHLEN X.40; and:

(69) F.L. LUCAS: 'The reverse of Aristotle', *CQ* 37, 1923, 98–104

Or is there a shift in the situation, which the audience is not invited to foresee? See:

(70) P. TURNER: 'The reverse of Vahlen', *CQ* 9, 1959, 207–15

ELSE X.32, connects the *peripeteia* with the hero's mistake (*hamartia*), and subsequent recognition. See also:

(71) D.W. LUCAS: 'Pity, terror and *peripeteia*', *CQ* 12, 1962, 52–60

(72) D.J. ALLAN: '*peripeteia quid sit, Caesar occisus ostendit*', *Mn* 29, 1976, 337–50

(73) O.J. SHRIER: 'A simple view of *peripeteia*', *Mn* 33, 1980, 96–118

(74) E. BELFIORE: '*Peripeteia* and discontinuous actions: Aristotle, *Poetics* 11, 1452a22–29', *CP* 83, 1988, 183–94

(E) Tragic Error

The tragic hero falls because of a *hamartia* or 'error': can a *hamartia* be a simple mistake, or must it be something more culpable? There is an eloquent exposition of the culpability view in:

(75) P.W. HARSH: 'Hamartia again', TAPA 76, 1945, 47–58
But the prevailing view allows that the hamartia may be a mere mistake.
See ELSE X.32, and:
(76) P. VAN BRAAM: 'Aristotle's use of hamartia', CQ 6, 1912, 266–72
(77) O. HEY: 'Hamartia: zur Bedeutungsgeschichte des Wortes', Phg 83,
1928, 137–63
(78) S.M. PITCHER: 'Aristotle's good and just heroes', Philological Quarterly 24, 1945, 1–11; 190–91
(79) I.M. GLANVILLE: 'Tragic error', CQ 43, 1949, 447–56
(80) S. OSTERUD: 'Hamartia in Aristotle and Greek tragedy', Symbolae
Osloenses 51, 1976, 65–80
(81) E. SCHÜTRUMPF: 'Traditional elements in the concept of hamartia in
Aristotle's Poetics', HSCP 93, 1989, 137–56
(82) N. SHERMAN: 'Hamartia and virtue', in RORTY X.45
The controversy is generously surveyed by:
(83) J.M. BREMER: Hamartia (Amsterdam, 1969)
On the connexions between Aristotle's theoretical views and the practice
of Greek tragedy see:
(84) J.T. SHEPPARD: The Oedipus Tyrannus of Sophocles (Cambridge,
Mass., 1920), pp.xxiv–xl
(85) M. OSTWALD: 'Aristotle on "hamartia", and Sophocles' Oedipus
Tyrannus', in Festschrift für Ernst Kapp (Hamburg, 1958)
(86) E.R. DODDS: 'On misunderstanding the Oedipus Rex', Greece and
Rome 13, 1966, 37–49 = his The Ancient Concept of Progress (Oxford,
1973)
(87) R.D. DAWE: 'Some reflections on atê and hamartia', HSCP 72, 1967,
89–123
(88) T.C.W. STINTON: 'Hamartia in Aristotle and Greek tragedy', CQ 25,
1975, 221–54 = his Collected Papers on Greek Tragedy (Oxford, 1990)

(F) Catharsis
Aristotle claims that through pity and fear, tragedy accomplishes the
catharsis of such emotions. Is it the audience which experiences catharsis, and is catharsis similar to a religious purification, or to a medical
purging? BERNAYS' article, favouring the medical view, has almost swept
the field:

(89) J. BERNAYS: Grundzüge der verlorenen Abhandlung des Aristoteles
über Wirkung der Tragödie (Breslau, 1957) = BARNES, SCHOFIELD, SORABJI
I.62
See also:
(90) A.W. BENN: 'Aristotle's theory of tragic emotion', M 23, 1914,
84–90
(91) W.J. VERDENIUS: 'Katharsis tôn pathêmatôn', in MANSION I.51
(92) F. DIRLMEIER: 'Katharsis pathêmatôn', H 75, 1940, 81–92
(93) W. SCHADEWALDT: 'Furcht und Mitleid?', H 83, 1955, 129–71
(94) M. POHLENZ: 'Furcht und Mitleid? Ein Nachwort', H 84, 1956, 49–74

(95) A. NEHAMAS: 'Pity and fear in the *Rhetoric* and *Poetics*', in RORTY X.45

The medical view has been challenged by ELSE X.32, commenting on *Poet* 6 and 14. Another heterodox view has been offered by:

(96) L. GOLDEN: '*Catharsis*', *TAPA* 93, 1962, 51–60

(97) L. GOLDEN: '*Mimêsis* and *catharsis*', *CP* 64, 1969, 145–53

(98) L. GOLDEN: 'The purification theory of *catharsis*', *JAAC* 31, 1973, 474–9

On the background to the theory (which has sometimes been seen as a reply to Plato, who criticized poetry for playing on the emotions: *Republic* 602–7), see GULLEY X.54; ELSE X.32 on *Poet* 14; and:

(99) H. FLASHAR: 'Die medizinischen Grundlagen der Lehre von der Wirkung der Dichtung in der griechischen Poetik', *H* 84, 1956, 12–48

(100) S. HALLIWELL: 'Plato and Aristotle on the denial of tragedy', *PCPS* 30, 1984, 49–71

(101) M.C. NUSSBAUM: 'Tragedy and self-sufficiency: Plato and Aristotle on pity and fear', in RORTY X.45

See also:

(102) D. KEESEY: 'On some recent interpretations of catharsis', *Classical World* 72, 1979, 193–205

(103) J. LEAR: '*Katharsis*', *Phron* 33, 1988, 297–326 = RORTY X.45

(104) R. JANKO: 'From *catharsis* to the Aristotelian mean', in RORTY X.45

(105) C.B. DANIELS and S. SCULLY: 'Pity, fear and catharsis in Aristotle's *Poetics*', *Nous* 26, 1992, 204–17

And, on the influence of the theory:

(106) I. BYWATER: 'Milton and the Aristotelian definition of tragedy', *JPh* 44, 1901, 267–275

(G) Comedy

The lost Book B of *Poet* contained Aristotle's views on comedy. Some scholars have seen the remnants of the lost book in the so called 'tractatus Coislinianus'. See:

(107) R. JANKO: *Aristotle on Comedy* (London, 1984)

For what can be gleaned about Aristotle's ideas, see:

(108) L. GOLDEN: 'Aristotle on the pleasure of comedy', *H* 115, 1987, 166–74 = RORTY X.45

(109) M. HEATH: 'Aristotelian comedy', *CQ* 39, 1989, 344–54

And note:

(110) L. COOPER: *An Aristotelian Theory of Comedy* (New York, 1922)

INDEX OF PASSAGES

385

INDEX OF NAMES

393

INDEX OF GREEK TERMS

INDEX OF SUBJECTS